[inside macromedia®]

FIREWORKS® MX

Dan Carr

Shannon Wilder

Scott J. Wilson, Ph.D.

THOMSON
DELMAR LEARNING™

Australia Canada Mexico Singapore Spain United Kingdom United States

THOMSON
DELMAR LEARNING

Fireworks [Inside Macromedia]
Dan Carr, Shannon Wilder, Scott Wilson, Ph.D.

Business Unit Executive:
Alar Elken

Executive Editor:
Sandy Clark

Acquisitions Editor:
James Gish

Editorial Assistant:
Jaimie Wetzel

Executive Marketing Manager:
Maura Theriault

Marketing Coordinator:
Sarena Douglass

Channel Manager:
Fair Huntoon

Executive Production Manager:
Mary Ellen Black

Production Manager:
Larry Main

Production Editor:
Tom Stover

Cover Design:
Brucie Rosch

Editorial:
Daril Bentley

Full Production Services:
Liz Kingslien
Lizart Digital Design, Chicago, IL

Printed in Canada.
1 2 3 4 5 XXX 06 05 04 03 02

For more information contact
Delmar Learning, Executive Woods,
5 Maxwell Drive, Clifton Park, NY 12065.
Or find us on the World Wide Web at
http://www.delmar.com

The authors would like to thank the following parties for allowing us to use their images in our book and exercises. The images may appear individually or as part of a collage.

PhotoDisc, Inc.
Digital Imagery © Copyright 2002

Website Pros
Screen captures in Chapter 3 developed during joint projects.

Library of Congress
Cataloging-in-Publication Data

Carr, Dan.
Fireworks MX [inside macromedia] / Dan Carr, Shannon Wilder, Scott J. Wilson.
p. cm.
ISBN 0-7668-2002-5
1. Computer graphics. 2. Web sites – Design. 3. Fireworks (Computer file) I. Wilder, Shannon. II. Wilson, Scott J. III. Title.
T385 .C388 2003
006.6'869--dc21

2002153171

NOTICE TO THE READER

Publisher does not warrant or guarantee any of the products described herein or perform any independent analysis in connection with any of the product information contained herein. Publisher does not assume, and expressly disclaims, any obligation to obtain and include information other than that provided to it by the manufacturer.

The reader is expressly warned to consider and adopt all safety precautions that might be indicated by the activities herein and to avoid all potential hazards. By following the instructions contained herein, the reader willingly assumes all risks in connection with such instructions.

The Publisher makes no representation or warranties of any kind, including but not limited to, the warranties of fitness for particular purpose or merchantability, nor are any such representations implied with respect to the material set forth herein, and the Publisher takes no responsibility with respect to such material. The Publisher shall not be liable for any special, consequential, or exemplary damages resulting, in whole or part, from the readers' use of, or reliance upon, this material.

All Web sites referred to in the exercises and examples in this book are intended to be purely fictional.

Introduction

Instructional Approach

Because of its many features and functions, Fireworks MX may at first seem intimidating.

We do not want to overwhelm you with a lot of details all at once, and therefore begin by introducing the aspects of Fireworks MX that are the most practical and most commonly used to build programs in the real world.

With this book, you have an opportunity to learn Fireworks MX in an intuitive way, while practicing some of the techniques and shortcuts typically used by developers using Fireworks MX for real-world applications. Each chapter builds upon the last, adding new features of Fireworks MX to your builder's toolbox.

Learning Activities

The learning activities used in these chapters are centered on the concept of "learning by doing." These activities are a synthesis of the authors' many years of experience teaching multimedia software and as authorized Macromedia Training Providers.

This book was written to help new users more quickly come up to speed in using Fireworks MX so that they can create high-impact designs. The learning activities found within the book are designed to accommodate different learning styles and situations. The following brief description of these activities may help you to better use the material presented within the book.

Guided Tours

Most chapters include a structured "walk-through" of how to perform tasks, such as making menu/window selections or looking at the various properties or options listed. A guided tour is not really an exercise, but follows the notion of learning by actively "looking and doing."

Practice Exercises

Most chapters will include hands-on experiences that introduce the basic skills of using the tools and techniques to create Fireworks designs typical of real-world applications. The scope of an exercise is fairly narrow, focusing on the concepts and skills introduced in the chapter. The content is generally simple so that the emphasis remains on learning and using techniques, and so that there is no dependence on preexisting artistic talent.

San Francisco Travel Guide

During the chapters in this book, you will create various aspects of the San Francisco Travel Guide web site. This is a fictional web site based on a variety of images of San Francisco and a professional layout of content as it might appear in an online travel guide. You will explore the site's features through a series of guided tours, as well as build the foundation of the site through a series of practice exercises.

Within the context of this fictional web site, you will get first-hand experience in web site layout and design, web site production using optimization, slicing and exporting, drawing with special effects, animation, and the process of combining functional code with your graphics using behaviors. In the end, you should have everything you need to get your site up and running using Fireworks MX as your design tool.

Using the Book on Your Own

Each book in the Inside Macromedia series has been designed to be used either on your own or within a classroom setting. Those of you who use this book to learn Fireworks MX on your own will find that you are guided through the process and are given the freedom to modify what you want. Keep in mind that there are generally several approaches to building something. You may end up performing exercises using steps (or sequences of steps) different from those outlined in this book, which is fine if your design does what it needs to do. Note also that the step-by-step instructions provide two levels of detail.

- *Numbered steps:* State what needs to be done.
- *Lettered substeps:* Describe how to perform particular steps.

Using the Book in the Classroom

As instructors for Fireworks MX, Flash MX, Dreamweaver MX, Authorware 6 (and other software), we believe these same learning activities (presented somewhat differently) are equally effective in the classroom. There, we use the book as a point of reference and organizational guide for the presentation of material. As a point of reference, we do not read from the book, nor ask students to do so (in class). Rather, we use the book to organize the classroom presentation. We encourage students to take notes, directly in the book.

About the Authors

Dan Carr

Dan Carr is lead designer, developer, and trainer for Dan Carr Design, based in San Francisco, California. He has over ten years of professional experience in art direction, graphic design, illustration, and multimedia development, including ongoing projects with Macromedia's Flash and e-Learning teams.

Dan began working professionally as an illustrator and designer in the late 1980s in Southern California. In the 1990s, he moved to San Francisco where he worked for a range of industry-leading clients in print and multimedia, and then founded Dan Carr Design in 1994.

In recent years, Dan has shifted his focus to web development and expanded his skills to include expert-level knowledge in front-end web technologies, including HTML, DHTML, XML, JavaScript, ActionScript, PHP, and ASP. He spends much of his time working with the Macromedia tools and teaching others how to become power users. Dan has developed e-Learning products that have shipped with Macromedia's Flash 5 and Flash MX, as well as served on the Macromedia advisory and beta teams for Flash and Fireworks.

Dan also teaches as a Macromedia Certified Trainer (Flash, Fireworks, Dreamweaver, and FreeHand), with a focus on beginning and advanced Flash development and web design. He has trained development teams for San Francisco's top companies for the past five years, including various Macromedia technical support personnel.

Dan has delivered outstanding work to industry-leading clients, including Intel, Macromedia, Oracle, PeopleSoft, Williams-Sonoma, CISCO, and Inktomi.

- *www.dancarrdesign.com*
- *dan@dancarrdesign.com*

Shannon Wilder

Shannon Wilder is an artist and educator with the University of Georgia. She currently works in the Office of Instructional Support and Development, where she teaches faculty development workshops and consults with university instructors who are exploring ways of integrating technology into their classrooms.

Her specializations and research interests include graphics and multimedia software, web development, video streaming technology, and applications of handheld technology in the classroom. Her other publications include *Flash 5* (Inside Macromedia series) and *Flash MX* (Inside Macromedia series).

Shannon is also an active freelance graphic designer and illustrator whose clients have included the Girl Scouts of America, the USDA Forest Service, and Rhone Merieux, Inc. She holds a B.F.A. in Art, an M.Ed. in Instructional Technology, and is currently working toward a Ph.D. in Art Education at the University of Georgia. Shannon currently resides in Athens, Georgia, with her husband, two cats, and a pug.

Scott J. Wilson, Ph.D.

Scott has extensive experience in the training industry, specializing in instructional design and management of the training function. He has managed the development of thousands of hours of multimedia and e-Learning applications.

Currently Scott is vice president of Instructional Architecture, a consulting firm helping corporations investigate, design, develop, and implement e-Learning solutions. He has given presentations at both national and regional conferences on many topics related to interactive multimedia and e-Learning.

Scott received his Ph.D. from Florida State University in Instructional Design and Research Methodology. Scott is the coauthor and instructional architect for the Thomson Learning Inside Macromedia series, which includes titles for Authorware 6, Flash MX, Dreamweaver MX, Fireworks MX, Director 8 and Lingo, Flash 5, and Dreamweaver 4.

- *www.InstructionalArchitecture.com*
- *ScottWilson@InstructionalArchitecture.com*

Acknowledgments

First and foremost we want to thank the thousands of students who have attended our classes over the last ten years. Through your enthusiasm and probing questions, you have not only given us enjoyment in teaching the classes but have helped us become better at what we do.

We would like to thank the many people at Macromedia with whom we have worked over the years, including those in the Authorized Training Program, Authorized Developer Program, Value Added Reseller Program, Technical Support, Marketing/Trade Events, and Development/Engineering teams.

We want to sincerely thank the many people at Delmar Learning for the help and encouragement they have provided: James Gish, for his continued help and support for the Inside Macromedia series; Thomas Stover, for his professionalism and work behind the scenes; Jaimie Wetzel, for keeping track of details and keeping us moving forward on time; Daril Bentley, for his continued help in making our manuscripts better; and Liz Kingslien (Lizart Digital Design) for your excellent production work and enjoyable working relationship.

From Dan

First, I'd like to thank those closest to me. To my parents for just being cool parents and having enough faith in me to let me pursue my own course through life and end up in this wonderful place. Thanks to Julie for sticking with me through all the late nights and frantic work and for your support and your continued love and friendship.

A special thanks to Scott for inviting me to participate in this project and for his continued enthusiastic support of my work and efforts. And thanks to Shannon for her great work and help with the book.

And finally, thanks to all my colleagues and peers who have made this such a great ride!

From Shannon

Thanks to all my colleagues at the University of Georgia for their advice and support during the writing process. I am so grateful to work in such an inspiring professional environment, and I have learned so much from my experiences in OISD. Thanks also to my parents for all the love and many hours of listening over the years. Finally, thank you to my husband, Lance, who always manages to bring me a cup of tea at just the right time, and who performs so many other small kindnesses that make our life together that much richer.

From Scott

Thanks to Dan and Shannon for all your hard work and professionalism throughout this project. It has been a pleasure to work with you both. Many thanks to my family, teachers, students, friends, colleagues, and fellow human beings – from whom I have learned so much along the way. God please give me the insight and strength to practice that which has been given to me. Marie-Claire, my wise and beautiful wife, thank you for your continued support, faith, and love.

Table of Contents

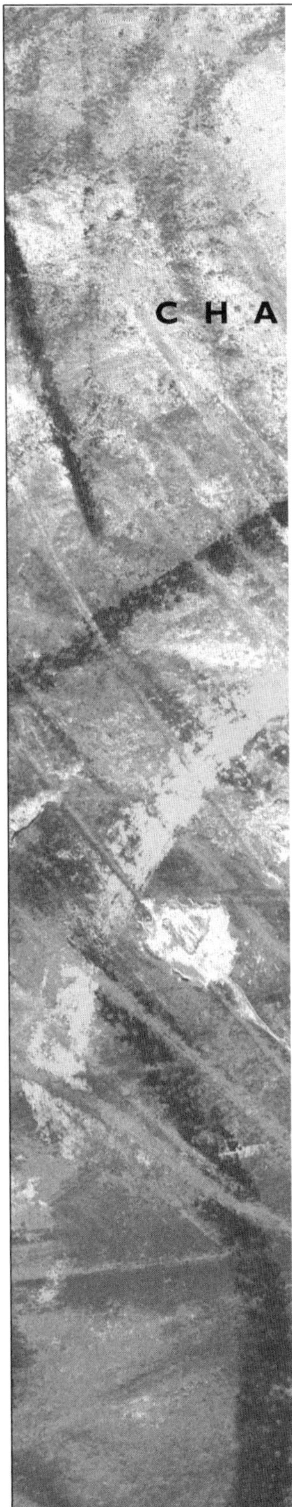

CHAPTER 1

Getting Started with Fireworks MX

Chapter Topics:

- *Introduction*
- *Guided Tour 1A: Opening Fireworks for the First Time*
- *Introduction to the Interface*
- *Guided Tour 1B: The Power of Fireworks Layers*
- *Guided Tour 1C: The Changing Look of the Properties Panel*
- *Guided Tour 1D: Working with Panels*

Introduction

As Macromedia has created and acquired new software products, it has continued to improve and standardize its software interfaces. This standardization has reached a new level with the MX software family, with essential components of the interface shared by Fireworks MX, Flash MX, and Dreamweaver MX. This shared MX interface allows users to cross over and begin to use the other MX software family products much more easily and quickly.

This chapter introduces you to the Firework MX interface, which consists of three primary components: menus, the Document window, and a variety of dockable panels. In this chapter you will receive a high-level overview of these interface components, with each explored in detail as encountered here and in subsequent chapters. By the end of this chapter, you will be able to:

- *Open the Fireworks MX program*
- *Create a new document, setting properties as you do so*
- *List the Fireworks MX menus*
- *Use the Document window options*
- *Briefly describe the concept of layers as interpreted within Fireworks MX*
- *Work with the Layers panel options*
- *Briefly describe the function of the Properties panel*
- *Dock and undock panels*
- *Reset panels to their factory default settings*

Let's begin by opening the program. Guided tour 1A takes you through the process of opening Fireworks for the first time. The instructions cover opening the program in both Windows and Macintosh environments.

Guided Tour 1A: Opening Fireworks for the First Time

This guided tour takes you through the process of opening Fireworks for the first time.

Windows Versus Macintosh

Fireworks MX, like most of Macromedia's software, looks and operates virtually the same way on both Macintosh- and Windows-based computers. Differences between the two include variations in a few keyboard keys and the absence of the right button on the Macintosh mouse. Table 1-1 compares the Windows and Macintosh keyboard keys.

Windows	Macintosh
Alt + another key	Opt + another key
Ctrl + another key	Cmd + another key
Right mouse button click	Ctrl + mouse click

Table 1-1: Fireworks MX Windows/Macintosh Keyboard Differences.

Throughout the book, these differences are minimized in that we most often make selections through the use of menu options, which are (unless otherwise noted) the same on both platforms. In the exercises, you will find Shortcut icons, which provide keyboard shortcuts to commands on both platforms.

To provide a consistent look for screen captures, most illustrations depict the Windows version of Fireworks MX. When needed, Macintosh screen captures are also provided. Before we begin to examine the Fireworks interface, you may find it useful to open your copy of the Fireworks program and look at the software screen, menus, and panels as they are discussed in the material that follows. The steps that follow take you through the process of opening Fireworks on both computer platforms.

Windows (PC) Computer

After you have successfully installed Fireworks MX on your computer, you can open it like any other Windows (PC) software program, as follows.

1. Click on the Start button on the Windows navigation bar to open the Windows main menu.
2. Select Programs, shown in figure 1-1.

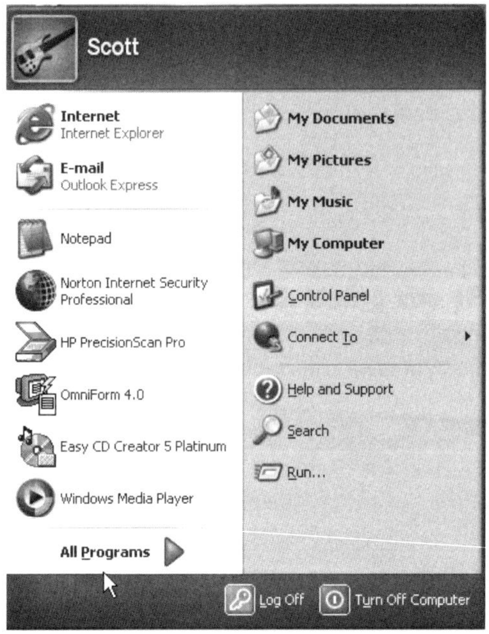

Fig. 1-1. Selecting Programs from the Windows main menu.

3. Select Macromedia | Macromedia Fireworks MX. See figure 1-2.

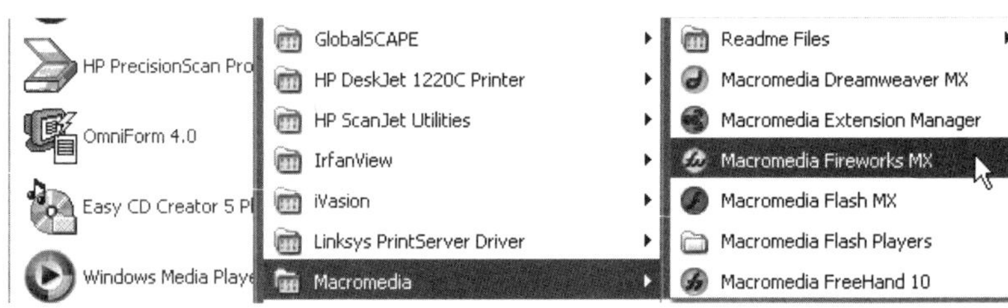

Fig. 1-2. Macromedia folder and Fireworks MX program.

4. As Fireworks MX opens, it presents an opening title screen. The exact appearance of this screen will differ, depending on whether you have a commercial version or an educational version.
5. Once Fireworks has loaded, you should see the Fireworks MX main interface, including the main menu and many panels, as they are located according to the factory default settings.

Continue with step 6, which follows the "Macintosh Computer" section.

Macintosh Computer

After you have successfully installed Fireworks MX on your computer, you can open it like any other Macintosh software program, as follows.

1. Double click to open the Macintosh hard drive where you installed Fireworks MX.
2. Select the *Macromedia* folder, shown in figure 1-3.

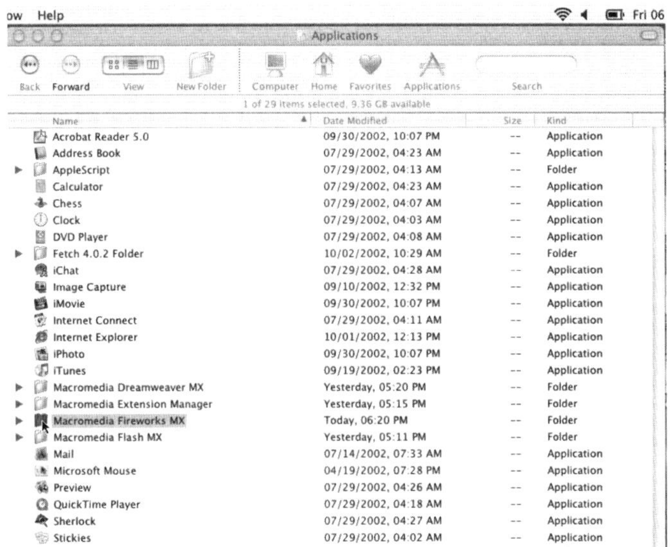

Fig. 1-3.* Macromedia *folder.

3. Select Fireworks MX, shown in figure 1-4.

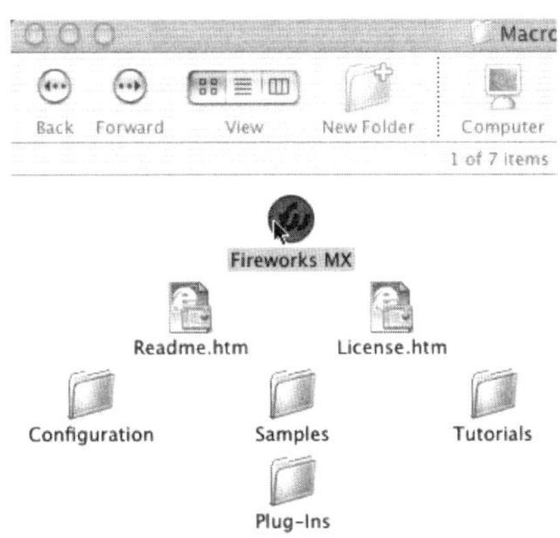

Fig. 1-4. Fireworks MX.

4. As Fireworks MX opens, it presents an opening title screen. The exact appearance of this screen will differ, depending on whether you have a commercial version or an educational version.
5. Once Fireworks has loaded, you should see the Fireworks MX main interface, including the main menu and many panels, as they are located according to the factory default settings.

Windows (PC) and Macintosh Continued

Continue with the following steps for both of the previous two sections.

6. Select the File menu.
7. Select the New option.

The New Document pop-up window, shown in figure 1-5, should have opened. The values you see in the Width, Height, and Resolution fields on your screen may be different than those shown here. However, this does not matter, as you are now going to change these values.

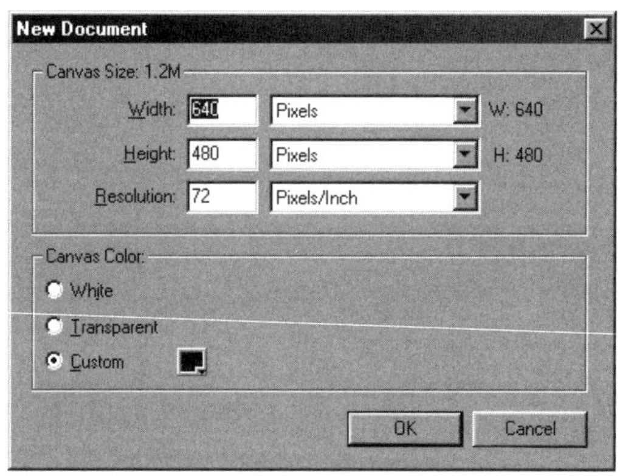

Fig. 1-5. New Document pop-up window.

8. If you are creating a new document (new graphic), the New Document pop-up window allows you to set the dimensions, resolution, and background color of the work area (the canvas). As you copy a graphic into the clipboard and then select File | New, the Width, Height, and Resolution fields will be preset, based on the characteristics of the graphic in the clipboard. Establish the settings in these fields by continuing with the following steps.
9. Click the mouse cursor in the Width field. Type in *640*. This defines the width of the canvas as 640 pixels. This is one width standard for web development (there are others).

10. Click the mouse cursor in the Height field. Type in *480.* This defines the height of the canvas as 480 pixels. This is one height standard for web development (there are others).

11. Note that the fields to the right of the Width and Height fields currently indicate that these dimensions are being defined in terms of pixels. Click on the down arrow on the right side of the Pixels field, to the right of the Width field. As you can see in the pull-down menu that opens, the measurement options for width are Pixels, Inches, and Centimeters. Leave the setting as Pixels, and simply click on Pixels to close this pop-up window. The options for Height are the same as for Width. Accepting the Pixels setting for Width also accepts the default for Height.

12. The next two fields are where you specify the resolution of the graphic. The first is where you can type in a number, and with the second you can use a pull-down menu to specify either Pixels per Inch or Pixels per Centimeter. Resolution for graphics to be used within the computer environment tends to be much lower than what you may have encountered for print-based media. Click the mouse cursor in the Resolution field. Type in *72*. Leave the second field as Pixels per Inch.

13. The last option in the New Document pop-up window is Canvas Color. Selecting White will set the canvas color to white. Selecting Transparent will set the canvas color to transparent. A gray-and-white checkerboard pattern represents a transparent background within the Fireworks Document window. The Custom field allows you to select any other available color. Click on the small color window to the right of the Custom option. You should now see a color palette in a pop-up window, as shown in figure 1-6.

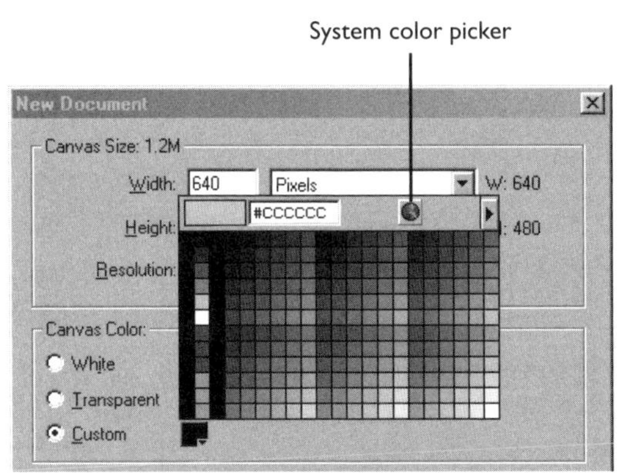

Fig. 1-6. Colors available for custom canvas color.

14. Change the canvas color by clicking on any color you see in the Color window, or by clicking on the System Color Picker icon in the upper right-hand corner of the Color pop-up window and selecting a color from the resulting color palette. (If you chose this second color palette, select a color and then click on the OK button.)
15. Click on the OK button to close the New Document pop-up window.
16. You are now looking at a new Document window with a colored canvas. (The Document window is examined in detail in material to follow.)

Introduction to the Interface

In addition to its new look and feel, the MX interface allows for greater flexibility in working with panels and customizing the setup within the Fireworks development environment. When you first open Fireworks, you may feel overwhelmed by the number of panels and options you see on screen. However, do not worry, as these panels and options are presented in a way that should make getting started with Fireworks a little easier.

As previously stated, the three major components of the Fireworks MX interface are menus, the Document window, and a variety of panels, as shown in figure 1-7. As you can see, menus are located across the top. The Document window occupies the central and largest portion of the screen. The Document window is the work area (canvas), in which you will be creating or modifying images. The areas to the left of the Document window, and those across the bottom and on the right, are where Fireworks will by default place the primary panel groupings. As you will see later, however, you can change the location and presence/absence of any of these panels.

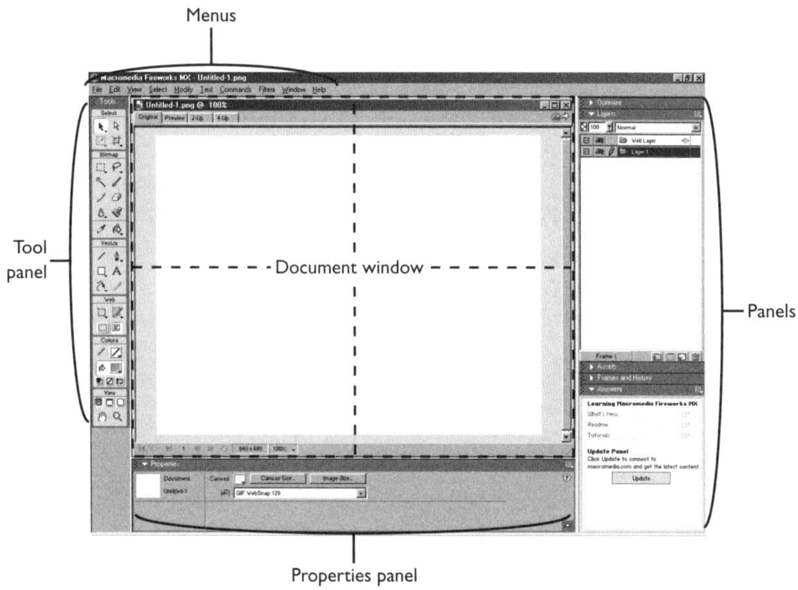

Fig. 1-7. Major components of the Fireworks interface.

Fireworks Menus

The menus that run along the top of the Fireworks interface (and many of the options within the menus) are fairly typical in organization and function to those found in many software programs. See figure 1-8. The sections that follow describe the functionality of each menu and the options found within it. You will examine these menu options in detail as they are encountered in guided tours and exercises.

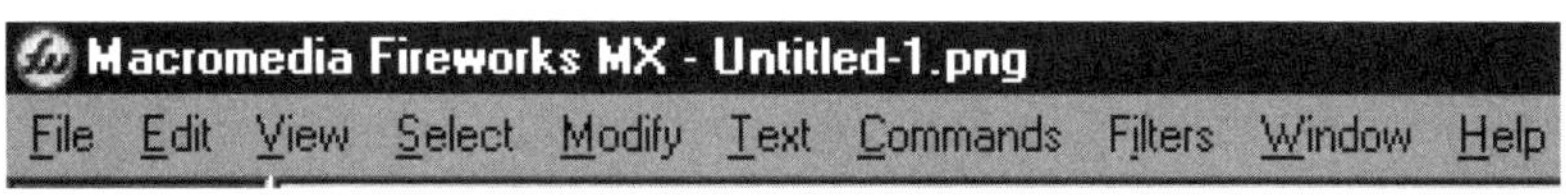

Fig. 1-8. Menus in Fireworks MX.

File Menu

Select the File menu and examine its options. Note that many of the menu options also include Keyboard Shortcuts. Keyboard Shortcuts for both Windows (PC) and Macintosh computers are included in the exercises that follow.

The options listed in the File menu pertain to operations you can perform on Fireworks files. Common functions include creating a new file (New), opening an existing file (Open), saving a file (Save), and several other functions common to most software programs. Open Recent presents a window that lists files you have recently had open. Fireworks can also Import and Export media elements, and includes a Batch Process option.

Edit Menu

Select the Edit menu and examine its options. Several of these options are the same as those you have used in many other software programs. These include Cut, Copy, Paste, and of course the indispensable Undo. The subcategories of these common options (such as Copy as Vectors, Copy HTML Code, Paste as Mask, Paste Inside, and Paste Attributes) provide you with extensive and specific capabilities. You will have a chance to work with these types of specific options throughout the book.

View Menu

Select the View menu and examine its options. The options in the View menu provide the capability to turn on or off a variety of display options (e.g., Rulers, Grid, Guides, Slice Guides, Slice Overlay, Hide Edges, and Hide Panels), and provide various types of zoom/display control (e.g., Zoom In, Zoom Out, Magnification, Fit Selection, and Fit All).

Select Menu

Select the Select menu and examine its options. The Select menu is probably a new one for you. Although you might have seen one of its options (Select All) listed in other program menus, the Fireworks Select menu offers a greatly expanded choice of what and how to select within the program. You will make use of several of these options in exercises you will encounter later.

Modify Menu

Select the Modify menu and examine its options. The Modify menu contains options that provide the capability to change the overall characteristics of the file (canvas) or of most images contained within the file. Some options are identical to those found in Flash MX and other programs, allowing you to Transform the shape or orientation of images, Arrange images from front to back, Align images, and Group images. Other options are specific to Fireworks MX: Animation, Mask, Combine Paths, and so on.

Text Menu

Select the Text menu and examine its options. Several of the options listed here should be very familiar to you, such as Font, Size, Style, Align, and Check Spelling. Others (such as Attach to Path and Detach from Path) are specific to Fireworks and are associated with its ability to attach text to curved shapes such as circles and arcs.

Commands Menu

Select the *Commands menu* and examine its options. Fireworks MX is capable of using and executing scripts controlled with the options listed in the *Commands menu.*

Filters Menu

Select the Filters menu and examine its options. These options (Adjust Color, Blur, Sharpen, and Other) provide the capability to change the appearance of the image. Other programs sometimes include these functions under a "Modify" (or similarly named) menu.

Window Menu

Select the Window menu and examine its options. These options control the display (or absence) of a variety of informational windows and panels. Panels opened and displayed by default include Tools, Properties, Answers, and Layers.

Help Menu

Select the Help menu and examine its options. These options offer a variety of methods for obtaining additional information. The options include Welcome, Using Fireworks, What's New, Fireworks Support Center, and Macromedia Online Forums, as well as options for registration.

Document Window

Another component of the Fireworks MX interface is the Document window. You should already have a new Document window opened from the previous guided tour. The Document window, shown in figure 1-9, is the large window at the center of the interface.

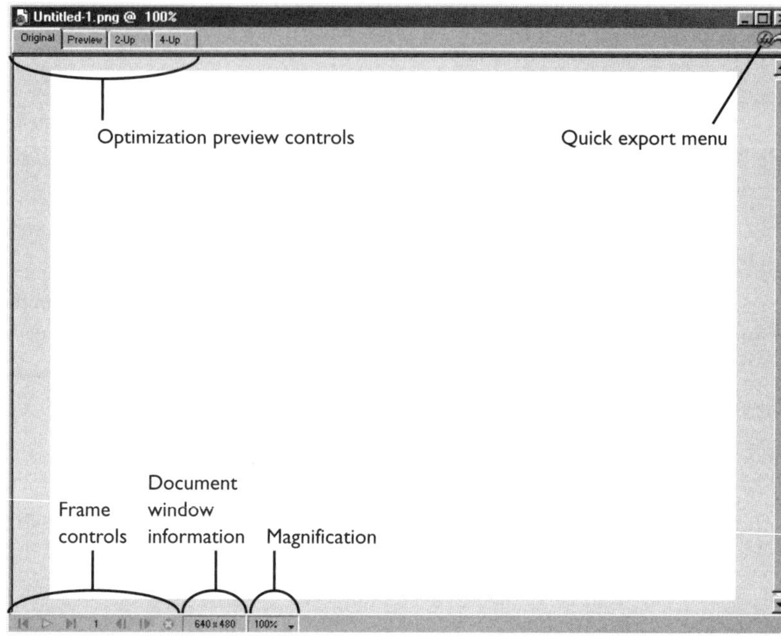

Fig. 1-9. Document window.

The Document window is where you create and view graphics, and where you view the optimized preview of your graphics. Note that the central colored area (whatever color you chose) is the actual viewable area (referred to as the canvas) of the graphic. Graphics cannot be seen if placed outside the canvas. Let's take a closer look at the Document window.

Note the Optimization (preview) controls in the upper left-hand corner of the Document window. See figure 1-9. The Optimization controls consist of four tabs: Original, Preview, 2-Up, and 4-Up. The Original tab (the default) shows the graphic in its current state. You can modify any object visible in the window by selecting this tab. Hidden layers and effects are not visible in any of the tab views. The Preview tab's window shows what the exported image will look like based on the optimization settings currently selected.

You can also use the Preview tab to test behaviors and rollovers before you export them. The next two tabs, 2-Up and 4-Up, can be used to compare the same graphic using different optimization settings. Click on the 2-Up tab. Unique settings can be assigned to each preview so that you can compare different settings side by side. The bottom of each preview window displays that window's settings, including file format, estimated download time, file size, current palette, and number of colors. Now click on the Original tab to return to the default display.

In the upper right-hand corner of the Document window, you can see the Quick Export menu, shown in figure 1-9. Go ahead and click on this menu. You will see that this menu displays options for exporting to Dreamweaver, Flash, FreeHand, Director, and other destinations. Click anywhere within the Document window to close the menu.

In the lower left-hand corner of the Document window, note the presence of the Frame controls option, shown in figure 1-9. If a document contains more than one frame (as it might in an animation sequence), these controls work much like VCR controls, providing navigational control within the document. A frame is somewhat analogous to a "page" in a flipbook animation. Most static graphics will contain a single frame, whereas an animation sequence created within Fireworks may contain several.

To the right of the Frame controls, note the Document window information bar, shown in figure 1-9. Clicking on this bar will display a pop-up window that specifies the current dimensions/attributes of the Document window, including width, height, and resolution information. Click anywhere within the Document window to close this pop-up. To the right of this area, note the Magnification pull-down menu option, shown in figure 1-9. Clicking on this option will display a menu that allows you to select another level of magnification from the options listed.

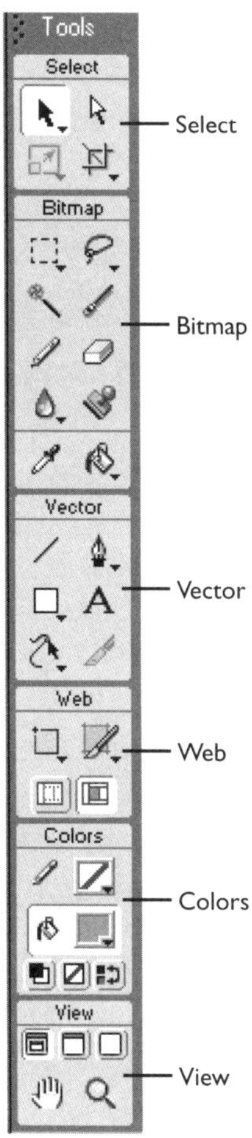

Fig. 1-10. Tools panel.

Panels

To this point, we have taken a quick look at two components of the Fireworks MX interface: the menus and the Document window. The remainder of the screen is full of a variety of panels. We do not want to overwhelm you, and therefore this chapter introduces just three primary panels: Tools, Layers, and Properties. We will begin with a "50,000-foot view" of these panels, and then proceed to a more in-depth examination of them as the book progresses. Other panels are introduced as they relate to ongoing discussion and instruction.

Tools Panel

The Tools panel has been enhanced in the current version of Fireworks. This is the vertical panel placed (by default) along the left edge of the interface, directly below the File and Edit menus, as shown in figure 1-10.

Note that the Tools panel consists of toolboxes for Select, Bitmap, Vector, Web, Colors, and View. Tools are grouped in these categories to reflect and logically organize the diverse needs developers have in creating and modifying graphics for use on the Web or within other media. In Chapter 2, you will have the opportunity to see how the tools in the Tools panel work, as you take a guided tour in the use of each.

Properties Panel

The Properties panel is also known as the Property Inspector. It is the horizontal panel that runs along the bottom of the interface. The Properties panel, shown in figure 1-11, is where you can very easily change the properties or characteristics of whatever object is currently selected. Figure 1-11 shows the Properties panel as it appears in a newly opened document. The Properties panel is context sensitive and will change in appearance and specific characteristics listed, depending on the type of object selected within the Document window. You will examine various configurations of the Properties panel in Guided Tour 1C.

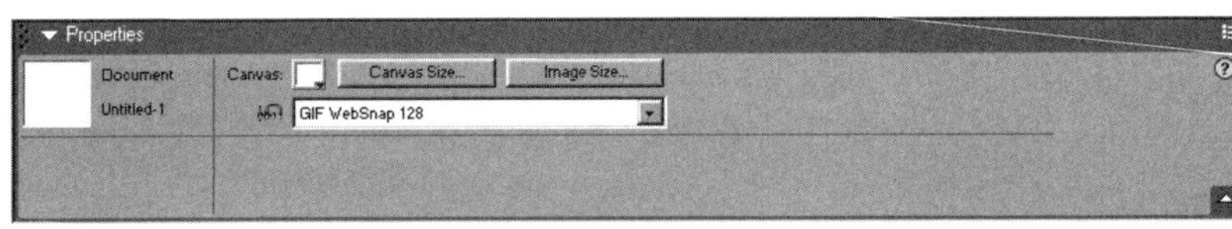

Fig. 1-11. Properties panel in a new document.

The Concept of Layers

Before working with the Layers panel, let's first take a quick look at layers themselves. Creating layers within a graphic represents a means of organizing graphic elements and keeping them separated from one another. The use of layers is fairly common within the world of computer graphics, and you will further explore the use of layers within Fireworks MX in a guided tour later in this chapter.

If you have previously worked with Flash, Photoshop, or other graphics packages, you may have encountered layers. If this is the case, you will need to pay attention as you begin to work with layers within Fireworks MX, as their application within Fireworks may differ from that which you have encountered previously. One of the primary differences is that within Fireworks every object created is assigned a sublayer. The organization of sublayers constitutes a layer.

For those of you unfamiliar with layers, let's start at the beginning and create, via analogy, an example of layer use within Fireworks MX. Assume you have a stack of tracing paper (in the old days it was called "onion skin," as you can see through it) totaling five sheets. You use a pencil to draw a tree in the left-hand portion of the first sheet. Call this first sheet the *Tree* sublayer. You then draw a house in the right-hand portion of the second sheet. Call this second sheet the *House* sublayer. You draw a small pond in the middle of the third sheet. Call this third sheet the *Pond* sublayer.

NOTE

The terms layer and sublayer are used in this text for purposes of distinction. There is no equivalent Macromedia terminology that clearly differentiates these layering possibilities.

Continuing, you draw a single image on each of the remaining two sheets. If you now pick up the stack of tracing paper and hold it in front of a light source, you can see the entire (composite) graphic, consisting of each image residing on its own piece of paper (i.e., sublayer). If you paperclip the stack together, it is analogous to a "single image," each piece of paper representing a "sublayer." The stack represents a "layer" of a "complete graphics image."

You might create another example, consisting of a *Sky* layer, in turn consisting of *Clouds*, *Sun*, and *Flying Birds* sublayers. Placing each image on its own sublayer gives you the flexibility of modifying an individual image without affecting any other image. Organizing related sublayers into layers also makes it easier to keep track of (and otherwise manipulate) the building blocks that constitute a completed graphics image.

Layers Panel

Fireworks MX's Layers panel is where you organize and access layers and sublayers. By default, the Layers panel is located along the right-hand side of the interface. Take a look at the Layers panel, shown in figure 1-12, on screen. As you can see, the panel currently contains a *Layer 1* label, but nothing exists in this layer. This should not be surprising, as currently you do not have anything in the Document window that would otherwise be displayed in this panel. In Guided Tour 1B you will examine the Layers panel in detail.

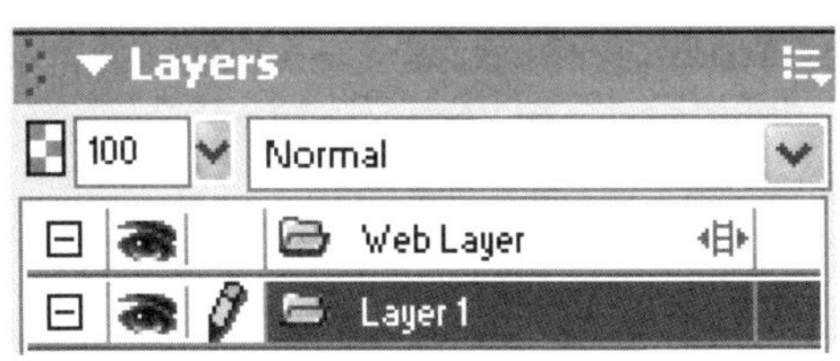

Fig. 1-12. Layers panel.

Answers Panel

The last panel to be examined in this chapter is the Answers panel. The Answers panel is a new feature of the MX family of software. This is where Macromedia has centrally placed reference material and web links that help you quickly obtain answers to questions you might have about the software.

By default, the Answers panel is located in the lower right-hand portion of the interface, as shown in figure 1-13.

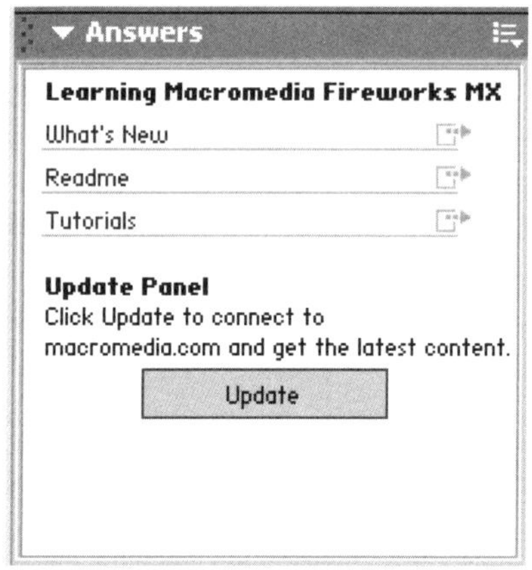

Fig. 1-13. Answers panel.

Guided Tour 1B takes a closer look at Fireworks layers, including the Layers panel.

Guided Tour 1B: The Power of Fireworks Layers

If you still have the untitled file from the previous guided tour open, close this file by clicking on the X located in the upper-right corner of the Document window. This will close the file without saving it.

In this guided tour you will open a file supplied on the companion CD-ROM. To take a closer look at how layers are used within the Fireworks environment, as well as use of the Layers panel, perform the following steps.

CD-ROM

1. Place the companion CD-ROM from the back of the book into the CD-ROM player of your computer.
2. Select the File menu.
3. In the menu that opens, select Open.
4. Verify that the Open Document dialog window has opened. See figure 1-14.

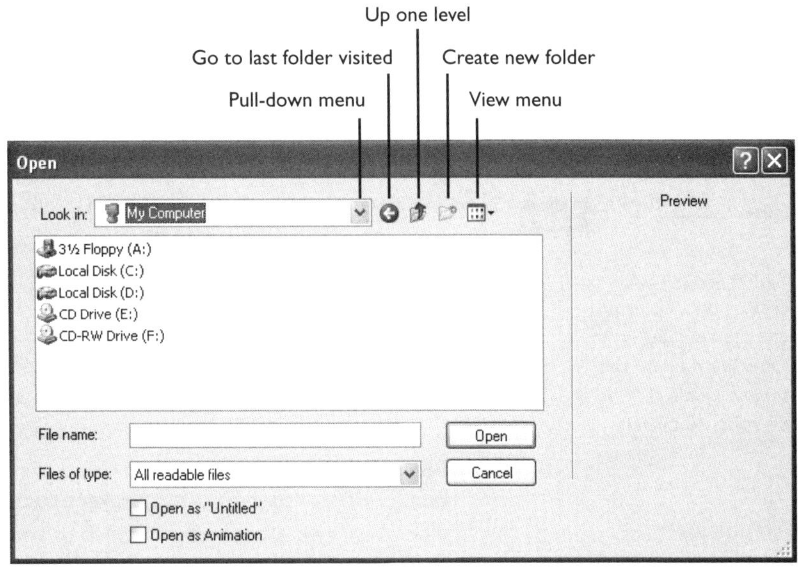

Fig. 1-14. Open Document dialog window.

Because this is the first time you have seen the Open Document dialog window, let's take a quick look around. This window is very similar to the "Open Document" (or similarly named) dialog window found in other software programs.

5. Note the Look In field at the very top of this dialog window. This field shows you what computer device (hard drive, CD-ROM, or removable disk), or folder within a device, is currently active. To the right of the Look In field is a down arrow, indicating a pull-down menu.
6. To the right of the Look In field down arrow are four graphic icons. Examine figure 1-14 to see what these icons represent.
7. Note below the Look In field a large, white area. The content of the currently active area (i.e., device, folder, and so on) is displayed in this area.
8. Note that the Files of Type field at the bottom of the Open Document dialog allows you to look (in the large, white area) at all files or just those you specify.
9. Note that a preview of the selected graphic, along with statistics about that graphic, is displayed in the right-hand side of the New Document window.
10. Click on the down arrow to the right of the Look In field, to open this option's pull-down menu.

11. Use the browse function associated with this pull-down menu to locate the CD-ROM player within your computer. Click on the CD-ROM player icon when you see it.
12. Double click on the CD-ROM icon to open it. Locate and double click on the *Chapter 1* folder, located on the companion CD-ROM.
13. Locate and click on the file *tour_1B.png*. Click on the Open button.
14. Examine the graphic image. This image will become (after some modifications) the splash screen for a sample web site you will create graphics for in subsequent chapters.
15. Examine the Layers panel at the right, shown in figure 1-15. As you can see, this image currently consists of three layers: *Web Layer*, *Logo and Text*, and *Interface*. As you will see in material to follow, the *Interface* layer contains several sublayers, each of which contains a different object. The *Logo and Text* layer contains two sublayers, each of which contains a text object. The *Web* layer stores objects such as hotspots and slices. No images are stored in the *Web* layer. (The *Web* layer is examined in more detail later in the chapter.)

·TIP· Rather than single clicking on a file name and then clicking on the Open button, you can simply double click on a file name to open it.

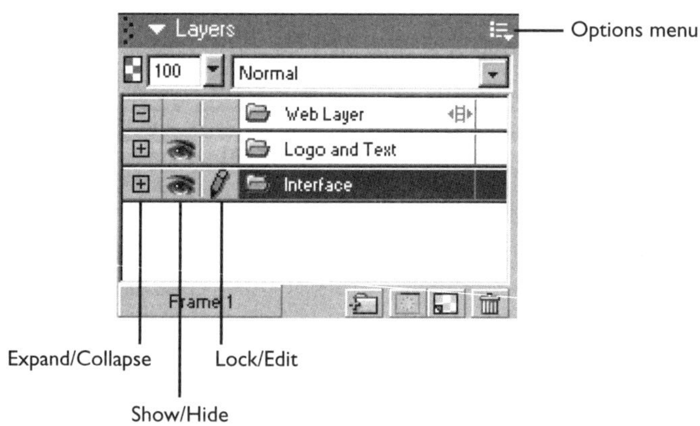

Fig. 1-15. Layers panel showing the* Web, Logo and Text, *and* Interface *layers.

Separating and placing graphics on different layers facilitates the organization of images and provides control over the attributes of constituent images. By placing graphic images on different layers, you are able to show/hide and lock/edit a graphic. These controls allow you to work on a specific section of the artwork without other sections getting in the way, and without the risk of accidentally changing these other sections.

16. Let's examine these controls for the *Interface* layer. Note the three columns to the left of the *Interface* label. You should see a Plus (+) icon in the first column, an Eye icon in the second, and a Pencil icon in the third.
17. Click on the Plus (+) icon to the left of the *Interface* layer. You have now expanded the *Interface* layer to reveal its sublayers. This layer contains six sublayers: *Group*, *Middle Bitmap*, *Left Bitmap*, *Right Rectangle*, *Line and Rectangle*, and *Block Rectangle*.
18. Click on the *Block Rectangle* sublayer located at the very bottom of the list. Note that there are now very small, blue "handles" around the large background rectangle located on the canvas (in the Document window).
19. Click on the *Line and Rectangle* sublayer, located directly above the sublayer you previously clicked on. Note that there are now blue handles around the very small, black rectangles and black line located at the bottom of the sublayer.

·TIP·

The blue handles indicate that this image is currently selected.

20. Click on the *Middle Bitmap* sublayer located at the top of the list. The blue handles now surround the photo located in the middle of the canvas.
21. Click on the Eye icon located to the left of the *Middle Bitmap* sublayer you just selected. Note that as the Eye disappears the bitmap photo is also hidden. Click on this same column to make the Eye and the bitmap photo reappear. Clicking on the Eye will *show* or *hide* an image contained within a sublayer.
22. Click on the Minus (–) icon to the left of the *Interface* layer to collapse the sublayers within this layer.
23. Click on the Eye icon associated with the *Interface* layer. This hides all images contained by the *Interface* layer. It may appear as though the *Logo and Text* layer has also disappeared, but it really has not. This layer is "invisible" because the white logo and text are not discernible against the white background. The point here is that the Hide/Show control applies to the selected folder only, not to the entire graphic. Click on this column again, so that the Eye and the *Interface* images reappear.
24. Click on the column showing the Pencil icon, to the left of the *Interface* layer. Note that the Pencil is now replaced with an icon of a lock. This means that all images within this layer are now locked and cannot be edited unless unlocked. Click on the Lock icon to redisplay the Pencil icon.
25. Double click on the *Interface* label. You should now see the Layer Name pop-up dialog window, in which you can modify the name of the layer. Type in *Background* and then press the Enter key to close the dialog window. You just renamed the layer as *Background*.

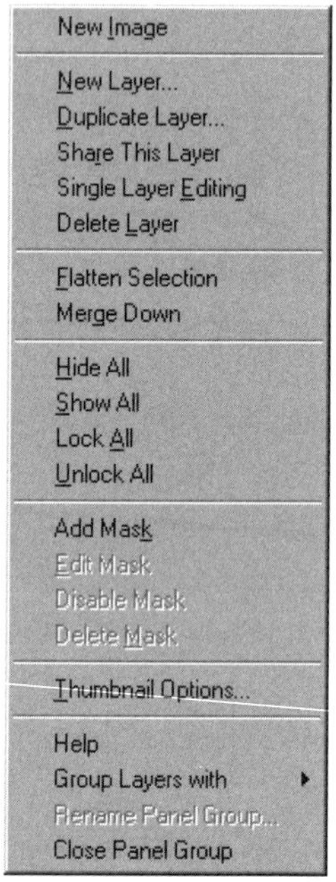

Fig. 1-16. Options menu.

26. Examine the top right-hand corner of the Layers panel. There is an Options menu icon located there. Click on this icon, shown in figures 1-15 and 1-17.

27. You have just opened a pull-down menu of layer options, shown in figure 1-16. At this point, we will examine just a few of the options available, with other options examined in exercises found later in the book.

28. Click on the New Layer option. Note that it opens the New Layer dialog window (very similar to the Layer Name dialog window you saw in step 25). Type in *Copyright* and click on the OK button. You have just added a new layer.

29. Select the *Background* layer. Click on the Plus (+) icon to expand the Folder list.

30. Click on the Options menu icon in the upper right-hand corner of the Layers panel. Toward the bottom of the list, select Thumbnail Options. In the dialog window that opens, select a larger-size thumbnail. Click on the OK button. You can see how easy it is to change the size of the thumbnail display. Click on the Options menu icon again. Select Thumbnail Options again, and this time select a smaller size. (It will be easier to work with a smaller thumbnail size as you continue through the tour.) Click on the OK button. Click on the Minus (–) icon to the left of the *Background* layer to collapse the sublayers.

·TIP·

Always name all of your layers with a simple and intuitive name, or you may later have difficulty finding where you placed your graphics.

31. Examine the lower right-hand side of the Layers panel, shown in figure 1-17. Note the four icons, and the labels indicating what they represent.

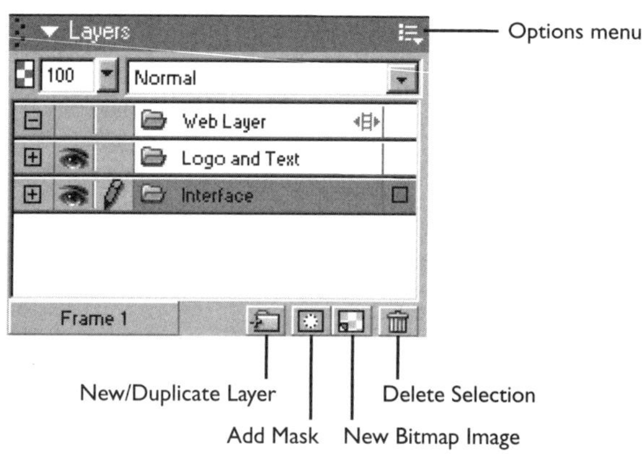

Fig. 1-17. Lower right-hand corner of Layers panel.

An important aspect of using layers is the ability to rearrange images in order to simulate "screen depth." Our eyes and mind perceive the 2D representation of an object in front of (and possibly partially covering) another object as an object closer to us than the object behind it.

Layers at the top of the Layer list will, as displayed on the canvas, appear to be "in front of" objects below them. By placing images in layers and then reordering these layers, you can manipulate whether objects are perceived to be in the background or foreground. The order in which layers appear (top to bottom in the list) is frequently referred to as the *layer stacking order*. Put another way, those items at the top of the stack (list) appear to be in the foreground, whereas those at the bottom of the stack (list) appear in the background. Just how near or far, relative to other items, an item appears in display is determined by the particular layer it is a member of.

The concept of stacking order applies to layers and sublayers. The stacking order can be changed at any time. Let's give it a try. Continue with the following steps.

32. Click on the *Logo and Text* layer. While you hold down the mouse button (left mouse button on the PC), drag the *Logo and Text* layer below the *Background* layer. As you drag the layer, you should see a thin black line, which corresponds to the position of the layer you are moving. Drop the *Logo and Text* layer below the *Background* layer. The text and logo should no longer be visible, because the *Background* layer (containing blue rectangles) now covers it up. That is, the *Background* layer is more toward the front (i.e., is higher in the stacking order) than the text and logo.
33. Let's change it back. Click on the *Background* layer and drag/drop it below the *Logo and Text* layer. You should now be able to see the text and logo again, because they are now higher in the stacking order.

This same reordering process can be applied to sublayers within a layer. Let's give it a try. Continue with the following steps.

Shortcut

To deselect all currently selected objects:
PC: Ctrl + D
MAC: Cmd + D

34. Select the *Background* layer. Click on the Plus (+) icon to expand the list of sublayers within the layer. You may find that all sublayers are selected. If this is the case, click the cursor anywhere in the white area of the Document window to deselect these sublayers. Note the Keyboard Shortcut at left, which provides keyboard commands for deselecting all currently selected objects.
35. Click on the *Block Rectangle* sublayer at the very bottom of the stacking order. Drag this sublayer to the very top of the list and drop it there. Note that all other images within this layer are now covered up. The reason you can still see the text and logo is that these objects are located in the *Logo and Text* layer, which is higher in the stacking order of layers.

36. Select Edit | Undo Layer Change to return the *Block Rectangle* sublayer to its original position. Now click on the Minus (–) icon to the left of the *Background* layer, to collapse the sublayers.
37. Leave this file open.

You will work extensively with the Layers panel as you continue with the exercises in this book. Let's now take a look at another primary panel.

Guided Tour 1C: The Changing Look of the Properties Panel

To explore the Properties panel, perform the following steps.

1. You should still have the file *tour_1B.png* open from the last guided tour. If not, open this file now. Figure 1-18 shows the Properties panel as seen upon opening the *tour_1B.png* file. If you kept the file open from the last guided tour, you may need to click on the white area of the Document window to view the document's Properties panel. Look at the options listed in the document's Properties panel.

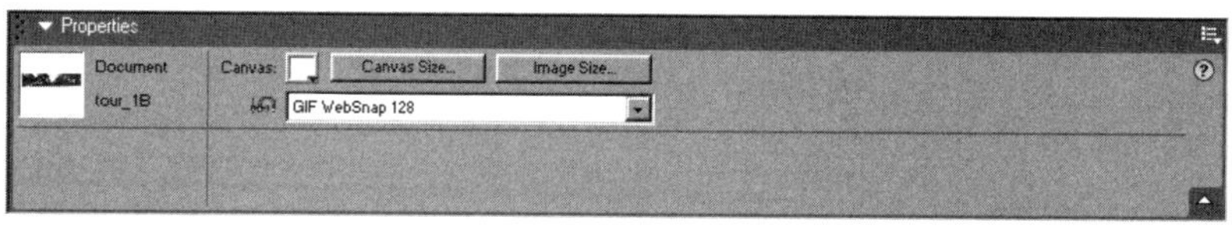

Fig. 1-18. Properties panel for tour_1B.png.

2. Select the *Background* layer from the Layers panel.
3. Click on the Plus (+) icon next to the Background layer, which will expand the list of sublayers inside the layer.
4. Click on the *Middle Bitmap* sublayer. Examine the Properties panel, shown in figure 1-19. This is how the Properties panel looks when a bitmap image is selected. Note that the options now listed are very different from those listed with the Document window. The Properties panel is context sensitive and will always show you the properties of the currently selected object.

Fig. 1-19. Properties panel for bitmap image.

NOTE

The difference between bitmapped and vector graphics is discussed in Chapter 2.

5. Click on the *Right Rectangle* sublayer. Examine the Properties panel, shown in figure 1-20. This is how the Properties panel looks when a vector image is selected.

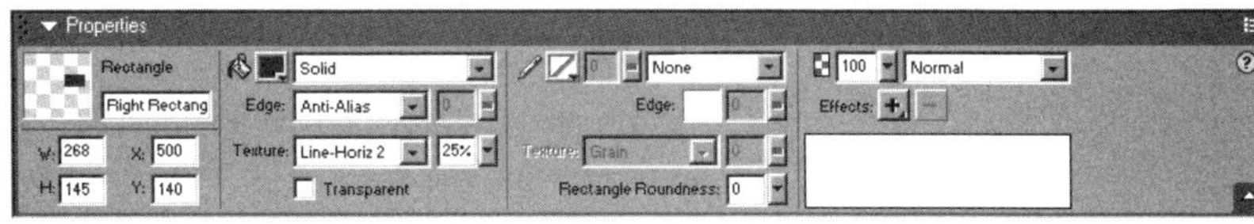

Fig. 1-20. Properties panel for vector image.

6. Click on the Minus (–) icon next to the *Background Layers* folder. This will collapse the list of sublayers.
7. Click on the Plus (+) icon next to the *Logo and Text Layers* folder. This will expand the list of sublayers inside the layer.
8. Click on the *Text* sublayer. Examine the Properties panel, shown in figure 1-21. This is how the Properties panel looks when a text image is selected.

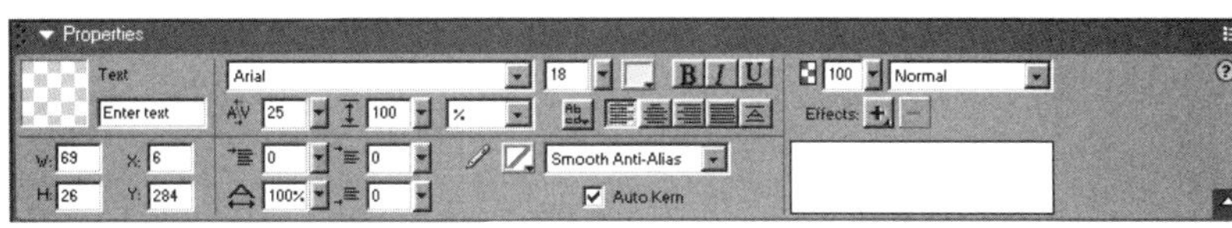

Fig. 1-21. Properties panel for text image.

You will explore the details of the options listed on each of the Properties panels as they are encountered in association with exercises throughout the book. In Guided Tour 1D you will continue to work with panels.

Guided Tour 1D: Working with Panels

In this guided tour, you will take a closer look at properties typical of all panels within Fireworks MX. The tour is fairly short and is organized around looking at how these general properties can be manipulated. All panels you have examined to this point have been positioned as they are by factory default. However, you can change this positioning scheme. Let's take a look.

Docking and Undocking Panels

By default, the panels on screen when you first open Fireworks MX are docked (attached to the side of the interface), making them immobile. However, you can easily undock a panel so that it is "free floating" and can be dragged to another location, as follows.

1. Let's look at the Tools panel first. Examine the upper left-hand corner of the panel. Note the panel gripper which appears as a "series of dots" in this corner.
2. Move the cursor over the panel gripper. Note that the arrow cursor now turns into a four-pointed cursor, which typically indicates that the object can be moved. Hold down the mouse button (left mouse button on PC) and drag the Tools panel to the center of the Document window. Drop the panel on top of the Document window.
3. Click on the very top of the Tools panel, and while holding down the mouse button drag the panel to the right and nestle it directly against the bottom portion of the menu bar and against the other panels at this location. Note that as you get in the general area Fireworks displays a highlighted rectangle, targeting where you can drop the panel. Actually, once you see this "target" rectangle, you can simply let go and Fireworks will automatically dock the panel. Note that it actually places the Tools panel to the right of the current panels.
4. Verify that the Tools panel is now docked at the right.
5. Let's now try undocking the Properties panel, now located below the Document window. Move the mouse cursor over the panel gripper until the arrow cursor changes to the four-pointed cursor. Click and hold the mouse button down (left button on PC) as you drag the panel up and position it above the Document window. Let go of the mouse button.

Grouping and Ungrouping Panels

Panels can be grouped by choosing Group Panel With from the Options menu in the upper right corner of each expanded panel. You may also access this option by right-clicking (Ctrl-clicking on Mac) on the panel's title bar to view the context menu. Grouped panels appear as a series of tabs within a panel group. If you try to drag a tab, an alert dialog will display and prompt you to use the Group Panel With option. To ungroup a panel, choose the Group Panel With option and select New Panel Group.

Note that panel groups may be docked to the Fireworks MX interface as described in the previous section or docked to other floating panel groups.

Collapsible Panels

You can expand or collapse any panel by clicking on the arrow in the upper left-hand corner of each panel or panel group, as shown in figures 1-22 and 1-23.

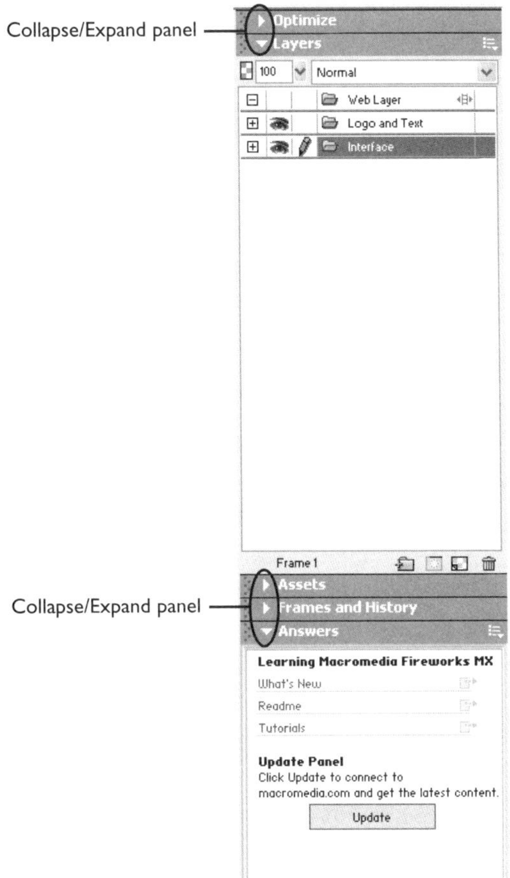

Fig. 1-22. The Layers and Answers panels in the expanded mode.

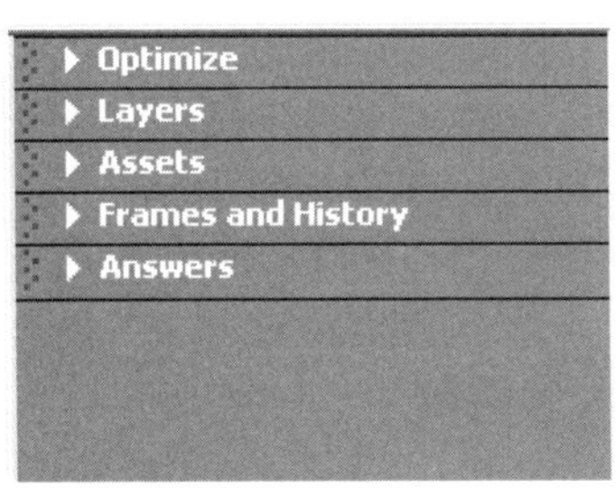

Fig. 1-23. The Layers and Answers panels in the collapsed mode.

Reset Panels to Factory Default

You can reset panels to their default settings by selecting Commands Menu | Panel Layout Set and then selecting the screen size your monitor is set to. Go ahead and do this. The panels should now look like they did when you first opened the program.

6. Click on the X in the upper right-hand corner of the Document window to close the file without saving it.

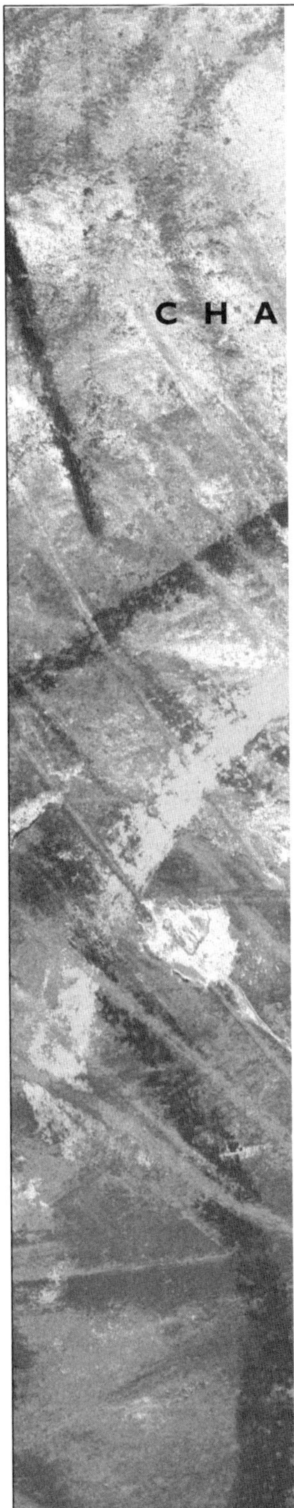

CHAPTER 2

Working with the Tools Panel

Chapter Topics:

- *Introduction*
- *Graphic Formats*
- *Guided Tour 2A: The Select Toolbox*
- *Guided Tour 2B: The Vector Toolbox*
- *Guided Tour 2C: The Bitmap Toolbox*
- *Guided Tour 2D: The Web Toolbox*
- *Guided Tour 2E: The Color Toolbox*
- *Guided Tour 2F: The View Toolbox*
- *Getting Your Computer Ready for Practice Exercises*
- *Practice Exercise 2-1: Drawing the Foundation for the Splash Page*

Introduction

Fireworks MX has a powerful set of drawing and painting tools that makes it possible for designers to create both vector and raster (bitmapped) objects to be used intact as graphic images, as well as the ability to process images for use on the Web – all within one program. Fireworks MX also allows you to import artwork created in other vector-based programs, such as Macromedia's FreeHand or a bitmap editor such as Adobe's Photoshop.

This chapter is focused on the needs of novice users who may not be familiar with the use of tools common to many graphics programs. More experienced users may want to browse through this chapter, as there may be tools in Fireworks MX with which you are not familiar. As you open up the Fireworks Tools panel, get ready to explore the many design possibilities available to you with these powerful tools. By the end of this chapter, you will be able to:

- *Briefly describe the difference between raster and vector graphic formats*
- *Use the Select tools*
- *Use the Vector tools*
- *Use the Bitmap tools*
- *Use the Web tools*
- *Use the Color tools*
- *Use the View tools*

Graphic Formats

When creating and using graphics, it is important to understand the difference between the two types of graphic file formats: raster and vector. The foundation of a raster graphic lies within a 2D matrix (basically rows and columns) consisting of individual pixels defined by (mapped by) specific X (row) and Y (column) coordinates. Raster graphics (more frequently referred to as a bitmapped graphics) are typically created in "paint" programs that build an image by electronically defining specific pixels. For example, to create a line in a bitmap format, pixels are "painted" (electronically turned on) as the drawing tool moves over the surface. The line consists of "painted" pixels, lying side by side, which define the length and width of the line.

A pixel is the smallest unit of measurement when working with bitmap graphics. Each graphic consists of many pixels of varying shades of color. These pixels are so small that when the graphic is viewed at normal size the pixels of various colors blend together to form an image recognizable to the human eye. Your computer monitor's resolution is also defined in terms of pixels: one standard monitor resolution is 800 by 600, or 800 pixels (along the X axis) by 600 pixels (along the Y axis). The larger the number of pixels, the more information (detail) the image contains.

The raster file must store the location and properties of each pixel. The strength of bitmapped graphics is that they are capable of very high resolution, with brilliant colors. The downside is that bitmapped graphics tend to have large file sizes (because of the large amount of information being stored) and are difficult to resize and otherwise manipulate. Bitmap graphics are the most common graphic type used on the Web today, because most web graphics are in either GIF or JPEG format, both of which are bitmap graphic types (compression formulas designed to reduce the size of specific types of graphics).

In contrast, vector graphic files contain algorithms (mathematical equations) used to generate the objects they represent. Algorithms can easily represent circles, arcs, lines, squares, and other such objects. As you might guess, vector graphics have file sizes that are much smaller than their bitmap cousins, but the downside is that they generally do not possess the thousands of colors and brilliance of bitmaps (which can contain complex color patterns consisting of potentially millions of colors).

Another benefit of using vector graphics is that they can be scaled proportionally to any size, larger or smaller, and still retain the same crisp shape and outline as their original size. This characteristic is not true of bitmap images, which are built around pixels. Looking at close-ups of two circles (one created as a vector image and the other as a bitmap) may help you see the difference between the two formats. (See figures 2-1 and 2-2.) Note that the circle in the bitmap image (figure 2-1) is pixilated (containing jagged edges), whereas the vector circle (figure 2-2) has a smooth, curved surface. The vector circle can easily be resized, whereas the bitmapped circle will become distorted as you try to enlarge it. Bitmapped images that include text frequently become difficult to read when either enlarged or reduced.

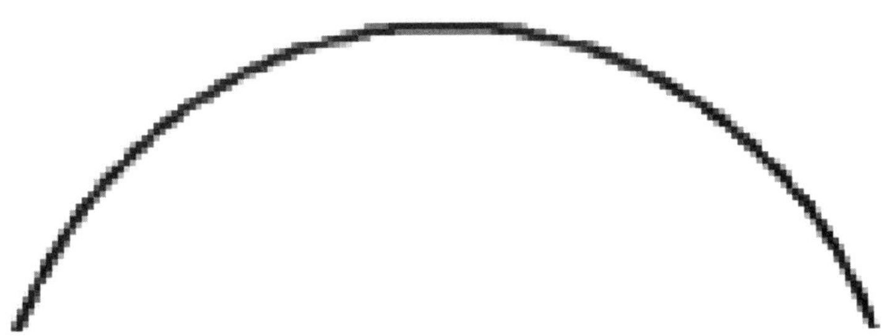

Fig. 2-1. Close-up of bitmapped circle image.

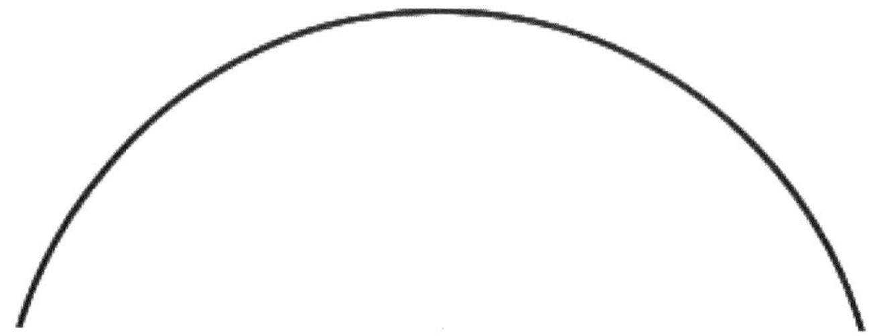

Fig. 2-2. Close-up of vector circle image.

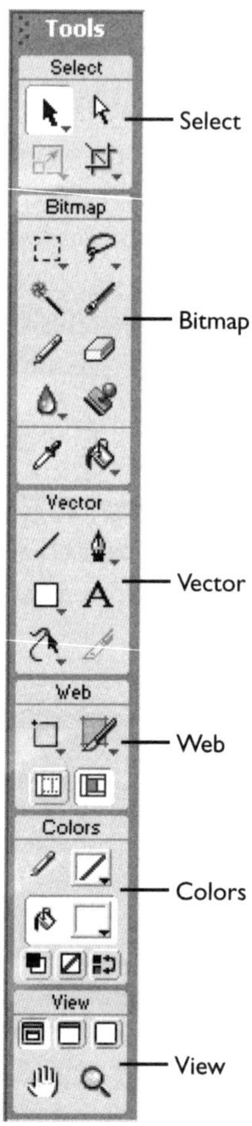

Fig. 2-3. Tools panel.

The beauty of Fireworks MX is that you can create and modify both bitmapped and vector images. As you work, each image is stored on a separate sublayer. When the file is saved in the native Fireworks format (PNG), all layers and sublayers are maintained with their various image formats. However, if you export or save the image in another format, all layers and sublayers are "flattened" (reduced) to whatever single bitmap graphic format you have selected.

The native Fireworks PNG is based on the standard PNG format, but it is not like an exported PNG file. Firework's PNG contains far more information in its header, to enable various Fireworks features. This is important because the basic file workflow requires two files: the master Fireworks PNG and whatever export format you choose. The master file can be edited with the separate layers intact, whereas the exported file is a "flattened" version. This means that the content of all layers has been combined into one background layer. The several guided tours in this chapter explore the tools that can be used with bitmap images, with vector images, with both types of images, and with those tools specialized for web use.

Guided Tour 2A: The Select Toolbox

In this chapter you are going to take a close look at the tools in the Tools panel. You saw this panel for the first time in Chapter 1. Note again that it divides the tools into six toolboxes: Select, Bitmap, Vector, Web, Colors, and View. See figure 2-3.

We have also divided the guided tours in this chapter to reflect the division of tools found in the Tools panel, so that each tour will be focused on just one section of the Tools panel. We hope this organization will help you come back to these guided tours for refreshers on how to use the tools, as you progress through the practice exercises found in subsequent chapters of the book. Let's get started.

CD-ROM

1. Locate the companion CD-ROM at the back of the book and place it in the CD-ROM player of your computer.
2. Select File | Open.
3. Verify that the Open Document dialog window has opened. See figure 2-4.

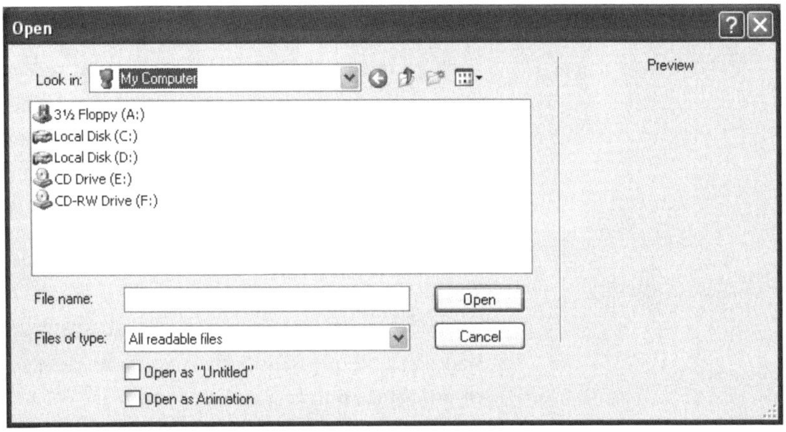

Fig. 2-4. Open Document dialog window.

4. Click on the down arrow to the right of the Look In field, to open the pull-down menu.
5. Using the browse function associated with this pull-down menu, locate the CD-ROM player within your computer.
6. Double click on the CD-ROM to open it. Locate and double click on the *Chapter 2* folder, located on the CD-ROM.
7. Locate and click on the file *Tour_2A.png*. Click on the Open button.
8. Take a moment to examine the graphic image. It is a graphic you worked with in Chapter 1.
9. Examine figure 2-3, which includes the Select toolbox, which you will work with in this guided tour.

TIP

You can also simply double click on the file name to open the file.

Why Do You Need to Select an Object?

Before you can copy, modify, transform, or otherwise do something to an object, you must first select it. Some people find the idea and necessity of selecting something before acting on it somewhat confusing. In this regard, perhaps an analogy will help.

Suppose you want to draw a picture of a sunny day at the beach. You decide to use a box of colored pencils. You first select the black pencil and sketch an outline of the seashore, with saw grass and sea oats. Next, you sketch the ocean and gently rolling waves breaking upon the beach. Then you add a few birds walking on the beach. Then you select the blue pencil and color in the ocean, and then a green pencil to add some shading to the ocean. You select a tan pencil, and then a light brown pencil, to color in the beach.

In each case you had to select a particular "object" (the ocean) and then the appropriate "tool" (color of pencil) for that object. Typically when you work with an image in Fireworks, that image will consist of many separate objects (just as our seaside picture consisted of different objects, such as the ocean, waves, beach, seashore, and birds). You have to tell Fireworks which object you want to work with, and which tool you want to use on that object. You do the "telling" by selecting the object and then selecting the tool.

If you are going to create a new object within Fireworks, you have to first select a tool to work with and then create the object you want. If you want to modify an object, you have to first select the object and then select the tool you want to use to modify it. In some cases, you will have to select a portion of an object before you can modify it.

The first group of tools you will examine are the tools Fireworks uses to select an object or a portion of an object. Let's take a closer look.

Pointer Tool

You can use the Pointer tool for general selection of bitmap and vector graphics. Selecting an object with the Pointer tool allows you to then be able to act on that object; that is, move it, transform it, or adjust the object's properties with the use of the Properties panel. Perform the following steps.

1. The Pointer tool should already be selected (by default, as you open the file). However, if it is not currently selected, click on the Pointer tool to select it.
2. Use the mouse to move the Pointer tool over the trolley car graphic to the left of the canvas. Note that this object now has a red highlight around it, as the cursor stays within the image's boundaries.
3. Move the Pointer tool over the street image in the middle of the canvas. Note that this object now has a red highlight around it, as will any object in an unlocked layer as the Pointer tool is rolled over it.
4. Go to the Layers panel (on the far right) and click on the plus (+) symbol next to the *Interface* layer, so that you can now see the sublayers within this layer.

·TIP·

You can change the highlight default color used to signify that an object is selected. Select Edit | Preferences and select a new Highlight color on the General tab that appears. You can "select" an object by clicking the Pointer tool on the object in the canvas or by clicking on the object in the Layers panel.

Shortcut

The keyboard shortcut for Edit | Undo is:
PC: Ctrl + Z
Mac: Cmd + Z

·TIP·

Holding the Shift key down as you click on multiple objects is a quick method of selecting a group of objects on the canvas.

Shortcut

You can select all graphics on unlocked layers at one time by simultaneously pressing:
PC: Ctrl + A
Mac: Cmd + A

You can deselect all selected graphics at one time by simultaneously pressing: PC: Ctrl + D
Mac: Cmnd + D

5. Go back to the canvas and click on the Pointer tool on the street image to select it. Note that the red highlight now turns blue, once the object has been selected. Note also that the *Middle Bitmap* sublayer is now highlighted in the Layers panel.
6. Examine the Properties panel, displayed at the bottom of the screen (unless you have moved it elsewhere). You might have to expand this panel by clicking on the white triangle to the left of the Properties label.

Once an object is selected, you can use the Properties panel to view or modify any of the properties displayed here. Let's try it. Continue with the following steps.

7. Click the mouse cursor inside the W field and highlight the current setting (249). Type in *150* and press the Enter/Return key. Note that you have just modified the width of the selected bitmapped object.
8. Select Edit | Undo Transform to return the image to the original image dimensions.
9. Let's try selecting multiple objects, one at a time. Click on the trolley car image on the canvas. As you hold the Shift key down, click on the street image. As you continue to hold down the Shift key, click on the light blue/white bar beneath both graphics. All of these objects should now have blue highlights around them.
10. You can deselect a selected object by clicking on any portion of the gray area outside the canvas. Go ahead and do that now. All highlights should disappear.
11. You can also use the Pointer tool to select a vector image. Move the Pointer tool over the text *san francisco travel guide*. Note that the entire phrase is highlighted, with four red corners showing. Click on these words. Note that the entire phrase is now selected and highlighted, showing four blue corners.
12. Click on the gray area surrounding the canvas to deselect the object.
13. In the Tools panel, you may have noticed the small black triangle at the lower right-hand corner of the Pointer tool. Click on the Pointer tool and hold the mouse button down for a few seconds. You should now see a pop-up window that offers another option: the Select Behind tool. The Select Behind tool is used for selecting graphics behind web objects such as slices and hotspots. When the *web* layer is visible, the slices are normally selected with the Pointer tool. You have to hide the slices in order to select the graphics beneath them, or use the Select Behind tool. Later

in the book you will be introduced to slices and hotspots. Close the pop-up window without changing the Pointer tool, by clicking on the gray area.

Subselection Tool

As you saw in step 11, you can use the Pointer tool for general vector selection. However, if you want to edit the points within a vector (perhaps to change the shape), you will have to use the Subselection tool from the Selection toolbox, as follows.

1. Click on the Subselection tool in the Tools panel (refer to figure 2-3, if you need to). Move the Subselection tool over the text *san francisco travel guide*. Note that the red highlight no longer shows a single object (actually, it is a group of objects). Instead, you now see the red selection over each shape in the logo. Using the Subselection tool, you can highlight and see the various objects that make up the text logo.
2. Click on the word *san* to select it. Note that all anchor points for the image now display as very small blue rectangles.
3. Click on any of these single anchor points to select them. Note that the small blue rectangle has now turned into a series of small, solid blue rectangles. You may also note small blue lines (depending on which point you have selected). Click on a point and hold the mouse button down (left button on PC) as you drag it away from the image. Let go of the mouse button. You should now see that you have altered the image by moving an anchor point of the line. See figure 2-5.

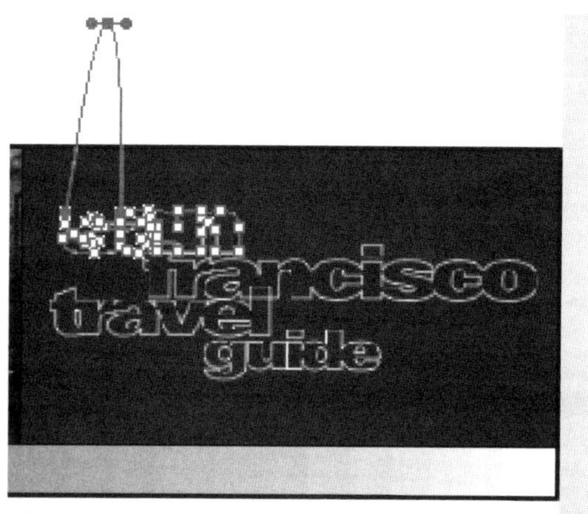

Fig. 2-5. Using the Subselection tool to alter a vector shape.

> **TIP**
> If you moved the anchor point more than once, continue to select Undo until you have returned the shape to its previous form. To set the number of multiple undos in Fireworks MX, select Edit | Preferences. On the General tab, type in the number of Undo Steps.

4. Select Edit | Undo Move Point to return the image to the original image shape.

Scale Tool

The Scale tool can be used with either bitmapped or vector objects to resize, move, or rotate a selected object. The resizing can be accomplished by adjusting either the height or width, independent of each other. Alternatively, you can resize the image with the width and height being changed in proportion to each other. In the steps that follow, you will practice using the tool in both of these ways.

> **TIP**
> When working with the Subselection tool and editing points along a path, it is often beneficial to zoom in on the area to see the edits more clearly. You will be introduced to the Zoom tool in the last guided tour of this chapter.

1. Click on the Pointer tool and click on the image of the trolley car.
2. Click on the Scale tool. You should see eight black rectangles outlining the image, with a black circle in the center of the image.
3. Move the cursor over the image and you will note the four-pointed cursor, indicating that you can move the object. Click and hold down the mouse button (left button on PC) as you drag the image slightly away from the current location. Now drag it back to the original location (or select Edit | Undo Transform).
4. Select the Scale tool again and move the cursor into the upper right-hand corner. You will note that the cursor changes to a double-headed arrow, indicating that you can now proportionally change the scale or size of the image. Click and hold down the mouse button as you move the cursor toward the center of the image. Let go of the mouse button. The image is now smaller, but keeps the same proportions (aspect ratio) it had originally. See figure 2-6.

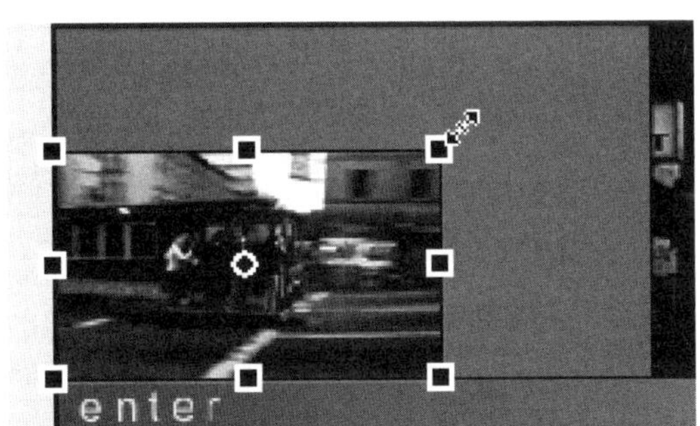

Fig. 2-6. Double-headed arrow with Scale tool to reduce image size (magnified view).

5. Move the cursor to the black rectangle in the middle of the right side. Click and hold the mouse button as you drag the right edge of the image

toward the middle. As you can see, you have just modified the width of the image, without changing the height. Try reducing the height of the image.

6. Move the cursor slightly away from the image. Note that the cursor is an arrow in the shape of a circle. This cursor indicates that you can now rotate the object. Click and hold the mouse button as you move the mouse upward. Let go of the mouse button. You should now see that you have just rotated the image counterclockwise. (See figure 2-7.) Select Edit | Undo to undo the scale-and-rotation operation.

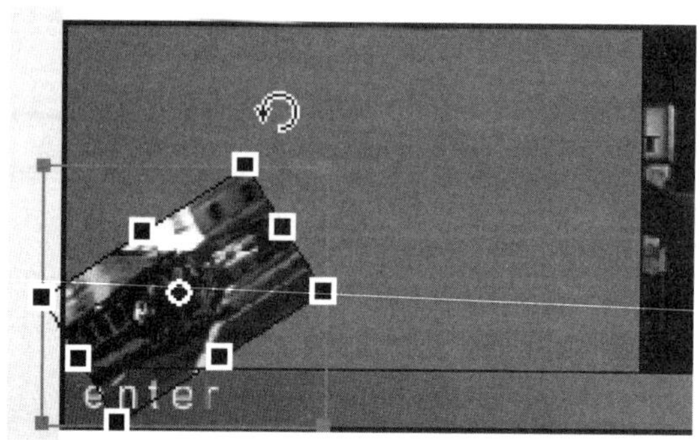

Fig. 2-7. Using the Scale tool to rotate an image (magnified view).

7. In the Tools panel, you may have noticed the small black triangle at the lower right-hand corner of the Scale tool. Click on the Scale tool and keep the mouse button down for a few seconds. You should now see a pop-up window that offers three tools: Scale, Skew, and Distort.
8. Click on the Skew tool. Click on the black rectangle in the middle of the right side of the image. As you hold the mouse button down, move the cursor up, and then down. As you can see, this tool allows you to skew the selected side in the direction you pull.
9. Click on the Scale tool and keep the mouse button down for a few seconds. From the pop-up window that appears, click on the Distort tool. Click on the black rectangle in the middle of the right side of the image. As you hold the mouse button down, move the cursor in different directions. This tool allows you to distort the image in whatever direction you move the mouse. Select Edit | Undo Transform to undo the distortion.

Crop Tool

The Crop tool is used to select a rectangular portion of an image. This selected area can then be cropped so that only the portion of the image inside the selection is retained. Anything outside the selected area is deleted from the image.

TIP

To cancel the selection, you can double click the Crop tool outside the selected area.

1. Click on the Crop tool. Move the cursor to the photo of the trolley car, up and left of where you see people standing in the doorway of the trolley car. Click the mouse and hold down the button as you drag toward the lower right-hand corner of the trolley doorway. Let go of the mouse button. Double click *inside* the selected area (you can also press the Enter/Return key). You should now see that the only portion of the image that remains is the section of the trolley doorway you just cropped. See figure 2-8.

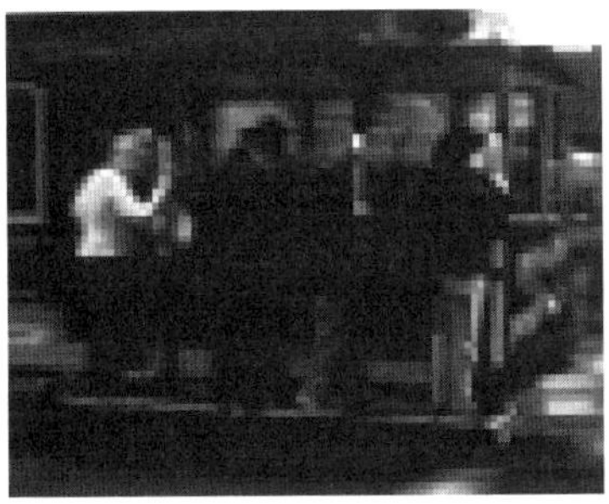

Fig. 2-8. Cropped image of the trolley doorway.

2. You may have noticed the small black triangle at the lower right-hand corner of the Crop tool. Click on the Crop tool and keep the mouse button down for a few seconds. You should now see a pop-up window that offers another option: the Export Area tool. The Export Area tool works the same way as the Crop tool. However, when you double click in the selection, the Export Preview window is launched automatically. This allows you to adjust compression settings and export just a portion of an image. When complete, the original picture is still the original size, with only the exported file being cropped.
3. Select File | Close. In the pop-window that appears, click on the No button to reject the saving of changes.

You have just completed a tour of the Select toolbox. In Guided Tour 2B you will explore the Vector toolbox.

Guided Tour 2B: The Vector Toolbox

You will probably find yourself drawing for the most part with the vector tools. This is a good idea, because vectors are far more flexible and editable than bitmaps, and transfer to other packages, such as Flash and FreeHand, more easily. In this guided tour, we will jump to the vector tools first, and then come back in the next guided tour to work with the bitmap tools.

1. Start with a new file by selecting File | New.
2. In the New Document window that opens, type in *500* for the Width, *500* for the Height, and *72* for the Resolution setting. Select a white canvas. Click on the OK button.
3. Use figure 2-9 as a reference for this guided tour on the Vector toolbox.

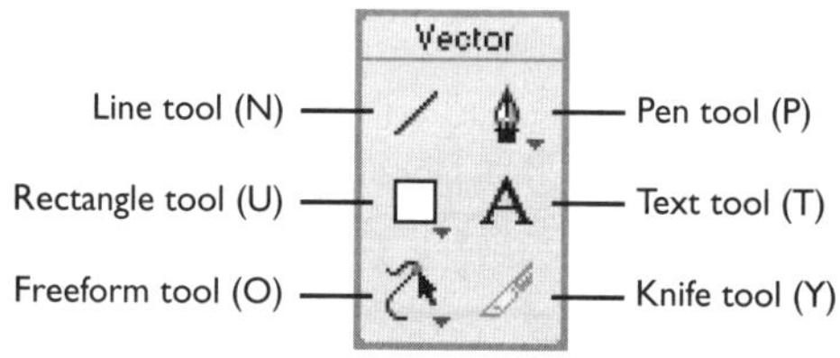

Fig. 2-9. Vector toolbox.

Line Tool

To work with the Line tool, perform the following steps.

1. Select the Line tool. Note that the cursor now looks like a crosshair.
2. In the Colors toolbox, click on the Pencil icon to open the Stroke color palette. Now select any color you wish (other than white).
3. Move the Line tool cursor to the lower left-hand portion of the canvas. Click and continue to hold down the mouse button as you drag the cursor to the right, a distance of about four inches. While still holding down the mouse button, move the cursor up, and then down. This shows you how a line can be adjusted as long as you keep the mouse button down. Now release the mouse button to form a line.

·TIP·

A quick and easy way to draw a straight line is to hold down the Shift key and draw the line with the Line tool. Holding down the Shift key constrains the line to a straight line that is either horizontal, vertical, or at a 45-degree angle.

Note that you could have drawn the first line at any angle you wished, prior to releasing the mouse button. Let's try a straight line. Continue with the following steps.

4. Press and hold down the Shift key. The Line tool should still be selected. Click the cursor anywhere on the canvas and as you hold down the mouse button (and keep the Shift key down), draw another line. As you can see, holding the Shift key down constrains the line to a straight line.
5. Clear the screen by selecting Select | Select All, and then press Del/Backspace.

Line Tool with the Properties Panel

You may have noticed that the lines you drew were all the same color as the color you chose with the Pencil icon in the Colors toolbox. You can also select and change the color and many other properties for vector lines by using the associated Properties panel. In figure 2-10, examine the Properties panel located below the canvas. Let's change the properties by performing the following steps.

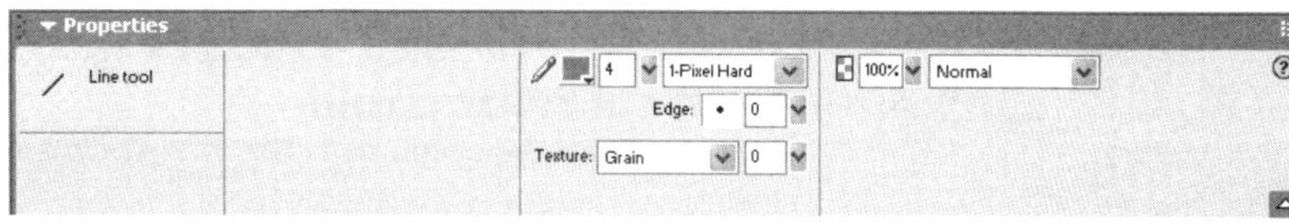

Fig. 2-10. Properties panel with Line tool selected.

1. The Line tool should still be selected. If it is not, select it. You should now see the line Properties panel below the canvas. In the middle of the Properties panel you should see an icon that looks like a pencil, with a color swatch next to it. This is the Stroke Color field. Click on the color swatch next to the Pencil icon. A color palette has now opened. Click on any color. The palette closes.
2. Next to the Stroke Color field is the Stroke Width field, consisting of both a data entry box (where you can type in a number to establish a stroke width) and a down arrow button (which opens a slider bar, from which you can select a stroke width). Use either method to set the stroke width to 10. Draw a few lines.
3. Next to the Stroke Width field is the Stroke Category field. Click on the pull-down menu and look at the options listed. (See figure 2-11.) These options alter the appearance or quality of the line. Note the black triangle next to each option, offering an additional pop-up menu of options for that particular stroke attribute.

·TIP·

Clicking on the Stroke Category field and selecting Stroke Options gives you access to extended and advanced stroke features, which you will use in subsequent chapters.

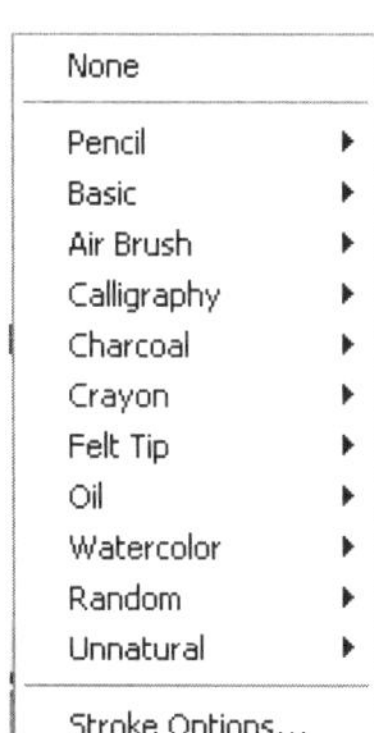

Figure 2-11. Properties panel showing Stroke Attributes pull-down menu.

4. Take a few moments and experiment with drawing lines with various stroke colors, widths, and attributes.
5. Examine the Color section in the Tools panel. Note that you can also select the stroke color using the first tool listed in this section. You will practice using this tool in Guided Tour 2E.

Pen Tool

Drawing point by point with the Pen tool is the most precise way of drawing complex vector shapes. Think back to when you last saw a "connect the dots" coloring book. Basically it consisted of a series of dots. The object was to draw lines between the dots to reveal an image. Once the dots were connected, the shapes could be filled in with color.

This is very similar to the process used when drawing with the Pen tool. You draw a series of points with the Pen tool, and the lines that connect them automatically appear when each point is added. The points are the anchors that the lines in a vector shape attach to. To adjust the curve of the lines between the points, you move a pair of handles that appear at each point to be edited. If the lines between the points are perfectly straight, you see no handles. If the lines between the points are curved, you see handles extending from the points as an "interface" used to modify the shape of the curve. Perform the following steps.

1. Let's clean up a bit first. Select Select | Select All (or use the keyboard shortcut Ctrl + A or Cmd +A). Press Delete (Backspace on Mac) or select Edit | Clear.
2. Select the Pen tool. Let's create a simple "house." Hold the Shift key down and click five points in the shape of a house (do not close the shape yet). After the second point and each consecutive point, a line is automatically drawn between the two points. Your drawing should look something like the illustration shown in figure 2-12, but do not worry about what it looks like. You will get a chance to modify the drawing in material to follow.

TIP

Holding the Shift key down and using the Pen tool works in a manner similar to using the Line tool. Holding the Shift key down constrains the points and paths to straight lines. This is often a good technique to use when drawing with the Pen tool: place the points, and then shape the curved lines between them.

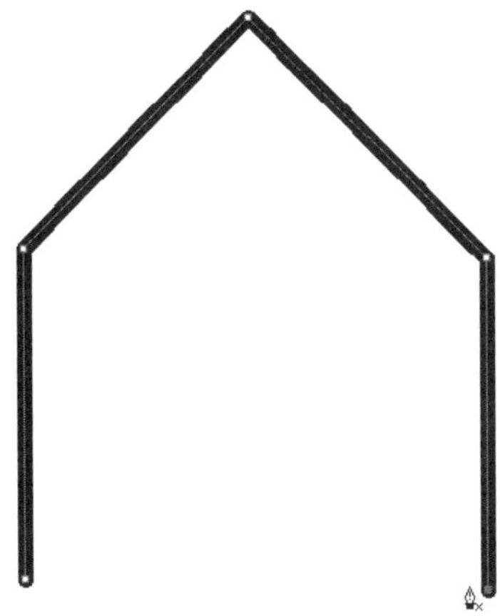

Fig. 2-12. Simple house drawn with Pen tool.

3. After you have drawn the fifth point, move the Pen over the first point you drew and note the circle icon (o) that appears below the Pen, as shown in figure 2-13. This indicates that clicking on this point will close the path of the shape. Click on that point to complete the path of the shape.

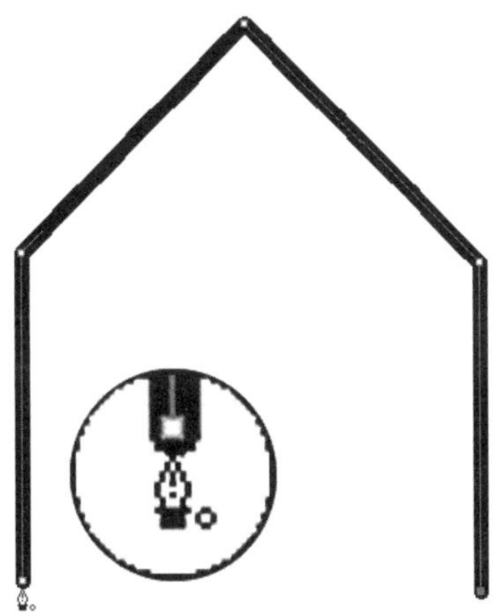

Fig. 2-13. Pen indicating that the image can be closed by clicking here (magnified view).

·TIP·

If you forget to select the Subselection tool and accidentally add anchor points with the Pen tool instead of moving a point, select Edit | Undo to get rid of the extra anchor points. Make sure to select the Subselection tool before trying to move an anchor point.

4. Adjust the location of a few points. First click on the Subselection tool, and then click on a point you want to relocate. As you hold the mouse button down, drag the point to a new location. Try another point.
5. Here is an easier way to work with the Pen and Subselection tools. Click on the Pen tool. Move the Pen tool toward a point whose location you want to change. Hold down the Ctrl (PC) or Cmd (Mac) key and you will note that the cursor changes to a small white arrow and that the Subselection tool becomes selected as long as the key is held down. With the Subselection tool activated, you can now adjust the location of this or any other point. When you release the Ctrl/Cmd key, the Pen tool returns as the active tool.
6. Let's add a point to the drawing. Select the house shape with the Pointer tool. Then select the Pen tool and click the Pen on any part of the path that does not already have a point. Look for the Plus (+) icon below the Pen tool before you click. (See figure 2-14.) Now you can click on the Subselection tool and move this new point, or hold down the Ctrl/Cmd key to toggle between the Pen and Subselection tool.

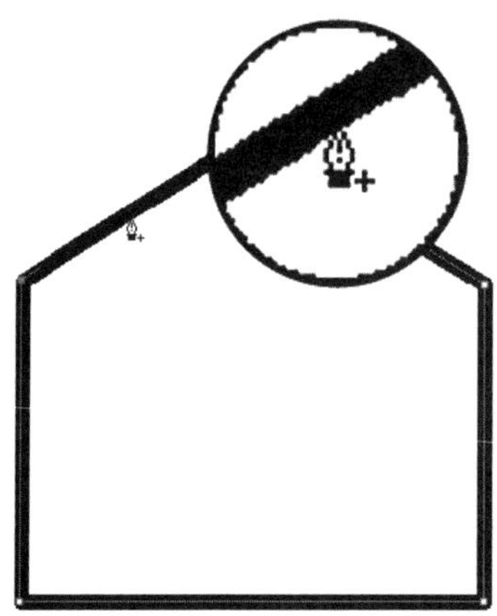

Fig. 2-14. Pen tool indicating that a point can be added here (magnified view).

7. Let's remove a point. Click on the Pen tool and move it to an existing point. (Remember, the shape must be selected first.) Look for the Minus icon (–) below the Pen tool (see figure 2-15) and then click on the point to remove it.

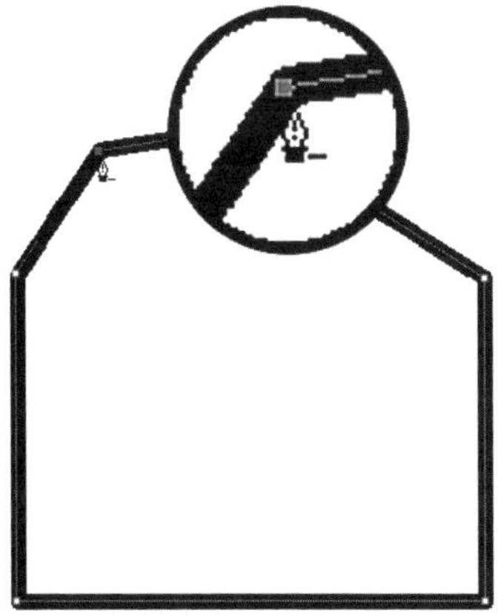

Fig. 2-15. Pen tool indicating that a point can be deleted here (magnified view).

·TIP·

Often the Pen tool is easiest to use if you trace a sketch or a screen shot. This way, you can connect the dots (points) over a rough image instead of guessing where to place the points. In Fireworks, you can easily import scanned photos or sketches to use as tracing images.

8. Now let's work with a curve. Move the Pen tool to an existing point. Click and drag a point with the Pen tool. Note that two handles appear (one for each line on each side of the point). See figure 2-16.

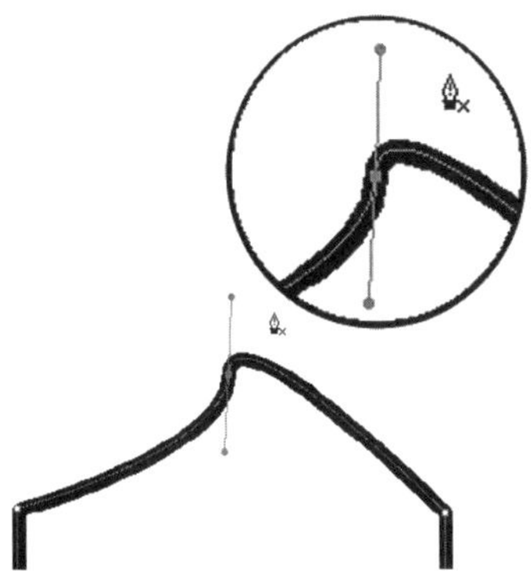

Fig. 2-16. Selected point and handles used to modify curve (magnified view).

9. When you first begin to drag with the Pen tool, the two lines move together, and subsequently the lines on both sides of the point move together. To move a single line in the pair, hold down the Alt (Option) key and click on the one end of a handle with the Subselection tool. See figure 2-17.

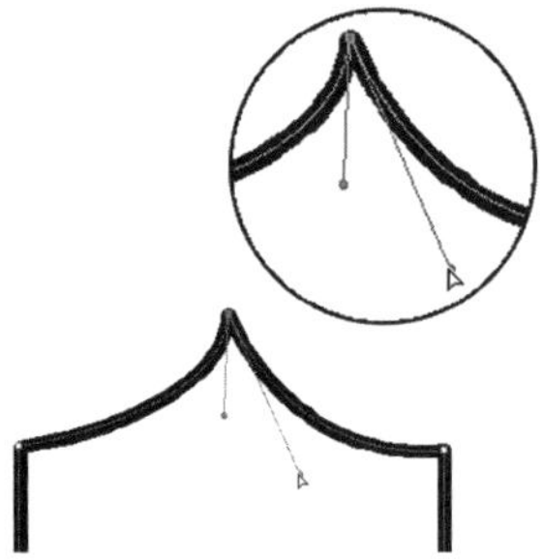

Fig. 2-17. Moving one end of the handles (magnified view).

Let's move on to the next vector tool, the Rectangle tool.

Shortcut

Press the U key on your keyboard to select the Rectangle tool, instead of clicking on the tool in the toolbox. As you press the U key repeatedly, it will cycle through the four shape options. Also carefully watch the Vector toolbox as you try this.

Rectangle Tool

The Rectangle tool is used to draw rectangular shapes. Refer to figure 2-9, if you need to. Note that the Rectangle tool has a small black triangle in the lower right-hand corner. Click on the Rectangle tool and hold the mouse button down for a moment, until the pop-up menu appears. As you can now see, this tool can be set to create rectangles, rounded rectangles, ellipses (circles), or polygons. Leave it on the rectangle setting for the moment.

1. Select the Rectangle tool and note that the cursor changes to a crosshair as you move it over the canvas.

TIP

Turning on the Caps Lock key changes a solid crosshair to a crosshair with a transparent center.

Before beginning to draw, let's pick some colors for the line and for the fill or internal portion of the rectangle. Continue with the following steps.

2. In the Colors section of the Tools panel (toward the bottom), click on the color swatch next to the Pencil icon (this will select the color of the line). In the color palette that opens, click on any color you wish. The palette will close. Click on the color swatch next to the Paint Bucket icon (this will select the color of the fill) in the Colors section. In the color palette that opens, click on any color you wish. The palette will close.
3. Move the cursor to the canvas area. Click and hold down the mouse button as you pull the mouse to the lower right-hand corner. You should now see a rectangle with the stroke color you selected, and with the fill color you selected.
4. Take a moment to look at the Properties panel associated with the Rectangle tool. Note the following fields in the lower left-hand corner of this panel: W (width), H (height), X (axis position), and Y (axis position). Click the cursor in the W field and type in a different width. Press the

Enter/Return key. Change any of these other three fields as desired. You have probably already noticed that there are many other properties in this panel. We will take a closer look at these properties in material to follow.

5. Click on the Rectangle tool and hold down the mouse button until the pop-up menu appears. Select any of the other shapes. Experiment with this tool, using whatever shapes, colors, and sizes you wish.
6. Note that when the Polygon tool is selected, the Shape field (far right side in the Properties panel) allows you to choose between a Star or a Polygon shape. Underneath the Shape field, you can specify how many sides the polygon or star has. Finally, the angle setting allows you to specify the angle used to create the anchor points of the shape.
7. By this time you have probably drawn several shapes on the canvas. Make sure that a couple of the shapes are overlapping each other, at least to some degree. Use the Pointer tool if you need to move them. Select one of the objects you have drawn, by clicking on it.

In the next section you will see how you can manipulate the appearance of the object you have just selected.

Path Operations

1. Select Window | Toolbars | Modify (place a check mark beside the Modify option). You probably noticed that a new panel of icons has been added, directly below the Properties panel.
2. Examine the icons that were just added. These represent a number of different functions that can be performed on a selected shape. See figure 2-18.

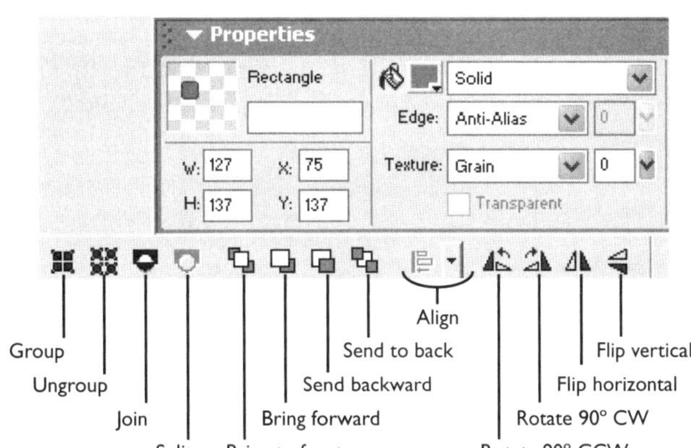

Fig. 2-18. Icons added below the Properties panel.

CAUTION

Some path operations (such as join and split) require two or more objects to be selected before they will work correctly.

3. Click on one of the shapes you have drawn. Experiment using these functions by clicking on the various icons, sending objects "to the front" and "to the back," as well as rotating them clockwise and counterclockwise.

As you have just seen, it is pretty easy to modify the orientation of images. Let's now take a look at adjusting the properties of vector objects.

Using the Properties Panel with Vector Objects

As you have seen in your initial work with vector objects, there are many options available in the Properties panel for working with vector objects. Some of these properties may or may not be available, depending on which type of vector object you currently have selected. Let's take a closer look at these properties. Perform the following steps.

1. Click on one of the rectangles you have drawn. Examine the Properties panel at the bottom of the screen. (See also figure 2-19.) Note the four sections of the Properties panel: Object, Fill, Stroke, and Effects. Vertical lines divide these sections.

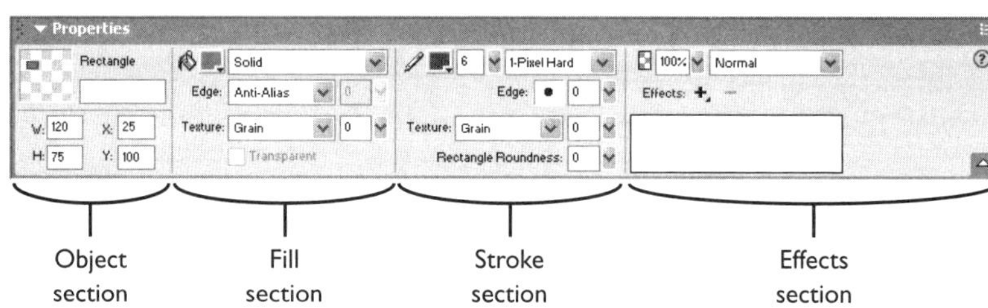

Fig. 2-19. Properties panel for rectangle vector shape.

2. Let's take a closer look at the options in each section. First, examine the options in the Object section, shown in figure 2-20.

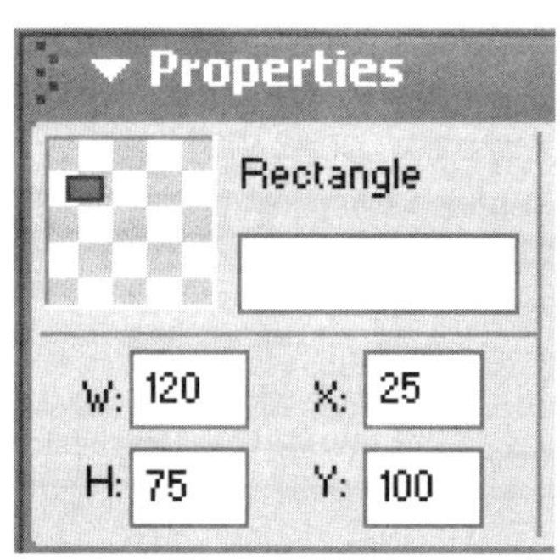

Figure 2-20. Object section within Rectangle Properties panel.

Table 2-1 outlines the fields available in the Object section, including descriptions of what each field does. Tables 2-2 through 2-4 outline the fields available in the other sections of the Properties panel.

Field	Purpose
Object Preview	Displays a thumbnail of the vector object.
Object Type	Displays the name of the object type currently selected: Path, Rectangle, Text, Bitmap, and so on.
Object Name	A blank field available so that you can type in a unique name for an object for use in a command or JavaScript reference.
W, H, X, Y	Fields that will display the current values for width, height, X axis, and Y axis. These fields show the values of an object if drawn freehand, or will allow you to type in values to resize and reposition the object based on the values you enter.

Table 2-1: Object Section Fields of the Properties Panel

Table 2-2 outlines the fields available in the Fills section, including descriptions of what each field does. See figure 2-21.

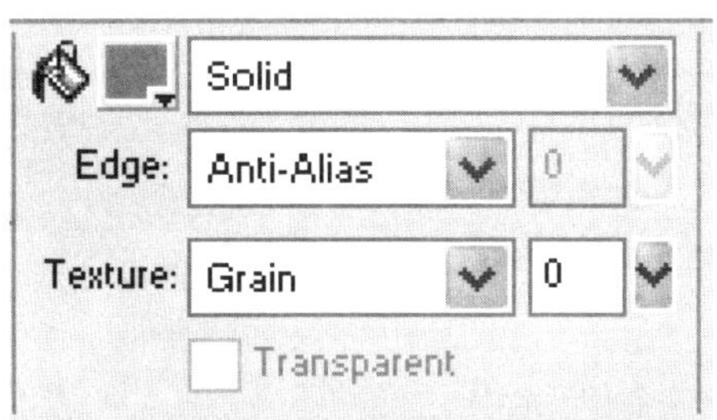

Fig. 2-21. Fill section within the Rectangle Properties panel.

Field	Purpose
Fill Color tool	Clicking on the Paint Bucket icon will display a pop-up panel used to select a color for the fill. You can simply click on a color, or you can type in a color's associated hexadecimal value (web-safe color) in the open field at the top of the panel. Note that the appearance of this panel will change if a Fill Category option is selected.
Fill Category	Clicking on the down arrow displays a pull-down menu from which you can select a variety of fill types, including solids, gradients, patterns, and others.
Edge/Amount	Clicking on the down arrow displays a pull-down menu from which you can select the edge style for the fill. The options are Hard, Anti-Alias, and Feather. You will use the Feather setting to create soft edge fills for effects later in the book. The Amount field adjusts the distance of the feathered edge.
Texture/Amount	Clicking on the down arrow displays a pull-down menu from which you can select an optional property that adds an overlay of a texture on the fill color. By default, the Amount field reads 0 (no texture). If you select a texture from the pull-down, the default changes to 50%. If you increase the amount, the texture will gradually blend with the fill.
Transparent	This field is related specifically to the Texture and Amount fields. Placing a check mark here will make an object's texture transparent to the degree of the value set in the Texture Amount field. The higher the number, the more transparent the fill.

Table 2-2: Fill Section Fields in the Properties Panel

Table 2-3 outlines the fields available in the Stroke section, including descriptions of what each field does. See figure 2-22.

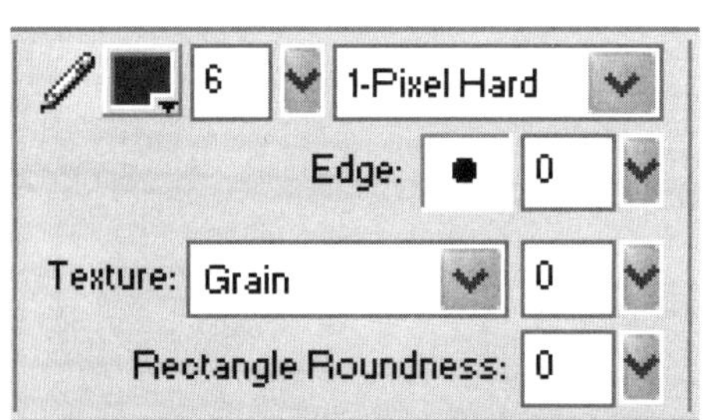

Fig. 2-22. Stroke section within the Rectangle Properties panel.

Field	Purpose
Stroke Color	Clicking on the Pencil icon will display a pop-up panel used to select a stroke color. You can simply click on a color, or you can type in the appropriate value in the hexadecimal entry field at the top of the panel.
Width	Clicking on the down arrow displays a slider bar you can use to set the width of the stroke. You can also type in a value in the entry field.
Stroke Category	Clicking on the down arrow displays a pull-down menu from which you can choose different categories of stroke styles. Some of the options are as simple as hard or soft edge, whereas others are more complex, such as the Unnatural option.
Edge	This field shows you what the edge will look like, depending on which option you selected in the Stroke category, and allows you to change the softness of the stroke edge. Use a setting of 0 for a crisp edge.
Texture/Amount	This is an optional property. Like the fill textures, you can add textures to the stroke. These textures are more noticeable if the width is 2 pixels or greater.
Rectangle Roundness	This field determines whether the rectangle will have square corners (with a setting of 0) or rounded corners, with a setting above 0.

Table 2-3: Stroke Section Fields in the Properties Panel

Table 2-4 outlines the fields available in the Effects section, including descriptions of what each field does. See figure 2-23.

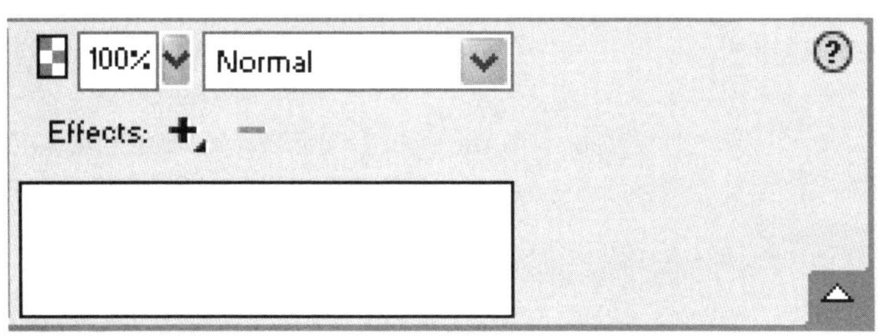

Fig. 2-23. Effects section within the Rectangle Properties panel.

Field	Purpose
Opacity	Clicking on the down arrow displays a slider bar you can use to set the degree of transparency for an image.
Blending Mode	Clicking on the down arrow displays a pull-down menu from which you can select a blending mode. Blending modes blend overlapping colors based on a variety of mathematical equations. You can use the blending mode on composite images to create special effects.
Effects	Clicking on the Plus icon (+) displays a pop-up menu offering a variety of special effects, including adjust color, bevel effects, and others. The effects can be added, removed, or edited at any time.

Table 2-4: Effects Section Fields in the Properties Panel

Let's work a little more with some of these options. Continue with the following steps.

·TIP·

Using the Colors toolbox, you can adjust the stroke and fill colors of a selected vector. You can also turn off a stroke or fill in the Colors toolbox by selecting the No Fill or No Stroke icon (this icon looks like an empty box with a red slash through it).

3. Make sure you have one of the vector rectangles selected. You have already seen the Fill Color field, but just to the right of it is the Fill Category field. It is probably currently set to Solid. Click on the pull-down menu for the Fill Category field and look at the other options. Click on the Starburst option. Click on any other options you would like to experiment with in the Fill section.
4. Click on the Fill Texture pull-down menu and examine its options. Click on a few to see how your choices change the appearance of the selected vector shape. Remember to use the Amount slider to increase or decrease the intensity of the fill texture.
5. Examine the options under Stroke (properties). To the right of the Stroke Color field is the Stroke Width field. Click on the pull-down menu and using the slider bar make the width 10, if it is not already.
6. To the right of the Stroke Width field is the Stroke Category field. Click on the pull-down menu and examine the options. Click on Airbrush, and then on Basic in the pop-up submenu that appears. Note the result of changes made to the selected object.
7. Locate the Edge field. Change its setting to 50, and note that the edges of the stroke appear harder.
8. Locate the Stroke Texture field. Click on the pull-down menu for Stroke Texture and experiment with its various options. Remember to use the Amount slider to increase or decrease the intensity of the texture.

9. Locate the Opacity field above the Effects pull-down. Click on the pull-down menu and use the slider bar to change the setting. Note the difference.

You have just taken a quick look at some of the properties associated with vector shapes, and have seen how easy it is to change these properties using the Properties panel. You will work with these settings in subsequent chapters. For now, let's continue with the vector tools and turn our attention to the Text tool.

Text Tool

To practice working with the Text tool, perform the following steps.

1. Let's clean up the screen. Select the menu option Select | Select All. Press the Delete key.
2. Select the Text tool from the Vector section of the Tools panel. Click the cursor on the canvas and type a word. You should see the text appear as you type. To make changes to the text, select the text with the Pointer tool, or use the Text tool to highlight the words and letters you would like to edit, much like you would do in a word processor. Try some experimenting with the Text tool.
3. Let's adjust some of the properties in the Properties panel for this selected text object. (See figure 2-24.) Continue with the following steps.

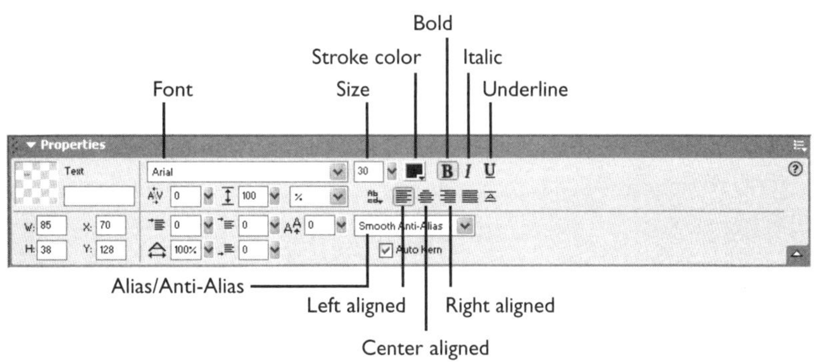

Fig. 2-24. Properties panel with text object selected.

4. Experiment with the Properties panel to adjust the properties of the selected text object. Try changing the following settings: Font, Size, Fill Color, Stroke Color, Bold, Italic, Underline, Left Aligned, Center Aligned, and Alias/Anti-Alias.

In general, the Properties panel will have the controls you need to modify text attributes, but there are a couple of options worthy of pointing out. These options are available in the Text menu only. Continue with the following steps.

5. In the menu bar, select Text | Editor. This opens a pop-up text editor. Note that this function remains inactive until you have created and selected a text object. The Text editor provides an easy option for changing the text itself, along with some of the most commonly used attributes. Click on the Cancel button to close the Text editor.
6. Select the Text menu again and note the Convert to Paths option. This option can be used if you need to break the text apart so that it is a series of paths (vector objects) instead of a text block. You may want to do this to send text to another computer that does not have a specific font installed, or to manipulate letterforms as graphic objects.
7. Note that the Text menu also includes Check Spelling, an invaluable option for most of us. You can set options for the Check Spelling feature by selecting the Spelling Setup option, at the very bottom of the Text menu. Close the Text menu by simply clicking anywhere in the gray area on screen.

CAUTION

If you choose to convert text to outlines, the text will no longer be editable as text.

The Text tool is pretty straightforward, so let's continue with other vector tools. Let's now take a look at the Freeform tool.

Freeform Tool

The Freeform tool allows you to paint distortions into a vector path using a brush, which can be adjusted in size. To work with the Freeform tool, perform the following steps.

1. Select the Rectangle tool and draw a rectangle about 2 inches in width.
2. With the rectangle still selected (you should see the blue points), select Modify | Ungroup. This will allow you to edit each side as a vector path.
3. Select the Freeform tool. Click the cursor about an inch to the outside of the rectangle, and then while holding down the mouse button drag the cursor over one of the rectangle's sides. Note that you can push/pull the shape around, just like paint on a canvas. See figure 2-25.

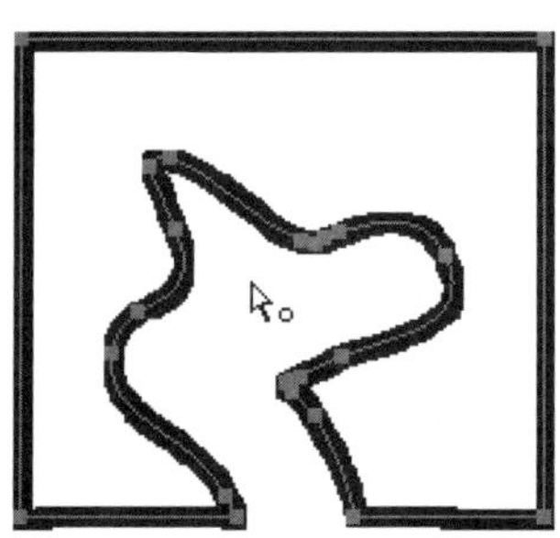

Fig. 2-25. Modifying a shape with the Freeform tool.

4. In the Tools panel, note the small black triangle, indicating that there is a pop-up menu associated with the Freeform tool. Click and hold the mouse button down on the Freeform tool, until the pop-up menu appears. There are some other options listed here. The Reshape Area tool allows you to distort a vector shape by pulling and "smudging" it around, as if you were dragging your fingers through finger paints and smudging the color onto the white of the paper. The Path Scrubber tools are designed to adjust vector paths that contain pressure-sensitive strokes. By varying the pressure and speed with which you pass over one of these paths, you can change the stroke properties. Let's try one of these other options.
5. Select the Rectangle tool and draw a rectangle about two inches in width.
6. With the rectangle still selected, select Modify | Ungroup. This will now allow you to edit each side as a vector path.
7. Select the Reshape Area tool, click in the center of the square, and pull a section off in a wavy line. Change the values for Size and Strength in the Properties panel as you continue to experiment.

We still have more vector tools to look at. Let's look at the Knife tool next.

Knife Tool

The Knife tool provides you with the capability of easily removing a section of a vector graphic or of splitting a vector path so that you can modify that path. This graphic tool works pretty much like a real knife: click and drag it across a vector object and it cuts any vector path it crosses over. Let's give it a try.

1. You first need to select a vector object to cut. Click on the Pointer tool, and then click on any vector object you have drawn. You should now see blue handles around the object.
2. Click on the Knife tool. Move the Knife so that it is to the left of the selected object. Click and hold the mouse button as you drag the Knife cursor to the right, crossing directly over the selected object and continuing until the Knife is to the right of the selected object. Let go of the mouse button.
3. Note that a new anchor point appears where you cut the segment. This indicates that you have cut the object into two sections.
4. Click on the Subselection tool, and click on the gray background to deselect all objects. Click the Subselection tool on one of the segments of the object you just cut. You should now see that only the portion you clicked on is selected. Press the Delete key.

5. Click the Subselection tool on the other portion of the object. Click on any of the path points. Click and hold the mouse button as you move the point anywhere you wish.
6. You have just used the Knife tool to break a single vector object into sections, and to delete one section and modify the shape of the other. Click on the X in the upper right corner of the Document window. Click on the No button to not save the file.

That concludes our tour of the vector tools. In the chapters to come, you will be given the opportunity to practice working with these tools. In Guided Tour 2C you will explore the Bitmap toolbox.

Guided Tour 2C: The Bitmap Toolbox

This chapter began with exploration of the vector tools because they include the basic drawing tools and those tools you are more likely to use at first, such as Text and Line. However, let's go back and take a closer look at the tools you can use to either create new bitmap objects or modify existing ones. You may find yourself needing to create a bitmap image to render a desired effect.

1. Select File | Open.
2. Verify that the Open Document dialog window has opened.
3. Click on the down arrow to the right of the Look In field to open the pull-down menu. Locate the CD-ROM player within your computer. Locate and double click on the *Chapter 2* folder, located on the companion CD-ROM.
4. Locate and click on the file *Tour_2C.png*. Click on the Open button. This file contains a bitmap image of a trolley car. You will use this image in the sections that follow.
5. Use figure 2-26 as a reference for the guided tour.

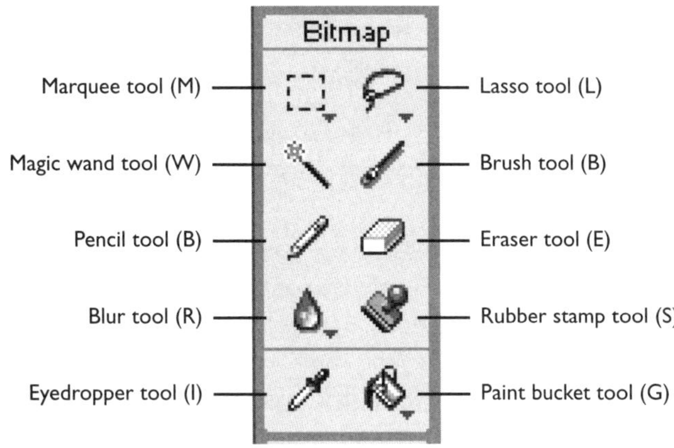

Fig. 2-26. Bitmap toolbox.

Marquee Tool

Whereas the Select and Subselection tools provide the capability to select a vector object, or section of a vector object, the Marquee and Lasso tools allow you to define and select a portion of a bitmap object. The Marquee tool allows you to easily define rectangular (or circular) areas for selection within bitmaps. In comparison, the Lasso tool allows you to draw an irregular or custom-defined area for selection within bitmaps. To work with the Marquee tool, perform the following steps.

1. Click on the Marquee tool. Note that it has a small black triangle in the lower right-hand corner. Click and hold down the mouse button on the Marquee tool, so that the pop-up menu appears. As you can see, you can select either a rectangular or circular shape for the selection marquee. Select the rectangular shape (the current and default setting).
2. Examine the Properties panel for the Marquee tool. (See figure 2-27.) As you can see in the lower left-hand corner, you can resize and move an area selected with the Marquee tool by typing in numbers in the W (width), H (height), X (axis), and Y (axis) fields. In the middle of the panel you will see the Style field, with a pull-down menu offering the following options: Normal, Fixed Ratio, and Fixed Size. When you change these settings, the portion of the image inside the marquee changes to fit these dimensions and moves to the specified location.

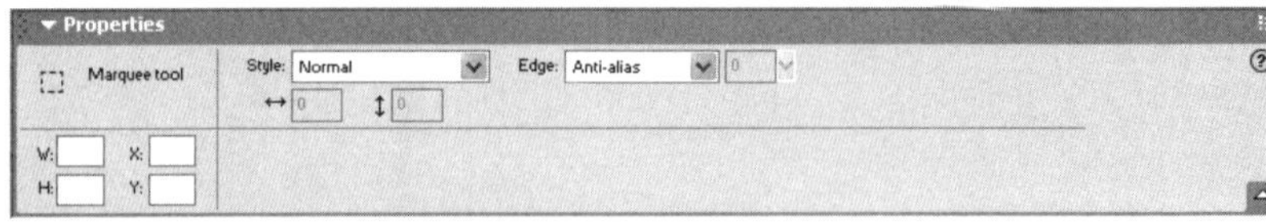

Fig. 2-27. Properties panel for the Marquee tool.

3. In the Style field, select the Fixed Ratio option. In the fields that now appear, the Fixed Ratio option allows you to constrain the ratio of the width compared to the height, according to whatever values you enter into these fields. Type some values into these fields (try *3* and *1*, or any other values you wish). Try making a selection with the Marquee tool by clicking and holding the mouse button as you drag the cursor. As you can see, the shape of the selection is now determined by the values you entered.

4. In the Style field, select the Fixed Size option. In the fields that now appear, the Fixed Size option allows you to constrain the size of the selection to the exact values you enter in these fields. Type some values into these fields (try *300* and *125*, or any other values you wish). Try making a selection with the Marquee tool. If you click the Marquee tool inside the selection and hold down the mouse button, you can move the selection to another location. Double click inside the selection to undo the selection.

5. Select the Normal option. The Normal option allows you to define the selection area by expanding the marquee selection to any size you wish. Try making a selection with the Marquee tool.

6. Move the cursor to the upper left-hand corner of the trolley door, where there are several people standing in the doorway. Click and hold down the mouse button as you drag the cursor below the trolley doorway on the right, expanding the marquee selection as you do so. Let go of the mouse. The borders of the marquee selection are now "crawling," indicating that the area has been selected.

7. Select Edit | Copy to copy the trolley doorway selection into the clipboard.

8. Select Edit | Paste. The copy should be pasted into the same location as it was copied from. Take a look at the Layers panel to see a new *Bitmap* sublayer, containing the content you just pasted into the document. Click on the Pointer tool and move it on top of the pasted object. Click and hold down the mouse as you drag this pasted copy to the white portion of the canvas. Let go of the mouse button. You can see that you can very easily select an area of a bitmap image, copy it, paste it, and move the pasted copy wherever you want. Note that this copied section has a hard, "crisp" edge.

Shortcut

To deselect the active selection, simultaneously press:
PC: Ctrl + D
Mac: Cmd + D

9 To disengage the active Marquee selection, make sure the Marquee tool is selected and click anywhere on the canvas or gray work area, or select Select | Deselect from the menu.

10. Let's try something a little different. Locate the Edge field. The Edge field allows you to select with a sharp, hard edge or to "feather" or fade out the edge of the selection. This field can help provide more artistic effects. Select the Feather option and set it to *50*.

11. Select the Marquee tool. Draw a selection around the trolley car door, as you did before.

12. Select Edit | Copy. The selected area is copied to the clipboard.

13. Select Edit | Paste. The selection should be pasted into the area it was copied from. Click on the Pointer tool and click and hold down the mouse button as you drag this pasted copy to an empty space on the white area of the canvas. Let go of the mouse button. Look at the differences between the two copied sections that are now located in the white area below the trolley car image. See figure 2-28.

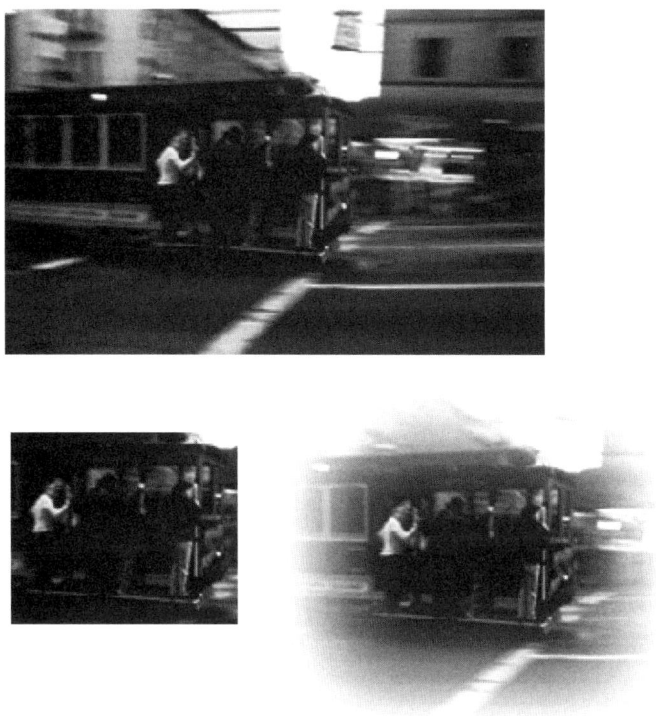

Fig. 2-28. Compare the images copied with hard and feathered edges.

14. Click on the Marquee tool and hold down the button until the pop-up menu appears. Select the oval option and experiment with making oval-shaped selections.

As you have just seen, the Marquee tool allows you to select either rectangular or circular selections on a bitmapped object. There will be cases, however, in which you will want to select an irregularly shaped section of a bitmapped object. The Lasso tool, explored in the following section, provides this capability.

Lasso Tool

You may not always want to select areas in a bitmap that are circular or rectangular. The Lasso tool allows you to define freeform or custom-defined shapes for selection. To work with the Lasso tool, perform the following steps.

1. Click on the Lasso tool. Note that it has a small black triangle in the lower right-hand corner. Click and hold down the mouse button on the Lasso tool, so that the pop-up menu appears. As you can see, you can select either the Lasso tool (as a continuous drawing tool) or the Polygon Lasso tool, which allows you to click anchor points to create a polygon-shaped area for selection. Select the Lasso tool (the current and default setting).
2. Examine the Properties panel options for the Lasso tool. The options found here are the same as those for the Marquee tool, minus a few.
3. Move the cursor over the image. Click and hold down the mouse button as you drag the Lasso tool around whatever area of the image you want to select. Finish the selection by bringing the cursor back to the point where you started. Let go of the mouse. The Lasso selection is now "crawling," indicating that the area has been selected.
4. Select Edit | Cut. The selected area is removed to the clipboard.
5. Select Edit | Paste. The selection is pasted into the area it was copied from. Click on the Pointer tool, and click and hold down the mouse as you drag this pasted copy to an empty area on the white section of the canvas. Let go of the mouse button.
6. To deselect the selected area, click on the Lasso tool again and then click anywhere on the gray work area or on the canvas.

> **·TIP·**
> For these types of procedures, you will find it easier to toggle back and forth to the Pointer tool by holding down the Ctrl (Cmd) key.

You have just seen how easy it is to make selections with the Lasso tool, by selecting an area. Now let's look at how you can make selections by using the Magic Wand tool to select colors.

Magic Wand Tool

The Marquee and Lasso tools allow you to select by defining an area. In contrast, the Magic Wand tool allows you to select by color or range of colors. To work with the Magic Wand tool, perform the following steps.

1. Select the Pointer tool and select the trolley image.
2. Click on the Magic Wand tool, located in the Bitmap toolbox. In the Properties panel, set Tolerance to 10.
3. Move the Magic Wand tool into the lower right corner of the image, over the section of the street that is dark blue. Click the Magic Wand tool in this area. You should now see a "crawling" selection marquee around a small section of color in the image.
4. Deselect the area by pressing Ctrl/Cmd + D.
5. In the Properties panel, set Tolerance to 70. Click in the same street section again. A much larger area should now be selected. Later in this toolbox section, you will see how you can use the Paint Bucket tool to change the color of this selected area.
6. Deselect the area by pressing Ctrl/Cmd + D.

Let's create some images by moving on to the Brush tool.

Brush Tool

The Brush and the Pencil are the two drawing tools within the Bitmap toolbox. They do roughly the same thing, which is to draw lines in bitmap images. The primary difference is that the Pencil tool draws lines using a single-pixel width, whereas the Brush has options for painting variable-width lines with adjustable line styles. Let's try it.

1. Close the current file without saving any changes. Select File | New to create a new file, with settings of *550*, *500*, and *72* and a white canvas.
2. Select the Brush tool from the Bitmap toolbox. Examine the Properties panel associated with this tool. You have seen these options in other Properties panels.
3. In the Properties panel, set the following attributes.
    - *Brush Color (color swatch next to the Pencil icon):* blue
    - *Tip Size (pull-down slider bar next to color swatch):* 10 pixels
    - *Stroke Category (to the right of Brush width):* Basic | Hard Line
4. Start on the left and draw a line to the right.

5. Change the attributes. In the Properties panel, set the following attributes.
   - *Tip Size:* 30 pixels
   - *Stroke Category:* Airbrush | Basic
   - *Edge:* 80
6. Start on the left and draw a line to the right.
7. Change the attributes again. In the Properties panel, set the following attributes.
   - *Stroke Category:* Airbrush | Textured
   - *Texture Field:* Sandpaper
8. Start on the left and draw a line to the right.
9. Try out whatever options you wish, as you experiment with the Brush tool.

Unlike the vector objects you drew earlier, each time you use a bitmap tool on a bitmap image, whatever you draw becomes an indistinguishable (and uneditable) part of the entire image. Examine the Layers panel. All objects you drew are located on one layer. In contrast, as you created the vector objects earlier, each object was placed on its own sublayer.

With vector drawings, each vector object remains separate and editable. With bitmap images, however, additions made with the bitmap tools instantly become part of the whole, and the "parts" can no longer be edited by themselves. Using the Brush tool on an image is like repainting a wall. Each brush stroke covers or paints over the pixels underneath. Let's move on and examine the Pencil tool.

Pencil Tool

As you might guess from its name, the Pencil tool can be used to draw freeform objects, much like you would using a real pencil. Let's give it a try.

1. Select the menu option Select | Select All and then press Delete (Backspace on Mac). You now have a clean screen to work with.
2. Click on the Pencil tool, located in the Bitmap section of the Tools panel. Examine the Properties panel at the bottom of the screen, displaying the options available for this tool. Click on the color swatch next to the Pencil icon in the Properties panel. In the color palette that opens, select a dark blue. Note that there is no field available for changing the width of the line.
3. Move the Pencil to the canvas. Click and hold down the mouse button as you draw a rectangle, making sure that as you finish, the last line touches

or crosses over the first line, so that the rectangle is closed. Do not worry about how it looks.

4. Click on the Subselection tool (used with vector objects to select a section of an object). Click on one corner of the rectangle. Click and hold the mouse button down as you move the corner toward the center. As you may remember, this type of action with a vector object would have changed the shape of the object (it would no longer have been rectangular, but would have a "squished" corner). With a bitmap, this action caused the rectangle to become smaller as its shape remained rectangular. Try pulling the corner out. The rectangle becomes larger but the shape remains rectangular. The shape itself cannot be edited, just resized.
5. Examine the lower left-hand side of the Properties panel for this bitmap object. As you can see, you change the width, height, X-axis placement, and Y-axis placement by typing numbers into the fields located here.
6. Click on the Pencil tool again and move it to an empty portion of the canvas. Click and hold as you draw several intersecting lines, so that it looks like a large asterisk.
7. Click on the Pointer tool. Note that both objects are selected and grouped as a single object at this point. In a later chapter you will learn how to place multiple bitmap objects on individual layers.

Eraser Tool

The Eraser tool is pretty straightforward, with just a few options. Let's take a look.

1. Click on the Eraser tool. Examine the Properties panel for the Eraser tool. In the first field you can change the size of the eraser tip. In the next field to the right, you can change the shape of the eraser tip. The Edge field allows you to change the edge characteristic in degrees from a clean, sharp erasure to a feathered/fading erasure. A zero (0) in this field will yield a sharp edge with no feathering, whereas a value of 100 will produce an edge that very gradually fades.
2. In the Properties panel, set Eraser Tip Size to 10. Click and drag the Eraser tool over any object currently on screen.
3. Change the settings. Set Eraser Tip Size to 30. Click and drag the Eraser tool over any object currently on screen. The difference between the two should be pretty obvious.

Blur Tool

With the bitmap tools you've had experience drawing new shapes and colors. You've erased sections of images. Now it's time to "blur" sections of images. To work with the Blur tool, perform the following steps.

1. Select File | Close. In the pop-up window that appears, click on the No button (to not save changes).
2. Select File | Open. Locate and open the file Tour_2C.png. You have now opened a "clean" copy of the file you were previously working with.
3. Select the Pointer tool and click on the trolley image to select it.
4. Click and hold the mouse button down on the Blur tool until the pop-up menu appears. As you can see, the options are Blur, Sharpen, Dodge, Burn, and Smudge. Let's take a quick look at two of the options here.
5. Select the Blur tool. Examine the Properties panel. You have seen most of these options previously.
6. In the Properties panel, set Tip Size to 15, Shape to Rectangular, Edge to 0, and Intensity to 100. Click and hold the mouse button down as you repeatedly drag the cursor back and forth over the people standing within the trolley door. What is happening here is that the Blur tool takes all pixel color values within a specified area and "averages" them to blend the individual color values, resulting in a blurred appearance. The Size field sets the overall area to be considered, whereas the combination of values for Edge and Intensity determine how the pixel color values within this area are averaged. Try changing the values of these settings, and use the Blur tool again on a different part of the image.
7. Click and hold on the Blur tool. Select the Smudge tool from the pop-up menu. Examine the Properties panel. You have seen most of these options previously, but there are a few new ones.
8. In the Properties panel, set Tip Size to 15, and Shape to Rectangular. Make sure there is a check mark in the Smudge Color field on the right. Click on the color swatch and select a color that contrasts with the colors already on screen. Set the Edge field to 50 and Pressure field to 50. Click and hold the mouse button as you drag the cursor over an object on the canvas. The result is similar to "smudging" with charcoal or pastel chalk.

Let's move on and try another "artistic" tool, the Rubber Stamp tool.

Rubber Stamp Tool

The Rubber Stamp tool is used to copy and "paint" an image to the canvas. This tool is most useful for touch-ups on images with textures too complex to paint with the other bitmap tools. To work with the Rubber Stamp tool, perform the following steps.

1. The canvas is pretty messy, so let's get another "clean" copy of the file we have been working with.
   a) Select File | Close. In the pop-up window that appears, click on the No button (to *not* save changes).
   b) Select File | Open. Locate and open the file *Tour_2C.png*.
2. Select the Rubber Stamp tool from the Bitmap toolbox. In the Properties panel, set the following attributes.
   - *Size:* 50
   - *Edge:* 30
   - *Source Aligned:* Place a check mark (activate)
3. Position the cursor in the center of the trolley doorway. Hold down the Alt (Opt) key as you click and release the mouse button to set the sample starting point.
4. Move the large circular cursor to the white area of the canvas. Click and hold the mouse button down as you continuously drag the mouse back and forth, "painting" another image of the trolley car. Note that the starting point where you sampled is the area that is copied. See figure 2-29.

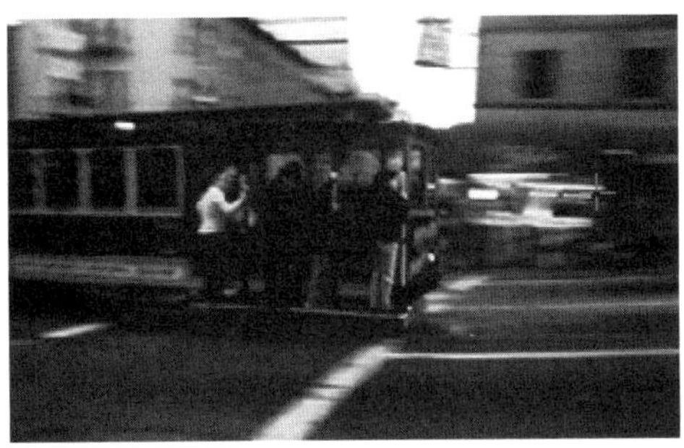

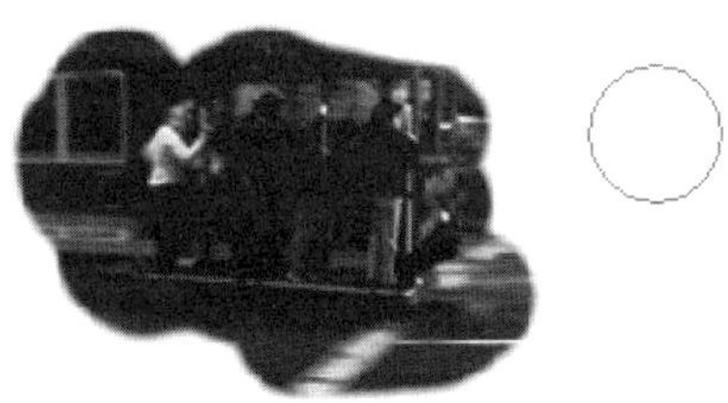

Fig. 2-29. Image created with the Rubber Stamp tool.

The Rubber Stamp tool is a little bit unusual to work with, but after you have experimented with it a bit, you will find that it provides a number of artistic possibilities. Let's now take a look at a more traditional "painting" tool.

Paint Bucket Tool

The Paint Bucket tool is a standard tool found in most paint programs. It allows you to "pour" a fill color or pattern into an object, to provide an interior color or pattern for that object. The Paint Bucket tool can be used on vectors and bitmaps, with each type of graphic. If you "pour" a fill into a vector shape, it will be confined within the vector. If you pour a fill within a bitmap, the fill may cover the entire canvas unless there is an object to contain it. To work with the Paint Bucket tool, perform the following steps.

1. Click on the Paint Bucket tool in the Bitmap toolbox in the Tools panel. Click on the Color Fill tool (Paint Bucket) in the Colors toolbox. In the pop-up color palette that opens, select a color for the fill by clicking on any yellow color.
2. Examine the Properties panel for the Paint Bucket tool. In addition to being able to change the fill color here, there are some other useful options. Note the Tolerance field in the middle section of the panel.

   Tolerance references how the fill color will be added to a bitmap's existing pixels. If Tolerance is set to 0, no other fill colors besides the color you click on with the Paint Bucket tool will be filled. If Tolerance is set to a larger number, a sampling of the surrounding color range will be filled also. In this example, using a higher Tolerance setting will allow the fill to flow into different shades of the blue area.
3. In the Properties panel, set the following attribute.
   - *Tolerance: 10*
4. Move the cursor (note that the cursor now looks like a small paint bucket) over the dark blue section of the street you worked with earlier (located in the lower right-hand side of the image). Click and release the mouse button. You should now see the yellow color you selected appear in a small section of the street – the section that was very dark blue. Change the Tolerance to 70 and click the Paint Bucket tool in another blue section of the street. As you can see, a larger Tolerance value allows the Paint Bucket to fill a larger variation from the initial color clicked on.
5. Let's try filling a vector image. Select the Rectangle tool from the Vector toolbox.

6. In the Properties panel, select any stroke color you wish.
7. In the Properties panel, select a different fill color.
8. Draw a rectangle on the canvas. You should see the stroke color and fill color you selected in the Properties panel.
9. Let's change the fill color. Select the Paint Bucket tool from the Bitmap toolbox. In the color palette window that opens, click on the Fill Options button, located at the bottom of the window. As you can see, another window now opens. In this new window, in the top field, select Pattern. In the field below Pattern, select Illusion. In the Texture field, select Sandpaper and set it to *50* (%).Click anywhere to close the Fill window.
10. Note that the Paint Bucket tool has a small black triangle, indicating a pull-down menu. Click on the Paint Bucket tool again, holding the mouse button down until the menu appears. Note that the other choice here is the Gradient tool. Select the Gradient tool.

The Gradient tool defaults to black and white, which can be used to very easily create masks. However, let's change the default colors to custom colors.

11. Select the Marquee tool and draw a rectangular selection somewhere on the trolley car.
12. Click on the Gradient tool.
13. In the Properties panel, establish whatever Fill Category, Edge, and Texture settings you like. To adjust the colors, click on the Fill Color tool. The gradient editor will pop up. Use the markers in the top panel to select and adjust the colors. To add markers, click along the panel where you want them. To remove markers, drag them off the gradient editor. See figure 2-30.

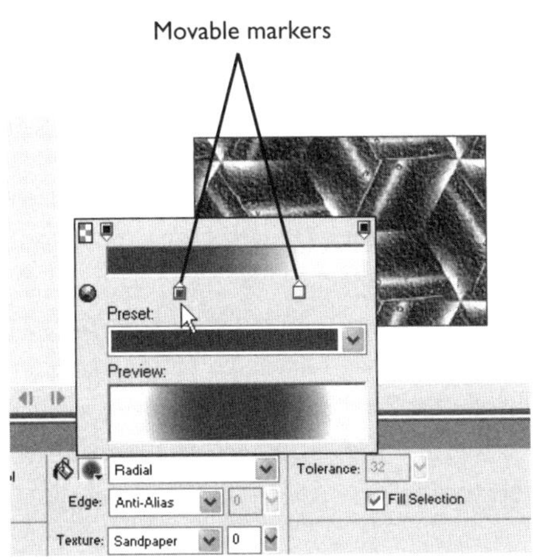

Fig. 2-30. The Gradient Editor accessible from the Fill Color palette.

14. Click the Gradient tool within the Marquee selection. You should now see the fill pattern you selected.
15. Press Ctrl + D (Cmd + D) to deselect the Marquee selection.

    Just like solid color fills, the gradient is uneditable after being applied to bitmap objects. We are now left with a pretty messy screen, but you have seen how to work with the Paint Bucket and Gradient tools. Now let's look at a tool that is frequently used with the Paint Bucket tool – the Eyedropper tool.

Eyedropper Tool

Shortcut

If you have the Paint Bucket tool selected, you can toggle to the Eyedropper tool by holding down the Alt (Opt) key.

The Eyedropper tool allows you to pick up a sample color from anywhere on the canvas and use the Paint Bucket tool to pour that color somewhere else. To work with the Eyedropper tool, perform the following steps.

1. Select the Pointer tool and click on the trolley car image to select it.
2. Click on the Eyedropper tool. Move the cursor over a light blue section of the image. Click the Eyedropper tool on light blue section. Examine the Paint Bucket fill icon in the Colors toolbox. It should now be the same color as the color you just clicked on.
3. Click on the Paint Bucket tool. Move the cursor over one of the areas you previously filled with yellow. Click the Paint Bucket tool on this area. You should have just "selected" one color with the Eyedropper tool and "poured" it into a second area.
4. Select File | Close. In the pop-up window that appears, click on the No button (to not save changes).

·TIP·

You can sample colors into either the Fill swatch or the Stroke swatch in the Colors toolbox. For example, you can sample a bitmap fill color to apply to a vector's stroke by selecting the Stroke swatch in the Colors toolbox and then taking a sample of the bitmap.

You have now completed working with all tools in the Bitmap toolbox. Let's move on to the Web toolbox.

Guided Tour 2D: The Web Toolbox

The Web toolbox contains tools for creating dynamic web content. For example, you can use hotspots (Hotspot tool) to create clickable linked areas over an image, or use slices (Slice tool) to cut a single graphic into multiple graphics that fit together in an HTML table. You can also use the Hotspot and Slice tools to create image areas to which you can attach JavaScript behaviors. The sections that follow introduce these tools, and in Chapters 3 and 6 you will explore them in more detail. Use figure 2-31 as a reference as you work with the Web toolbox.

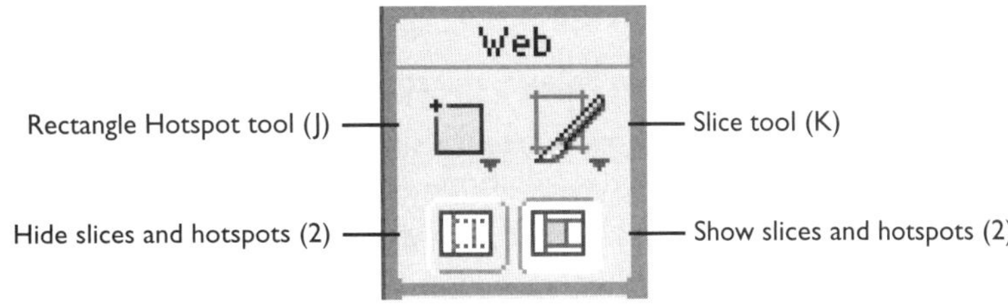

Fig. 2-31. Web toolbox.

Rectangle Hotspot Tool

A hotspot is most often used to create image maps (multiple clickable areas) within one image. (See Chapter 3 for more on working with hotspots.) To begin working with the Rectangle Hotspot tool, perform the following steps.

1. Create a new file by selecting File | New and inputting the following settings: W at *500*, H at *500*, R at *72*, and a white canvas.
2. Draw a rectangle using the Rectangle tool.
3. Select the Rectangular Hotspot tool and draw a selection over the rectangle.
4. Examine the hotspot. Note that the selection appears as a transparent blue object, that the hotspot appears in the *Web* layer within the Layers panel, and that hotspot attributes are shown in the Properties panel.
5. You can select the hotspot with the Pointer tool and move or size it as desired.
6. In the Layers panel, to the left of the *Web* layer, click on the Eye icon to hide the *Web* layer. Click on this same column to redisplay the Eye icon and the *Web* layer.

Let's now look at the next web tool.

Slice Tool

The Slice tool marks areas that will be sliced (cut up) upon export. This is often done to create the illusion of faster downloads, to embed animated GIF files into an image layout, to include GIF and JPG images in a layout, or to isolate buttons in a tight graphic composition. (See Chapter 6 for more on slicing.) To begin working with the Slice tool, perform the following steps.

1. Select the Slice tool.
2. Draw a selection completely around the rectangle you previously drew.
3. Examine the slice. Note that the slice appears as a transparent green object, that the slice object appears in the *Web* layer of the Layers panel, that slice properties are shown in the Properties panel, and that slice guides (horizontal and vertical lines) appear around the slice on the canvas.
4. You can select the hotspot with the Pointer tool and move or size it as desired.

Let's move on to the next web tool.

Hide Slices and Hotspots Tool

The Hide Slices and Hotspots tool merely hides web objects. Because slices and hotspots obscure the graphics they cover, you will have the need to variously show and hide them. All these buttons do is hide the *Web* layer. To work with the Hide Slices and Hotspots tool, perform the following steps.

1. Click on the Hide Slices button.
2. Note that the hotspots and slices are no longer visible, but they are still available in the *Web* layer.

Show Slices and Hotspots Tool

The Show Slices and Hotspots tool does just as its name implies. To use the Show Slices and Hotspots tool, perform the following steps.

1. Click on the Show Hotspots button.
2. Note that the hotspots and slices are now visible in their previous location.

As previously mentioned, you will begin to actually work with these web tools in Chapters 3 and 6. You will probably find that these tools will make more sense once you begin to work with them in context, in the exercises found in these chapters. Let's move on to Guided Tour 2E, in which you will work with the Colors toolbox.

Guided Tour 2E: The Colors Toolbox

You have been using the Colors toolbox in conjunction with tools previously introduced. However, let's look a little more closely at the tools found here, as well as some of the options available. Use figure 2-32 as a reference.

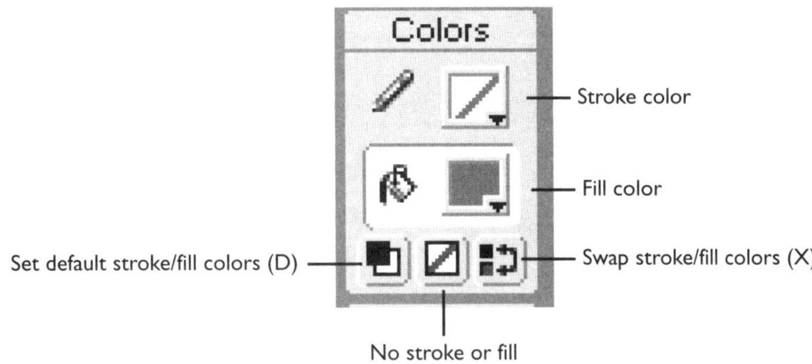

Fig. 2-32. Colors toolbox.

1. Start with a new file by selecting File | New.
2. In the New Document window that opens, type in *500* for the Width and *500* for the Height. Select a white canvas. Click on the OK button.
3. So that you have an object to work with, click on the Rectangle tool in the Vector toolbox. Draw a rectangle on the canvas.
4. Examine the Properties panel for the rectangle you just drew. Note that the panel includes the fields Fill Color (Paint Bucket icon) and Stroke Color (Pencil icon). These same tools exist in the Colors toolbox, to provide access to the same properties.
5. In the Colors toolbox, click on the Stroke Color tool (Pencil icon). Let's take a little closer look at the pop-up window that has opened. See figure 2-33.

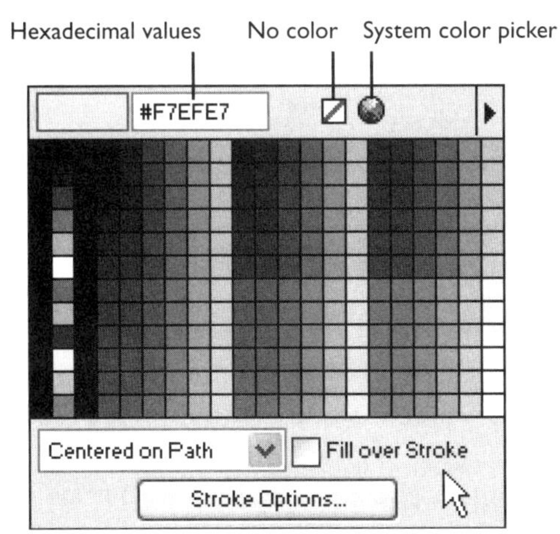

Fig. 2-33. Stroke Color palette (pop-up window) from the Colors toolbox.

6. Selecting a color is pretty easy. Click the cursor (note that the cursor is in the shape of the Eyedropper tool) on the color you want. If you are trying to exactly match a color and you know the color's hexadecimal code, you can alternatively type this code into the entry field at the top of the pop-up window.

7. In the top right-hand corner of the current pop-up window, there are two other options. The first, the button with the red line through it, allows you to set the stroke to Transparent or to no stroke color. To the right of this is a button that opens another pop-up window for the System color picker. Click on this button. You should now be looking at the pop-up window shown in figure 2-34. This window is generally used by more advanced designers, as they create and save a custom color palette. Click on the Cancel button to close the System color picker.

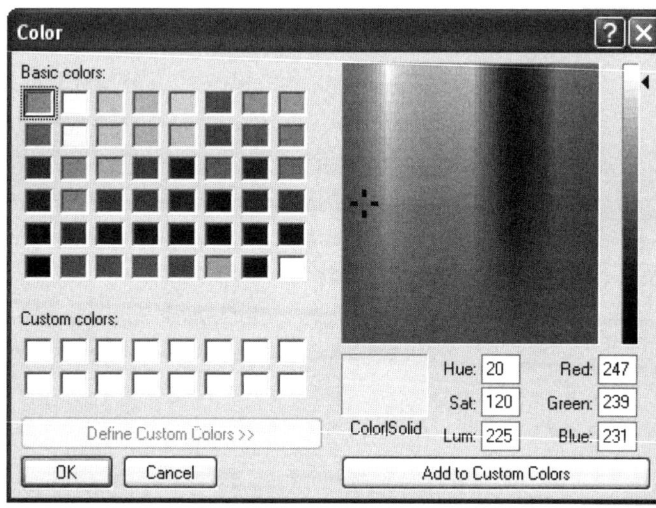

Fig. 2-34. System color picker.

8. The Stroke Color palette should still be open. In the lower left-hand corner of this window you will see a field that allows you to set the location of the stroke, relative to the path. You will most often use the default setting, Centered on Path, as you draw objects. On the other hand, when very precise size and placement are required, such as getting two or more separate graphic elements to "fit together," you may end up using the other options (Inside Path or Outside Path), along with typing in entries for the W (width), H (height), X (axis), and Y (axis) fields in the Properties panel. Select Centered on Path. The window will close.

9. Select Stroke Color to open the pop-up window again. In the lower right-hand corner there is the Fill Over Stroke option. If you place a check mark beside this option, the fill will cover the stroke.
10. At the very bottom of the pop-up window is a Stroke Options button. Click on this button. Click on the pull-down menu and select the Air Brush option. The options found here are the same as those in the Properties panel of the vector object you have drawn. Note that there is an additional button, Advanced, which provides further options for the characteristics of a custom stroke. Click on the background to close the window.
11. In the Colors toolbox, click on the Fill Color tool (Paint Bucket). Let's take a little closer look at the pop-up window that has opened. This color palette looks identical to the pop-window for Stroke Color, with the exception of the Fill Options button at the bottom. Click on this button. Again, you can see that this additional pop-up window offers the same Fill options offered in the Properties panel of the vector object you have drawn. Click on the background to close the window.
12. There are three more icons located in the bottom row of the Colors toolbox. The leftmost button is Set Default Stroke/Fill Colors. The middle button is No Stroke/Fill. This button is operational if either the Stroke Color or Fill Color tool is currently selected. The rightmost button is Swap Fill/Stroke. This button applies to those colors currently selected for the Stroke and Fill options.

As you have seen, all the options available with the use of the Colors toolbox are also available through the Properties panel when a vector object is selected. Now let's look at the last section of the Tools panel, the View toolbox.

Guided Tour 2F: The View Toolbox

There are three view mode options available in the top row of the View toolbox. Each view mode provides a different view of the Document window. The tools in the bottom row of the View toolbox help you examine the current view mode more easily. Use figure 2-35 as a reference for this guided tour. Let's take a closer look.

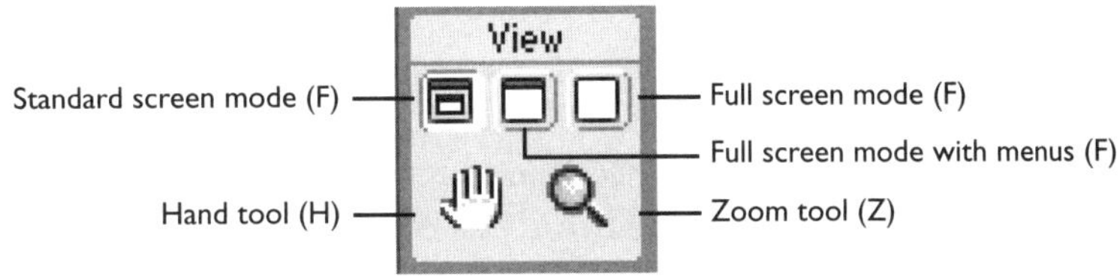

Fig. 2-35. View toolbox.

CAUTION

The Full Screen Mode button drops the Main menu out of the viewable area. To retrieve it, click on either of the other two modes.

TIP

The Zoom tool has been enhanced in Fireworks MX to zoom in on a specific area if you click-drag a selection around that area before releasing the mouse.

TIP

Double clicking on the Zoom tool in the toolbox will return you to 100% scale in the Document window.

Shortcut

Alternatively, you can use the following keyboard shortcuts to perform step 7.

Mac: Zoom In: Cmd + (+)

Zoom Out: Cmd + (–)

PC: Zoom In: Ctrl + (+)

Zoom Out: Ctrl + (–)

1. Continue to work with the file open from the last guided tour. If this file is not available, open a new file and draw a couple of objects.
2. By default, the Standard Screen Mode option in the View toolbox is selected when a file first opens. Click on the second button located there, the Full Screen with Menus Mode button. Note that the very top row of the program disappears as the work area becomes somewhat larger.
3. Click on the third button, Full Screen Mode. Now the top two rows disappear, including the menus.
4. Click on the Standard Screen Mode button to restore the screen to its normal mode.
5. Click on the Zoom tool. Move the cursor to a corner of an object on the canvas. Click the mouse button and drag the marquee to cover a portion of the object. Let go of the mouse button. You are now looking at a magnified view of the section of the object you selected with the Zoom tool.
6. Chapter 1 noted the Magnification field, located in the middle of the status bar, below the work area and canvas. Click on the small black triangle to open a pull-down menu. Select another value for Magnification.
7. With the Zoom tool still selected, perform one of the following, depending on which system you are using. PC users: right mouse click to open a pop-up menu for magnification. Mac users: Ctrl-click to open a pop-up menu for magnification.
8. Click on the Hand tool. Move the Hand tool anywhere on screen. Click and hold the mouse button down as you drag the Hand tool in any direction. Let go of the mouse button. As you can see, the Hand tool allows you to move the canvas around within the viewable area. The Hand tool is especially useful when viewing a portion of the canvas in a magnified view.

In the guided tours in this chapter, you were introduced to all of the tools within the Tools panel. Now it is time for you to try using these tools within a realistic context. In Practice Exercise 2-1 you will draw the foundation of a Splash page.

Getting Your Computer Ready for Practice Exercises

Throughout the course of this book, you will be creating many Fireworks MX files that you will want to save on your computer. To make it easier to locate these files and to communicate to you about these files, it is strongly recommended that you create a new directory (folder) on your computer's hard drive to store these files. You can do this by performing the following steps.

1. Create a directory (folder) on the root directory of your computer's hard drive.
2. Name the directory (folder) *SaveWork*.
3. Save all files into this *SaveWork* directory (folder).

Practice Exercise 2-1: Drawing the Foundation of a Splash Page

Description

In the introduction to this book, a description was provided for the San Francisco Travel Guide web site, a fictional site we are using to provide a "real-world" context for the practice exercises (and several guided tours) that you will encounter in this book. In this first practice exercise, you will build the framework for the Splash page graphic you first looked at in Chapter 1. You will continue to work with the finished results of this exercise as you move through the guided tours in Chapter 3. As a convenience, a completed version of the current exercise is provided on the companion CD-ROM, so that you can use it for the guided tours you will encounter later in the book.

This exercise provides you with the opportunity to practice using many of the tools you were introduced to in the guided tours in this chapter. You will also use the vector tools to build the artwork. In the next chapter you will import the bitmap images and vector logo to supplement this artwork.

Preview of Completed Exercise

Before beginning the exercise, let's examine the exercise in its completed state so that you can clearly see what you are about to build. The objects you draw may be somewhat different from those shown in the completed exercise file, which is okay. Feel free to take artistic license in making modifications.

CD-ROM

1. Select File | Open and in the pop-up window, locate on the companion CD-ROM the directory named *Chapter 2*. Within this directory, locate and double click on the file named *Exercise2_1(complete).png*.
2. Verify that file *Exercise2_1(complete).png* appears in your copy of Fireworks MX.
3. Examine the Layers panel. The layers *Logo and Text* and *Interface* should have a minus (–) sign, indicating that they are displaying the sublayers within them. If not, click on the plus (+) sign to activate display of the sublayers within both layers.

4. Within the *Interface* layer, click on each sublayer so that you can see which object is being referred to and where it is located on the canvas.
5. Within the *Logo and Text* layer, click on the sublayer *Text* to see where this is located.
6. Examine the image on the canvas. Note that the color in the bottom rectangle begins as a medium blue in the left-hand corner, gradually fades to a lighter blue, and then eventually fades to white at the far right-hand corner.

Storyboard: On Screen

Figure 2-36 shows what the canvas will look like within the Fireworks program after you have completed the exercise.

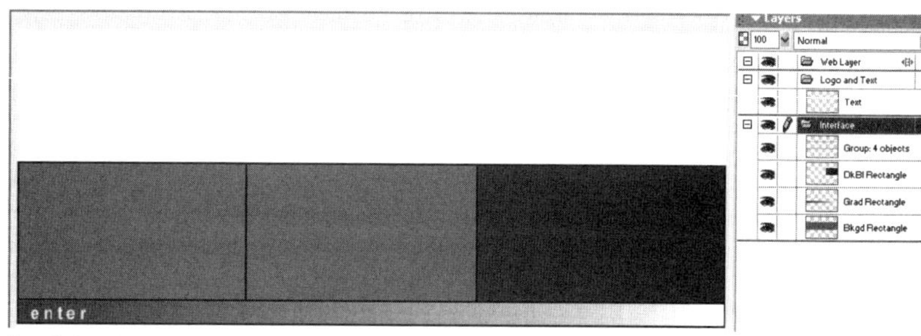

Fig. 2-36. Canvas display of completed exercise.

Step-by-Step Instructions

1. Let's start by creating a new file.
   a) Select File | New.
   b) In the New Document window that opens, type *770* in the Width field, *500* in the Height field, and *72* in the Resolution field. Verify that Canvas Color is set to White.
   c) In the section immediately preceding this exercise ("Getting Your Computer Ready for Practice Exercises"), you were asked to create a folder (directory) on your computer and to name it *SaveWork*. If you have not yet created the *SaveWork* folder, do so now. See the section "Getting Your Computer Ready for Practice Exercises" if you need to.
   d) Select File | Save and use the pop-up window to locate and point to the *SaveWork* directory. Save the file with the name *Exercise2_1.png*.
2. Before beginning the graphic, rename the layer.

a) Locate the Layers panel on the far right of the screen. Note that the first layer is by default named *Layer 1*.

b) Double click on the layer title (*Layer 1*). The Layer Name pop-up window appears. Type in the new name *Interface* and press Enter/Return.

TIP

You might ask yourself where we got the numbers (values) we are using throughout this exercise and those that will follow. The answer is that we have designed the elements of the exercises so that the step-by-step instructions can guide you through the development process. "In real life" you will not have these numbers (values) predetermined, but you will need to determine their values by using whatever settings make the best artistic rendering.

3. Now let's create the foundation graphic for the image. You are going to start by drawing a rough rectangle, and then you will use the Properties panel to modify its characteristics.

a) Select the Rectangle tool in the Vector toolbox.

b) Move the cursor to the canvas and draw a rectangle. Do not worry about the size or location; you will modify these in material to follow.

c) In the Layers panel, double click on the layer label that now reads *Rectangle*. Type in the new layer name *Bkgd Rectangle* and press the Enter/Return key.

d) In the Properties panel, establish the following field settings.

- *Width:* 770
- *Height:* 170
- *X:* 0
- *Y:* 140
- *Fill Color:* #0099FF
- *Stroke Color:* No Stroke

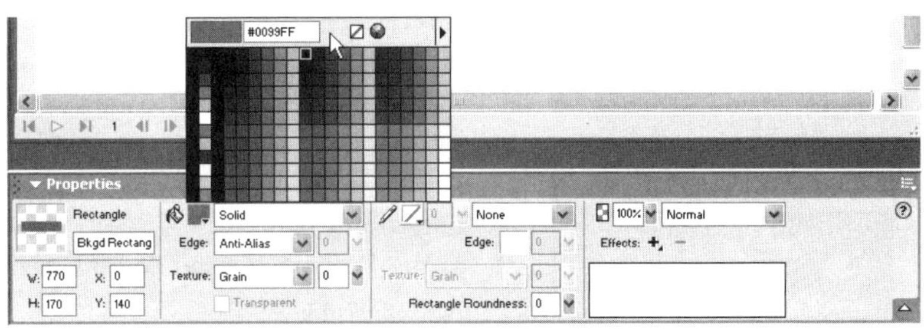

Fig. 2-37. Rectangle Properties panel with field settings.

Note that you will be typing in a hexadecimal code for the blue color. Click the cursor in that field and type over the current value, and then press Enter/Return. See figure 2-37.

e) Verify that your graphic looks like that shown in figure 2-38.

Fig. 2-38. Blue background rectangle on canvas.

4. Next, you will draw another, smaller rectangle that will sit on the bottom edge of the first shape. This second rectangle will have a gradient applied to it.
   a) Select the Rectangle tool and draw a rectangle on the canvas. Do not worry about what it looks like; you will use the Properties panel to modify its characteristics.
   b) Double click on the layer label (for the new layer) that now reads *Rectangle*. Type in the new layer name *Grad Rectangle* and press Enter/Return.
   c) In the Properties panel for this second rectangle, establish the following field settings.
      - *Width:* 770
      - *Height:* 25
      - *X:* 0
      - *Y:* 285
      - *Fill Category:* Linear
      - *Stroke:* No Stroke
   d) Click on the Fill Color tool in the Properties panel. The top display area shows dark blue on one side, gradually fading to a medium blue on the

other side. Note that immediately below the display area is what looks like a dark blue marker and a mid-blue marker. See figure 2-39.

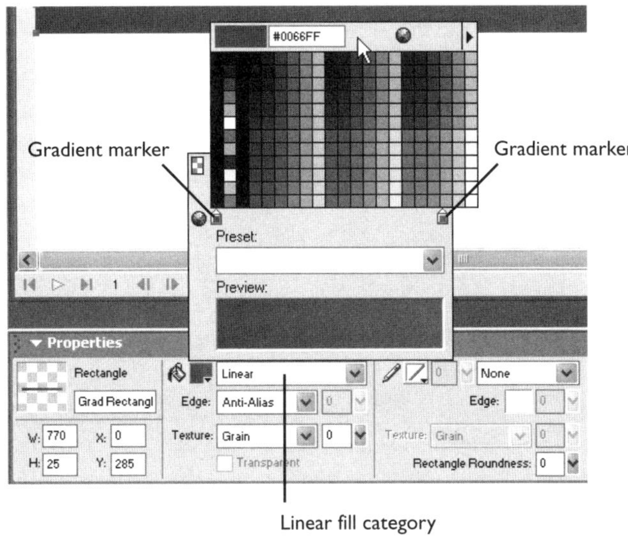

Fig. 2-39. Fill Color window with Linear Fill category selected.

e) Click on the marker located on the left. Click the cursor in the top color field, type in *#0066FF*, and press Enter/Return. If the marker is not already located on the far left, move it there now by clicking on it and while holding down the mouse button dragging the marker to the far left.

f) Click on the marker located on the right. Click the cursor on the white color swatch in the open palette. Your settings should now look like those shown in figure 2-40.

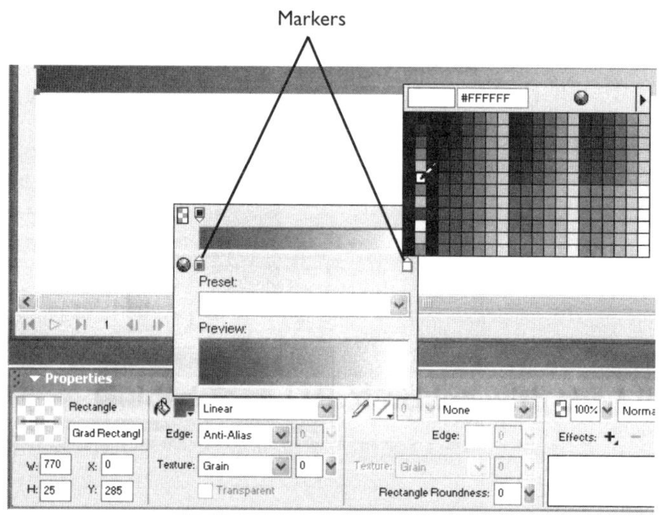

Fig. 2-40. Settings for left and right markers within Linear Fill window.

g) You should now see a linear color gradient in the smaller rectangle on the canvas. See figure 2-41.

Fig. 2-41. Linear color gradient as displayed on the canvas.

5. You will now draw a series of outlines to frame the two rectangles and to divide the top area into three sections. These sections will hold the photos and the logo that you will import in an exercise in the next chapter.
   a) Select the Rectangle tool and draw a rectangle on the canvas. Do not worry about what it looks like; you will use the Properties panel to modify its characteristics.
   b) Locate the Properties panel for this third rectangle and establish the following field settings.
      - *Width:* 768
      - *Height:* 170
      - *X:* 1
      - *Y:* 140
      - *Fill Color:* No Fill (select None in the Fill category)

- *Stroke Color:* Black
- *Stroke Width:* 2

c) Select the Line tool and set the Stroke setting to black and its width to 2 pixels. Draw a horizontal line that spans the entire canvas. Use the Pointer tool (or settings in the Properties panel) to place the line at the top edge of the smaller rectangle at a Y value of 285. Your canvas should now look like that shown in figure 2-42.

·TIP·

Remember that it is much easier to draw a straight line by first pressing and holding down the Shift key, before and as you draw the line. Holding down the Shift key constrains the line to a 45-, 90-, or 180-degree angle.

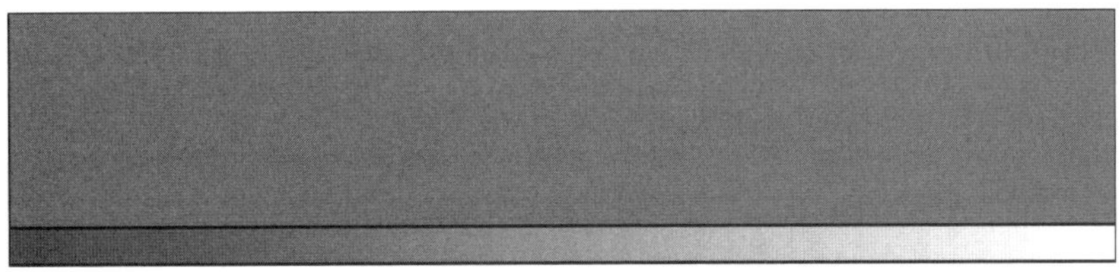

Fig. 2-42. Canvas in progress.

Shortcut

The keyboard shortcut for duplicating selections is:

PC: Ctrl + Alt + D

Mac: Cmd + Opt + D

d) Select the Line tool and set the Stroke option to black and its width to 2 pixels. Draw a vertical line spanning the top section of the graphic but stopping before the smaller gradient rectangle. Use the Properties panel to set the X value to *250* and Y value to *140*.

e) Duplicate the vertical line by selecting Edit | Duplicate and using the Properties panel to place the copy at an X value of *500* and a Y value of *140*.

f) Let's group these divider lines for easier handling. Press and hold the Shift key as you click on the three lines and rectangle you just created (the top four sublayers in the *Interface* layer). Select Modify | Group. Note that the name of the layer changed to *Group: 4 objects*. To see what this now looks like on the canvas, see figure 2-43.

Fig. 2-43. Canvas in progress, showing divider lines.

6. Let's now draw a final rectangle in the top right-hand section to add a darker color to that area.
   a) Select the Rectangle tool and draw a rectangle on the canvas. Do not worry about what it looks like; you will use the Properties panel to modify its characteristics.

b) Double click on the layer label that now reads *Rectangle.* Type in the new layer name *DkBl Rectangle* and press Enter/Return.

c) In the Properties panel for this final rectangle, establish the following field settings.

- *Width:* 268
- *Height:* 145
- *X:* 500
- *Y:* 140
- *Fill Color:* #0000CC (dark blue)
- *Texture:* Line-Horiz 2
- *Amount of Texture:* 25%
- *Stroke Color:* No Stroke

d) Move the cursor to the Layers panel. Click on the *DkBl Rectangle* layer object and hold the mouse button down as you drag this layer object below the *Group: 4 objects* object layer, so that the grouped outlines come to the foreground. See figure 2-44.

Fig. 2-44. Canvas in progress, showing the dark blue rectangle.

7. To finish the framework of the graphic, let's add a new layer with some text.

   a) Locate the four icons at the bottom of the Layers panel. See figure 2-45.

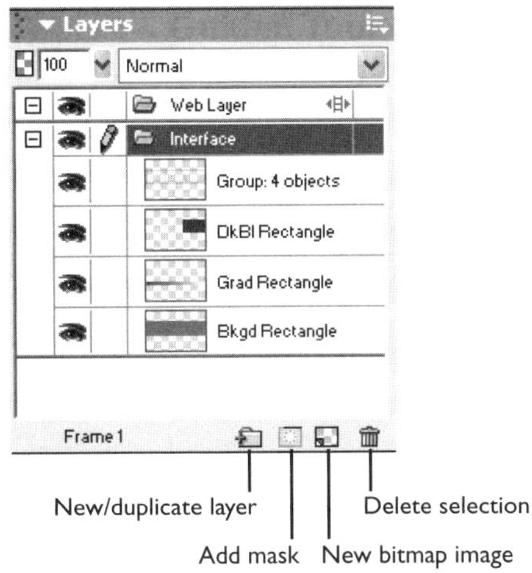

Fig. 2-45. Icons at the bottom of the Layers panel.

b) Click on the New/Duplicate icon to add a new layer.

c) Double click on the new layer label and name it *Logo and Text*. Press Enter/Return.

d) Select the Text tool and click the cursor in the white area of the canvas to open the Text window. Type the word *enter*. Do not worry about the placement of the entry; you will use the Properties panel to modify its characteristics.

e) In the Properties panel for this text object, establish the following field settings. (To apply these settings to text that has already been typed, make sure you have either highlighted all the text with the Text tool or that you have selected the text object with the Pointer tool.)

- *Font Face:* Arial
- *Font Size:* 18
- *Fill Color:* #CCFFFF (light blue)
- *Kerning:* 25
- *X:* 10
- *Y:* 288

8. Figure 2-46 shows what your canvas and Layers panel should look like at the completion of this exercise.

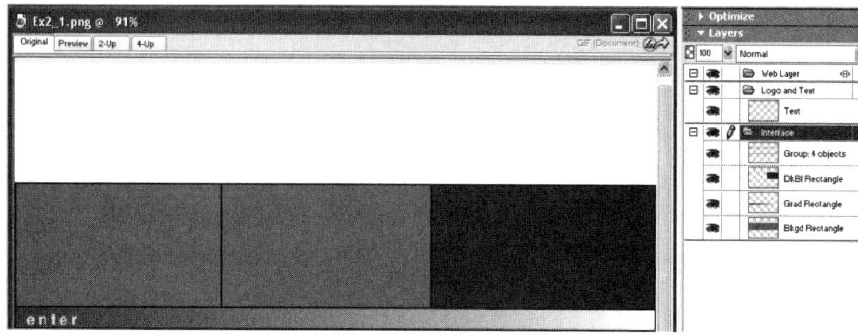

Fig. 2-46. Canvas and Layers panel at completion of exercise.

9. Save the file.

CHAPTER 3

Importing Resources and Editing Web Graphics

Chapter Topics:

- *Introduction*
- *Guided Tour 3A: Importing and Capturing Bitmap Artwork*
- *Guided Tour 3B: Importing Vector Artwork Created in Other Software*
- *Guided Tour 3C: Applying Transformations to Vectors and Bitmaps*
- *Guided Tour 3D: Adding Hotspots to Web Graphics (Making Image Maps)*
- *Designing Screens and the User Interface*
- *Practice Exercise 3-1: Designing and Editing a Web Site Interface*

Introduction

In the previous chapters, you learned the basics of working with the Fireworks interface and using the bitmap and vector tools to create original artwork. You will find that a significant part of your design work will require you to also manipulate existing images for incorporation within your designs. Whether these resources include screen shots, stock photos, scanned images, or artwork supplied by a client, learning to enhance, edit, and combine these images is an essential part of the creative process. The files you worked with in previous chapters consisted of designs with multiple images, photographs, text, and vector shapes. Fireworks MX incorporates many tools for manipulating imported images to create collage effects for your designs. By the end of the chapter, you will be able to:

- *Import and manipulate images in Fireworks MX*
- *Apply effects, transformations, and color corrections to bitmap images*
- *Edit imported vector images*

This chapter includes guided tours and a practice exercise focused on importing and manipulating various types of images in Fireworks. Previously you worked with Fireworks documents that contained bitmap and vector images that had been imported for you. This chapter begins with helping you learn the steps for importing and placing artwork yourself.

Guided Tour 3A: Importing and Capturing Bitmap Artwork

In this guided tour you will continue to work on the splash page for the travel web site you started working on in the practice exercise in Chapter 2. We will use the splash page as the context for the content, as you learn how to use the Fireworks features to import bitmap artwork.

1. Let's continue to work with the completed version of a file you worked with in Practice Exercise 2-1. You can use either the file you created and saved on your hard drive or the file provided on the companion CD-ROM. These files should be identical, containing some blue rectangles and lines that will form the foundation of the splash page begun in the last chapter. See figure 3-1.

Fig. 3-1. Image on canvas as you begin the guided tour.

Go Solo

a) If you want to use your file, select File | Open. Locate the *SaveWork* folder on your hard drive and then select the file *Exercise2_1.png*. Click on the Open button.

b) If you want to use the file on the companion CD-ROM, select File | Open. Locate and double click on the CD-ROM player within your computer. Double click on the *Chapter 3* folder, and click to select the file *Tour_3A.png*. Click on the Open button.

Importing Bitmaps

Importing bitmap artwork is a process used to place images such as photographs, bitmap clip art, and screen shots into your current Fireworks file. Once imported, the new images are placed on the canvas of the Fireworks MX document. They can then be manipulated with the appropriate tools.

CAUTION

Be careful to not compress your images too much before you import them into Fireworks. You should start your design with the highest quality of images possible. You might import TIF or high-quality JPG images. This is also true when scanning images directly from the Scan command.

1. Let's start by importing two photos for use on the splash screen. Click to select the *Interface* layer in the Layers panel. Selecting this layer will ensure that the imported bitmaps will be placed on a sublayer within the *Interface* layer.

2. Select File | Import and browse for the *trolley.jpg* image in the *Chapter 3* folder on the companion CD-ROM. When you select the file, note the thumbnail preview and the format and file size information in the Import window (shown in figure 3-2), to the right of the file list. This information can be helpful if you are searching for images with nondescript file names. Click on Open.

TIP

You can open standard bitmap formats directly into Fireworks without importing and placing the image into an existing Fireworks document. Select File | Open to open common bitmap formats such as JPG, GIF, TIF, and EPS into individual files.

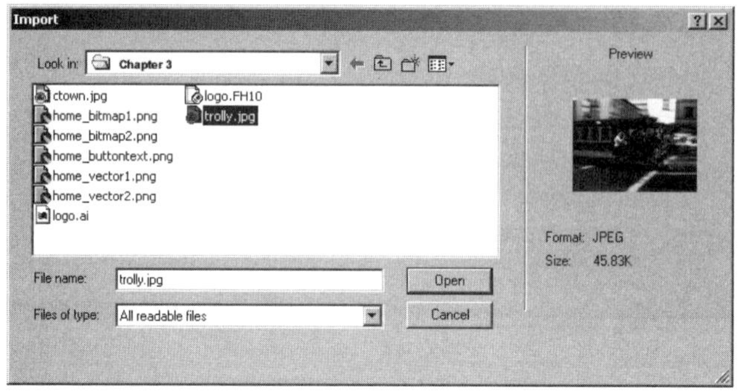

Fig. 3-2. Thumbnail and file size preview of **trolley.jpg.**

3. Note that the cursor has now changed to the shape of a right angle. (See figure 3-3.) The right angle indicates where the top and left edges of the imported graphic will be placed on the canvas after you anchor the location by clicking the mouse button. Place the cursor in the upper left of the canvas and click with the mouse button (left mouse button on PC) to import the image. Do not worry about the location right now. You will change that later.

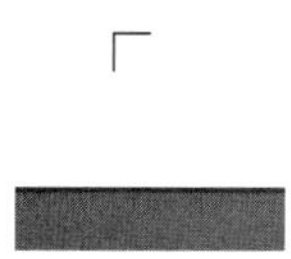

Fig. 3-3. Cursor changes to right angle after File | Import.

4. The image now appears in the place where you clicked your mouse. As you can see, it is too large for our design and is not positioned correctly. Therefore, you need to scale it down and reposition it, which you will do a little later in this guided tour.
5. You may need to open the *Interface* layer by clicking on the (+) symbol next to this layer. Double click on the *Bitmap* sublayer label in the Layers panel that contains the trolley image. Type in *Trolley*, and then press Enter/Return to rename the sublayer. See figure 3-4.

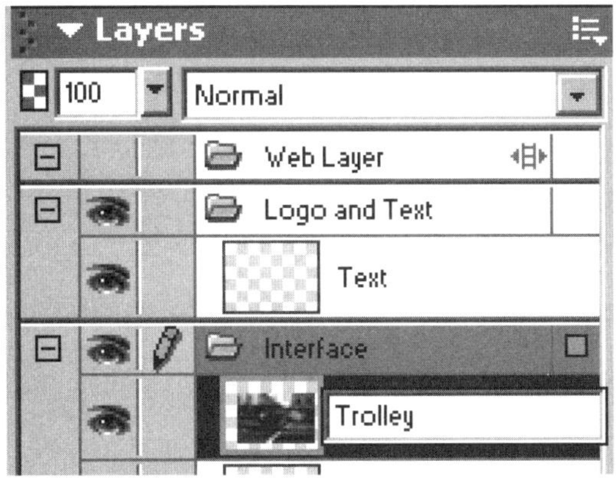

***Fig. 3-4. Renaming the* Bitmap *sublayer to* Trolley.**

6. For now, let's hide this bitmap object so that we can continue importing other objects. In the Layers panel, click on the Eye icon next to the *Trolley* sublayer.
7. Repeat steps 1 through 6 to import the *ctown.jpg* image and place it in the middle of the canvas. Again, we will come back later in this guided tour to reposition and resize this graphic. Be sure to rename this sublayer *Street Scene*, and use the Eye icon in the Layers panel to hide this graphic.
8. Your canvas and Layers panel should now look like those shown in figure 3-5.

Fig. 3-5. Bitmap images do not show on canvas, but are displayed in Layers panel.

9. Save the file as *Tour_3A.png* in the *SaveWork* folder on your hard drive.

Capturing Bitmap Artwork Using the Scan Command

In addition to importing artwork directly into your current document from other files, you can capture images directly from your scanner, digital camera, or other peripheral device. You can do this by using the File | Scan command.

The Scan command accesses any peripheral devices on your computer that use the industry standard TWAIN module. For example, when you first attach a scanner or other peripheral device to your computer, you will probably be asked to install software that allows you and your computer to communicate with the device. Often this software automatically installs the TWAIN module necessary for you to acquire the scanner or other peripherals through various software packages, such as Fireworks MX. The TWAIN module bridges the gap between Fireworks, the scanner software, and the scanner hardware.

·TIP·

If you have peripheral input devices attached to your computer and are not able to view these peripherals using the steps provided here, try reinstalling the device's software. You might want to also check for updates to this software from the manufacturer's web site. If this does not work, double check that your device is TWAIN compliant.

If you have installed software with the TWAIN module for a scanner, digital camera, or other peripheral on your system already, try completing the following steps. If you do not have access to a peripheral, the following steps provide a general overview of the Scan command.

1. Select Menu | File | Scan | Twain Select.
2. All TWAIN-compliant devices should show up in the dialog box that appears. For example, if you have a scanner and a digital camera installed, you should have options for selecting either device.
3. Highlight the peripheral you want to use, and then click on Select.
4. The software for that peripheral will then open within the Fireworks workspace. Select your settings for the device and scan or acquire your images.
5. When finished, the software will close and the scanned image will appear in Fireworks.

·TIP·

Photoshop files can also be imported or opened in Fireworks. Unlike TIF and JPG files, which import as a single flattened image, Photoshop files can be imported with their layer structures intact. Fireworks MX also features enhanced support for maintaining Photoshop 6 text layers.

Bitmap images can be manipulated with the bitmap tools in Fireworks MX. Remember, the main difference between bitmap and vector images is that bitmaps consist of pixels of different colors, whereas vector graphics are images created by a mathematical equation that defines a path or outline of an image. The Fireworks MX toolbox has tools for creating and manipulating both types of images. However, there are other programs, such as Macromedia FreeHand, that can be used to create vector artwork. This artwork can be imported into Fireworks MX with the unique features of vector artwork intact. In Guided Tour 3B you will learn how to import vector artwork created in other software programs and place it in Fireworks MX for use within your designs.

Guided Tour 3B: Importing Vector Artwork Created in Other Software

The process for importing vector artwork is very similar to importing bitmap artwork. The only difference is that vector artwork allows you to enter a series of options before you import it. Once imported, the vectors become Firework's vectors and can be handled as if they were created locally. In this guided tour, you will continue to build the splash page you have been working on in previous exercises.

1. If the *Tour_3A.png* file from the previous guided tour is still open, you can continue working with it, or you can use our completed version of the previous exercise.
2. If you want to use the file on the companion CD-ROM, select File | Open. Locate and double click on the CD-ROM player within your computer. Double click on the *Chapter 3* folder on the companion CD-ROM and click to select the file *Tour_3B.png*. Click on the Open button.
3. Save the file as *Tour_3B.png* in the *SaveWork* folder on your hard drive.

Now let's import the vector logo for the splash screen. This file was created in Macromedia FreeHand, but you can use this method to import any vector graphic (such as an Illustrator file or an EPS file) created with a vector software program.

4. Look in the Layers panel and click to select the *Logo and Text* layer so that the logo will automatically import to a sublayer within this layer.
5. Select File | Import and browse for the *logo.fh10* file.
6. Select the file, and click on Open. Note the following properties in the Vector File Options window, shown in figure 3-6.
    - *The Scale, Width, Height, and Resolution settings can be customized so that vectors can be set to any size.*
    - *The Anti-Alias Paths and Text options allow you to maintain editable text and to control the appearance of vector edges.*
    - *Include Invisible Layers allows layers that were hidden when the file was saved to be revealed in the Fireworks document.*
    - *Render as Images converts vectors to bitmaps, given specified conditions.*

TIP

When importing a FreeHand document, the only difference between the Vector File Options dialog box and the FreeHand dialog box is that the FreeHand dialog box has a few more options for handling FreeHand-specific attributes. These options include the File Conversion settings Open a Page and Include Background Layer, along with the Render as Images option Blends Over. These options are grayed out for other vector file types, such as Illustrator files.

CAUTION

Fireworks MX can export vector graphics to Flash or export an SWF document, but it cannot import an SWF file. To export graphics from Flash MX to a Fireworks-compatible format, you need to export the Flash graphics in Illustrator format. In addition, Fireworks MX does not allow import of Windows Meta Files (WMF), which is a common export format for some types of vector clip art.

Shortcut

The keyboard shortcut for File | Import is:
PC: Ctrl + R
Mac: Cmd + R

·TIP·

In addition to vectors and bitmaps, Fireworks will import a variety of text file formats, including RTF, HTML, and ASCII.

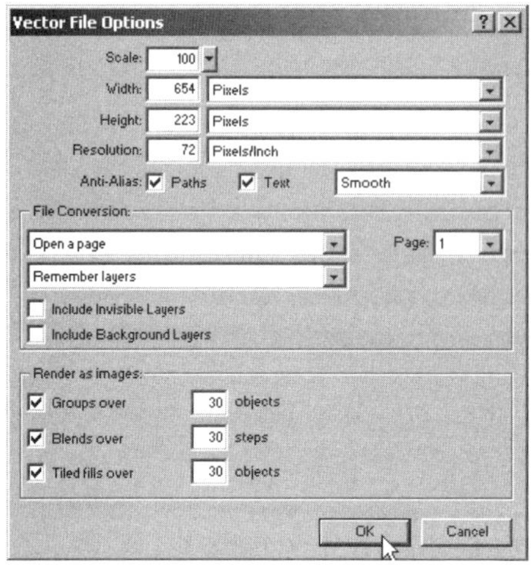

Fig. 3-6. Vector File Options window.

7. Let's use the default options, so just click on OK.
8. Note that the cursor has now changed to a right angle for import placement. Click in the upper left corner of the canvas to place the vector logo on the canvas. Once again, the file is too large for the design and needs to be repositioned on screen. We will come back and do this in another guided tour in this chapter.
9. In the Layers panel, double click on the label *Group: 3 objects* for the new sublayer, which contains the imported image. Rename this sublayer *Logo*.
10. For now, let's hide this vector object. In the Layers panel, click on the Eye icon next to the *Logo* sublayer. Your canvas and Layers panel should now look like those shown in figure 3-7.

Fig. 3-7. Vector image does not show on canvas, but is displayed in Layers panel.

11. Save a copy of the file as *Tour_3B.png* in the *SaveWork* folder on your hard drive.

Once you have imported artwork into a Fireworks MX document, you may want to alter or manipulate the image in some way. Sometimes this can be as simple as scaling an object to the appropriate size for your design, or rotating the artwork. In Guided Tour 3C you will learn how to alter the physical dimensions and orientation of the imported graphics so that they will meet the needs of your graphic design.

Guided Tour 3C: Applying Transformations to Vectors and Bitmaps

In the last two guided tours you learned how to import both bitmapped and vector images into Fireworks. In those exercises you left the imported images just as they were when you imported them. We told you that you would come back later to resize and reposition the images. In this guided tour you will now learn how to adjust the images so that they will fit properly within the splash page.

Applying Physical Transformations

Applying physical transformations simply means to select a graphic, either vector or bitmap, and change the physical characteristics of the artwork in some way. The physical characteristics of an object include the width and height dimensions, as well as the rotation and distortion of an image. A simple and versatile way to alter these physical characteristics in Fireworks MX is to use the Scale tool in the Select toolbox. The Scale tool and the tools grouped with it will allow you to scale, rotate, skew, and distort the image.

1. If the file *Tour_3B.png* from the previous guided tour is still open, you can continue working with it, or you can use our completed version of the previous exercise.
2. If you want to use the file on the companion CD-ROM, select File | Open. Locate and double click on the CD-ROM player within your computer. Double click on the *Chapter 3* folder on the companion CD-ROM and click to select the file *Tour_3C.png*. Click on the Open button.
3. Save the file as *Tour_3C.png* in the SaveWork folder on your hard drive.

You need to now scale the logo and the two photos so that they will fit properly on the splash page layout. First, however, let's reveal the trolley bitmap. Continue with the following steps.

4. In the Layers panel, click on the Eye icon next to the *Trolley* sublayer. You should now be able to see the large cable car photo.

TIP

Before you begin to resize the image, you can use the Pointer tool to select and drag the upper left-hand corner of the trolley image to the correct location on the screen. You can also use the arrow keys to nudge the image in smaller increments for precise placement.

5. Select the Scale tool from the Select toolbox (see figure 3-8) and click on the trolley photo.

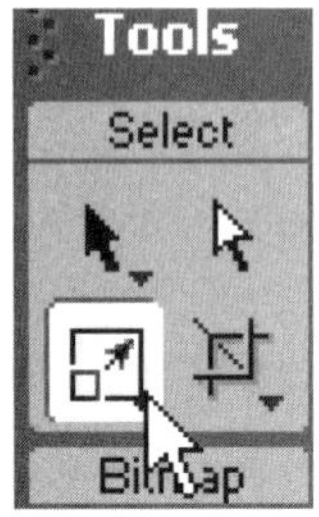

Fig. 3-8. Scale tool in the Select toolbox.

A series of "handles" now appears around the image. See figure 3-9.

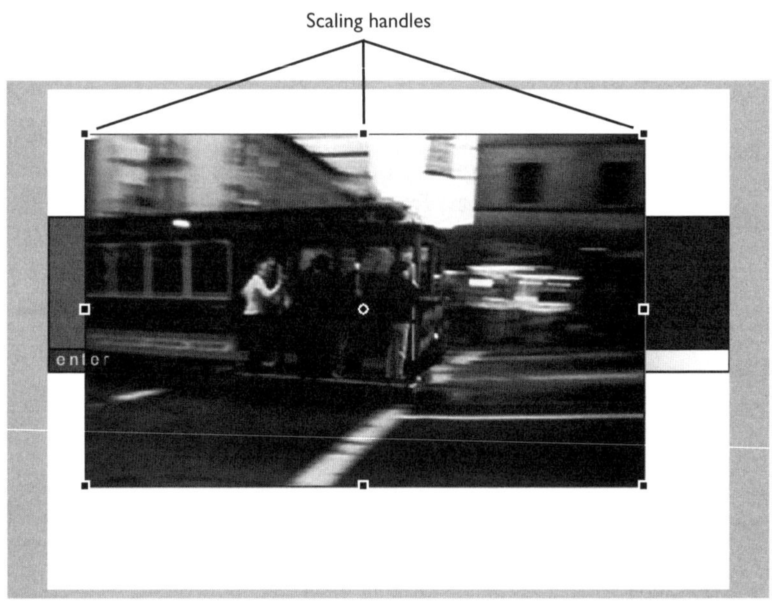

Fig. 3-9. Scaling "handles" appear around the selected image.

6. Let's make the image smaller so that it will fit. Click on the handle located in the lower right-hand corner and pull it toward the middle of the image. This will proportionately reduce the scale of the image. See figure 3-10.

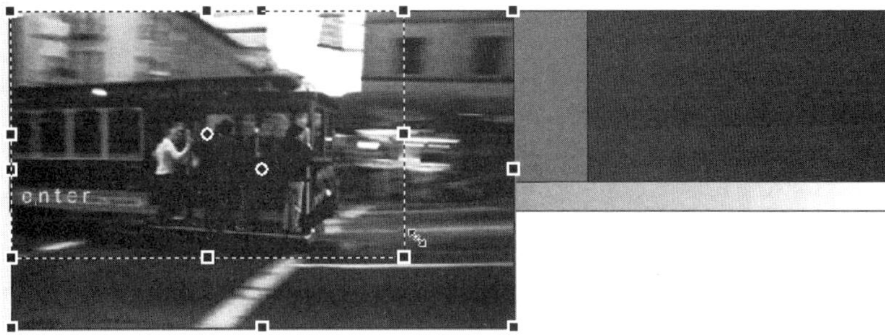

Fig. 3-10. Pull scaling handle toward middle of image to reduce size.

7. Note that the image probably also needs to be scaled horizontally so that it will fit inside the rectangle. To scale the image horizontally (make it wider), use the handles in the middle of either side of the image. Keep pulling on various scale handles until you have adjusted the size of the image so that it fits perfectly into the light blue rectangle on the left side of our splash page. See figure 3-11.

Fig. 3-11. Trolley image scaled to fit within the leftmost light blue rectangle.

8. Double click inside the selection to release the Scale tool and fix the size.
9. In the Select toolbox, click on the Scale tool icon and hold down the mouse button until the pop-up menu appears. As you can see, there are two other options displayed here: the Skew tool and the Distort tool. (See figure 3-12.) As noted in Chapter 2, each of these other tools provides additional capability to modify the physical attributes of the selected image.

·TIP·

In general, scaling photographic images by stretching them disproportionately is considered risky. Make sure the distortion is not noticeable if you do this. In this exercise, the horizontal distortion is not noticeable.

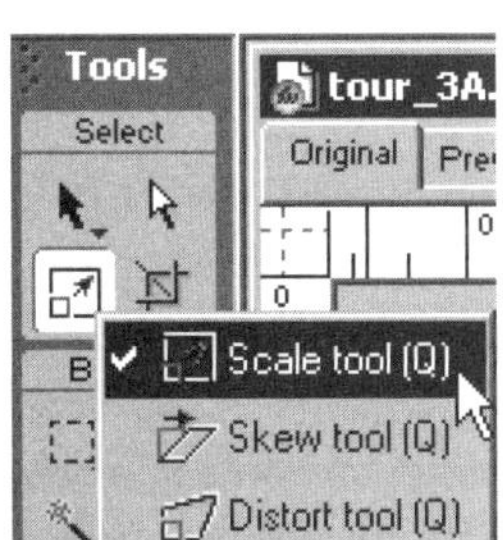

Fig. 3-12. Scale, Skew, and Distort tools listed within the pop-up window for the Scale tool.

·TIP·

The Scale tool can also be used to rotate a selected object. First select the object, and then select the Scale tool in the toolbox. Place the cursor just outside the handles until the cursor turns into a circular arrow. Click and drag in a circle to rotate the object.

10. In the Layers panel, click on the Eye icon (next to the Street Scene sublayer) so that you can see the image. Repeat the process we used on the Trolley image to scale and fit the image within the center rectangular section of the splash screen.

11. In the Layers panel, click on the Eye icon (next to the *Logo* sublayer, within the Logo and Text layer) so that you can see the image. Repeat the process you used with the Trolley and Street Scene images to scale and fit this text within the rectangular section on the far right of the splash screen. Note that the text is centered within the rectangle and does not completely fill the entire space. When you are finished, your canvas should look similar to that shown in figure 3-13.

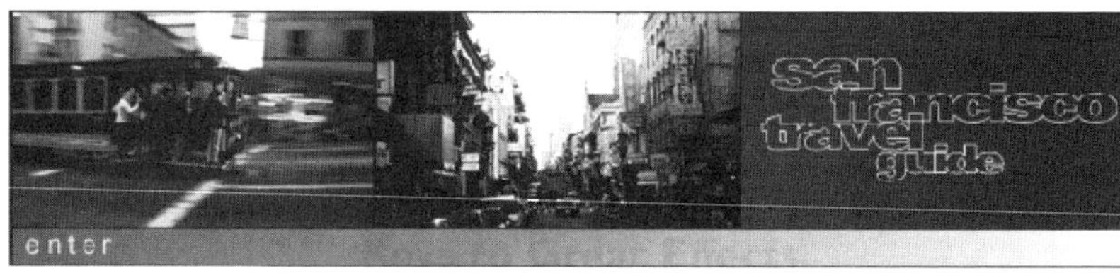

Fig. 3-13. Two bitmapped images and text image scaled and positioned on splash screen.

NOTE

Do not save the changes made in this section. We are using this file to introduce you to some useful transformations, but do not want you to save the file with these transformations.

12. Save a copy of the file as *Tour_3C.png* in the *SaveWork* folder on your hard drive.

Transforming Objects

In addition to the transformation tools available in the Select toolbox, there are Transform options available in the Modify menu. Select Modify | Transform to see what options are available. As you can see by looking at the options listed here, you can transform an object by resizing, distorting, rotating, or flipping it either horizontally or vertically. Note that if you do not have anything selected on the canvas these commands are grayed out. To transform objects, perform the following steps.

1. You should still have the previous file open. If it is not, open *Tour_3C.png* now.
2. Let's first try the Flip Horizontal transformation.
   a) Using the Pointer tool, select the image of the street scene in the center of the layout. This image is located on the sublayer *Street Scene*.
   b) Select Modify | Transform | Flip Horizontal.
   c) The image appears in the same spot but perfectly flipped. This is a great trick for creating mirror images of graphics. Select Edit | Undo to undo this transformation.
3. Now let's see what the same image looks like when it is flipped vertically.

   a) Select Modify | Transform | Flip Vertical.
   b) Now the image looks upside down. Select Edit | Undo to undo this transformation.

4. Try experimenting with some of the other transformation commands found in the Modify menu, such as Rotate and Numeric Transformation.
5. Do *not* save the file with the changes you have made. Simply close the file without saving (File | Close, selecting the No button to not save changes).

The splash page we have been working on serves as an entry point (or "front door") to the home page for the San Francisco Travel Guide web site that we will build later. Because this is a front door to the site, it stands to reason that we need to give our visitors a way of opening that door. On a web page, clicking on links opens doors. In Guided Tour 3D, you will learn how to use hotspots to turn a static image into a link.

Guided Tour 3D: Adding Hotspots to Web Graphics (Making Image Maps)

In Fireworks MX, a hotspot is defined as an area that has HTML code attached to it. Generally, the HTML code makes the hotspot interactive so that by clicking on it, the user can jump to another page. You can add hotspots over text so that the user can click on the text to jump to another web page, or you can place a hotspot over part of a graphic image. When hotspots are applied to a graphic image, it is generally referred to as an image map.

Hotspots can be drawn using a rectangle, a circle, or a multisided polygon. The hotspots you draw will only be visible in Fireworks. Once you export your graphics, these hotspots will be turned into code in an HTML page that Fireworks MX automatically generates for you, containing the code to make your image display properly on a web page.

In this guided tour, we will add a hotspot in order to make an area of an image link to another page. We are going to add a hotspot to the *enter* text that you created in Chapter 2 to turn this graphic into a link. You will be working with the Hotspot tool in the Web toolbox. This tool will allow you to create hotspots over any area of a graphic.

1. We are going to continue to work with the completed version of a file you worked with in the last guided tour. You can either use the file you created and saved on your hard drive or the file provided on the companion CD-ROM. These files should be identical.

a) If you want to use your file, select File | Open. Locate the *SaveWork* folder on your hard drive and then select the file *Tour_3C.png*. Click on the Open button.

CD-ROM

b) If you want to use the file on the companion CD-ROM, select File | Open. Locate and double click on the CD-ROM player within your computer. Double click on the *Chapter 3* folder on the companion CD-ROM and click to select the file *Tour_3D.png*. Click on the Open button.

c) Save the file as *Tour_3D.png* in the *SaveWork* folder on your hard drive.

2. Select the Hotspot tool from the Web toolbox, shown in figure 3-14.

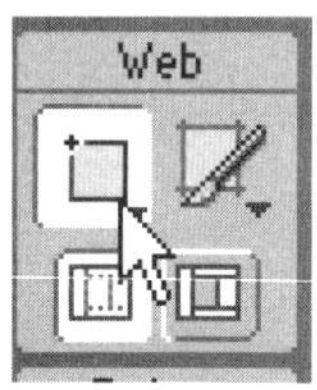

Fig. 3-14. Hotspot tool in the Web toolbox.

3. Take a quick look at the Properties panel specific to the Hotspot tool. Click on the down arrow for the Shape field to open the pop-up menu. See figure 3-15.

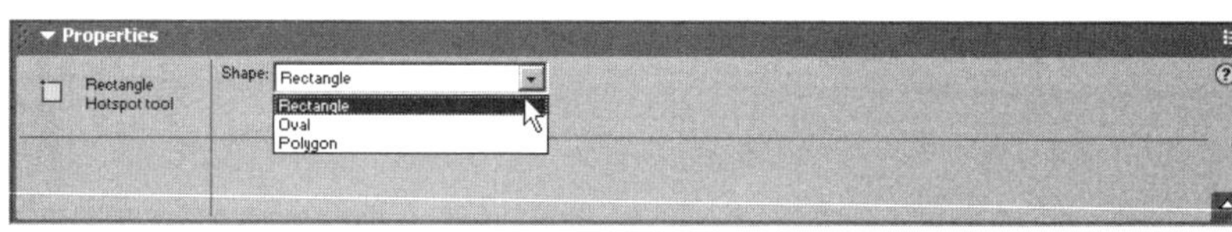

Fig. 3-15. Hotspot Properties panel with Shape pop-up menu open.

4. You can see this same list of options by looking at the Hotspot tool. Click and hold the Hotspot tool, until the pop-up menu displays the options available. (See figure 3-16.) Select the Rectangle Hotspot tool. This is the default shape, and the shape we want to use for this task.

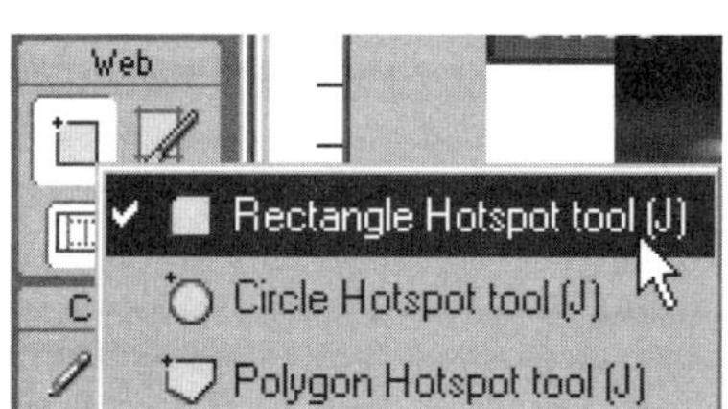

Fig. 3-16. Options listed in pop-up menu from the Hotspot tool.

5. Now let's create a hotspot over the text *enter*, so that users can click on the hotspot to enter the web site.
   a) To draw the hotspot area, move the cursor to the upper left-hand corner of the text *enter*. Click and drag the Rectangle Hotspot tool over the text, ending up in the lower right-hand corner of the text area. Note that a transparent blue rectangle now covers the area where you drew the hotspot. See figure 3-17.

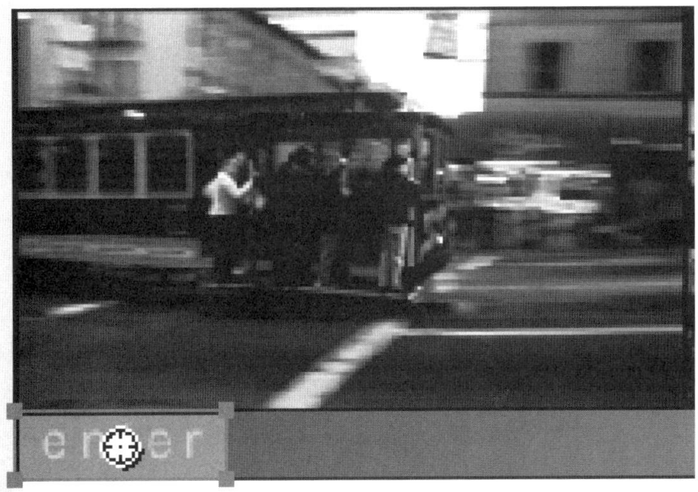

Fig. 3-17. Blue rectangle indicates where the hotspot has been drawn.

   b) In the Layers panel, note that there is now a new *Hotspot* sublayer within the *Web* layer. (See figure 3-18.) The *Web* layer is specifically designed to store hotspots and slice regions, as you may remember from Chapter 2.

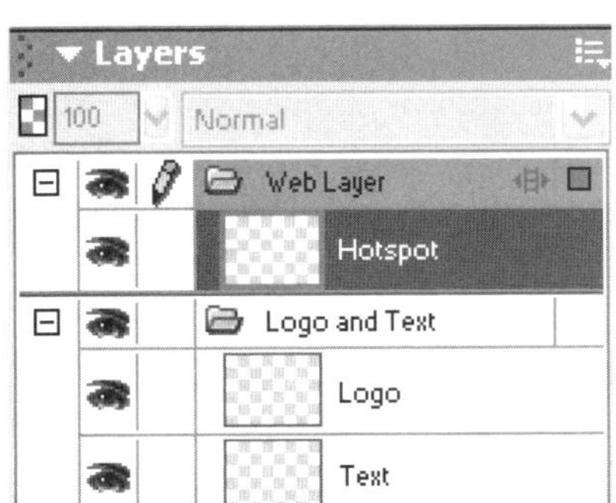

***Fig. 3-18. Addition of* Hotspot *sublayer within the* Web Layer.**

6. To show or hide a hotspot, click on the Eye icon, next to the *Hotspot* sub-layer in the *Web* layer.
7. To select a hotspot on the canvas, use the Pointer tool, as you would for any other object. Once selected, you can resize the hotspot by dragging any of its corner points. Resize the hotspot so that it is about the same size and position as shown in figure 3-17.
8. Select the hotspot and enter the following values into the fields displayed in the associated Properties panel.
   - *Link:* home.html
   - *Alt:* Enter the travel site. (This is the text that appears in a web browser when the viewer rolls over the image.)
   - *Target:* Leave this field blank. This allows you to target a frame within an HTML frame set.
9. The Properties panel in your file should now look like that shown in figure 3-19.

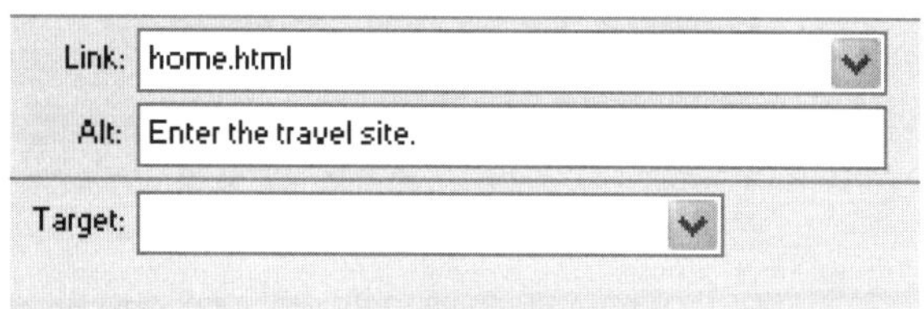

Fig. 3-19. Properties panel for the hotspot.

10. Save a copy of the file as *Tour_3D.png* in the *SaveWork* folder on your hard drive.

You have now completed the content and linkage aspects of the splash page for the San Francisco Travel Guide web site. Over the last several exercises, you have learned how to draw vector shapes, import and rescale bitmapped objects, import and rescale vector objects, and place a hotspot on the image so that the user can jump to the next page, the home page of the web site. You now need to create the home page.

Designing Screens and the User Interface

There are a variety of types of screens you can use within your web application. You have just completed creating a splash screen, the first screen a web surfer will see when he encounters our San Francisco Travel Guide web site. Other types of screens include content screens (with a variety of screen layouts); message, feedback, or overlay screens; contact screens; questionnaire screens; and e-commerce screens.

Each of these screens should include common graphic and design elements that promote a unifying "look and feel" across all of these screen types. This unifying "look and feel" helps identify all screens within the application as being part of that particular application, and generally contributes to the project as being perceived in a more professional light.

To help you see what we mean about the unifying "look and feel" of a professionally created web site, let's take a close look at sample screens created for a client. This sample web site is also a travel site. Let's first look at the splash screen – something you should now be familiar with. (See figure 3-20.) Note the images, and the text *Click to Enter* (yes, it is a hotspot).

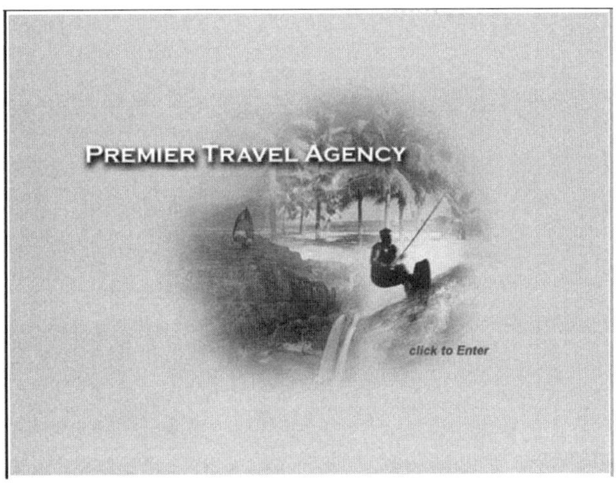

Fig. 3-20. Example of a splash screen.

Each type of screen is also designed to serve a different and distinct purpose. To help users more quickly identify what type of screen is currently being displayed (and its underlying purpose), many developers will design each type of screen with its own distinct appearance (different design, different screen layout, and perhaps different colors).

At the same time, these different screen appearances still include the common graphic/design elements that help make all screens part of the same application. Look closely at figures 3-21 through 3-28, which show a group of screen captures illustrating a variety of different types of screens, with different screen layouts. Look for the unifying "look and feel" in each screen.

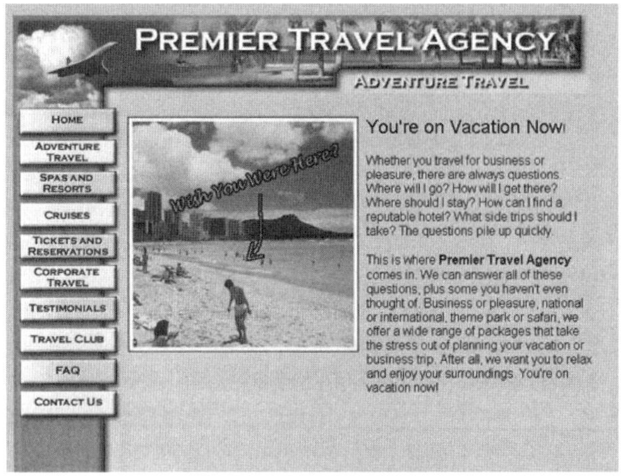

Fig. 3-21. Example of a home page screen.

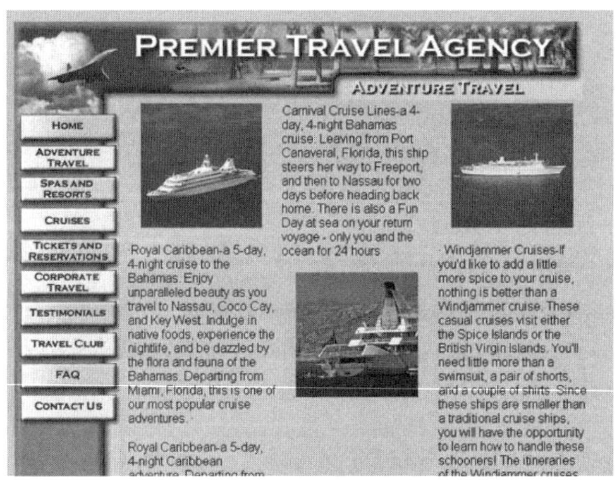

Fig. 3-22. Example of a content page, with three columns per screen.

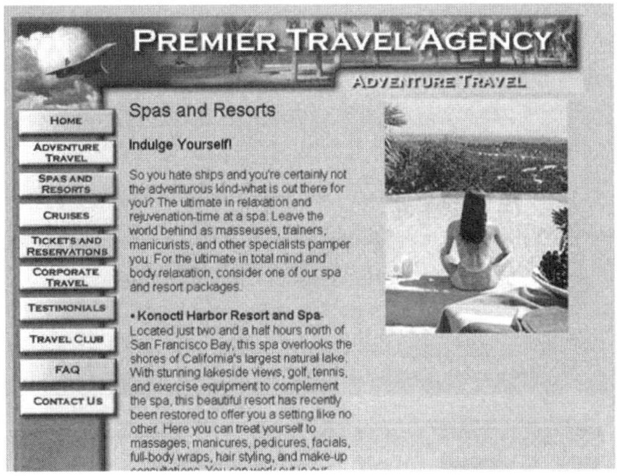

Fig. 3-23. Example of a content page, showing text on left and photo on right.

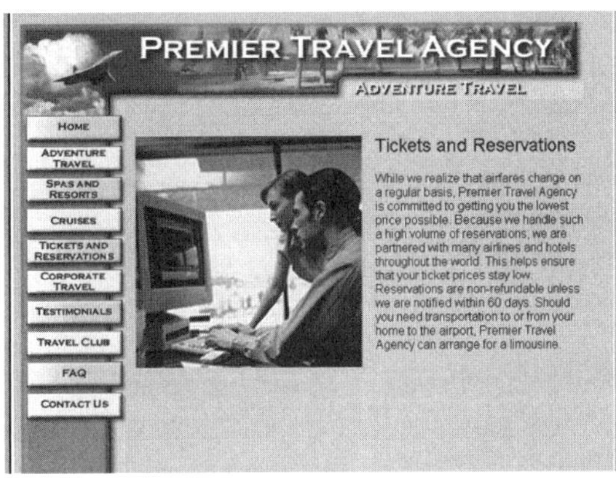

Fig. 3-24. Example of a content page, showing text on right and photo on left.

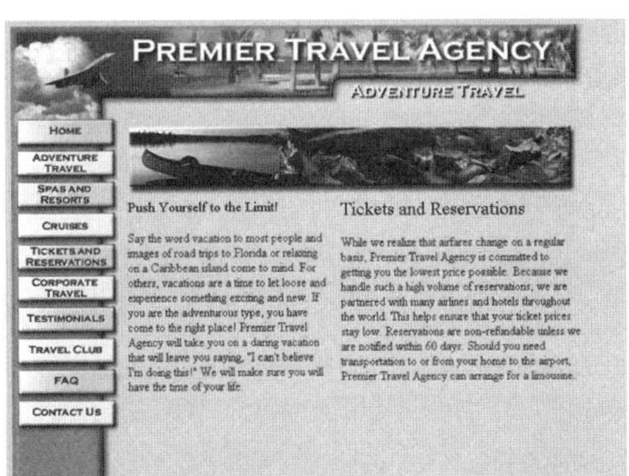

Fig. 3-25. Example of a content page, showing two text columns and banner photo.

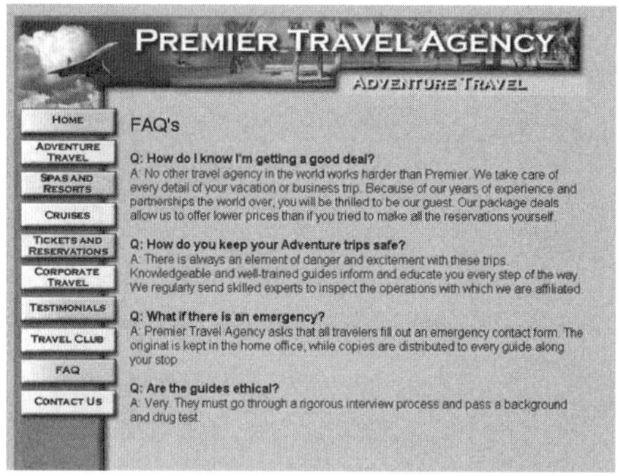

Fig. 3-26. Example of a Frequently Asked Questions page.

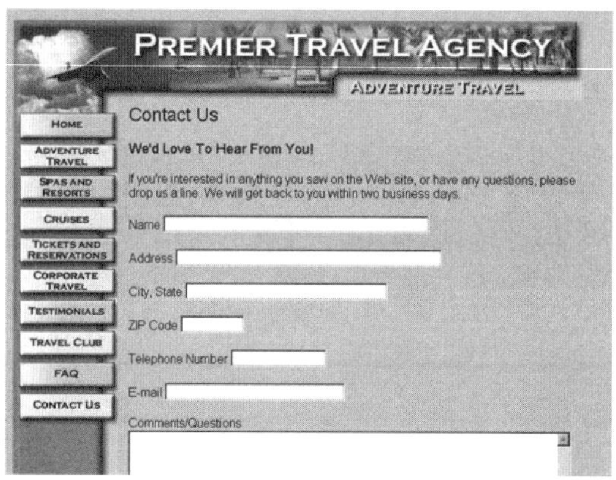

Fig. 3-27. Example of a Contact Us page.

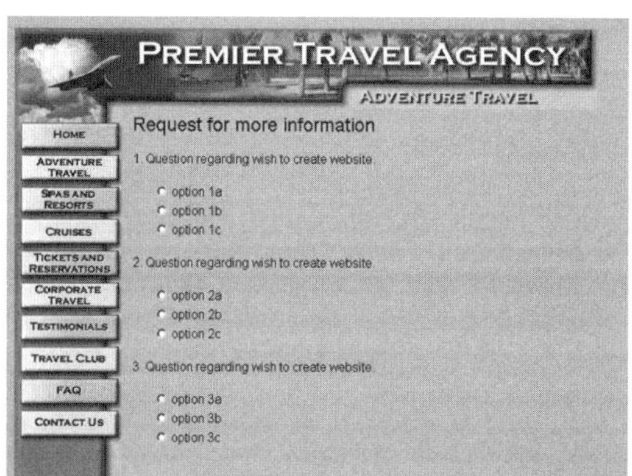

Fig. 3-28. Example of a Request for More Information page.

Let's take a closer look at the details of these screens. Within each screen, there are two very distinctly separate areas: a section that contains all of the navigational controls and web site information, and the main content area.

The first area is the user control panel (or user interface). This area contains all functional means (buttons or menus) to provide the user with the ability to move about within the web site. The user interface should be consistently located in the same place on every content screen. Figure 3-29 shows the user interface for this sample web site.

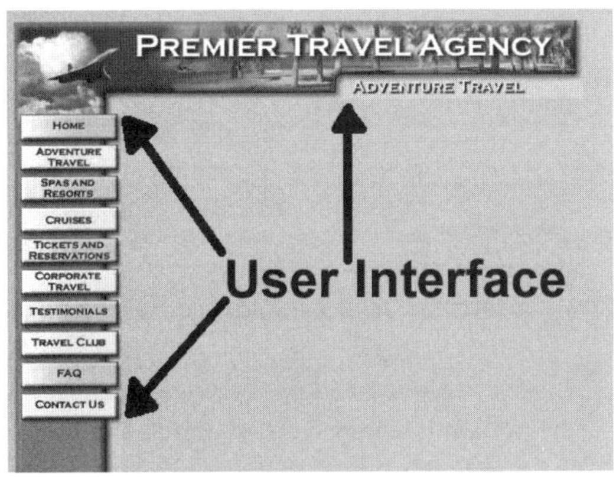

Fig. 3-29. User interface for a sample web site.

Note that in our sample web site interface, the name of the company is prominently displayed across the top of the screen, along with a very inviting beach scene and a plane suggesting how we might travel to that beach. This top banner is a crucial part of the user interface and is a common aspect of every screen within the web site.

Most web designers will place the user interface at the top or left portions of a web screen. Multimedia developers may also place the user interface across the bottom of each screen. Wherever you decide to place it, be consistent and always place it in exactly in the same location, with exactly the same look and functionality.

Consistency is important in regard to the user interface. However, simplicity and ease of use is equally important. The user should be able to easily interpret the information located here, as well as easily make the appropriate functional selections. In our sample web site, the user can very easily select a different page to visit by clicking on the subject buttons located on the left portion of the user interface. These buttons provide complete navigation from any page of the web site to any other page within the site. Each button includes a hotspot to link to the appropriate page. The button/hotspots include Home, Adventure Travel, Spas And Resorts, Cruises, Tickets And Reservations, Corporate Travel, Testimonials, Travel Club, Frequently Asked Questions, and a Contact page. See figure 3-30.

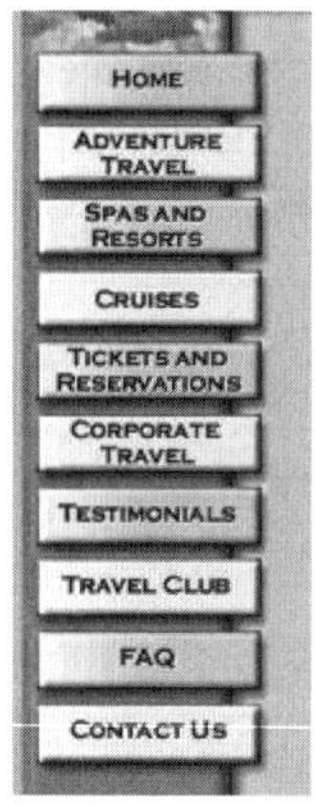

Fig. 3-30. Close-up of buttons/hotspots in user interface for the sample web site.

Given the design and placement of the user interface, the rest of the area on the screen is where you will place the content. The content area is where a variable combination of text (headlines, body text, and text bullets), graphics, photographs, and animation can be displayed. See figure 3-31.

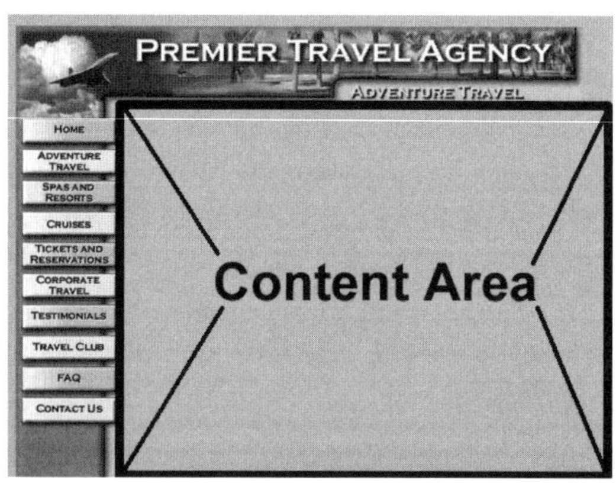

Fig. 3-31. Content area for screens in the sample web site.

This content area can be designed and the elements laid out in any number of ways, depending on the nature of the project. You may want go back and review figures 3-21 through 3-28.

The content area and the user interface should be logically and visually organized so that these two areas can be immediately distinguished from each other. Consistency and simplicity mitigate against user distraction. In other words, the user/viewer can concentrate on the subject matter and does not need to "think about" how to perform functions. In Practice Exercise 3-1 you will gain some practice designing and editing a web site interface.

Practice Exercise 3-1: Designing and Editing a Web Site Interface

Description

In this exercise, you will build the framework for the home page and user interface for the San Francisco Travel Guide web site. You will incorporate the design principles that were just presented in the preceding topic. You will import vector and bitmap artwork. You will also set up a series of text buttons and add hotspots to them.

Preview of the Completed Canvas

Before beginning the exercise, let's take a look at the graphic in its completed state so that you can clearly see what it is you are about to build.

1. Use the menu option File | Open and locate the *Chapter 3* folder on the companion CD-ROM. Find the file named *Exercise3_1(complete).png*. Double click on this file to open it.
2. Take a look at the completed images on the canvas, making note of the content and structure of the Layers panel.
3. Figure 3-32 shows what the canvas will look like when this exercise is completed.

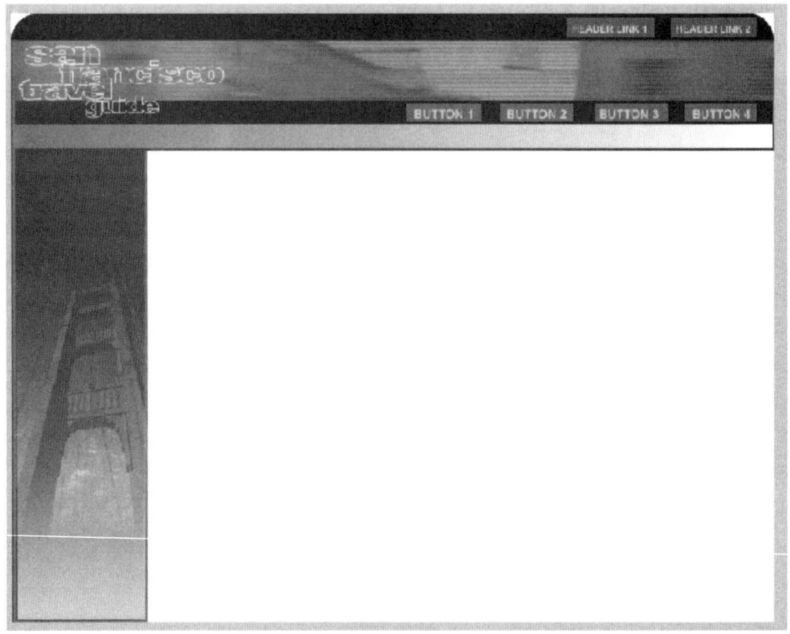

Fig. 3-32. Completed canvas upon completion of the exercise.

4. Figure 3-33 shows what the Layers panel will look like when this exercise is completed.

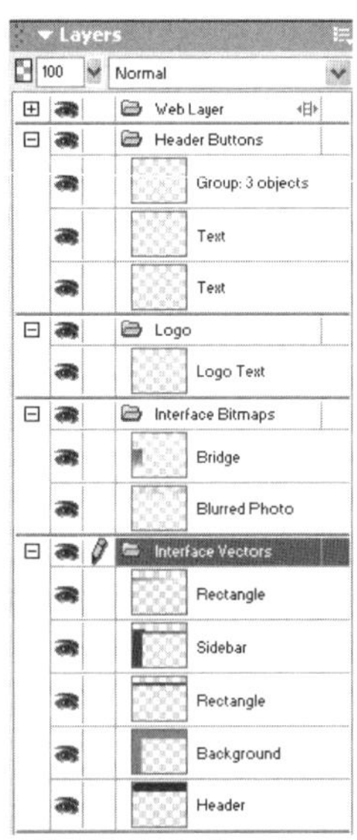

Fig. 3-33. Completed Layers panel upon completion of the exercise.

Step-by-Step Instructions

1. Select File | New and set the canvas size to 770 x 600. Set the Canvas Color to white, and leave the Resolution at 72. Save the file as *Exercise3_1.png* in the *SaveWork* folder on your hard drive.
2. Change the name of *Layer 1* to *Interface Vectors* by double clicking on the layer name and typing in the new name.
3. Next, let's import and place the first group of interface graphics on the canvas.
   a) Select File | Import, and double click on the *home_vector1.png* file from the *Chapter 3* folder on the companion CD-ROM. (The files you will be importing for this exercise were created in Fireworks MX.)
   b) Note that the cursor has now turned to a right angle. Click the cursor in the very upper left-hand corner of the canvas, so that the graphics will appear in this location. After importing, note that two vector graphics now appear on the canvas. Figure 3-34 shows what your canvas and Layers panel should look like at this point.

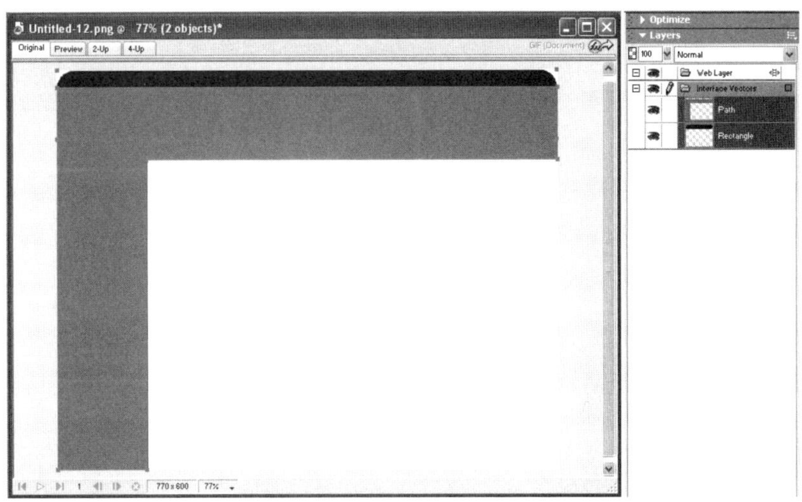

Fig. 3-34. Canvas and Layers panel in progress.

   c) In the Layers panel, select the blue graphic (*Path* sublayer) and rename it *Background*.
   d) In the Layers panel, select the black graphic (*Rectangle*) and rename this sublayer *Header*.
   e) Select the Pointer tool. Hold down the Shift key and click to select both graphics on the canvas. In the Properties panel, type *0* in both the X and Y fields. Press Enter/Return to set the values. Setting the

X and Y coordinates to 0 aligns the graphics to the top and left of the canvas.

4. Next, let's import and place the second interface graphic on the canvas.
   a) Select File | Import to import the *home_vector2.png* file from the *Chapter 3* folder on the companion CD-ROM.
   b) The cursor now turns to a right angle. Click the cursor in the very upper left-hand corner of the canvas, so that the graphics will appear in this location. After importing, note that only one vector graphic appears on the canvas, and only one sublayer has been added (*Path*).
   c) In the Layers panel, select the new *Path* sublayer and rename it *Sidebar*.
   d) Select the Pointer tool, and then select the new graphic. Use the Properties panel to set the X coordinate to *4* and the Y coordinate to *86*.
   e) Figure 3-35 shows what your canvas and Layers panel should look like at this point.

·TIP·

We included this note in the first practice exercise and will only include it again this second time. You might ask yourself where we got the numbers (values) used in this exercise and those that follow. The answer is that we have designed the elements of the exercises so that the step-by-step instructions can guide you through the development process. "In real life" you will not have these numbers (values) predetermined for you, and will need to determine their values by using whatever settings make the best artistic rendering.

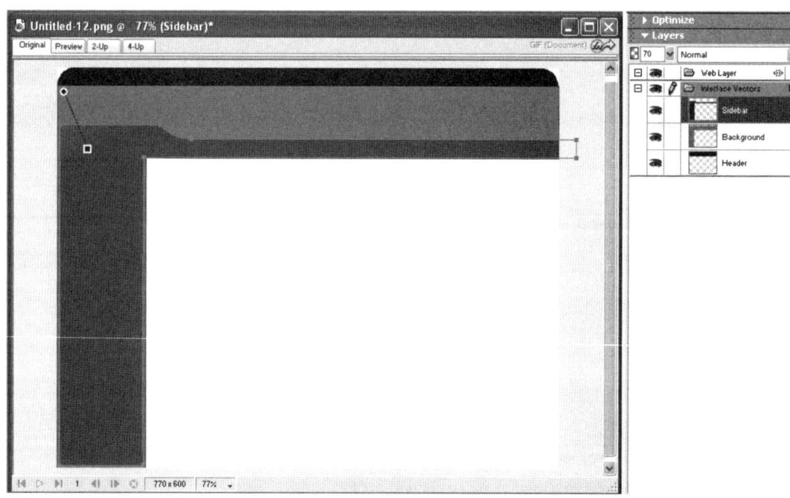

Fig. 3-35. Canvas and Layers panel in progress, showing new graphics.

5. Save the file as *Exercise3_1.png* in the *SaveWork* folder on your hard drive.

6. Next, let's draw and arrange several rectangles on the canvas to complete the basic design.
   a) Select the Rectangle tool from the Vector toolbox, and draw a horizontal rectangle that spans the entire width of the medium blue area of the header. You will adjust the location and size in the next step.
   b) Select the rectangle you just created and enter the following values in the Properties panel.

- *Width:* 765
- *Height:* 23
- *X:* 4
- *Y:* 86
- *Fill Category:* None
- *Fill Color:* #330066 (Click on the Fill color swatch and in the pop-up window that opens, type the number in the hexadecimal field at the top of the window.)
- *Texture:* Smoky
- *Amount of Texture:* 10%
- *Stroke Color:* No Stroke (Remember, no stroke is indicated by the white square with a red line through it.)

c) Click on the *Rectangle* sublayer and drag it below the *Sidebar* sublayer in the Layers panel, so that the sidebar graphic comes to the foreground.

d) Figure 3-36 shows what your canvas and Layers panel should look like at this point.

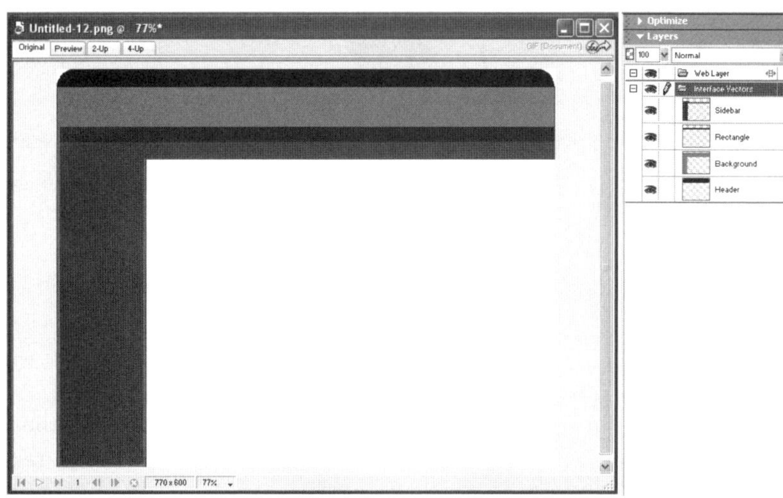

Fig. 3-36. Canvas and Layers panel in progress,progress, showing the new sidebar graphic.

7. Now let's draw another rectangle about the same size and location.

a) Select the new rectangle and enter the following in the Properties panel.

- *Width:* 765
- *Height:* 23

- *X:* 4
- *Y:* 109
- *Fill Category:* Linear
- *Fill Color:* Left Gradient Marker - #3399FF; Right Gradient Marker – White (Select the Fill color swatch. On the pop-up window that appears, there are two small markers on either end of the gradient. Click on each marker to change the colors in the gradient.)
- *Texture:* Smoky
- *Amount of Texture:* 0%
- *Stroke Color:* No Stroke

b) Figure 3-37 shows what your canvas and Layers panel should look like at this point.

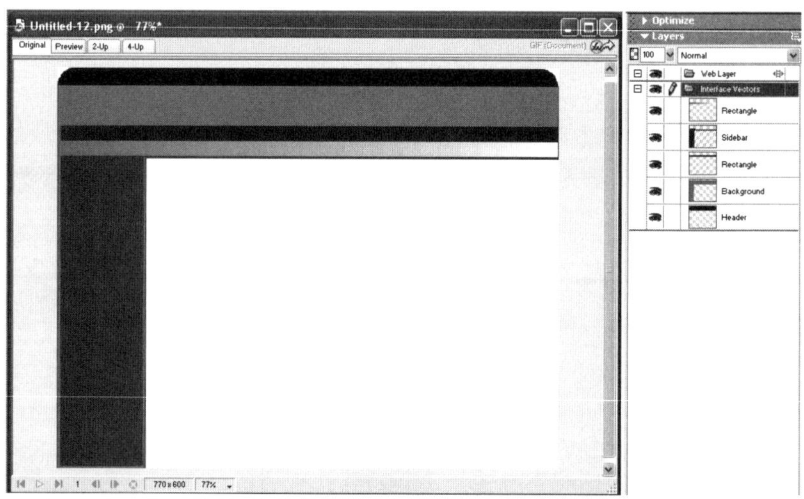

Fig. 3-37. Canvas and Layers panel in progress, with the gradient added.

That completes the vector shapes that contribute to the interface. Next, let's import some bitmap images to add some texture to the interface.

8. Let's import the first bitmap file.
   a) Click on the New/Duplicate Layer icon at the bottom of Layers panel, to add a new layer. Name the layer *Interface Bitmaps*. See figure 3-38.

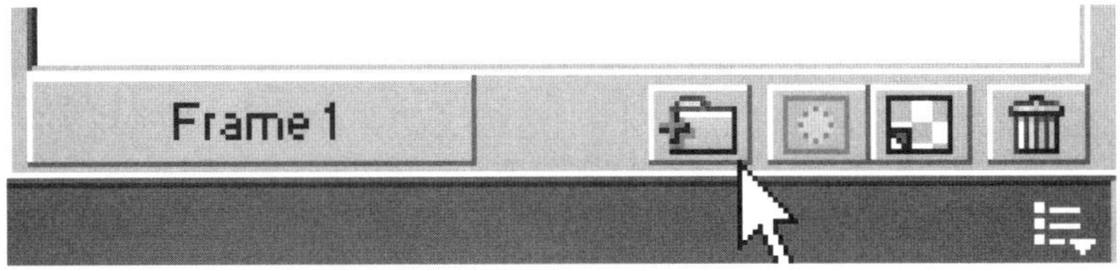

Fig. 3-38. New/Duplicate Layer icon in the Layers panel

b) Select File | Import, and select *home_bitmap1.png*.
c) Click the cursor in the upper left corner of the canvas, so that the graphics will be placed in this location.
d) Select the bitmap and use the Properties panel to set the X value to *0* and the Y value to *27*.
e) In the Layers panel, rename the new sublayer *Blurred Photo*.
f) Figure 3-39 shows what your canvas and Layers panel should look like at this point.

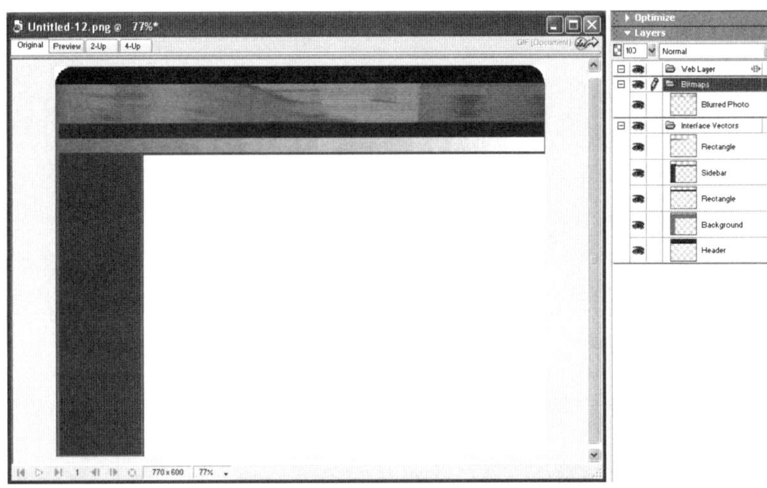

Fig. 3-39. Canvas and Layers panel in progress, with the blurred graphic added.

9. Let's import the second bitmap file.
   a) Select File | Import, and double click on *home_bitmap2.png*.
   b) Click the cursor in the top of the dark blue sidebar area to place the graphic in this location.
   c) In the Layers panel, rename the sublayer *Bridge*.
   d) Select the bridge image and use the Properties panel to set an X value of *2* and a Y value of *238*.
10. To make this graphic blend into the sidebar better, let's try a new setting. Click on the bitmap in the Layer panel to select it. In the Blend Mode

pull-down menu located at the top of the Layers panel, change the current setting of Normal to Lighten. Note that the hard edge of the bridge image now blends into the color of the sidebar. (See figure 3-40.) Blend modes are explored more later in the book.

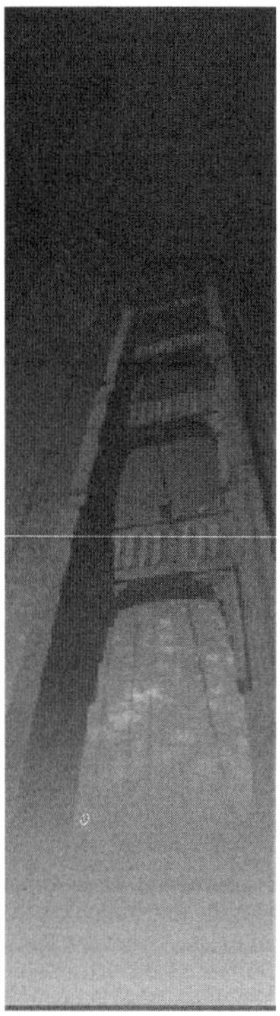

Fig. 3-40. Second bitmap "lightened" using the Blend Mode menu.

11. Now let's import the logo and place it the header.
    a) Add a new layer and name it *Logo*. Drag the *Logo* layer and drop it just below the *Web* layer.
    b) Make sure the *Logo* layer is selected. Select File | Import, and then select *logo.fh10* from the *Chapter 3* folder on the companion CD-ROM.
    c) On the Vector File option window, accept the default settings and click on OK.
    d) Click the cursor in the top left of the canvas to place the graphic in this location.
    e) In the Layers panel, rename the sublayer *Group: 3 objects* as *Logo Text*.
    f) Select the Scale tool and use it to reduce the size of the logo to fit in the upper left of the header area just below the black bar, as shown in figure 3-41. It is okay for the logo to flow over the purple bar somewhat at the bottom.

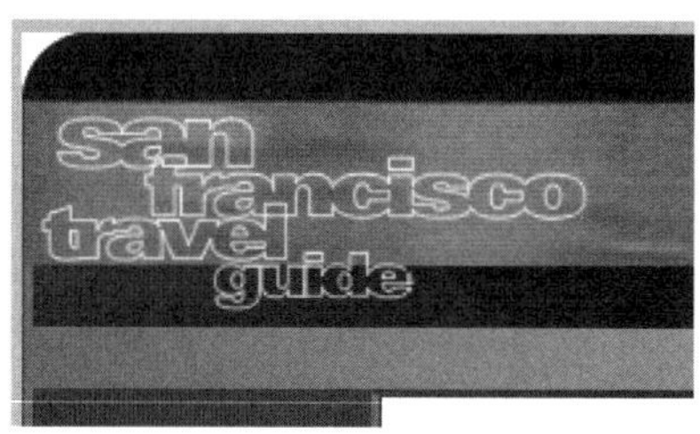

Fig. 3-41. Logo placement on the canvas.

12. Save the file as *Exercise3_1.png* in the *SaveWork* folder on your hard drive.
13. Now let's import some text that we will use for buttons.
    a) Add a new layer and name it *Header Buttons*. If you need to, drag this new layer so that it rests directly under the *Web* layer.
    b) Make sure the *Header Buttons* layer is selected, and then select File | Import. Double click to select the *home_buttontext.png* file in the *Chapter 3* folder on the companion CD-ROM.
    c) Click the cursor in the top middle of the header area, so that the graphics are placed in this location.
    d) With the button text still selected, use the Properties panel to set the X value to *406* and the Y value to *10*.
    e) Figure 3-42 shows the placement of the button text.

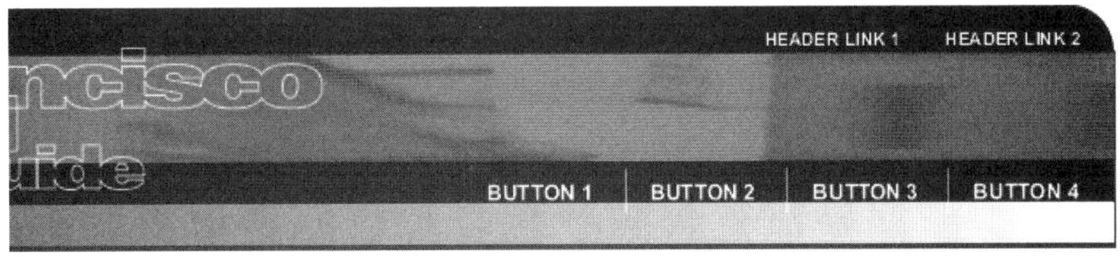

Fig. 3-42. Placement of the button text.

14. Now let's add a hotspot to each of the buttons we just added.
    a) Select the Hotspot tool from the Web toolbox and draw a rectangular hotspot above each graphic. The hotspots do not have to be exact, as they will be invisible to the user. See figure 3-43.
    b) You can also use the Properties panel to help with the positioning and size of each hotspot.

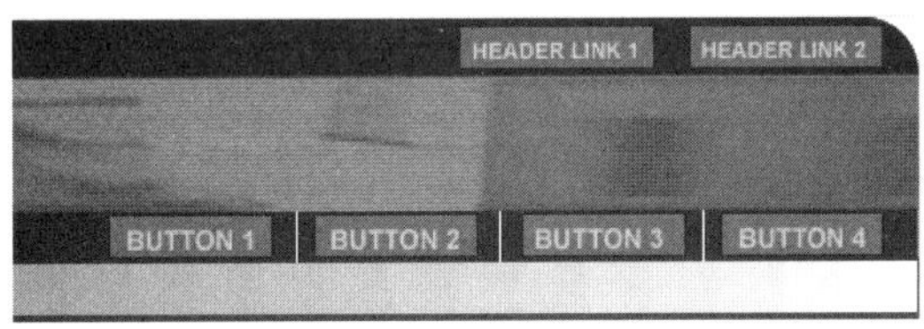

Fig. 3-43. Placement of the hotspots over each button text object.

15. Next, let's add a link to each of the hotspots.
    a) Select the *Button 1* hotspot and enter the following information in the Properties panel.
        - *Alt:* Button 1
    b) Select the *Button 2* hotspot and enter the following information in the Properties panel.
        - *Alt:* Button 2
    c) Select the *Button 3* hotspot and enter the following information in the Properties panel.
        - *Alt:* Button 3
    d) Select the *Button 4* hotspot and enter the following information in the Properties panel.
        - *Alt:* Button 4
    e) Select the *Header Link 1* hotspot and apply the following information in the Properties panel.
        - *Alt:* Header Link 1

f) Select the *Header Link 2* hotspot and apply the following information in the Properties panel.

- *Alt:* Header Link 2

g) Figures 3-44 and 3-45 show the canvas and Layers panel as they should appear at the completion of the exercise.

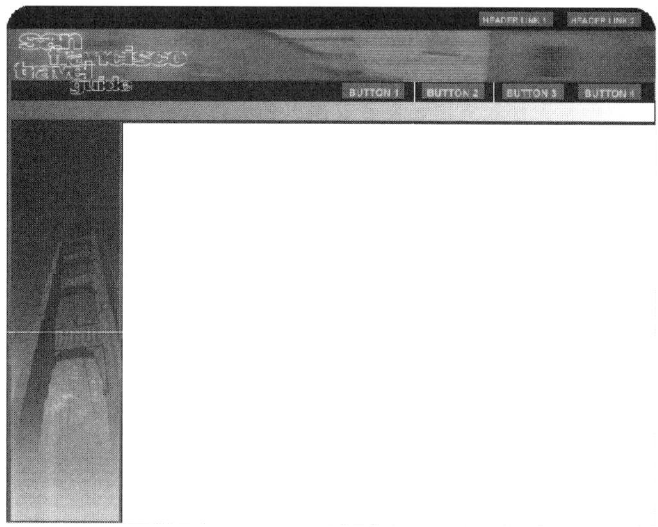

Fig. 3-44. Completed canvas.

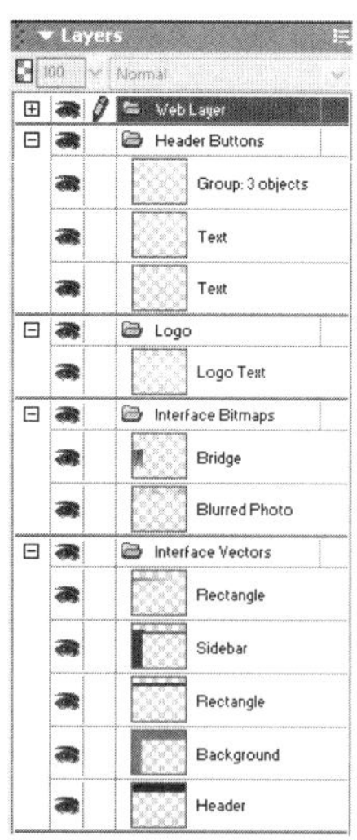

Fig. 3-45. Completed Layers panel.

16. Save the file as *Exercise3_1.png* in the *SaveWork* folder on your hard drive.

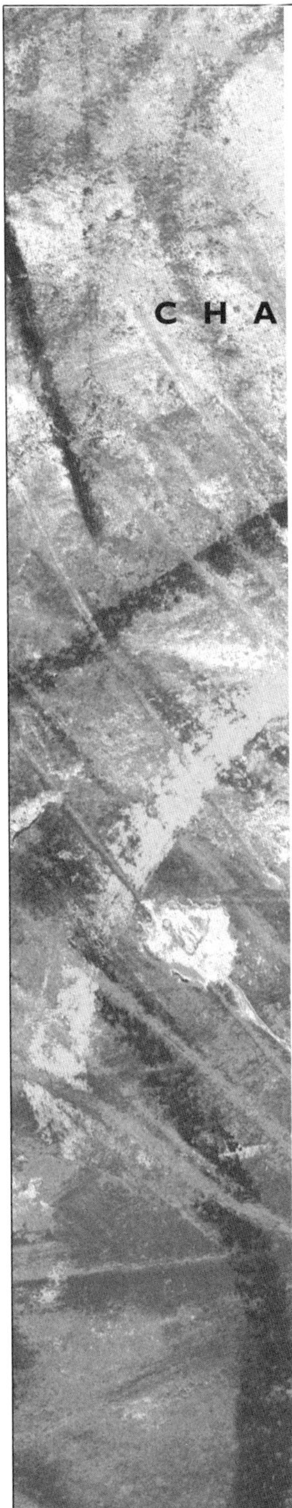

CHAPTER 4

Handling Color in Fireworks MX

Chapter Topics:

- *Introduction*
- *Understanding Color for Web Production*
- *Guided Tour 4A: The Fireworks MX Color Controls*
- *Guided Tour 4B: Controlling Color Using Find and Replace*
- *Guided Tour 4C: Saving a Custom Palette from the Color Table*

Introduction

Color is a key element in graphic design. When designing with color on a computer monitor, it is important to understand how these colors are displayed, how colors translate when printed, and how colors in web designs may display differently on the PC and Mac and from monitor to monitor. Web designers will discover that there are functional as well as aesthetic issues that make understanding color usage vital. Issues such as file size and compression, as well as bandwidth, make creating designs for the Web a challenge. This chapter provides an overview of color management in Fireworks MX, designed to cover important color concepts and to introduce you to the Fireworks system for handling color.

You were introduced to the Colors toolbox and Properties panel (containing the Stroke and Fill Color fields) in Chapter 2, and you had a chance to work with them in Chapter 3. In this chapter, you will work with some of the additional details concerning color editing and manipulation through a series of guided tours. By the end of the chapter you will be able to:

- *Describe the general capabilities and properties of the Fireworks MX color panels*
- *Work with RGB and hexadecimal color naming and controls*
- *Use the Fireworks MX Find and Replace feature to control color*

Understanding Color for Web Production

Before we get into the guided tours, clarification on a few concepts will help get you started. When creating graphics for the Web, the creation and application of color is only a small part of the entire process. You must also be able to choose colors deliberately and choose file formats that best support optimization of those colors.

As you have been surfing the Web, you more than likely have encountered a web page that has evoked the gut response of – yuck! It might have been the clashing circus of colors, overuse of font styles, or overall lack of design. Beginning developers frequently make the same mistake: given many options, use them all!

The common mistake with color is to use too many colors in the background, as part of the graphic screen treatment, or as part of graphic illustrations. Some colors just do not look good together on screen. This is where some artistic talent or discrimination is needed. As a general suggestion, use a small number of colors that complement one another, and use them consistently, especially in the user interface and overall screen background.

Limiting Colors with Bit Depth

The bit depth of an image refers to the number of actual colors included in an image. A single bit depth holds two colors. Two-bit color depth equals four colors, three-bit color depth equals eight colors, and so on. When working with the Fireworks optimization controls, you will notice the numbers 8, 24, and 32 next to the export file type options. These numbers are actually references to the bit depth of an image, which is the number of actual colors in the exported image.

8-bit Images

8-bit images are useful for graphics with flat color and a very limited number of colors. Simple drawings are usually saved in an 8-bit format. 8-bit images are limited to a maximum of 256 actual colors, and can be reduced to as few as four colors. The advantage of limiting the number of colors is that it creates smaller file sizes, which in turn means faster downloads. The disadvantage of 8-bit color is that complex detail, such as photographic detail, does not render very well. For the Web, the most common 8-bit export format is GIF. The GIF file format was designed to compress images with few colors. As a result, photographic images often look flat when they are saved as GIF files, because the GIF format cannot handle subtle color information.

24-bit Images

Most photographic images or drawings with complex textures and detail are 24-bit images, in that this format is used for graphics that contain millions of colors. The advantage of 24-bit color is the detail rendered by this bit depth. The disadvantage is that larger file size accompanies the increased color information. For the Web, the most common 24-bit format is JPG. Just as the GIF format specializes in compressing images with fewer colors, the JPG format is designed to compress images with millions of colors. As you prepare graphics for export, be aware of the particular characteristics of the GIF and JPG formats, which are outlined in Table 4-1.

GIF Characteristics	JPG Characteristics
Used for compressing images with 256 or fewer colors (e.g., graphic logos, simple clip art, and text)	Used for compressing images with millions of colors (e.g., color photos and detailed illustrations)
Supports transparency	Does not support transparency
Supports animation (animated GIF)	Does not support animation
Lossy compression format	Lossy compression format
.gif file extension	.jpg file extension

Table 4-1: Comparison of GIF and JPG File Format Characteristics

32-bit Images

32-bit images share the same qualities as 24-bit, but contain a larger range of colors. As a result, they can also support features such as transparency. This is particularly useful for high-quality PNG images for export into applications such as Flash and Director.

Web-Safe Color Palette

·TIP·

In addition to dealing with differences of color across computer platforms, gamma settings are also displayed differently on the Windows and Macintosh computer platforms. The gamma setting is used to adjust midtones in images so that they will not appear too dark when displayed on a monitor. The Windows gamma correction setting is higher than the Mac's setting, and therefore colors often display much darker on Windows. You will have to pay attention to this issue if you are designing for cross-platform audiences. To preview cross-platform gamma correction, select View | Macintosh (or Windows) Gamma. This option simulates the gamma display on different platforms.

Consider for a moment the people who look at web pages, and the equipment they use to do their web surfing. They are using computers with operating systems that include Macintosh, Windows 95/98/2000/XP, Linux, and a variety of other operating systems. And do not forget WebTV and the new handheld devices. Each of these operating systems has its own organization of how colors are processed and displayed on screen. In other words, the 256 colors Windows uses are not the same 256 colors (or even the same order) used with the Macintosh.

Luckily, most web browsers (e.g., Internet Explorer and Netscape) use the same color management scheme, consisting of 216 colors. These 216 colors are the same for the browsers no matter which computer platform they are running on. These 216 common colors are often referred to as "web-safe" or "browser-safe" colors.

Using the Web-Safe color palette ensures that browsers render the colors in our graphics as we intend, without color shifts that may arise when using colors outside this palette. As a general suggestion, when designing in Fireworks, use the Web-Safe color palette to produce the most reliable results on the Web.

The web-safe colors are the default colors in the Fireworks interface. Web-safe colors are also known as hexadecimal colors because of the six-character letter-and-number combination used to represent the color in the HTML code of a web page. The Fireworks MX color palette displays color swatches, as well as the corresponding hexadecimal number. For more experienced web designers, this palette allows you to type the hexadecimal number directly into the number field located at the top of the Web-Safe color palette. See figure 4-1.

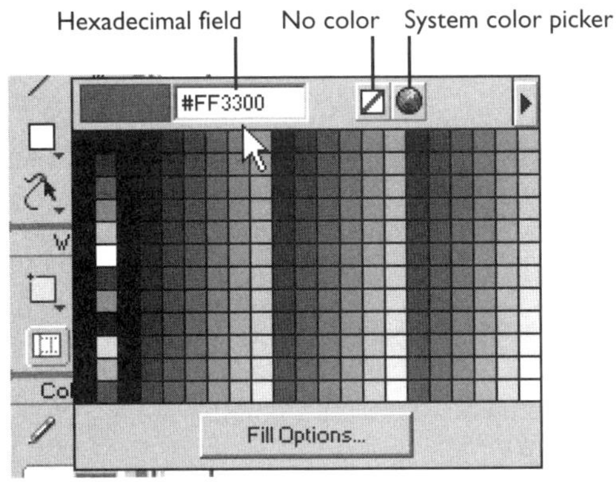

Fig. 4-1. Hexadecimal field in the Fireworks MX Web-Safe color palette.

Color Models

Color models are simply different ways of referencing a color. For example, RGB (red, green, blue) is the common model that computer monitors use to represent color. Hexadecimal (Hex) is the common system that web pages use to reference color (Fireworks uses Hex by default). CMYK is a common model for printing and desktop publishing. All these models can reference the same color(s), they just use different methods. Knowing that you have access to all of these options (and more in Fireworks) gives you an advantage for sharing images from other resources. In Guided Tour 4A, you will work with the Fireworks MX tools for controlling color.

Guided Tour 4A: The Fireworks MX Color Controls

In Chapter 2 you used some of the Fireworks MX panels to select color as you were using the drawing tools. In particular, you adjusted the Stroke and Fill color options in the Tools panel (Colors toolbox) and in the Properties panel. These two panels are also frequently used to select and set other color properties of an object. Fireworks MX provides much more control over color properties than you have applied so far. This guided tour introduces you to some of these other color properties.

Selecting Color with the Eyedropper Tool

At times you may want to perfectly match a color already on screen. Fireworks MX provides a means of "sampling" a color from one area of the sreen and reusing that same color elsewhere. The Eyedropper tool is the means to "sample" color. Let's try it. To select color using the Eyedropper tool, perform the following steps.

1. Select File | New, and set the canvas size to 500 x 500. Leave the Resolution at 72 and the Canvas Color on white.
2. You used the Eyedropper tool (shown in figure 4-2) in Chapter 2, while exploring the Bitmap toolbox. As you may recall, the Eyedropper works by sampling a color from a vector or a bitmap. In addition to selecting a color from an image using the Eyedropper, the Eyedropper tool also appears as an icon whenever you are selecting colors from the Swatches panel, Mixer panel, or any of the color palette pop-ups in the Colors toolbox and Properties panel. The Eyedropper is your visual cue that you can sample and select a color.

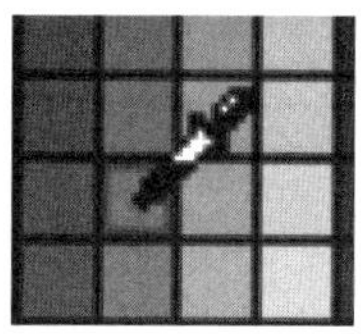

Fig. 4-2. The Eyedropper tool over a color palette.

3. Select the Rectangle tool and draw three rectangles on the canvas. Use a different fill color for each. Make sure to deselect all rectangles by pressing Ctrl/Cmd + D.
4. Let's now use the Eyedropper tool to select a color we might want to use.
   a) Select the Fill Color tool in the Colors toolbox.
   b) Select the Eyedropper tool from the Bitmap toolbox, and click it within each of the rectangles you just drew, one at a time. Note that as you click the Eyedropper tool on a new color in each rectangle, that new color appears in the Fill Color tool inside the Colors toolbox. See figure 4-3.

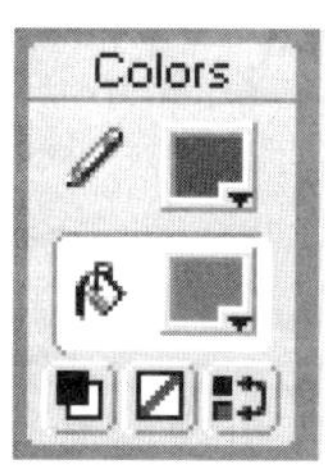

Fig. 4-3. Fill Color selected in the Colors toolbox, with new color picked using Eyedropper tool.

   c) Select the Stroke Color tool in the Colors toolbox.
   d) Select the Eyedropper tool and click it within each of the rectangles. Note that as you click on a color in each rectangle, that new color

appears in the Stroke Color tool inside the Colors toolbox. See figure 4-4.

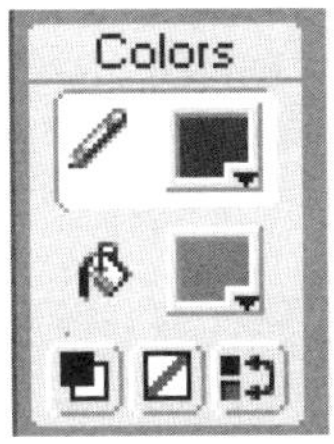

Fig. 4-4. Stroke Color selected in the Colors toolbox, with new color picked using Eyedropper tool.

CAUTION

This direct sampling and filling of an object will only work on vector graphics. Bitmap colors can be sampled the same way, but the Marquee or Lasso tool needs to be used to indicate a selection where you want to "pour" the new color.

5. Now let's use the color palette from the Fill Color tool.
   a) Click on the color well in the Fill Color tool, inside the Colors toolbox. A pop-up color palette has now opened. As you have seen before, the cursor now looks like (is) the Eyedropper tool. Click the Eyedropper tool within one of the rectangles you have drawn. As you can see, the Fill Color has now changed to that color.
   b) Click on the Paint Bucket tool and click the cursor on another rectangle. You have now taken a color from one area and "poured" it into another area.
6. To apply no color to a fill or stroke, select a rectangle and click on the No Fill button. This button is available on the pop-up color palette associated with the Stroke Color or Fill Color tool in the Colors toolbox, in the Properties panel, or in the Mixer panel. The result is an empty color well with a red line drawn through it. See figure 4-5.

·TIP·

The No Color indication appears in various places within the Fireworks MX interface. It always looks the same (an icon of an empty color well with a diagonal line through it).

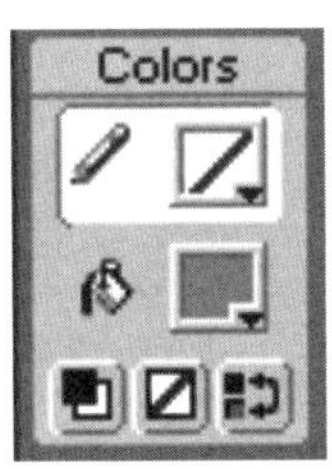

Fig. 4-5. No stroke color, as indicated in the Stroke Color tool in the Colors toolbox.

Adjusting Color with the Mixer Panel

Now let's take a look at another method of selecting colors. This method involves use of the Mixer panel. The Mixer panel allows you to choose stroke or fill colors using any one of five different color models. The unique thing about the Mixer is that you can choose any color in the spectrum instead of being limited to the colors displayed on the pop-up color palette.

1. Select Window | Color Mixer to open a new color panel. Note that the Mixer panel opens grouped together with the Swatches panel. See figure 4-6.

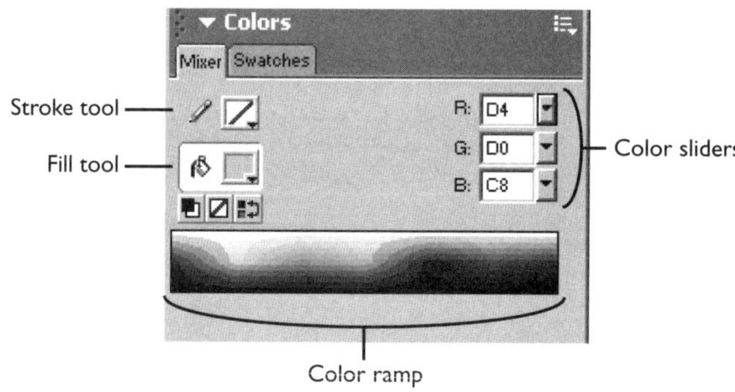

Fig. 4-6. Color Mixer panel.

2. Let's draw a new shape.
   a) Select the Ellipse tool, and on the canvas draw an ellipse of any size and color.
   b) Select the Fill Color tool.
   c) Using the Pointer tool, select the shape you just drew. This way, any changes made in the Mixer panel will be applied directly to the shape.
3. Examine the Mixer panel. The following are three methods available via this panel for adjusting color.

   - *The color ramp:* This is the horizontal spectrum of color at the bottom of the panel. Note that when you move the cursor over this color spectrum, the Eyedropper tool appears. You can simply click on any color in the spectrum to select it. Try it out, by clicking on a color. Note that as you clicked on a color, that color now appears in the color well of the Fill Color tool, as well as within the fill of the object you drew. Try clicking on a few other colors.
   - *The Fill Color and Stroke Color:* These are located on the left side of the panel, and duplicate the function of these same tools found in the Colors toolbox, in the Tools panel. The Web-Safe color palette is used by default. These same tools are found in the Properties panel when a vector graphic is selected.
   - *Color sliders:* The color slider controls are on the right side of the panel, next to each of three color fields. These controls change as

you change the color models (you will do this in step 5). By default, these fields reference RGB values. However, the other mode options available are CMY, HSB, Grayscale, and Hexadecimal.

4. Click on the Fill Color tool in the Mixer panel and experiment in selecting different fill colors using all three methods for adjusting color—the color ramp, the color wells, and the color sliders.
5. What if you need to change the color model? (By default, the hexadecimal model is being used.)
   a) The Mixer panel should still be open. If it is not open, select Window | Color Mixer.
   b) You should see a series of alphanumeric characters next to the R, G, and B sliders that represent the current color.
   c) To change the color model, click on the Options menu icon (looks like a series of small bullets and lines), located in the upper right-hand corner of the Mixer panel. The Options menu now opens. See figure 4-7.

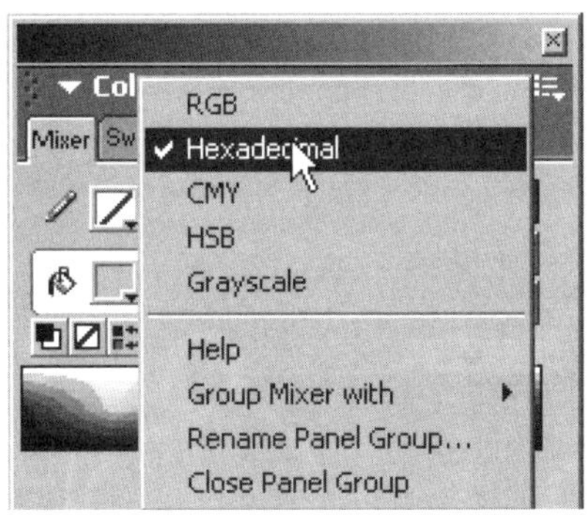

Fig. 4-7. Options menu opened within the Mixer panel.

·TiP·

CMY is the equivalent of CMYK for printing. K stands for the black ink that is necessary for some dark colors to print appropriately. This color is unnecessary for web-related design, and therefore the basic color mix is referenced as CMY in Fireworks.

   d) Select RGB from the menu. You should see that the alphanumeric hexadecimal numbers have now changed to regular numbers, ranging from 0 to 255. These numbers can be used to represent standard RGB values.
   e) Take a moment to explore the other color models, outlined in the following.

      - *RGB:* Refers to red, green, and blue. Standard naming system used by computer monitors and most graphic applications.
      - *Hexadecimal:* Standard system used for referencing colors on web pages.
      - *CMY:* Refers to cyan, magenta, and yellow. Standard system used in certain types of printing.

·T/P·

The HSB model can be used for selecting tints of a color by adjusting the saturation and brightness sliders.

·T/P·

The Swatches panel can show any preset or custom palette independently of the Colors toolbox, Properties panel, or Mixer panel. In this way, you can have the default color palette available, as well as the Swatches showing a custom palette.

- *HSB:* Refers to hue, saturation, and brightness. Common to many graphics programs, HSB is a standard system that represents colors as they are seen on a color wheel.
- *Grayscale:* Presents one slider, labeled K for black, which adjusts the grays between black and white.

Using the Swatches Panel for Custom Control

The Swatches panel holds preset and/or custom swatch color palettes. A swatch is simply a selectable representation of a color, whereas a palette is a collection of color swatches. Often a developer will use the Web-Safe (Hexadecimal) palette while designing a web site to keep colors from shifting across platforms. However, there are times you may need to create a custom swatch palette to store a particular color scheme for a graphic or an entire web site, toward consistently using the same colors.

Let's explore the Swatches panel by saving and managing a custom set of colors.

1. The Mixer panel should still be open. If so, simply click on the Swatches tab. If the Mixer panel is not open, you can open the Swatches panel directly by selecting Window | Swatches. Either action displays the Swatches panel, shown in figure 4-8.

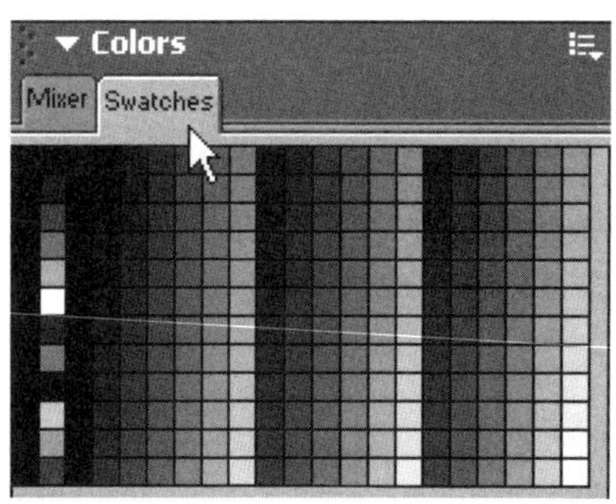

Fig. 4-8. Swatches panel.

2. With the Rectangle tool, draw a rectangle of any size and color on the canvas.
3. Select the rectangle with the Pointer tool. Note the presence of the *Rectangle* sublayer in the Layers panel.
4. In the Properties panel, set the Fill Category option to Cone, to create a cone-shaped gradient of colors. (See figure 4-9.) Note the gradient fill on the canvas.

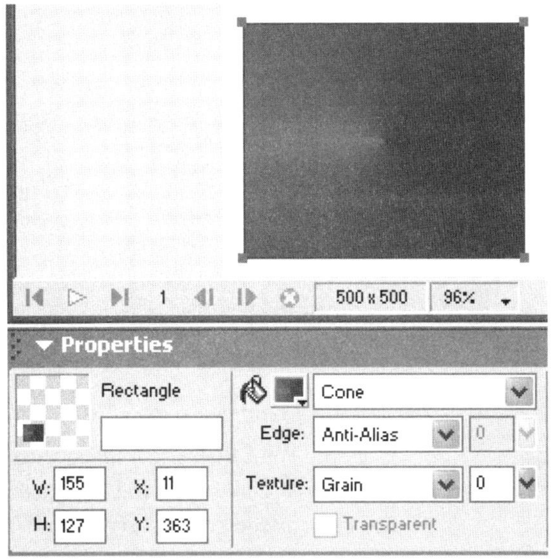

Fig. 4-9. Cone fill in the Properties panel and result on canvas.

5. With the rectangle still selected, select Modify | Flatten Selection to change the vector to a bitmap. Examine the Layers panel. The *Rectangle* sublayer (a vector object) has now been replaced with a *Bitmap* sublayer, indicating that the object is now a bitmap image.
6. Now let's select the different pixel colors from this bitmap image.
   a) Select the Eyedropper tool from the Bitmap toolbox and hold the mouse down as you drag the Eyedropper over the gradient to sample the color directly below the tool. Release the mouse button when you have found the color you want. Note that as you move the Eyedropper over the gradient, the Fill Colors tool provides a preview of the selected color.
   b) To add this fill color sample to the Swatches panel, move the cursor to the gray area at the bottom of the Swatches panel until the cursor turns into a Paint Bucket. See figure 4-10.

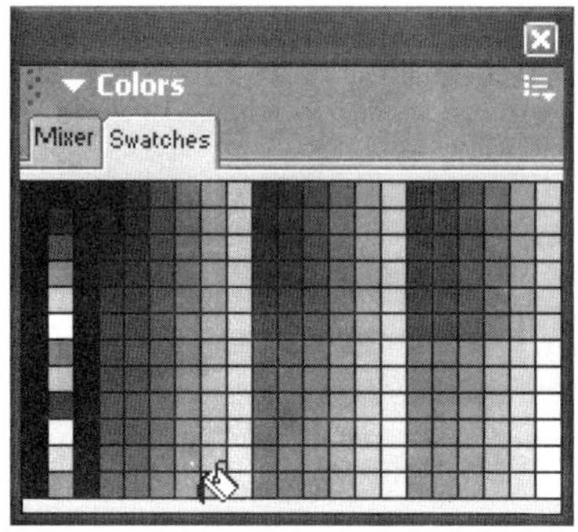

Fig. 4-10. Swatches panel with Paint Bucket over gray area.

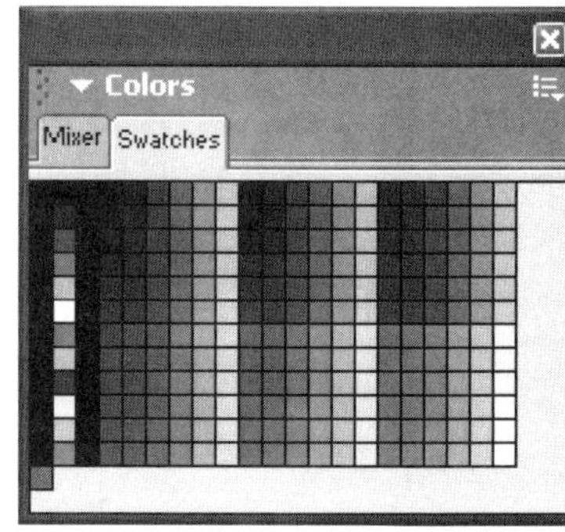

Fig. 4-11. Swatches panel with new swatch added to bottom row.

c) Click the Paint Bucket cursor in the gray area and note that the color palette has reduced in size to make more room, and that a new swatch has been added to the very bottom of the palette. (See figure 4-11.) This swatch can now be applied to different objects on the canvas.

d) Repeat steps 6a through 6c to create a few new color swatches.

7. Now let's change or update one of the new color swatches.
   a) Select a new color with the Eyedropper. Move the cursor (Eyedropper) into the Swatches panel, and over one of the new swatches you created. Press the Shift key. You should note that the Eyedropper has now changed to a Paint Bucket (you may have to move the cursor slightly).
   b) Click the Paint Bucket cursor in the color swatch you want to change.

8. Now let's remove one of the new swatch colors in the custom palette.
   a) Move the cursor over one of the new swatches you created.
   b) Press the Ctrl key (Cmd on Mac). The cursor has now changed to a pair of scissors. Click the scissors icon on the color square you want to delete – and it should now be gone.

9. It is easy to store a custom palette of colors from your document in the Swatches panel. These custom swatches will be saved with your document and will be available each time the document is opened. With Fireworks MX you can also save the custom palette for reuse in other documents. For other options related to custom palettes, open the Swatches Options menu (located in the upper right of the panel) and use any the following options. See figure 4-12.

·TIP·

In addition to adding custom swatches to your palettes, you can change the default preset swatch view from Web-Safe to the Windows System, Macintosh System, or Grayscale setting by using the Swatches Options menu in the upper right-hand portion of the panel.

Shortcut

To reset the Swatches panel to the default web palette, from the Swatch Options menu, select Clear Swatches and then select Color Cubes.

TIP

You can also load a GIF image into the Swatches panel by selecting Add Swatches or Replace Swatches from the Swatch Options menu. These commands display the color index (custom palette) saved in the GIF file in the Swatches panel.

Shortcut

The preset palette for the color wells in the Colors toolbox, the Properties panel, and the Mixer panel always shows the same view and does not reflect changes to the Swatches panel. You can quickly switch to the Swatches panel by clicking on a color well. From the pop-up color window, select the arrow at the top right of this window. Select Swatches Panel from the menu.

- *Save Swatches:* Saves the current palette into an Active Color Table file (extension .act).
- *Clear Swatches:* Clears the existing palettes in the Swatches panel.
- *Add Swatches:* Loads a palette of swatches from a file and appends them to the existing swatches.
- *Replace Swatches:* Loads a palette from a file and replaces the existing swatches.

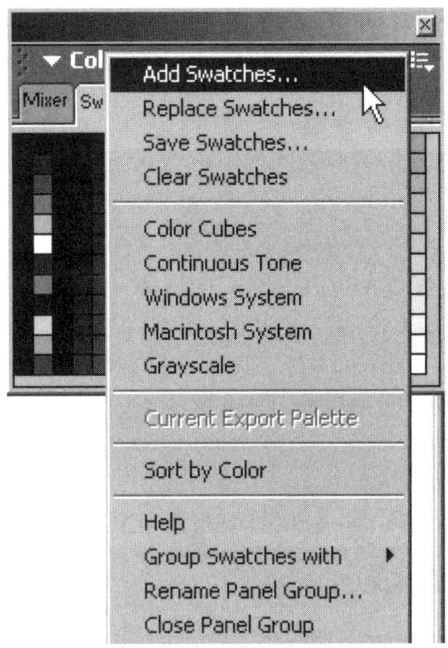

Fig. 4-12. Swatches Options menu.

Now that you have explored the various color panels in more depth, let's move on to color control. Guided Tour 4B introduces you to using the Find and Replace feature for managing global color changes within a document.

Guided Tour 4B: Controlling Color Using Find and Replace

Fireworks MX's Find and Replace feature can be very handy for finding specific colors and replacing them with the color of your choice. There are two options available for this task. The first allows you to search for a specific color and replace it with a specific color. The second option allows you to search for all non web-safe colors and convert them automatically to the closest web-safe equivalent. You will have the opportunity to try both in the steps that follow.

1. Select File | New and create a file with a canvas size of 500 x 500. Set the Resolution at 72 and leave the canvas white.
2. Let's first replace a specific color in the document with a new color. Use the rectangle tool to draw a rectangle on the canvas, setting the following options in the Properties panel.
   - *Stroke color:* medium blue
   - *Stroke width:* 5
   - *Fill:* light green.
3. Now let's make three copies of this rectangle and place all four rectangles so that they do not overlap one another.
   a) To duplicate the rectangle, select the rectangle using the Pointer tool.
   b) Select Edit | Duplicate three times, to make three copies. You will need to use the Pointer tool to move the rectangles so that you can see them on the canvas.
   c) You should have four rectangles. Move them to different parts of the canvas so that they do not touch one another.
   d) Select Select | Deselect to deselect all objects. See figure 4-13.

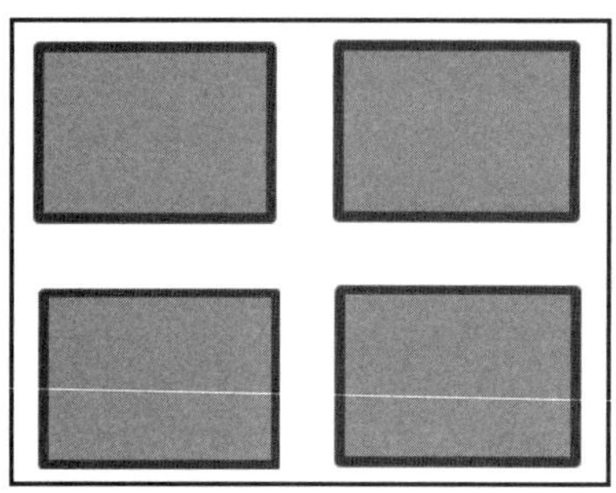

Fig. 4-13. Four rectangles on the canvas.

Shortcut

The keyboard shortcut for Duplicate is:
PC: Ctrl + Alt + D
Mac: Cmd + Opt + D

·TIP·

You can also use Edit | Copy and Edit | Paste to make duplicates of objects on the canvas.

4. Now let's try out the Find and Replace feature to replace a color in the document.
   a) Select Edit | Find and Replace. The Find and Replace window now opens. See figure 4-14.

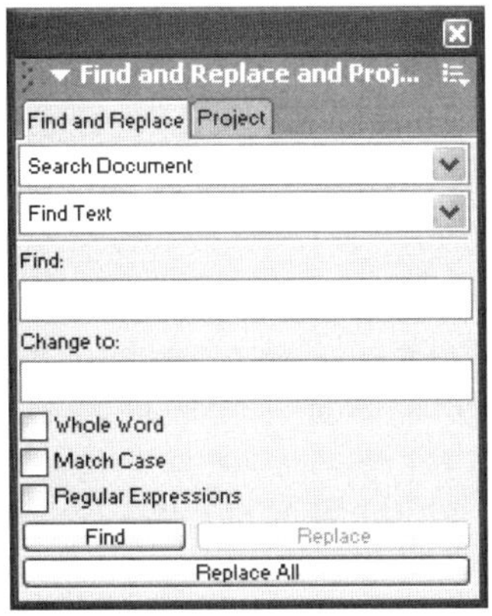

Fig. 4-14. Find and Replace window when first opened.

b) In the Find and Replace window, enter the following values.

- *Search menu:* Search Document.
- *Find menu: Find Color.* Note that the window options now change. See figure 4-15.
- *Find color:* Click on the color well and move the Eyedropper over the green fills within one of the rectangles. Click the mouse button to sample this fill color.
- *Change to color:* Click on the color well and select a different color from the color well.
- *Apply to:* Fills.

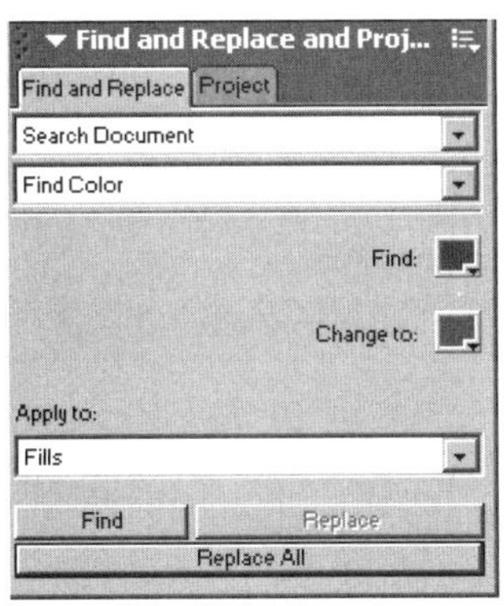

Fig. 4-15. Find and Replace window after Find Color has been selected.

c) Click on the Replace All button at the bottom of the window. Note that all four rectangles on the canvas are selected and update their fill color. A window opens displaying the results of the search. Click on the OK button to close it.

d) Try repeating steps 4 a-c, but this time sample and change the stroke color. Remember to change the *Apply to* setting to Stroke in order for this to work. Close the panel when you are finished.

5. Next, let's try to dynamically convert colors to web-safe equivalents.

a) Select Window | Color Mixer to open the Color Mixer panel. Open the Options menu (located in the upper right-hand corner) and verify that the Hexadecimal color model is selected.

b) Hold down the Shift key and use the Pointer tool to select all four rectangles on the canvas.

c) We need to obtain a color that is not part of the Web-Safe color palette. Next to the color sliders, type in the following values to change the fill colors in each of the rectangles to a non-Web-Safe palette color.

- *R:* 6C
- *G:* F5
- *B:* 45

d) The color you now see as the fill in the rectangles is not a Web-Safe palette color.

e) Select Edit | Find and Replace. In the window that opens, enter the following values.

- *Search menu:* Search Document
- *Find menu:* Find Non-Web216
- *Apply to:* Fills & Strokes

f) Click on Replace All. You may have noted a slight shift in color within all four rectangles as Fireworks automatically substituted the closest web-safe color. A window opens displaying the results of the search. Click on the OK button to close it. Close the Find and Replace window.

·TIP·

Find and Replace can also be accessed through the Window menu. Select Window | Find and Replace to open this panel.

·TIP·

Find and Replace does not work on complex textures in vectors or with pixels in bitmap images. The primary use for Find and Replace is for updating vector strokes and fills, and to effect color change.

You have learned to create a custom color palette by adding swatches to the Swatches panel. To use this palette in more than one document, you must save the palette. In Guided Tour 4C you will learn the process for saving and using these custom palettes in multiple Fireworks MX documents. For developers who are using Fireworks to create graphics for extensive web site designs or print publications, the information in this tour can help you manage color consistency from document to document.

Guided Tour 4C: Saving a Custom Palette from the Color Table

A color table is a listing (index) of colors used in an exported image. This table consists of a maximum of 256 colors, and sometimes as few as four. The indexing process involved in creating a color table allows you to limit the number of colors in an image and to replace colors with those that are closely matched using a different palette, such as the Web-Safe color palette.

A color table is created via the Optimize panel and the Export Preview window as you are exporting images to an 8-bit format. Common 8-bit file formats include GIF, PNG8, TIFF8, and BMP8 (Win)/PICT8 (Mac). In this guided tour, we will take a peek at how color tables are created and see how we can capture a custom group of colors from an image. After this is done, you will learn to save the custom color palette and load it into the Swatches panel for use in other files.

1. Select File | New to create a new file, with a canvas size of 500 x 500. Leave the Resolution at 72 and set the canvas color to white.
2. Select the Rectangle tool from the Vector toolbox and on the canvas draw a rectangle of any size and color. You will change the size and color in material to follow. Verify that the rectangle is selected, and set the following options in the Properties panel.
   - *Width:* 350
   - *Height:* 100
   - *Fill Category:* Starburst
   - *Fill Color:* Red, Green, Blue gradient preset (click on the Fill color well, and in the window that opens select the Preset pull-down menu)
   - *Stroke Color:* No Stroke
3. You should now see on the canvas a colorful rectangle with a starburst-shaped fill. (See figure 4-16.) You will use this spectrum of colors to sample colors for the custom palette.

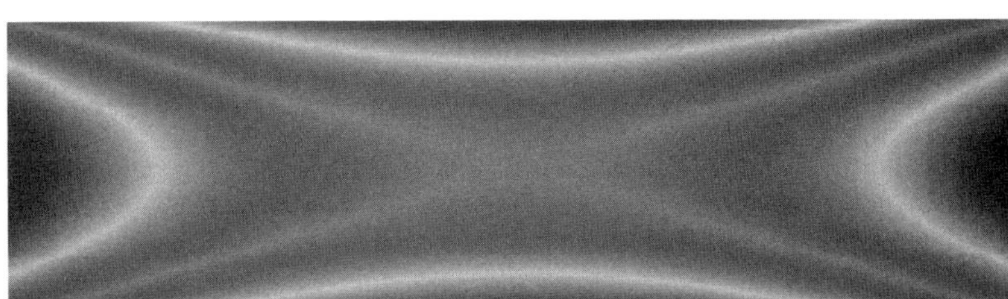

Fig. 4-16. Rectangle on the canvas after settings in the Properties panel are applied.

4. Select Window | Optimize to open the Optimize panel, if it is not already open. (By default it is located on the right, as part of the panels grouped there. See figure 4-17.)

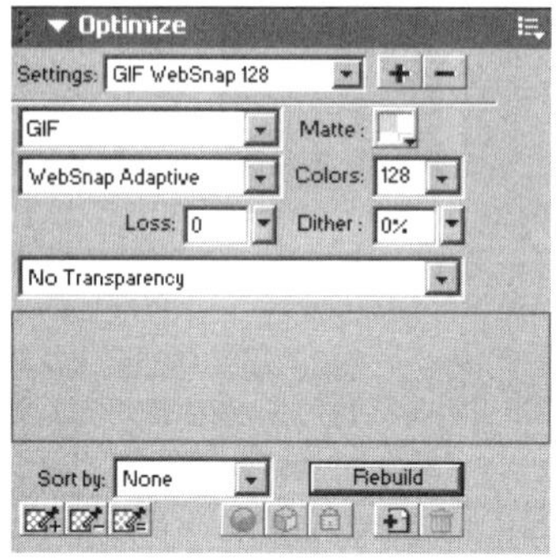

Fig. 4-17. Optimize panel.

5. To better see the color table, you may need to extend the lower portion by dragging the bottom right-hand corner down and away from the panel.
6. In the Export File Format field at the top of the panel (see figure 4-17), select GIF if it is not already selected.
7. Set the Indexed Palette field to WebSnap Adaptive. (The WebSnap Adaptive setting will represent the colors in the image accurately and try to shift them to the closest web-safe color possible.)
8. Use the Colors drop-down menu to change the number of allowable colors to 64.
9. Click on the Rebuild button at the lower right-hand corner of the panel. You should see the previously blank color table (gray area in center of panel) fill with swatches of colors found in the image on the canvas. Any web-safe colors in the palette have a diamond icon on top of them. See figure 4-18.

·TIP·

You can click on the Preview tab at the top left of the Document window at any time to preview the effect of the optimization settings on the quality of the graphic.

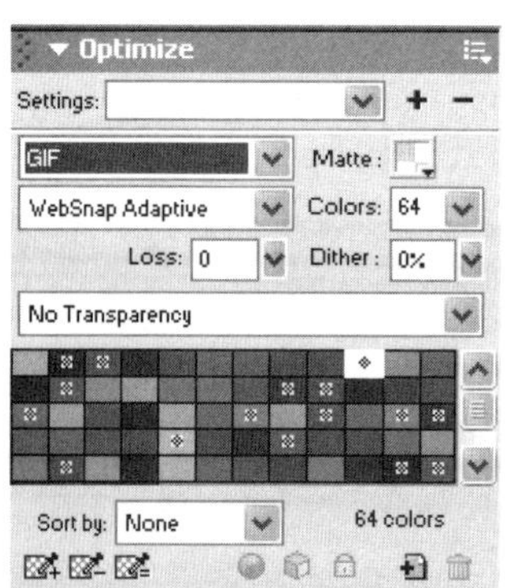

Fig. 4-18. Web-safe colors indicated by a diamond icon.

10. To export the new custom palette, open the Options menu, located in the top right-hand corner of the panel. Select the Save Palette option from this menu. See figure 4-19.

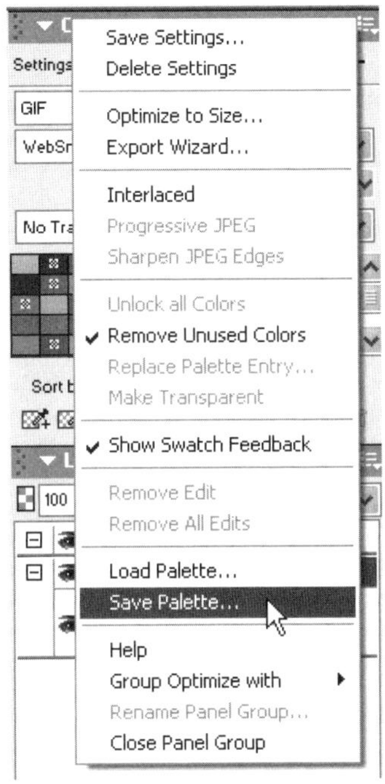

Fig. 4-19. Save Palette option within the Optimize options menu.

11. Note that a Save window opens to provide you with the opportunity to specify a folder and file name. Click on the Cancel button to cancel the save. This was just an experimental palette, so there is not need to save it.

12. If we had continued with the Save As, we could have saved the palette as an ACT file that can be loaded into the Swatches panel and used in other files or for batch processing. This feature may be particularly handy if you need to optimize a large number of files using the same limited color palette.

CHAPTER 5

Optimizing and Exporting Graphics

Chapter Topics:

- *Introduction*
- *Guided Tour 5A: Using the Fireworks Export Tools*
- *Guided Tour 5B: Using the GIF Export Format*
- *Guided Tour 5C: Using the JPEG Export Format*
- *Guided Tour 5D: Other Export Formats*

Introduction

If you frequently use the Web, the following scene should sound familiar. You energetically sit down to your computer to do some web surfing. You connect to the Internet and type in a web address — and then wait. Seconds seem like minutes as you watch the status bar in your browser and wait for an image to download and appear. Although it is true that some images are worth the wait, a web site design that forces a visitor to wait for buttons and logos to appear is usually a web site that will lose even the most interested viewers.

On the Web, the larger the file size, the longer the wait to download, so it should be obvious that small file sizes are highly desirable. Smaller file sizes are usually achieved by compressing graphic files. Unfortunately, most file formats that apply compression to images also result in a degradation of the image quality. The process of compressing file sizes in balance with required image quality is known as *optimization*.

Fireworks MX contains optimization tools that make choosing the appropriate file compression settings easy. These tools also allow you to preview and adjust the image quality of your optimized graphics once they have been compressed. In this chapter, you will explore a number of Fireworks MX compression formats and options for optimization. As you work through this chapter, you will explore the Fireworks MX optimization and export controls. By the end of the chapter you will be able to:

- *Describe the benefits and issues related to file optimization and compression*
- *Use the Optimize panel to modify and define export file types and optimization settings*
- *Use a number of file format types for export*
- *Use the Export menu to export your images*

In Guided Tour 5A, you will begin exploring the Fireworks export tools.

Guided Tour 5A: Using the Fireworks Export Tools

The following sections take you on a tour of the interface components and functionality involved in using Fireworks MX export tools. The Optimize panel is the starting point.

·TIP·

The Color Table panel that existed in previous versions of Fireworks has been incorporated into the Optimize panel in Fireworks MX. It no longer exists as an independent panel.

·TIP·

When working with the Optimize panel, it is often easier to undock it and use it as a floating panel. However, this is really a matter of personal preference.

CD-ROM

The Optimize Panel

In the Fireworks MX workspace, the Optimize panel is the primary area for adjusting the file settings that will be used once the graphic is exported. This panel allows you to access all optimization formats available and allows you to customize the properties associated with each.

The various optimization settings are explored in depth in the next chapter. For now, let's take a close look at the structure of the Optimize panel, and the options it contains.

1. We are going to continue to work with the completed version of a file you worked with in the practice exercise in Chapter 3. You can use either the file you created and saved on your hard drive or the file provided on the companion CD-ROM. These files should be identical.
   a) If you want to use your file, select File | Open. Locate the *SaveWork* folder on your hard drive and then select the file *Exercise3_1.png*. Click on the Open button.
   b) If you want to use the file on the companion CD-ROM, select File | Open. Locate and double click on the CD-ROM player within your computer. Double click on the *Chapter 5* folder, and then click on (2) the file *Tour_5A.png*. Click on the Open button.
   c) Save the file as *Tour_5A.png* in the *SaveWork* folder on your hard drive.
2. Select Window | Optimize to open the Optimize panel, shown in figure 5-1, if it is not already open. If the panel is docked (attached) to the interface, you may want to undock it by clicking on the panel gripper icon in the upper left-hand corner of the panel and dragging it into the workspace. Note the following features of the Optimize panel, as shown in figure 5-1.
   - *Settings:* You can select from Fireworks' pull-down menu of preset optimization settings or add and remove your own settings using the Plus (+) and Minus (–) buttons located to the right of the Setting field.
   - *Export File Format:* Use the pull-down menu to select the file type for export.
   - *Option area:* This encompasses the fields adjacent to the Export File Type field. The options displayed in this area change according to which file format is chosen.
   - *Color table and controls:* These are located in the lower area of the panel. The color table is available when using one of the 8-bit file formats.

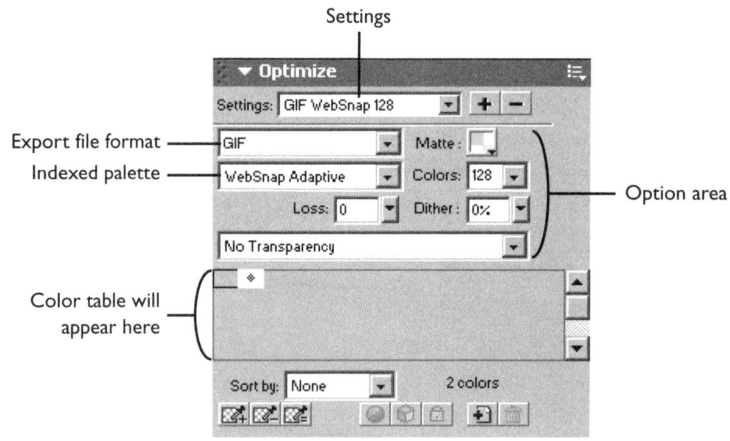

Fig. 5-1. Optimize panel.

Preview Modes in the Document Window

Along with a wide range of export options in the Optimize panel, you also have the ability to preview these settings in the workspace before exporting. Fireworks MX provides the capability to use split-window previews to compare different settings so that you can determine the optimal balance between file type and compression level.

1. Continue working with the *Tour_5A.png* file, which you created in the previous guided tour. Please be advised that we are not going to save the changes to this file, we are just going to use it to demonstrate the optimization features.
2. Preview the export settings for the objects on the canvas.
   a) In the Document window, click on the Preview tab in the top left corner of the window. See figure 5-2.
   b) Clicking on this tab takes you into preview mode. In this state, you can see a preview of the affects of the optimization settings you have selected.

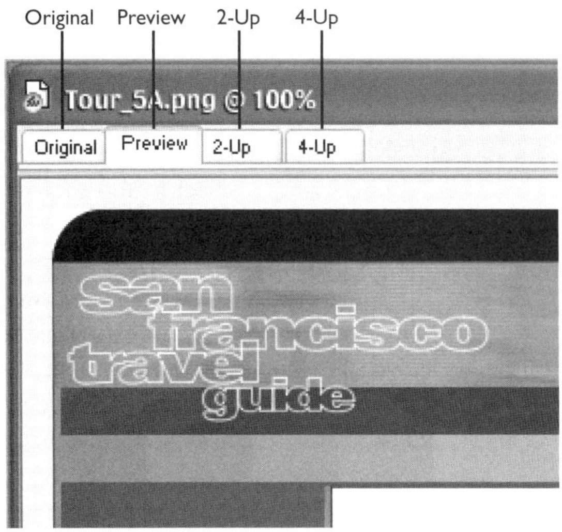

Fig. 5-2. Preview tab located in upper left-hand corner of the Document window.

3. We have not changed any settings yet, but let's take a look at the other preview options. Click on the 2-Up tab to see two comparisons of settings. Click on the 4-Up tab to see four comparison views. See figure 5-3.

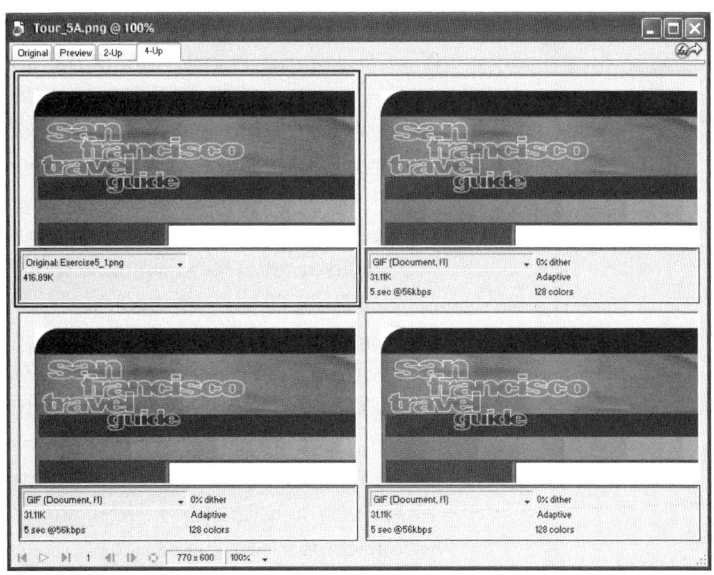

Fig. 5-3. 4-Up comparison preview on canvas.

4. While we are still in the 4-Up mode, from the Optimize panel, let's select different optimization settings for each view.

a) Examine the preview displayed in the upper left-hand corner. In particular, look at the file statistics, located in the left-hand portion of the panel, below the graphic. The file size of the original graphic is about 417K.

b) Select the Pointer tool and then click on the Preview pane in the upper right to select it. You should see a black highlight around the pane when it is selected.

c) Let's make some adjustments to settings in the Optimize panel. In the Settings field, use the pull-down menu to select JPEG – Smaller File. This preview should now look a little bit fuzzy, especially when compared to the preview in the upper left-hand corner.

d) Use the Quality field pop-up slider and select a quality setting of 30. This is a low-quality setting, and the result is that the image is now very fuzzy. Note the statistics for this preview pane. The file size is only about 8K. Although the file size is small, the trade-off of poor quality of image is unacceptable.

e) Let's go to a high-quality setting. Use the Quality field pop-up slider and select a quality setting of 100. This is the highest-quality setting for this export format. Look at the statistics for this preview. The file size is about 138K. This file size is considerably smaller than that of the original, and the improvement in image quality is significant. For the moment, leave these settings as they are.

f) Click on the Pointer tool in the bottom left pane to select it. Let's try a different group of settings. In the Settings field, use the pull-down menu to select JPEG – Better Quality. The Quality setting is probably set at 80. Look at the image quality and file size (about 42K). The image looks about the same as the pane in the upper right, but our current file size is considerably smaller. Try increasing the Quality setting to 90. This image now looks about the same as the original, and has a file size of about 66K.

g) Click on the Pointer tool in the bottom right pane to select it. Note that the default settings are GIF, WebSnap, and 128. This image quality seems to be about the same as that of the JPEG image in the lower left, but the GIF settings produce a file size of about 31K.

h) Note the file size and download time indicator beneath each preview, as shown in figure 5-4. These statistics are an important part of the file comparison. The object of previewing files and comparing file settings is to find the best balance between quality of image and file size, in the context of intended use.

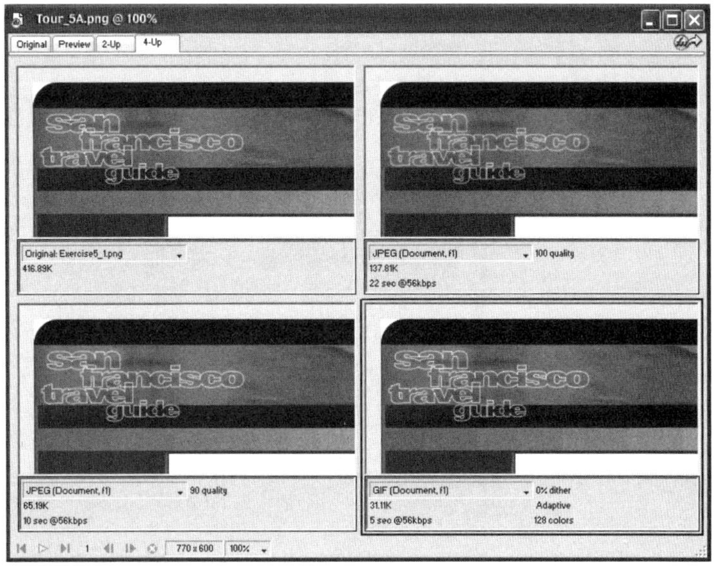

Fig. 5-4. Four different settings with various file sizes and download times.

TIP

You can resize the view dimensions of all previews using the Document window's magnification control, the Magnifying Glass tool, or any of the other shortcuts for document magnification.

5. To leave preview mode and return to editing mode, click on the Original tab.

The Export Preview Window

The Export Preview option under the File menu lets you edit the Optimize options, preview mode, and export size all from one window. Frame control is also available from this panel for optimizing multiframe files such as GIF animations. Let's take a look.

1. To view the Export Preview window, select File | Export Preview.
2. The Export Preview window appears, which looks similar to a combination of the Optimize panel and the preview mode, as shown in figure 5-5.

TIP

You cannot edit images on the canvas if the Preview tab is selected. The Original tab must be selected in order to use the drawing and editing tools. If you attempt to draw on the canvas while in preview mode, the tool cursor becomes locked when placed over the canvas.

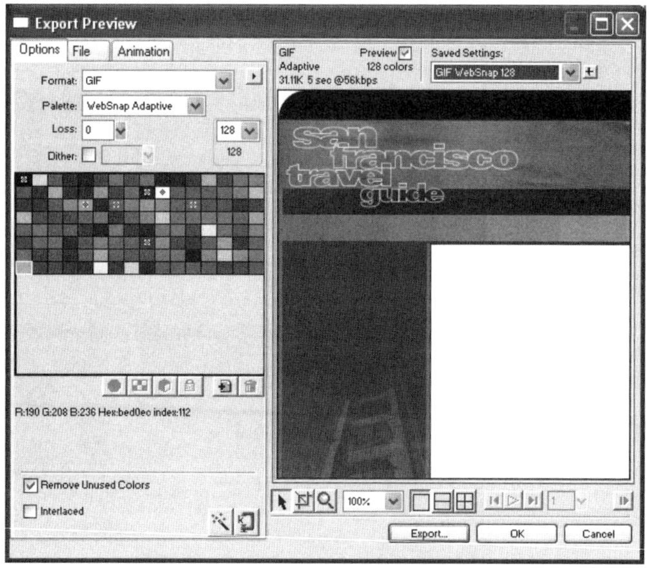

Fig. 5-5. Export Preview window.

3. As you can see in figure 5-5, the window is split into two sides. The left side contains three tabs: Options, File, and Animation. The right side consists of the preview image and a variety of options, which perform the same functions as those options examined previously.

4. Click on each tab on the left-hand side of the window and note the following features.

   - *Options tab:* This tab contains the same options as the Optimize panel.
   - *File tab:* This tab contains settings for scaling the export file. By default, this is set at 100%. Alternatively, you can use the Export setting to type in dimensions for cropping an image to specific coordinates. You can also establish width and height settings.
   - *Animation tab:* This tab contains animation settings for multiframe animations.

5. At the bottom of the preview section on the right side of the window, note the controls, which are as follows.

   - *Pointer tool:* Allows you to reposition the canvas within the preview area.
   - *Crop tool:* Allows you to customize which portion of the preview image will be exported. This is a great tool for cropping out extra space around an image on the canvas.

- *Magnifying Glass tool:* Allows you to zoom in and out of selected areas of the preview.
- *Magnification menu:* Menu for zooming in and out of the preview image.
- *1-Up, 2-Up, 4-Up preview controls:* Allow you to compare previews with different settings.
- *Frame playback controls:* Play, stop, and rewind frame-based animations created in Fireworks MX.

6. Click on the 2-Up preview button. Select the Pointer tool and click within the preview area of one of the panes. Hold the mouse button down as you drag the image within the Export Preview window, so that the upper left-hand corner of the image is displayed. See figure 5-6.

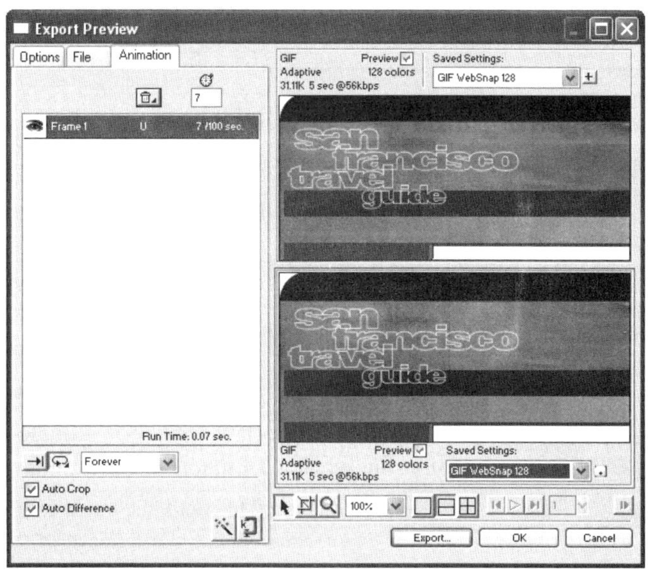

Fig. 5-6. Export Preview window with Animation tab and 2-Up preview.

·TIP·

If you want to export only a portion of the image, use the Crop tool to crop the area to be exported.

7. Note the three buttons at the bottom of the Export Preview window. Clicking on the OK button will save the settings within the Fireworks PNG file. Clicking on the Export button will open the Export dialog box. Clicking on the Cancel button will close the window without saving any of the settings.
8. Click on the OK button to close the window with the current settings.

The Export Dialog Box

If you have already previewed your export settings in the Optimize panel and are ready to export your images, you can go directly to the Export command by simply selecting File | Export. This is a streamlined procedure for when you have already saved export settings with the file and are ready to export the file for use in another application program. Let's take a quick look.

1. Continuing with the same file, select File | Export to launch the export options. Note the following options in the Export window that has now opened. See figure 5-7.

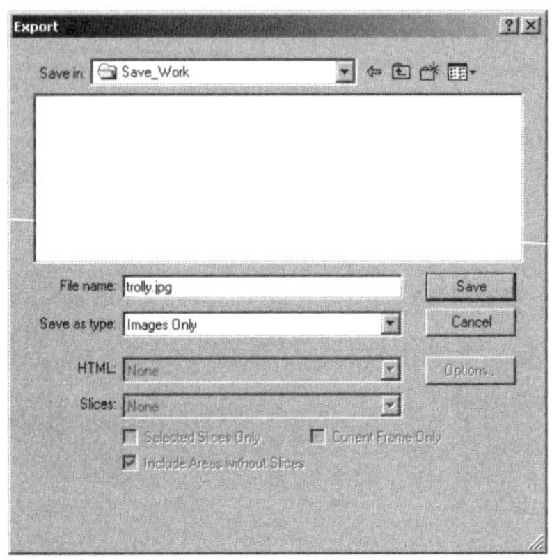

Fig. 5-7. Export window.

- *Save In:* Use this field to select a location on your hard drive where you want to save your file.
- *File Name:* Use this field to name the file you are exporting.
- *Save as Type:* This field allows you to choose a file type. The Images Only setting will save the image in the format you specified in the Optimize or Export Preview options. You can also export your file in other graphics formats (such as Illustrator, Flash SWF, and Photoshop) or as other combinations of text files and graphics (via such options as CCS Layer and HTML and Images). The HTML and Images setting will activate the grayed-out settings below the Save as Type option. All of these options are discussed in the next chapter.

2. In the File Name field, type in the name *TestExport*. Set the Save as Type option to Images Only, and save the file to your *SaveWork* folder.

As you see, in Fireworks, exporting images is as easy as choosing your settings, previewing and comparing, and saving the image file. In Guided Tour 5B you will explore the use of the GIF export format.

TIP

The Export Snapshot tool (grouped with the Crop tool in the Select toolbox) will allow you to create a crop selection that will automatically launch just the selected area into the Export Preview window for optimization.

TIP

The Export wizard is available to walk you through file type and compression settings. You can launch the wizard from the Optimize panel options menu or by using the Magic Wand and Size icons at the bottom middle portion of the Export Preview window.

Shortcut

You can use the Export to Size option from the Optimize panel options menu to choose a file size to match during file compression. Fireworks will examine the image and automatically establish the appropriate format and settings for optimal output file size.

Guided Tour 5B: Using the GIF Export Format

In Guided Tour 5A you had the opportunity to take a general look at the ability to preview export settings within Fireworks MX. Now, let's take a closer look at one of the options you are likely to use in your work as you continue to use Fireworks MX for your design projects.

1. Continue working with the file from Guided Tour 5A.
2. The Optimize panel is probably already open. If it is not, select Window | Optimize panel.
3. Select GIF as the Export File Format setting, if it is not already selected.

GIF and JPG are the most widely used file formats on the Web. GIF images are 8-bit indexed color files that contain a maximum of 256 colors. With GIF compression settings, exported files tend to be very small, which increases download speed. GIF compression is based on limiting the amount of colors within the image. GIF images are commonly used for graphics with flat color or limited numbers of colors. Simple images (such as cartoons, banner ads, and logos) are commonly found in GIF format. See Chapter 4 for a brief table comparing GIF and JPEG characteristics.

In addition to creating files that are small in file size, GIF has the advantage of being able to use transparency to create transparent backgrounds. GIF files can also contain multiple frames and are often used to create small animations.

·TIP·

GIF is the only standard web format to support transparency. PNG also supports transparency, but it is not a widely used and supported format on the Web.

4. Note the following options in the Optimize panel for the GIF format. See figure 5-8.
   - *Matte:* Matte applies a canvas color to the image even if the canvas color of the Fireworks document is a different color. This is very handy when exporting artwork for use on backgrounds of various colors.
   - *Indexed Palette:* WebSnap Adaptive is the default palette. This option selects a range of colors representing true colors, but snaps colors to their closest web-safe equivalents if they are near the respective true color value.
   - *Number of Colors:* Limits the number of colors in the color table.
   - *Loss:* Creates smaller file size by removing pixel information.
   - *Dither:* Dither will create a greater range of perceived colors from the palette by putting colors side by side to produce the illusion of new colors. This is useful for smoothing areas of color transitions, such as the banding in a gradient. Dithering does increase the file size of the image.

·TIP·

The Custom setting under Indexed Palette allows you to import a custom-saved palette either as an Active Color Table (ACT) file or as a GIF file.

·TIP·

When working with the GIF format, select the Interlace option in the Optimize panel options or the Export Preview options to create a GIF file that will be viewable as it downloads. The GIF file will appear to gradually fade in while downloading.

·TIP·

You can also select the colors in the color table associated with the indexed image, but often it is easier to simply select the colors on the canvas via the Add Color to Transparency button.

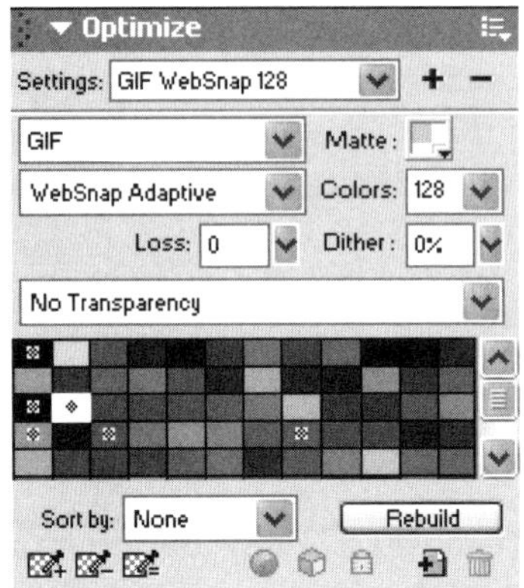

Fig. 5-8. GIF options within the Optimize panel.

Creating Transparent GIFs

GIF images also allow one or more colors to be marked as transparent, and thus invisible on the web page. This is a great option for creating transparent backgrounds and the illusion of image files that are not rectangular.

1. Continue working with the file you already have open.
2. To create a transparent background, select the Preview tab in the Document window.
3. In the Optimize panel, click on the Add Color to Transparency button in the lower left of the panel (see figure 5-9). Note that the cursor has now turned into the Eyedropper tool.

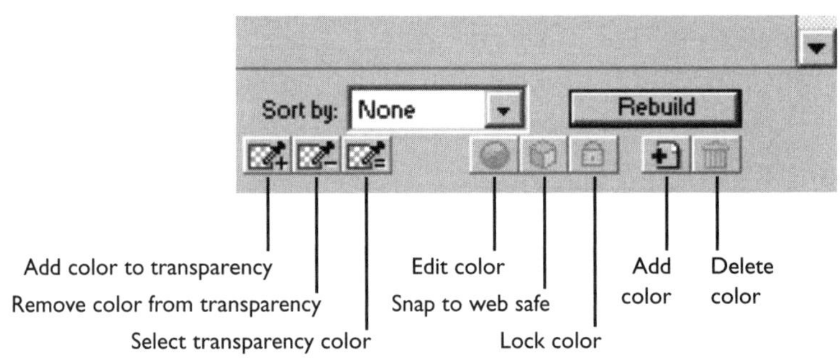

Fig. 5-9. Transparency buttons at the bottom of the Optimize panel.

4. Click the Eyedropper tool on the white background where the web page content would normally be. Note that Fireworks has now turned the white into a checkerboard pattern. This pattern indicates that the white areas in the image are now transparent. See figure 5-10.

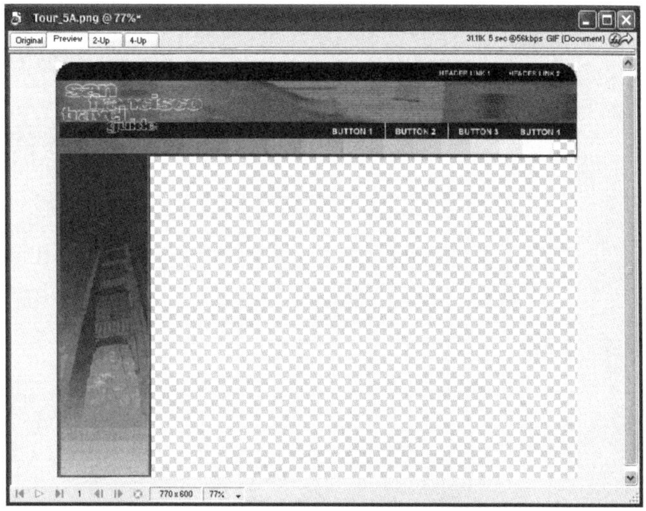

Fig. 5-10. White areas on canvas are now transparent.

5. To restore the white background color, click on the Remove Color from Transparency button on the lower left of the Optimize panel and then click on the transparent background. The white background color returns. See figure 5-11.

·TIP·

The Type of Transparency field (just above the color table) updates as you make colors transparent or remove transparent colors. For GIFs, use either No Transparency or Index Transparency. These settings turn a pixel color on or off. The Alpha Transparency setting allows you to create degrees of transparency. This is also a feature of PNG files that appears in the GIF setting.

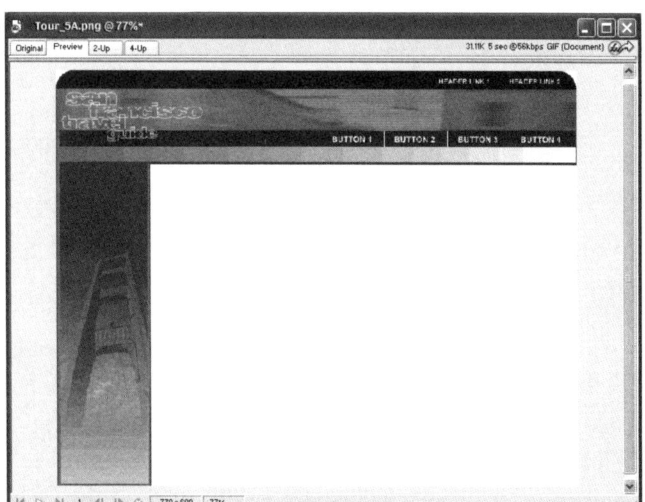

Fig. 5-11. Transparent areas returned to original white color.

The Animated GIF Settings

The Animated GIF settings are available in the Export Preview area under the Animation tab or in the Frame panel settings. You will take a closer look at these options and will create animated GIF files in Chapter 8.

Now that we have covered all of the GIF settings in the Optimize panel, in Guided Tour 5C we will turn our attention to JPEG settings.

Guided Tour 5C: Using the JPEG Export Format

To begin using the JPEG export format, perform the following.

1. Continue working with the file from the previous guided tour.
2. In the Optimize panel, select JPEG as the Export File Format, as shown in figure 5-12.

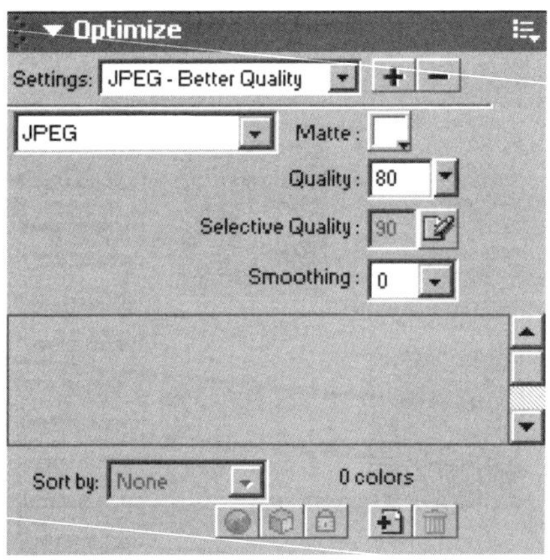

Fig. 5-12. JPEG export settings in the Optimize panel.

The JPEG format is used to export photographic images that contain detailed color information, often containing millions of colors. These exported images often contain 24-bit or 36-bit color. The JPEG format compresses color information by removing pixels, which is why this is called a lossy compression format. GIF files are also lossy compression formats because information is discarded from the image during compression. You adjust the quality settings so that the loss of pixel information is not noticeable when viewed on screen.

3. Note of the following options in the Optimize panel with the JPEG setting activated. See figure 5-10.
   - *Matte:* This option controls the canvas color, as is the case in the GIF settings.

TIP

Usually a quality setting of 60 to 80 works well for most photographic images. Use the Preview mode to view the affects of various quality settings on images.

TIP

The Smoothing option works great for curve-shaped images, but tends to dramatically blur images with sharp text or lines.

TIP

Make sure the Sharpen JPEG Edges option is checked in the Optimize panel options or Export Preview options to keep your edges looking clear when using lower-quality settings.

- *Quality:* This setting controls the amount of compression (or degradation of pixels) that occurs. The lower the setting, the smaller the file size and the lower the image quality.
- *Smoothing:* This setting blends pixels to cover up degradation due to lower-quality settings. Smoothing tends to create a slightly smaller file size, but also results in blurring of the image.

Setting the Progressive JPEG Option

Progressive JPEGs are simply JPEG files with a slightly extended capability, which is that you can see them in the process of being downloaded. In principle, the Progressive JPEG option works just like an interlaced GIF. The standard JPEG format requires that the JPEG image download entirely before you can see any part of it. In contrast, progressive JPEGs allow the viewer to preview the image as it begins to download. The appearance is slightly different from the interlaced effect in the GIF format, but has the same functionality. Download performance is similar between standard and progressive JPEG, and therefore the choice of progressive or standard is generally a matter of preference.

1. To activate the Progressive JPEG function, click on the JPEG Export File Type field.
2. Open the Optimize options menu (located in the upper right-hand corner of the panel) and select Progressive JPEG, shown in figure 5-13.

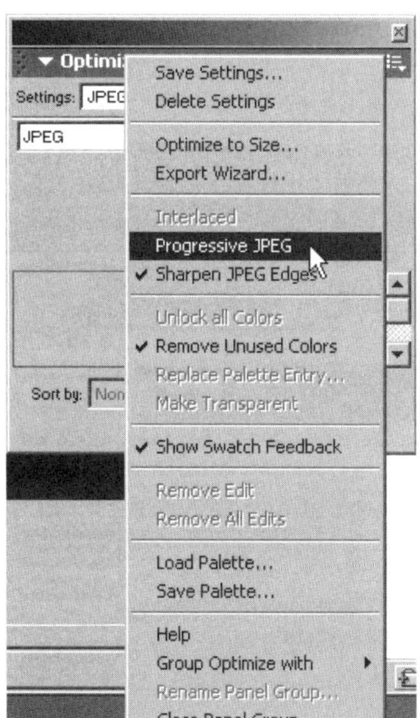

Fig. 5-13. Progressive JPEG option in the Optimize options menu.

·TIP·

Progressive JPEG files will not open in some older graphics applications. Be sure you are aware of this when sharing files with other users.

Using the Selective JPEG Option

The Selective JPEG option allows you to compress different areas of the JPEG at different quality settings. This is accomplished by defining each compression area of a bitmap with a selection and then saving the selection as a selective JPEG mask. Let's try it.

1. Continue working with the previous file. Select the Original tab if you still have the Preview tab selected.
2. Draw a marquee selection around an area of the image you wish to compress differently.
   a) Select the Rectangular Marquee tool in the Bitmap toolbox.
   b) Use the Marquee tool to select the dark blue area with the bridge, located on the left of the canvas.
3. Select Modify | Selective JPEG | Save Selection as JPEG Mask. This adds a slightly tinted box that represents the regions of the JPEG mask. Click on the Marquee tool on the white canvas to deselect the area. The tinted area should now be apparent.
4. To modify the mask settings, select Modify | Selective JPEG | Settings to open the Selective JPEG Settings window, shown in figure 5-14. You can also access this window by clicking on the Edit Selective Quality Option button, located on the Optimize panel under the JPEG options.

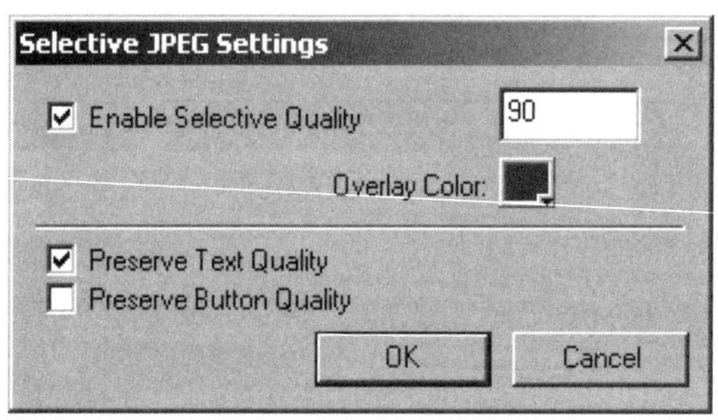

Fig. 5-14. Selective JPEG Settings window.

5. In the window that appears, you can now select the amount of compression to apply to the masked area. This is usually a different setting from what was used in the basic JPEG setting specified in the Optimize panel. Note that you can also specify the Selective quality setting, below the standard Quality setting in the Optimize panel. We are not going to make or save any setting, so simply click on the Cancel button.
6. To remove a selective JPEG mask, select Modify | Selective JPEG | Remove JPEG Mask. Go ahead and make this selection. As you can see, the mask

has now been removed. You can also select Modify | Selective JPEG | Restore JPEG Mask as Selection to release the mask and revert to the original marquee selection.

TIP

The Selective JPEG option allows you to compress an image with low-quality settings and use selective masks to add less compression to the areas of the image that have started to degrade.

Now that we have reviewed optimization settings for the most commonly used file types, GIF and JPEG, in Guided Tour 5D we will turn to other file optimization settings available from the Optimize panel.

Guided Tour 5D: Other Export Formats

As mentioned previously, GIF and JPEG are the image file formats most commonly used on the Web, but there are other export options available in Fireworks MX that might be used in other applications. Each of the formats discussed in the sections that follow shares similar properties as reviewed with the GIF and JPEG formats. Let's start with a brief overview.

Continue working with the file from the previous tour. You will select each of the formats discussed in the sections that follow from the Export File Type menu and review the options for each.

The PNG Format

To begin an examination of the PNG format, perform the following.

1. Continue working with the file from the previous guided tour.
2. In the Optimize panel, select PNG 8 as the Export File Format setting.

CAUTION

Even though the PNG format is native to Fireworks MX, the Fireworks PNG format contains many enhancements for handling all properties of the application. Make sure you export to a standard PNG file if you wish to create PNG files that are compatible with other programs.

Note that there are three PNG options (8, 16, and 32). The PNG format is a high-quality compression format that can be used for web pages, but it is still in the early stages as far as acceptance by web browsers. Although the major browsers can display PNG files, many of the finer features (such as transparency and gamma correction) are still not supported. PNG files tend to create images of slightly higher quality than JPEG, but also at a slightly larger file size. For these reasons, JPEG still dominates the Web for compressed photographic images.

Although PNG might not be your first choice for the Web, it has many strong points that make it ideal for exporting graphics to Director, Flash, and FreeHand, and other multimedia and graphics programs. PNG 32 supports 256 degrees of transparency for any color. This will allow you to export high-quality bitmap images with transparent backgrounds for use in other applications.

The TIFF Format

To begin an examination of the TIFF format, perform the following.

1. Continue working with the file from the previous guided tour.
2. In the Optimize panel, select TIFF 8 as the Export File Format setting.

Note that there are three TIFF options (8, 16, and 32). The TIFF format is mainly used for high-quality print images, or images for on-screen slide presentations, such as PowerPoint presentations. Use the Fireworks TIFF settings to produce files for use with print applications. Use the TIFF 8 version to create print-ready files with reduced colors.

·TIP·

You may find yourself working at a higher file resolution if you need to export your graphic in TIFF format for printing. Common high-resolution settings range from 300 to 1,200 pixels per inch (ppi). Set the resolution in the Image Size settings, or when you create a new file.

The WBMP Format

To begin an examination of the WBMP format, perform the following.

1. Continue working with the file from the previous guided tour.
2. In the Optimize panel, select WBMP as the Export File Format setting.

Fireworks MX can import and export the WBMP format. WBMP is used for graphics intended for mobile devices in the Wireless Application Format (WAP). This format converts all graphics to 1-bit depth of color, meaning two colors (black and white).

Other formats

The remaining Fireworks MX formats are BMP (Windows) and PICT (Mac). These are both platform-specific formats and should generally only be considered if designing graphics strictly for applications within the respective platform. Each format contains an 8-bit, 24-bit, and 32-bit setting.

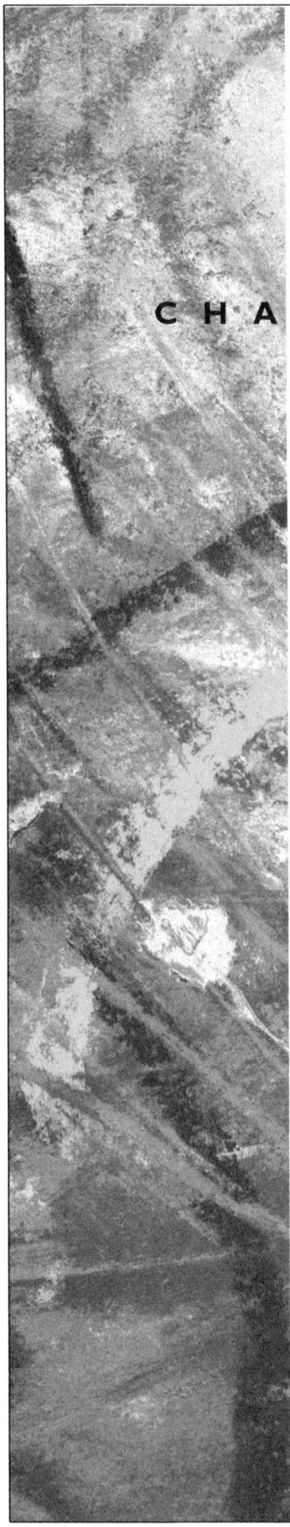

C H A P T E R 6

Slicing Web Graphics and Exporting HTML

Chapter Topics:

- *Introduction*
- *The Slicing Concept*
- *Guided Tour 6A: Using the Slice Tools*
- *Guided Tour 6B: Optimizing Slices*
- *Practice Exercise 6-1: Exporting Slices and HTML*
- *Practice Exercise 6-2: Slicing and Exporting the Home Page Graphic*

Introduction

Slicing may sound like something you do in the kitchen, but within Fireworks MX, slicing is a powerful feature that allows you to create sophisticated web layouts that can be "sliced and served" to users of your web site. With the Fireworks MX slice tools, designers can divide a single image into multiple images by defining slice regions within a document. This is important because in using this process, you can significantly decrease an image's download time, while optimizing the quality of its display characteristics.

Once images have been sliced, you can assign individual optimization settings to each slice. This means that conceivably you could assign GIF and JPEG settings to different slices in the same image. Not only can you choose optimization settings most appropriate for each part of your layout, slicing also allows you to break large graphics up into smaller files that can then be downloaded more quickly.

This chapter reviews the slice tools and offers practice applying slices to the user interface for the travel web site we have been constructing in previous chapters. By the end of the chapter you will be able to:

- *Describe and use the functions of the Slice tools*
- *Select and insert slices using rulers and guides*
- *Edit slices and use draggable slice guides*
- *Export slices and generate a web page for the layout*

The Slicing Concept

Slicing a graphic is a simple process of cutting a single image into a number of smaller images. As you continue with your own design work with Fireworks, you will probably find that you will want to use different file or compression types in different areas of an image. Once you have created slices for a layout, Fireworks MX names and exports the slices, along with a custom formatted HTML page that automatically reassembles the sliced graphics into a table. Think of your slices as puzzle pieces, and the HTML page as the completed puzzle.

If you are not familiar with HTML coding, do not worry. Fireworks does all the coding for you, based on the arrangement of your slices in your Fireworks MX document. All you need to do is "apply" the slices, and Fireworks automatically creates a web page with the sliced images assembled according to your original layout. After using the Slice tools, you can immediately export the collection of images and the web page that holds them—all ready to publish or to import into web page editing software, such as Dreamweaver MX.

Figure 6-1 shows the splash page graphic you worked with in previous chapters. Note how the slices now divide the graphic into sections. Each slice has its own optimization setting. Some slices are set for compression as GIF files, some as JPEG. As mentioned previously, each slice is like a puzzle piece that is assembled on the HTML page as part of the completed puzzle.

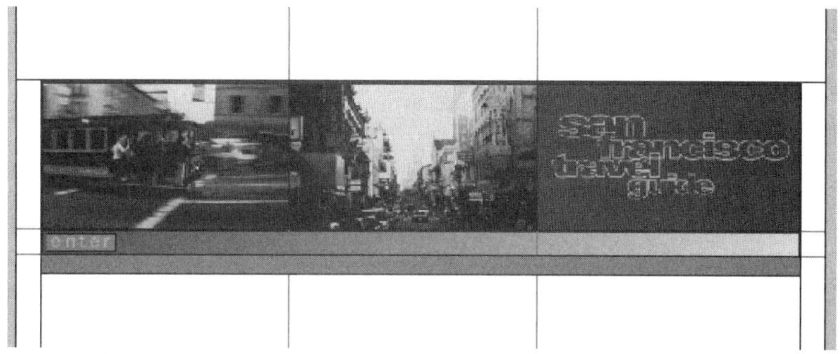

Fig. 6-1. Slices on the splash page graphic.

Figure 6-2 shows the exported slices that have been reconstructed by HTML code on a web page. When the HTML page is viewed in Dreamweaver MX, you can see how a table holds the "puzzle pieces" together.

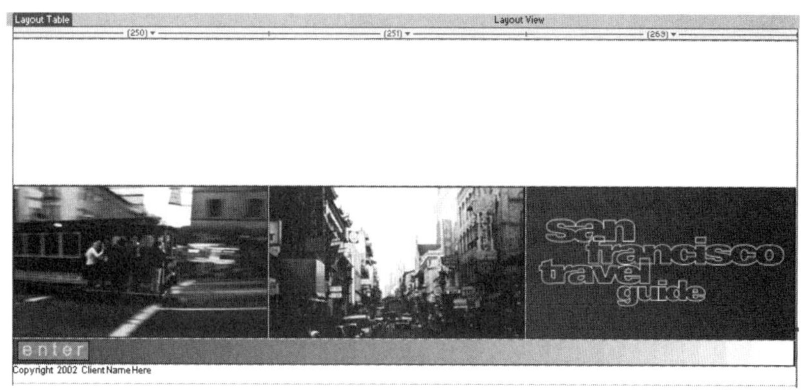

Fig. 6-2. Slices reconstructed on a web page in Dreamweaver MX.

In Guided Tour 6A you will get some practice using the Slice tools to divide the splash page graphic into pieces.

Guided Tour 6A: Using the Slice Tools

To use the Slice tools to divide the splash page graphic into pieces, perform the following steps.

1. Select File | Open. Locate and double click on the CD-ROM player within your computer.
2. Double click on the *Chapter 6* folder on the CD-ROM and click to select the file *Tour_6A.png*. Click on the Open button. This file contains a completed version of the splash page graphic used in previous guided tours.

Slice Tool and Web Layer

The Slice tool is designed to draw rectangular sections across any area of your image, so that you can define how an image will be segmented.

1. Select the Slice tool (see figure 6-3), and click and drag to draw a rectangle on top of the middle graphic (street scene) on the splash page.

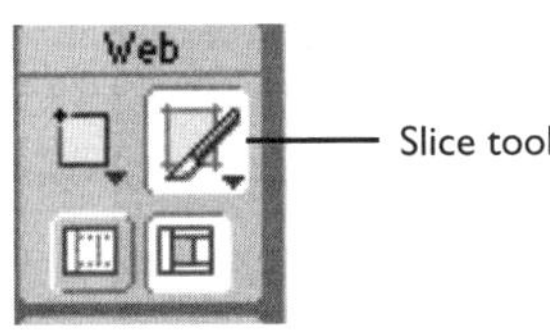

Fig. 6-3. Slice tool.

2. A slice appears as a transparent green block, and several lines now divide the canvas. See figure 6-4.

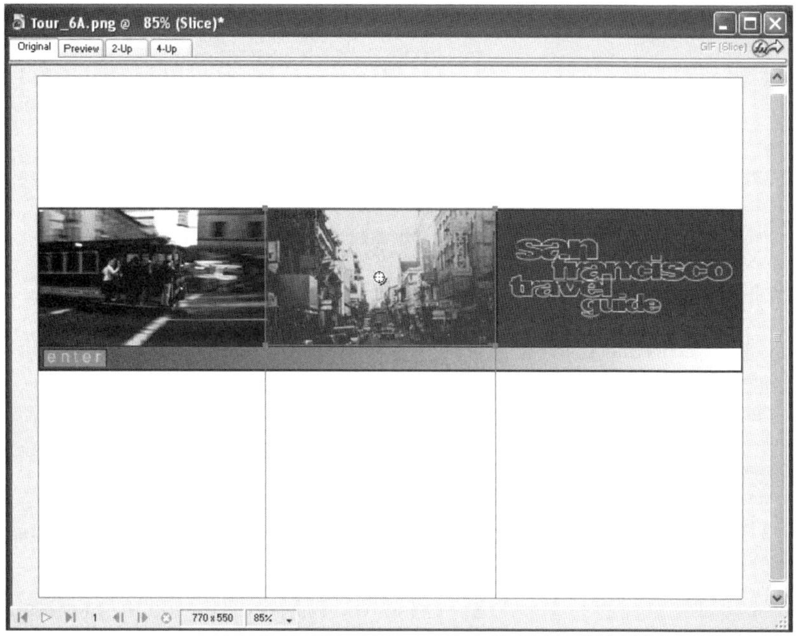

Fig. 6-4. Slice indicated by the green block and red lines.

3. Once you have drawn the slice, note that this green slice also appears in the *Web* layer in the Layers panel. Slices and hotspots are always placed on the *Web* layer and cannot be added to any other layer. See figure 6-5.

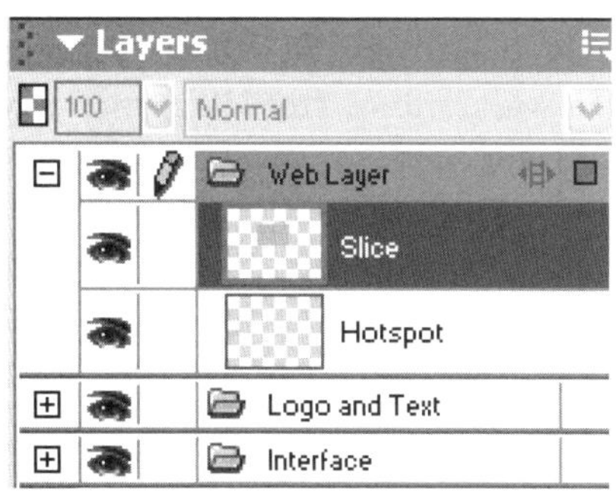

Fig. 6-5.* Web *layer with slice.

4. The *Web* layer is a special type of layer that contains invisible elements, including slices, hotspots, and JavaScript behaviors (used to generate HTML code once the file is exported).
5. Note that the *Web* layer is always the top layer and that it cannot be moved from this location.

Polygon Slice Tool

The Polygon Slice tool allows you to draw geometric shapes with more than four sides.

·TIP·

The Polygon Slice tool allows you to draw polygon slice selections around any portion of your image. Fireworks then builds a series of supporting rectangular slices that will make the area fit within the rectangular cells of an HTML table.

1. To use this tool, click and hold the cursor on the Slice tool until the pop-up menu appears. See figure 6-6.

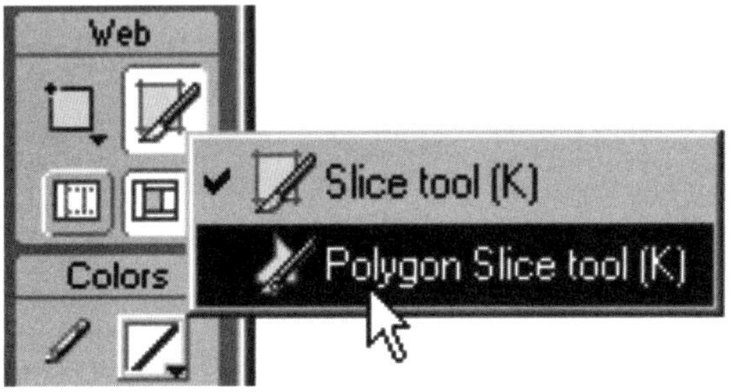

Fig. 6-6. Polygon Slice tool within the pop-up menu from the Slice tool.

2. Select the Polygon Slice tool from the menu.

Using this tool is similar to drawing shapes with the Pen tool. Instead of clicking and dragging to form a shape, you will click to establish the corner points of the polygon shape you are drawing.

3. Let's draw a slice around another part of the splash graphic, now using the Polygon Slice tool.
   a) Use the Polygon Slice tool to click dots directly around the cable car image, located on the left portion of the splash page. As with the Pen tool, drawing a shape with the Polygon Slice tool is like playing "connect-the-dots."
   b) Note the transparent green slice, and that the series of horizontal and vertical slice guides now extends around the image you drew. (See figure 6-7.) Also note that this new slice has been added to the Web layer.

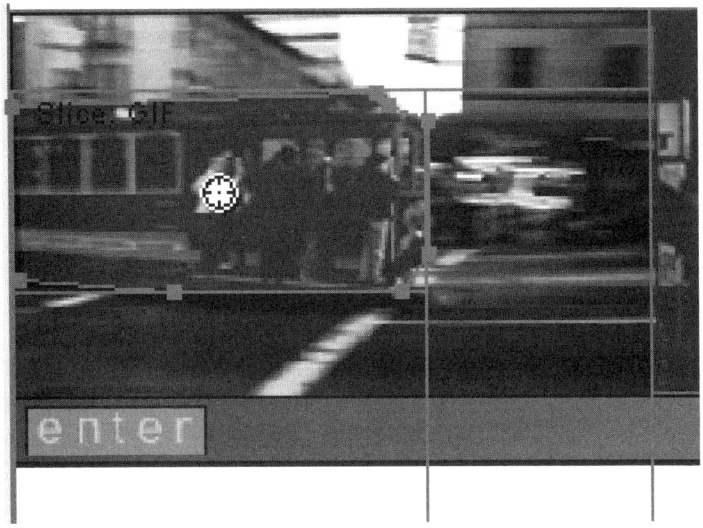

Fig. 6-7. New slice created with the Polygon Slice tool.

c) To move the entire shape, select the Pointer or the Subselection tool and click in the middle of the shape to drag it to a new location. Try moving it. Then select Edit | Undo Edit Slice.

d) To edit the location of the corner points, select the Pointer or Subselection tool and then click and drag the anchor points to move them to a new location. Try moving an anchor point. Then select Edit | Undo Edit Slice.

TIP

To change a slice color, make sure the slice is selected and look in the Properties panel. Next to the Type field, note the color swatch that displays the currently selected color of the slice. Select the swatch, and then select a new color from the pop-up color palette that appears.

Show/Hide Slices

Once you have drawn a slice, you may need to edit the artwork beneath the slice at some point. Usually the easiest way to do this is to hide the slice or the *Web* layer from view, and then show it again when you need to edit the slices on the *Web* layer. This can be accomplished with the Show/Hide Slices and Hotspots buttons or with the Show/Hide icon in the Layers panel. Let's try it.

1. Click on the Hide Slices and Hotspots button in the Web toolbox. (See figure 6-8.) Note that both slices have disappeared from the canvas view.

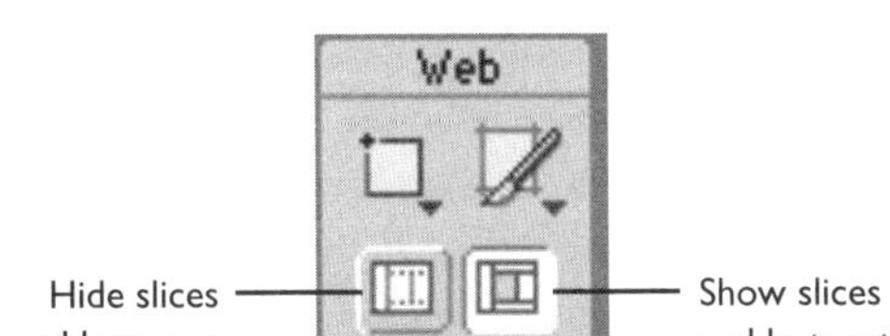

Fig. 6-8. Show/Hide Slices and Hotspots buttons.

2 Click on the Show Slices and Hot Spots button to once again reveal the slices on the canvas.

3. The same effect can be achieved with the Show/Hide icon in the Layers panel.
   a) In the Layers panel, click on the Eye icon (Show/Hide icon) next to the sublayer containing the *cable car* slice. The slice for the cable car is now hidden.
   b) Click on the Eye icon next to the *cable car* sublayer a second time to reveal this slice again.
   c) Let's hide all sublayers at once by clicking on the Eye icon (Show/Hide icon) next to the *Web* layer.
   d) Click on the Eye icon next to the *Web* layer a second time to reveal all slices again.

·TIP·

You can also rename the sublayers containing the slices in the *Web* layer, just as you did previously with other layer and sublayer names. Simply double click on the slice name and type in a new, more descriptive, label to rename the sublayer.

Adding, Selecting, and Removing Slices

1. To add more slices to your splash page image, you could choose the Slice tool from the Web toolbox and draw another slice over a different part of the image. Instead, let's try a new technique for inserting slices.
   a) On the right (in the text logo), using the Pointer tool, select the text *san francisco travel guide.* Remember, you can tell when an image is selected by looking for the blue highlight and anchor points that appear.
   b) With the text logo selected, right-click (Mac: Ctrl + click) on the selected text logo and then select the Insert Slice option from the pop-up menu that appears. (See figure 6-9.) A slice is now automatically inserted on top of the text logo image.

·TIP·

You can also add a slice over an object by selecting the object and then selecting Edit | Insert | Slice. This will add a slice covering the area of the object.

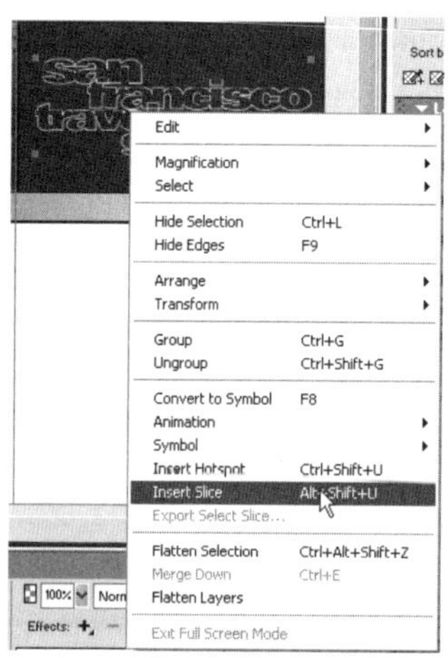

Fig. 6-9. Insert Slice option from the pop-up menu.

2. To select a slice, simply click on it with Pointer tool.
3. To select multiple slices, press and hold the Shift key as you click on each slice. Select all three slices you have inserted into your image.
4. Use the menu option Select | Deselect to deselect all slices.
5. Let's delete the slices you just created.
   a) Select the Pointer tool and then click on the *cable car* slice. Press the Delete key. The *cable car* slice is deleted.
   b) You may also delete a slice by selecting the slice and clicking on the Trash Can (Delete Layer) icon at the bottom of the Layers panel.
   c) Using either method, delete all three slices. All slice sublayers should now be gone. See figure 6-10.

TIP

Remember that it is possible to lock the *Web* layer in the Layers panel. If you accidentally lock the *Web* layer, you will be unable to select any of the slices on this layer. To unlock, click on the Lock icon in the *Web* layer.

Shortcut

You can also select a single slice or multiple slices by clicking on the slice(s) in the *Web* layer. Hold down the Shift key as you click to select multiple slices.

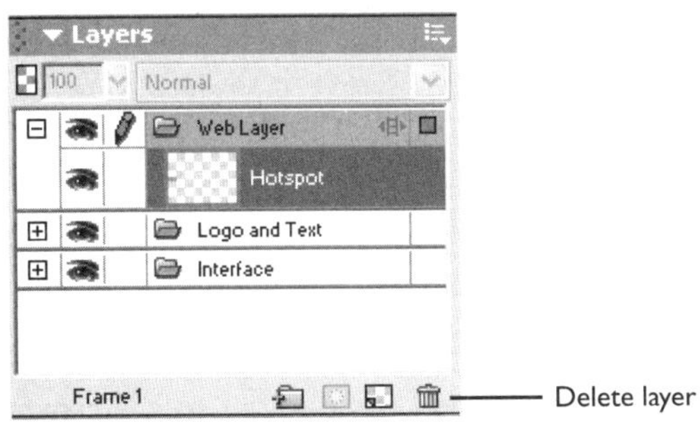

Fig. 6-10. Trash Can (Delete Layer) icon in the Layers panel. Note that all slice sublayers have been deleted.

Using Rulers and Guides for Slice Control

Using rulers and guides to lay out slice areas allows you to control the placement of slices. You can use the ruler's pixel increments for exact placement, and use guides to "snap" slice borders into place. Let's try them both.

1. Select View | Rulers to activate the rulers in the open document, as in figure 6-11. Rulers are by default set to zero at the top left corner and display measurements for the X (horizontal) and Y (vertical) axes of the canvas. See figure 6-11.

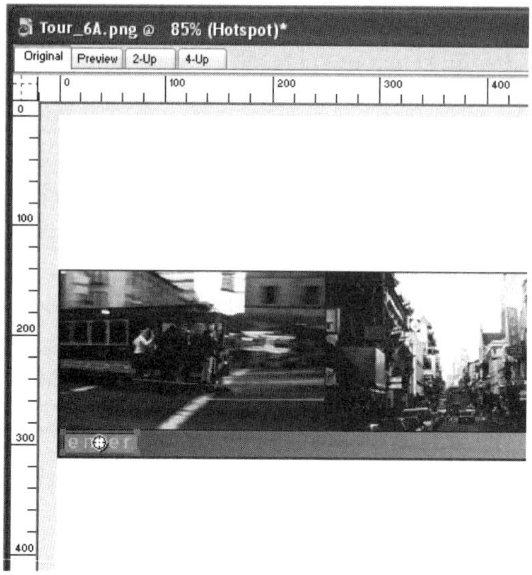

Fig. 6-11. Rulers along the X and Y axes.

2. As you move your cursor on the canvas, note that a black line appears on the X and Y axes of the rulers to indicate the position of your cursor.
3. Now let's add some guides to the canvas. You can use these temporary guideposts to help you align objects on the canvas. As you will see, you can "pull" a guide from the horizontal ruler running across the top of the document.
   a) Place your cursor over the horizontal ruler and click and drag toward the center of the canvas. As you drag, the guideline will appear and can be dragged to any location on the canvas, as shown in figure 6-12.

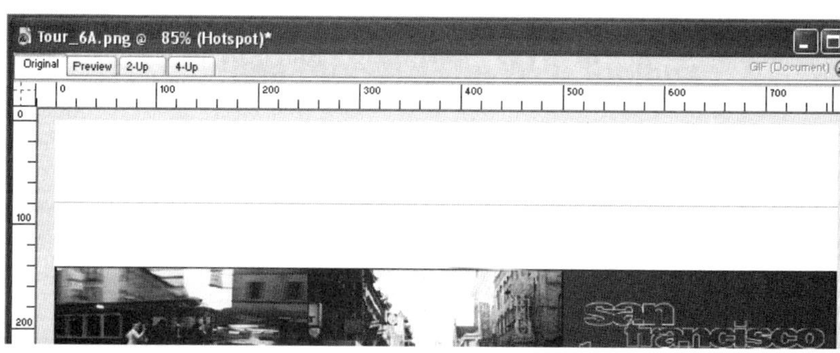

Fig. 6-12. Add a guide by "pulling" it from the horizontal ruler.

   b) Create a second guideline.

c) Place the guidelines so that one is directly on the top edge and the second is directly on the bottom edge. See figure 6-13.

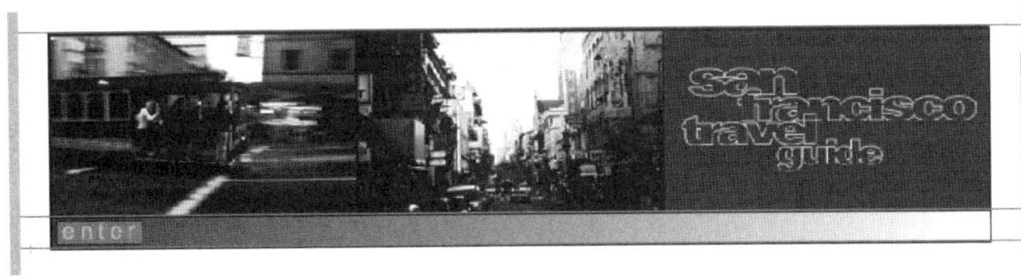

Fig. 6-13. Horizontal guides on the splash screen graphic.

d) Add two vertical guides between each photo and the logo by pulling them from the vertical ruler, as shown in figure 6-14.

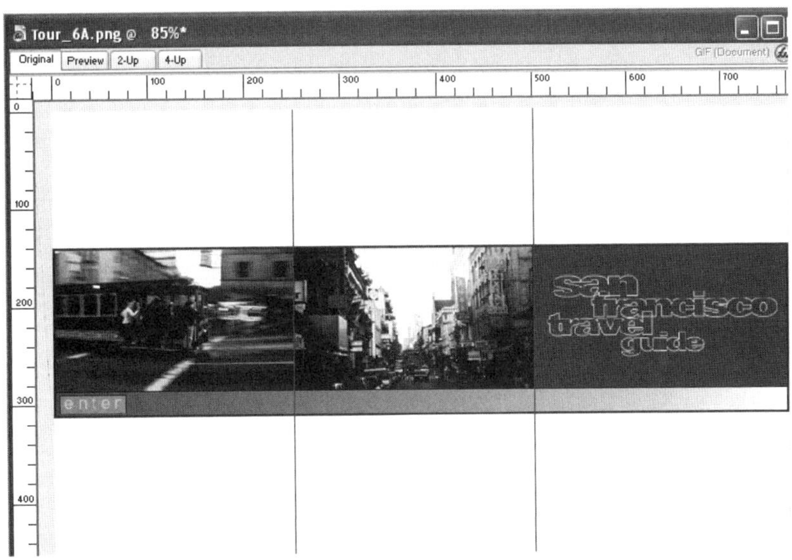

Fig. 6-14. Vertical and horizontal guides on the splash screen graphic.

4. Now let's use the Slice tool to draw slices based on the guides you just created on the canvas.
   a) Select the Rectangular Slice tool from the Web toolbox.
   b) Select View | Guides | Snap to Guides to turn the snapping feature on. If Snap to Guides already has a check mark next to it, this feature is on. The Snap to Guides feature makes each guide act like a magnet. As you draw slices, when your cursor gets close enough to the "magnetized" guide, the cursor will snap to the line. Using Snap to Guides makes it easier to draw specific shapes on the canvas.

c) With the Slice tool, start drawing the slice at an intersection point of the grid lines at the top left of the cable car photo (this way you're sure to cover the entire area). Pull down to the lower right of the photo.. You should notice that the Slice tool snaps to the guide as the cursor gets near.

5. Draw slices over the remaining images.
   a) Draw a slice over the *China Town* image (middle street scene).
   b) Draw a slice over the logo area.
   c) Draw the final slice over the entire width of the enter button panel.
   d) Your canvas should now look like that shown in figure 6-15.

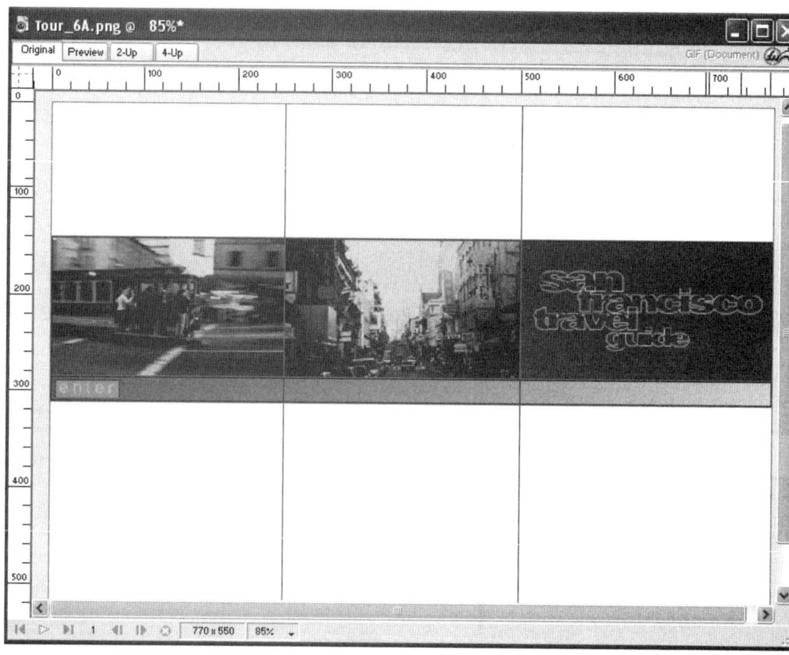

Fig. 6-15. Canvas with four slices applied.

TIP

Note that the hotspot is still present from our previous work. Hotspots and slices can work together. In this case, the slice is marking the area that will be exported (the entire Enter Button graphic), and the hotspot is marking an isolated clickable area within that graphic.

6. You might want to move the *Hotspot* sublayer to the top of the *Web* layer stack so that it can be easily selected for editing. In the Layer panel, select the *Hotspot* sublayer and drag it to the top of the stack of sublayers within the *Web* layer, as shown in figure 6-16.

7. Save the file to your *SaveWork* folder, naming the file *Tour_6A.png*.

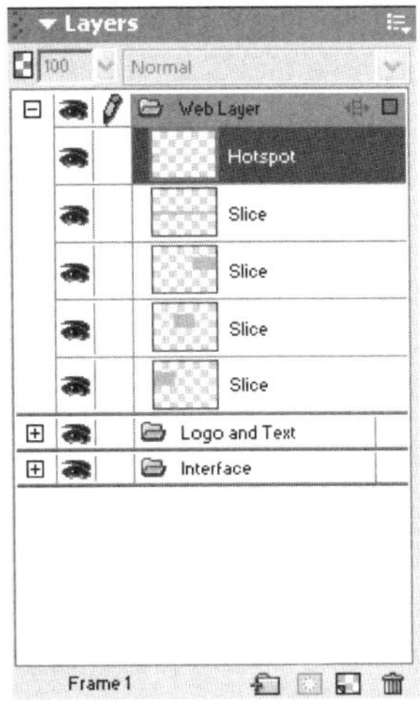

Fig. 6-16. Moving the* Hotspot *sublayer to the top of the stacking order.

Now that you have learned how to draw slices, the next step is to determine optimization settings for each slice. In Guided Tour 6B, you will learn to apply these optimization settings so that Fireworks will know how to compress the image within each slice upon export.

Guided Tour 6B: Optimizing Slices

In the sections that follow, you will learn how to optimize slices.

Adjusting and Repositioning Slices

Once you have drawn a slice, you can move and transform that slice just like another object on the canvas. You can use the Pointer tool to select and move a slice, or you can use the Subselection tool to move the anchor points of a slice. You can also use any of the Transform tools to scale, skew, or rotate the slice.

TIP

Slices should not overlap. If this happens, Fireworks MX will assign priority to whichever slice is highest in the *Web* layer stacking order when the file is exported or when a JavaScript behavior is attached to the slice.

1. We are going to continue to work with the completed version of a file you worked with in the last guided tour. You can use either the file you created previously or the file provided on the companion CD-ROM. These files should be identical.
   a) If you want to use your file, it should still be open from the last guided tour.
   b) If you want to use the file on the companion CD-ROM, select File | Open. Locate and double click on the CD-ROM player within your

CD-ROM

computer. Double click on the *Chapter 6* folder on the CD-ROM and click to select the file *Tour_6B.png*. Click on the Open button.

c) Save the file as *Tour_6B.png* in the *SaveWork* folder on your hard drive.

2. First, let's turn off the rulers and guides we used in the previous tour. Select View | Rulers and remove the check mark in the menu to turn off the rulers on the canvas. Then select View | Guides | Show Guides to turn off the guides.

3. Using the Pointer tool, select the slice over the *China Town* photo and drag it so that it overlaps the *cable car* slice, as shown in figure 6-17. Remember that slices define the pieces of a puzzle that will be put together by the HTML code in a web page. When slices overlap, Fireworks is unable to understand where one puzzle piece begins and one ends, so overlapping slices is never a good idea. (We will move it again in material to follow.)

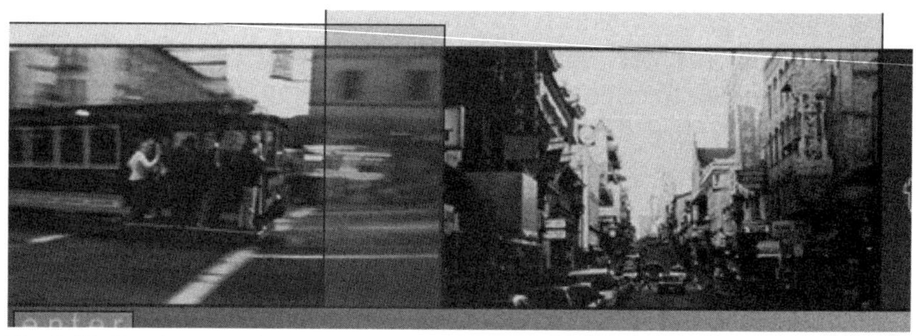

Fig. 6-17. Overlapping slices.

4. With the slice still selected, select the Scale tool in the Select toolbox. See figure 6-18.

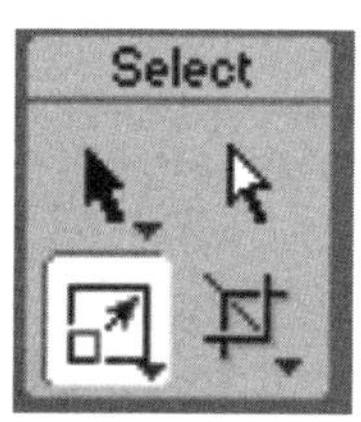

Fig. 6-18. Scale tool in the Select toolbox.

5. Note that scale handles appear around the edges of the slice selection. Use the handles to drag the slice back into place over the *China Town* photo, as shown in figure 6-19.

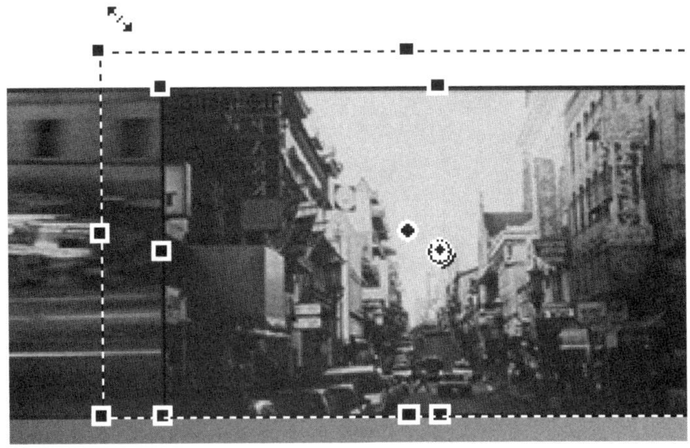

Fig. 6-19. Scaling a slice object.

6. Press Enter/Return to apply the scaling.

Working with Slice Guides

Slice guides are the red guidelines that mark the edges of all rectangular slice areas. Slice guides have been enhanced in Fireworks MX to allow shared slice boundaries to be edited by dragging them to the desired location. This is great for making adjustments to all slices that share a slice border. Let's try it.

1. Click and drag the red slice guide between the shared edge of the two photos, as shown in figure 6-20.

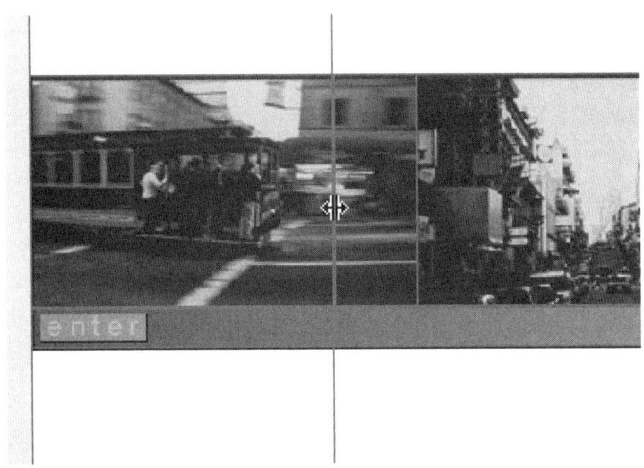

Fig. 6-20. Slice guide between photos.

2. When you release the mouse, note that both slices resized themselves based on the position of the slice guide.
3. Drag the slice guide back to its original position, or press Ctrl + Z (Mac: Cmd + Z) to undo the move.

·TIP·

Using the Draggable Slice Guide feature is the best method of avoiding overlaps and potential problems that can occur from repositioning slices.

Setting Slice Options Using the Properties Panel

As mentioned previously, one of the benefits of slicing images is that each slice can be treated individually in regard to unique properties, including export file type, variations in compression, URLs and <*alt*> tags, and individual slice names. To do this, we will use the Properties panel for a selected slice.

1. With the Pointer tool, select the slice that covers the cable car image. Take a look at the Properties panel, as shown in figure 6-21, and note the options listed there. These options are described in the following.

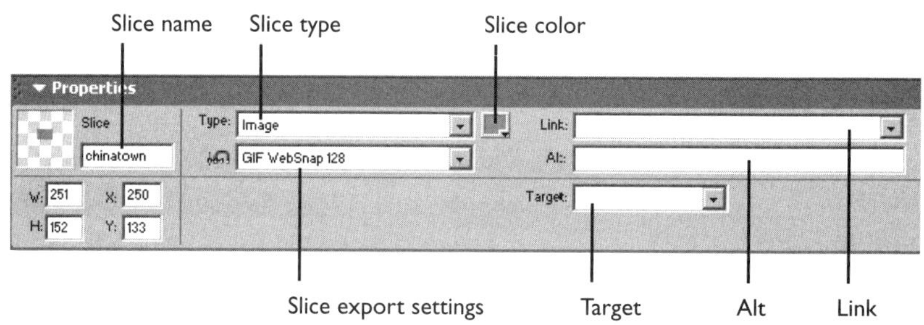

Fig. 6-21. Properties panel with a slice object selected.

- *Slice Name:* By default, the slice name automatically assigned corresponds to row and column numbers, but can be renamed to any name of your choice. This name is used in the *Web* layer as the slice name. It is also the default name that will be used for this slice image when it is exported.
- *Slice Type:* Slice Type options are Image and HTML. Leave the Image option selected for normal image export. Select HTML if you want to create a slice that can be used to insert HTML code and text in that area once the code is exported.
- *Slice Export Settings:* Select from a menu of preset options.
- *Slice Color:* Allows you to change the color of the slice.
- *Link:* Insert a URL that can be attached to the slice. Once exported, this will make the image clickable in an HTML document.
- *Alt:* Add an <*alt*> tag to the slice. An <*alt*> tag is a text description of the image. This description is used by screen readers and browsers that do not support in-line image viewing. Within most web browsers,

this is also the text that appears when you move the mouse cursor over an image.

- *Target:* Specifies which browser window the link associated with this slice will open in. The following options are available.
  - *_blank:* Loads the page in a new browser window that pops up above the open window.
  - *_self:* The implied default, which therefore does not necessarily need to be specified.
  - *_top:* Loads the page into the full browser window and is normally used to replace a frame set.
  - *_parent:* Used with frames to load the link into the window that contains the page.

2. To optimize the image slice, select the slice and select a preset export setting from the Properties panel.
   a) With the Pointer tool, select the *cable car* slice and then in the Slice Export Setting field, select JPEG – Better Quality from the pull-down menu. The Slice Export Settings menu allows you to set compression options for the image associated with each slice.
   b) Select the *China Town* slice and select GIF Web 216 from the Slice Export Settings menu.
   c) Once you have established a setting for a slice, you can then preview that slice. Select the *cable car* slice again, and then click on the 2-Up tab (shown in figure 6-22) to preview what the image will look like using this slice setting, as well as to preview the file size and estimated download time.

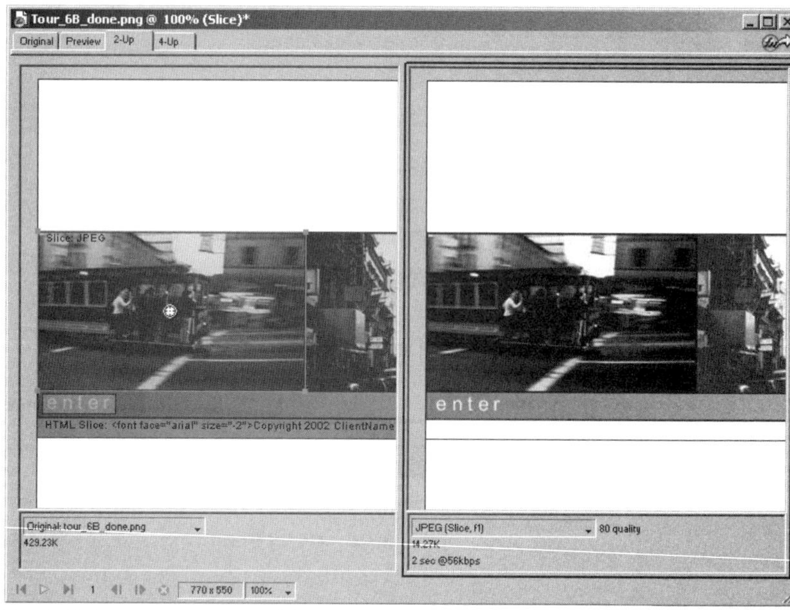

Fig. 6-22. 2-Up preview of cable car slice.

d) To see other slices in the preview area, select the Hand tool in the View toolbox. (See figure 6-23.) Click and drag with the Hand tool in the preview area to reposition the image in the window, so that the *China Town* image (street scene) can now be seen.

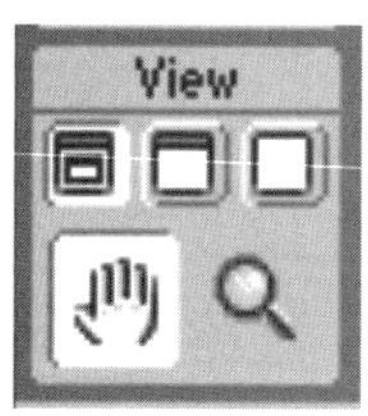

Fig. 6-23. Hand tool in the View toolbox.

e) With the Pointer tool, select the *China Town* slice in the left-hand pane and note that preview statistics in the right-hand pane now change to reflect the GIF setting on the *China Town* slice. Take a look at how the GIF setting alters this photographic image. You may note that the GIF Web 216 setting does not export as well as the JPEG setting.

f) Select the Original tab to return to editing mode.

3. You can also use the Optimize panel to adjust slice settings if you do not want to use a preset or custom setting.

a) Select Window | Optimize to open the Optimize panel, if it is not already open.
b) Select the *China Town* slice and note the GIF settings that were applied in the Properties panel. Use the Export File Format menu in the Optimize panel to change the setting to JPEG, as shown in figure 6-24.

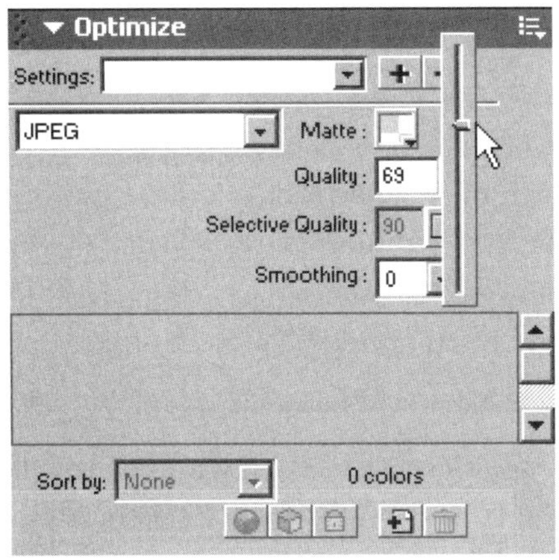

Fig. 6-24. Optimize panel.

c) Use the Quality slider in the Optimize panel to adjust the quality of the image. Toggle back and forth from Preview to Original to see the effects of adjusting the quality slider. The lower the number on the quality slider, the lower the quality of the image.

Creating an HTML (Text) Slice

From the previous tour of the Slice Properties panel, you may remember that Fireworks MX allows you to designate slices as images or as HTML code. Image is the most frequently used slice type because most slices exported from Fireworks are associated with images created on the canvas. The HTML slice type, however, can be useful if you want to create designated areas in your layout that will be used for text and other HTML coding. When you designate a slice as HTML, no image will be exported into that area. Once you have exported your file, you can open the HTML file generated by Fireworks within Dreamweaver or any other web-editing program and enter text or other HTML code in the blank slice area.

1. Select the Slice tool and draw another horizontal slice spanning the white area of the canvas below the bottom edge of the splash graphic, as shown in figure 6-25.

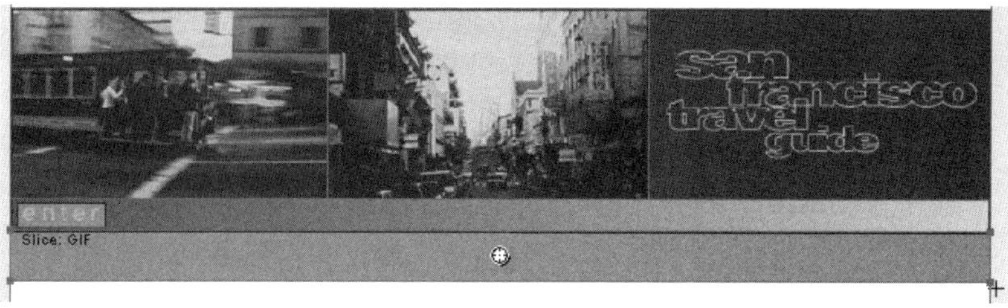

Fig. 6-25. HTML slice on the canvas.

2. With the Pointer tool, select the new slice, and then select HTML from the Type field in the Properties panel.
3. Note that an Edit button now appears below the field. Click on the Edit button and type the following phrase into the window that appears.

   <font face="arial" size="-2">Copyright 2002 ClientName</font>

   a) Click on the OK button when you have finished typing in the phrase. What you just typed is HTML code that defines the font style to be used (arial) and the font size (-2). Note that the HTML code is surrounded by brackets (< >). The words outside the brackets will actually appear on screen (in this case, *Copyright 2002 ClientName*).
   b) The code now appears in the slice. When this file is exported to HTML, the text inserted into the slice will appear as *Copyright 2002 ClientName*, and none of the HTML code will be visible.
   c) An alternate way of working with an HTML slice, if you are unfamiliar with HTML coding, is to insert the slice and set it to HTML. Then, leave it blank. You can always insert text, links, or other elements into this area once the file has been exported and you open it in Dreamweaver MX or any other HTML editing program.

TIP

You can tell the difference between an Image slice and an HTML slice by either looking at the Properties panel or by looking for the label HTML or the export file type on the selected slice.

After creating and applying optimization settings, the last step is to export your file. In Practice Exercise 6-1 you will learn how to simultaneously export the image slices and a customized HTML file, which recreates the layout of the splash page graphic.

Practice Exercise 6-1: Exporting Slices and HTML

Description

In Chapter 5 we explored the export options for a single image. In this practice exercise, we will revisit the Export Options panel and explore the HTML export options available from the same panel. By the end of this practice exercise you will be able to:

- *Insert slices and set optimization settings for each*
- *Export slices along with an HTML file*

Preview of Completed Exercise

Before beginning the exercise, let's take a look at the graphic in its completed state so that you can clearly see what it is you are about to build.

1. Use the menu option File | Open and locate the *Chapter 6* folder on the companion CD-ROM. Find the file named *Exercise6_1(complete).png*. Double click on this file to open it.
2. Take a look at the completed layout and make sure to also note the structure of the Layers panel. Figure 6-26 shows you what the slices on the Fireworks canvas will look like when this exercise is completed.

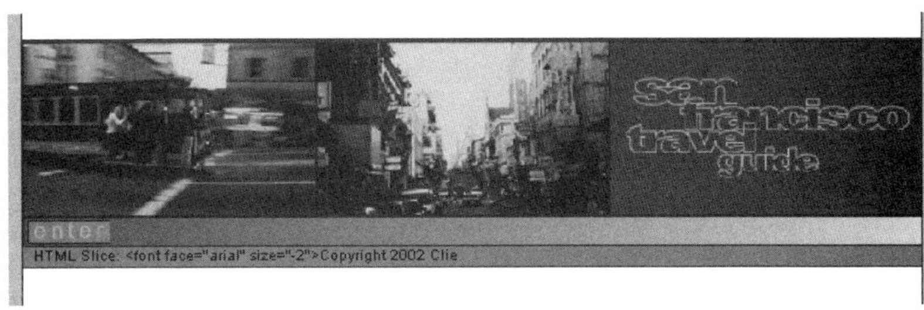

Fig. 6-26. Canvas when the exercise is completed.

3. To view the completed HTML file that will be exported from the Fireworks file in this exercise, minimize or hide Fireworks MX. Use your computer's browse function to locate and view the content of the companion CD-ROM. Find the file named *splash.htm* and double click to automatically open the file in your web browser, as shown in figure 6-27. The *splash.htm* page is linked to a number of image files that are located within an *image* folder, located within the *Chapter 3* folder on the companion CD-ROM.

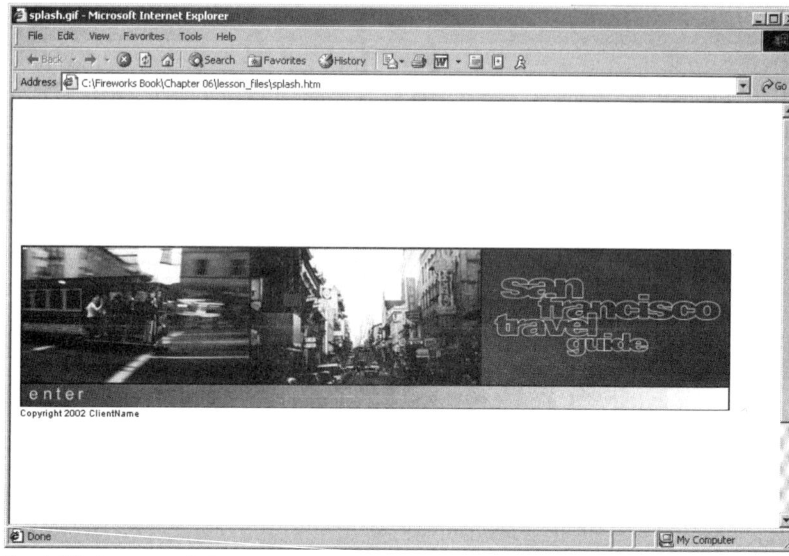

Fig. 6-27. Preview of the exported HTML file in a web browser.

Step-by-Step Instructions

1. We are going to continue to work with the completed version of a file you worked with in the last guided tour. You can use either the file you created or the file provided on the companion CD-ROM. These files should be identical.
   a) If you want to use your file, it should still be open from the last guided tour.
   b) If you want to use the file on the companion CD-ROM, select File | Open. Locate and double click on the CD-ROM player within your computer. Double click on the *Chapter 6* folder on the companion CD-ROM and click to select the file *Exercise6_1.png*. Click on the Open button.

CD-ROM

2. Save the file as *Exercise6_1.png* in the *SaveWork* folder on your hard drive.
3. First, we will set export options for each of the four image slices on the splash graphic.
   a) Let's first work with the slices of the photos of the cable car and China Town. The Optimize panel should already be open (if not, select Window | Optimize). Now select the *cable car* slice. In the Optimize panel, in the Export File Format field, select JPEG from the pull-down menu. Use the Quality slider to set the Quality option to 75%. Select the *China Town* slice and apply these same settings.

b) Select the *cable car* slice on the canvas. In the Properties panel Name field, name this slice *streetcar*. See figure 6-28.

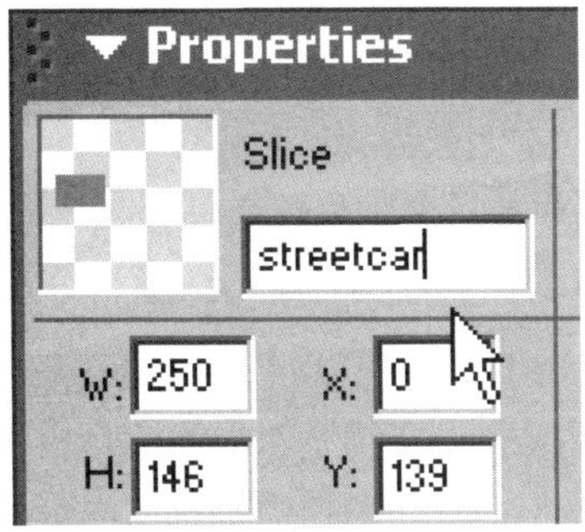

Fig. 6-28. Naming a slice in the Properties panel.

c) Select the *China Town* slice and in the Properties panel name it *chinatown*.

d) Select the *logo* slice and in the Properties panel select the GIF WebSnap 128 option. (See figure 6-29.) Name this slice *logo*.

e) Select the slice along the bottom that contains the Enter button, and in the Properties panel select the GIF WebSnap 128 option. Name this slice *enter*.

f) Select the slice that contains the HTML code, and in the Properties panel name this slice *html*.

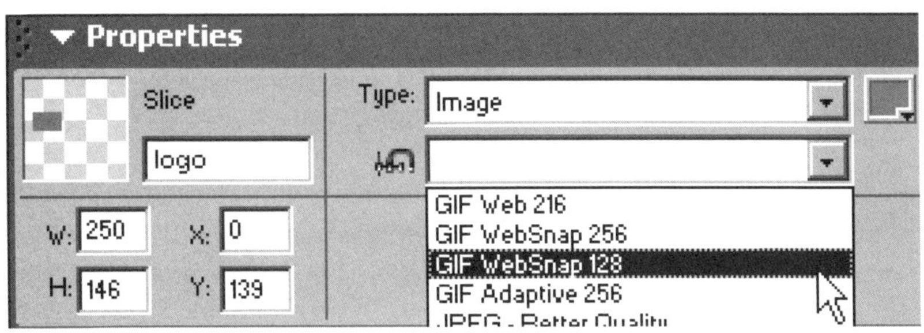

Fig. 6-29. GIF WebSnap 128 option in the Slice Export field within the Properties panel.

4. Now that you have set the export compression options for each slice, Fireworks MX can export the slices and save them with these file types and compression settings. Remember that each slice in the splash graphic layout is like a piece of a puzzle. The pieces are put together by the HTML code that is automatically generated by Fireworks MX when the file is exported.

5. Select File | Export to open the Export window, shown in figure 6-30. These options change depending on what file type you are exporting. Note the following options for exporting HTML and images.

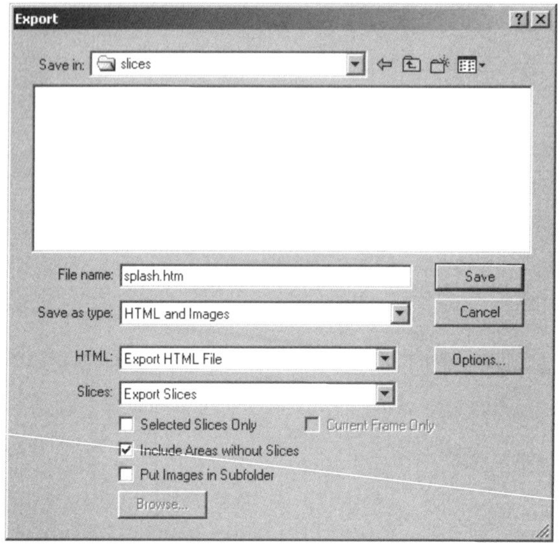

Fig. 6-30. Export window.

·TIP·

You can use *.htm* and *.html* interchangeably as the file extension for web pages.

CAUTION

Make sure not to use any space or special characters such as &, *, or $ in your file names. Many web servers do not allow file names with spaces and special characters. You can use a hyphen (-) or an underscore (_) to simulate a space in a file name.

- *Save In:* Allows you to select a location or folder on your computer to save your file into.
- *File Name:* The name of the HTML file that will be generated upon export, or the name of whatever type of file is selected in the Save as type field. Make sure to not use spaces or special characters such as &, *, or $ in your file names. Many web servers do not allow file names with spaces and special characters.
- *Save as Type:* Always set to HTML and Images when slices are being exported. Use this menu to determine which file type(s) to use for export. Options include HTML and Images (used for slices), Images Only, Dreamweaver Library *(.lbi)*, CSS Layers *(.htm)*, Director *(.htm)*, Layers to Files, Frames to Files, Lotus Domino Designer, Macromedia Flash SWF, Illustrator 7, and Photoshop PSD.
- *HTML:* Used for HTML and Image settings. This field allows you to select Export to HTML File or Copy to Clipboard in order to pass the HTML into another document, such as a Dreamweaver document.
- *Slices:* Select None, Export Slices, or Slice Along Guides to determine how Fireworks MX exports images on the canvas. If you have drawn slices and set optimization settings for them and want to export all slices, select Export Slices. If you do not want to export any slices,

select None. To have Fireworks MX automatically determine slices based on guides on the canvas, select Slice Along Guides.

- *Include Areas without Slices:* Check this box if you want Fireworks MX to create transparent spacer graphics (blank "space savers") for any areas that do not have slices in order to maintain the current layout.
- *Put Images in Subfolder:* Check this box if you want to create a subfolder named *images* for containing all image slices exported from Fireworks MX. Use the Browse button to select an alternate subfolder on your hard drive if you do not want Fireworks to create a folder for you. Note that the HTML file generated when saving via the HTML and Images option will be not be placed inside the *images* subfolder, but will be placed one level up in the directory structure.

Shortcut

Slice Along Guides allows you to export slices based on guides on the canvas without having to draw slices with the Slice tool.

·TIP·

Spacer GIFs are 1-pixel by 1-pixel transparent GIF images that can be scaled to any size to fill a table cell for spacing and alignment purposes.

6. In the open Export window, fill out the following options for the splash page graphic.
   - *Save In:* Create a new folder within the *SaveWork* folder on your hard drive. Name this new folder *slices*. Select this as the folder where your documents will be saved.
   - *File Name: SplashPage.htm*
   - *Save as Type:* HTML and Images
   - *HTML:* Export HTML File
   - *Slices:* Export Slices
   - *Include Areas without Slices:* Deselect (remove check mark)
   - *Put Images in Subfolder:* Select (add check mark). This will automatically create a subfolder named *images* in the *slices* folder.
7. Click on the Save button.
8. To view the exported files, use your computer's browse function and locate the *SaveWork* folder on the hard drive. Now look inside the *slices* folder.
   a) Note that this folder contains the *SplashPage.htm* file and the *images* folder, as shown in figure 6-31.

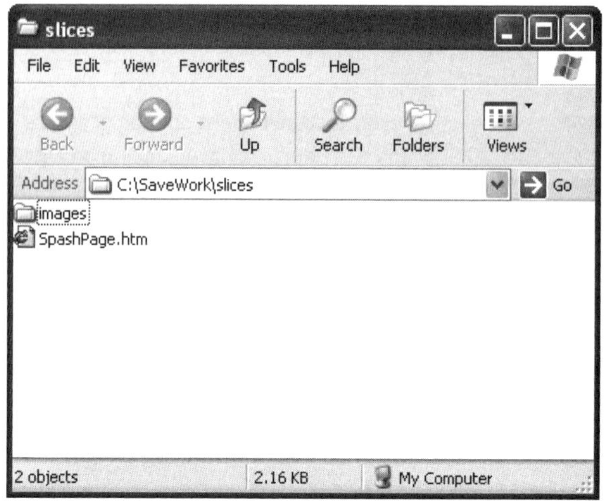

Fig. 6-31. **HTML** *file and* **images** *folder.*

b) Open the *images* folder. You should have five image files that correspond with the four image slices in your Fireworks MX document and the spacer graphic, as shown in figure 6-32.

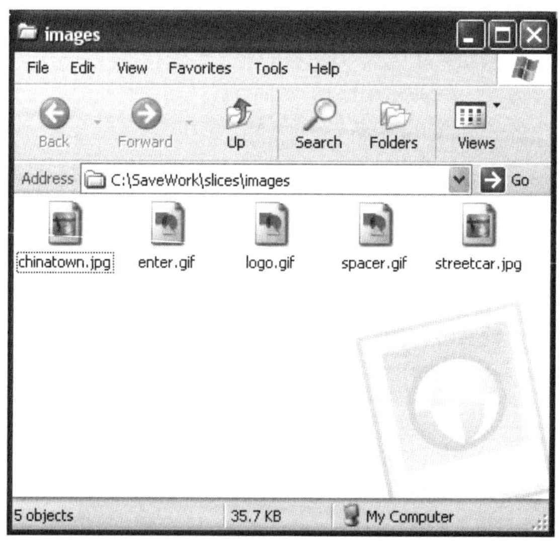

Fig. 6-32. Files within the **images** *folder, within the* **slices** *folder, within the* **SaveWork** *folder.*

Note that the file extensions correspond to the optimization setting selected for each slice. For example, the *chinatown* image is a JPEG file, whereas the *logo* image is a GIF file. Also note the fifth image, the *spacer.gif* image. A spacer image is a transparent GIF image Fireworks uses by default to force the HTML table holding the slices into exact width and height increments that will not shift during browser resizing.

c) If you did not name your slices, your files are automatically assigned a name that includes the HTML file name along with an extension of row and column numbers. In the example shown in figure 6-33, GIF was selected for all export settings.

Name	Size	Type
spacer.gif	1 KB	GIF Image
splashpage_r2_c1.gif	18 KB	GIF Image
splashpage_r2_c2.gif	24 KB	GIF Image
splashpage_r2_c3.gif	6 KB	GIF Image
splashpage_r3_c1.gif	4 KB	GIF Image

Fig. 6-33. Image files with names automatically assigned by Fireworks MX.

d) Go back up a directory level to the *slices* folder. Double click on the *SplashPage.htm* file to automatically open it in your web browser. This file contains HTML code that reassembles all images in the *images* folder into a layout that is just like the Fireworks MX document. Fireworks does this by creating an HTML table that forms the skeleton of the layout.

9. Select File | Save.

Adjusting the HTML Setup

To adjust the HTML output settings, the spacer GIF settings, and the dynamic slice export naming, you can use the HTML setup window available from the Options button in the Export window, or the HTML setup option under the File menu.

1. Select File | HTML Setup to take a look at the HTML settings. The General tab has several options, as shown in figure 6-34. These options are described in the following.

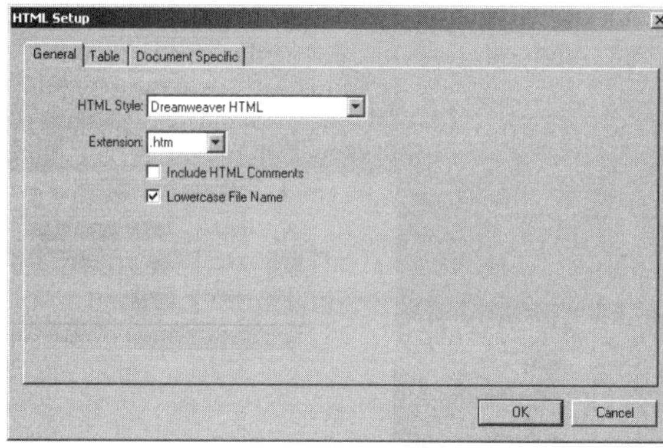

Fig. 6-34. General tab in the HTML Setup window.

- *HTML Style:* Note that you can adjust the HTML style setting to match a specific format, such as Dreamweaver HTML and GoLive.
- *Extension:* Select from *.htm, .HTM, .html, .HTML,* or *.asp* as the default file extension for exported HTML or ASP files.
- *Include HTML Comments:* Check this box if you want Fireworks to automatically add descriptive comments into the HTML code.
- *Lowercase File Name:* Check this box to have Fireworks MX automatically lowercase all file names upon export if the name was typed in with capital letters.

2. Select the Table tab and note the following options, shown in figure 6-35.

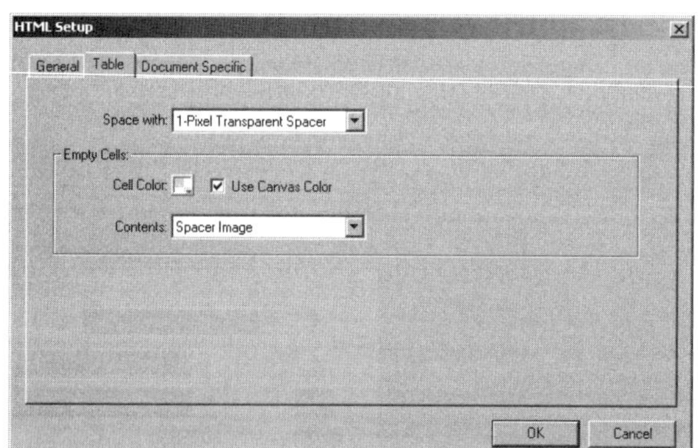

Fig. 6-35. Table tab in the HTML Setup window.

- *Space with:* Allows you to choose between using spacer images or tables as spaces in exported HTML tables.

- *Empty Cells:* Choose a background color for empty cells in any tables generated by Fireworks MX. Also select from None, Spacer Image, or Non-breaking Space for the content of empty cells.

3. Select the Document Specific tab and note the options available, as shown in figure 6-36.

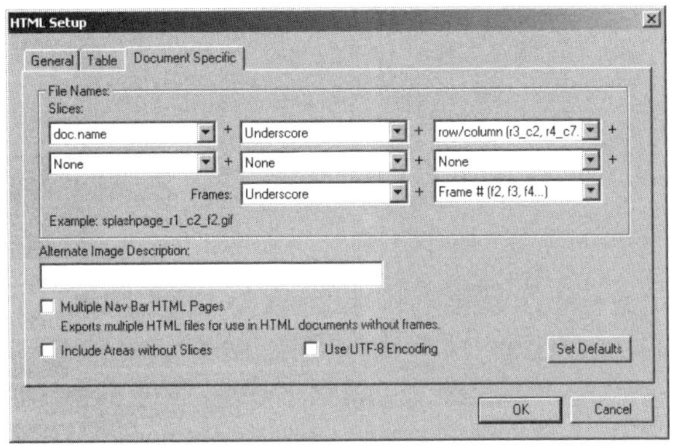

Fig. 6-36. Document tab in the HTML Setup window.

There are many options on this tab, but pay particular attention to the File Name section. This allows you to customize the dynamic naming properties Fireworks uses when generating slices. If you want to use this feature instead of manually naming each slice, you can customize this to your specifications.

4. Click on the Cancel button to close the HTML Setup window.

Exporting a Single Slice

It is also possible to export slices individually. This is useful if you need to make minor changes to an image slice, but not to the entire layout, and want to update the image in this slice by exporting again. You may also want to export an individual slice for use in some other application.

1. To export a single slice within the splash image, select the *logo* slice.
2. Right-click (Mac: Ctrl + click) to view the context menu, shown in figure 6-37.

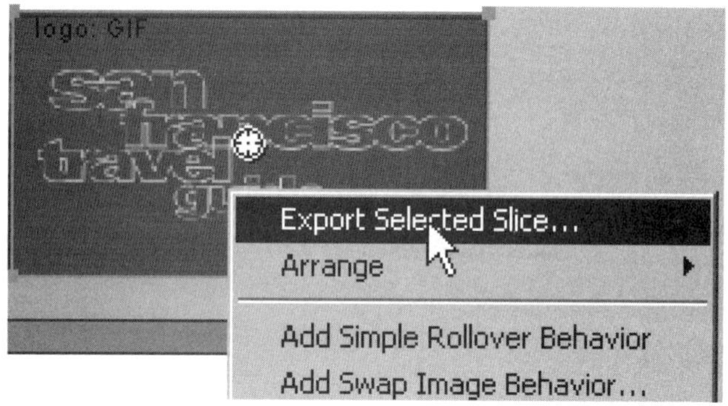

Fig. 6-37. Using the Context menu to export a single slice.

3. Select Export Selected Slice from the menu that opens.
4. Apply the following options in the Export window that opens.
   - *Save In:* Save in the *slices* folder.
   - *File Name:* This is automatically set to the slice name. Leave this setting.
   - *Save as Type:* Images Only.
   - *HTML:* Grayed out because we are only exporting a selected slice, not an HTML page.
   - *Slices:* Export Slice.
   - *Selected Slices Only:* Automatically checked because we are exporting a single slice.
   - *Current Frame Only:* Checked by default. Uncheck this option if you have more than one frame in your document that should be exported as well. This is often used for rollover images or animated GIFs created in Fireworks.
5. Click on the Save button to export the single *logo* slice.

Let's now move on and do some more "slicing and dicing." In Practice Exercise 6-2 you will slice and export a home page graphic.

Practice Exercise 6-2: Slicing and Exporting the Home Page Graphic

Description

In this exercise you will work with the home page design of the San Francisco Travel Guide web site. You will practice setting up slices and optimization settings in preparation for export. Finally, you will export the home page slices, along with an HTML page that displays the home page layout.

Preview of Completed Exercise

Before beginning the exercise, let's take a look at the graphic in its completed state so that you can clearly see what it is you are about to build.

1. Use the menu option File | Open and locate the *Chapter 6* folder on the companion CD-ROM. Find the file named *Exercise6_2(complete).png*. Double click on this file to open it.
2. Take a look at the completed layout and make sure to examine the structure of the Layers panel. Figure 6-38 shows you what the slices on the Fireworks canvas will look like when this exercise is completed. Carefully look at the slices that appear on the canvas. Note that each element of the splash page has been divided into slices.

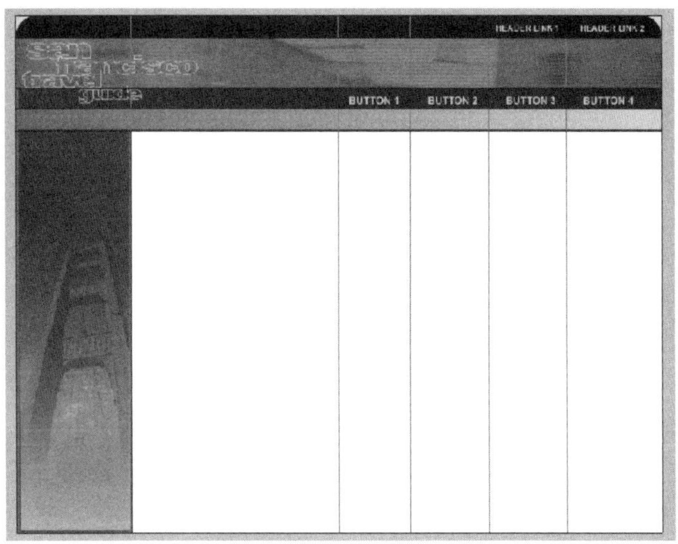

Fig. 6-38. Home page with slices.

Step-by-Step Instructions

1. Select File | Open and locate the *Chapter 6* folder on the companion CD-ROM. Find the file named *Exercise6_2.png*. Double click on this file to open it.
2. Now that we know how to export via the slicing method, let's replace the button hotspots (created in an earlier chapter) with slices. We can then

attach URLs to the image slices instead of using hotspots. In this way, the buttons will be prepared for further development, such as the addition of rollover states, covered in a later chapter.

a) Select the Pointer tool and while holding down the Shift key, select all hotspots in the *Web* layer.

b) Delete the hotspots by clicking on the Trash Can icon.

3. Next, let's set up a series of horizontal and vertical guides that split the horizontal and vertical areas of the home page graphics, as shown in figure 6-39.

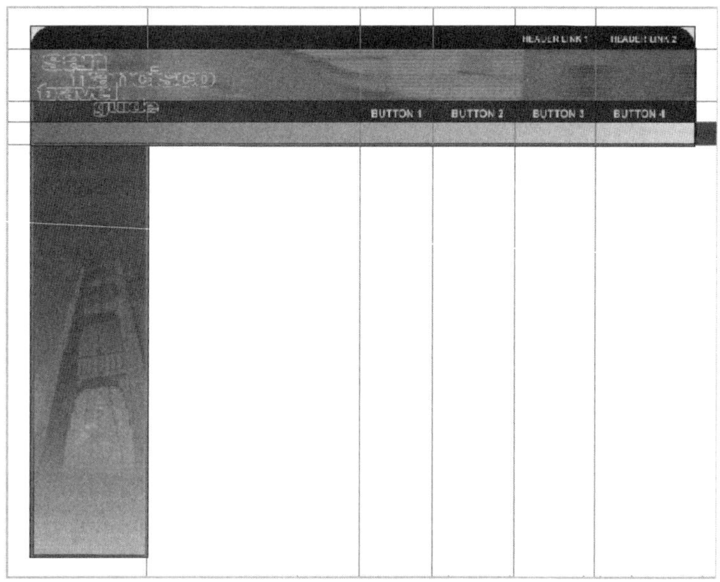

Fig. 6-39. Guide placement on the home page canvas.

a) Select View | Rulers to turn rulers on.

b) Select View | Guides | Show Guides to turn guides on.

c) "Pull" guides from the horizontal and vertical rulers so that each element is segmented. (See figure 6-39.) Pull four horizontal guides (below black bar at top, above the bar containing buttons 1 through 4, below the bar containing buttons 1 through 4, and below the light blue bar that lies below the buttons). Pull five (5) vertical guides (on the right edge of the bridge image, to the left of button 1, between buttons 1 and 2, between buttons 2 and 3, and between buttons 3 and 4).

4. Now let's draw the slices.

a) Select View | Guides | Snap to Guide.

b) Select the Slice tool in the Web toolbox.

c) Following the guides, draw three slices across the black bar at the top of the header. Span the first slice across the top and stop short of the first button text. The other two slices should cover the buttons (Header Link 1 and Header Link 2). See figure 6-40.

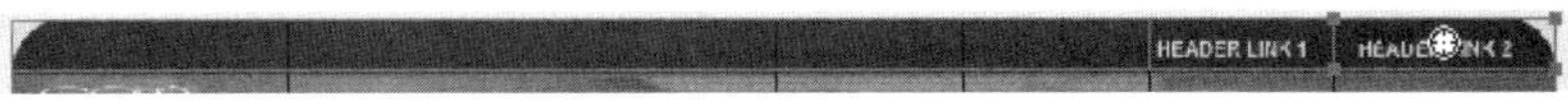

Fig. 6-40. Three slices over the black bar at the top of the canvas.

d) Draw a long horizontal slice between the black bar at the top and the medium blue bar with buttons (this will cover the medium blue section that contains the text *san francisco*, as well as all of the blue area to the right). See figure 6-41.

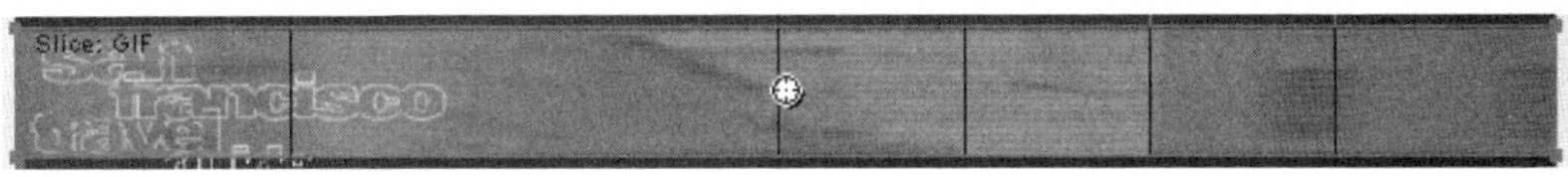

Fig. 6-41. Long horizontal slice over the medium blue section.

e) Draw five (5) slices over the dark blue bar with the buttons on it. The first slice should span from the left edge of the image to the left edge of the first button. Then add four more slices covering each button. See figure 6-42.

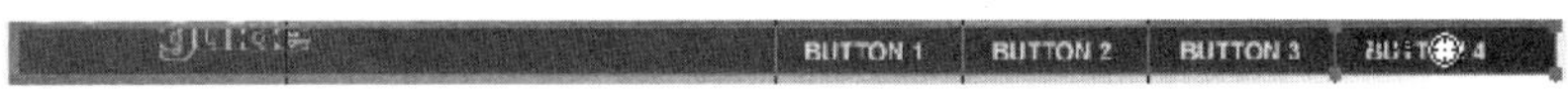

Fig. 6-42. Five slices over the dark blue bar with buttons.

f) Draw a single, long horizontal slice spanning the light blue gradient under the buttons. See figure 6-43.

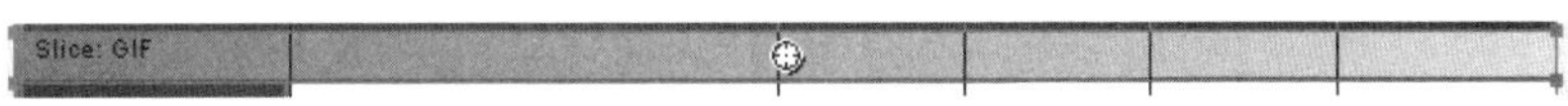

Fig. 6-43. Single slice over the light blue gradient.

g) Finally, draw a single vertical slice covering the entire *bridge* graphic on the left. (See figure 6-44.) We will work more with this area later in the book.

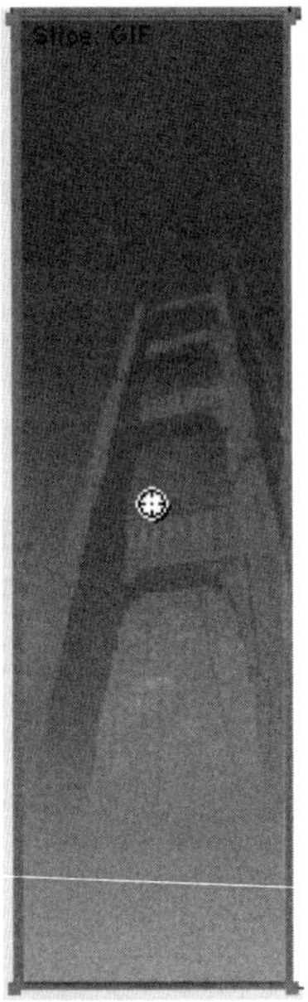

Fig. 6-44. Single slice over the bridge image on the left.

5. Now let's give each slice a name.
   a) Select the large vertical slice on the left containing the *bridge* photo and in the Properties panel name it *bridge*. See figure 6-45.

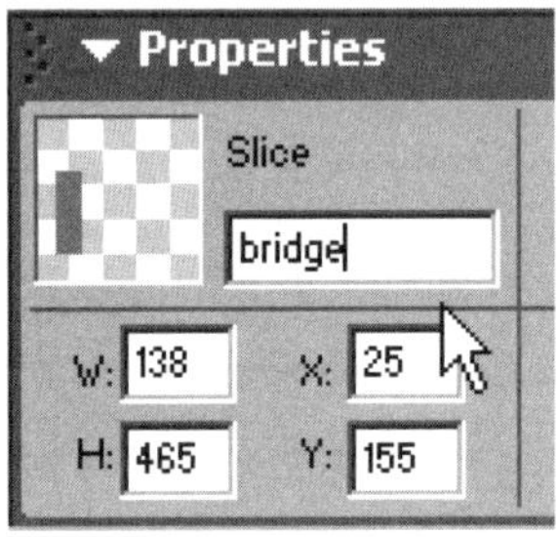

Fig. 6-45. Renaming the bridge photo.

   b) Select every slice on the canvas and give each a unique name in the Properties panel. Choose any names you wish. The names we used are shown in figure 6-46.

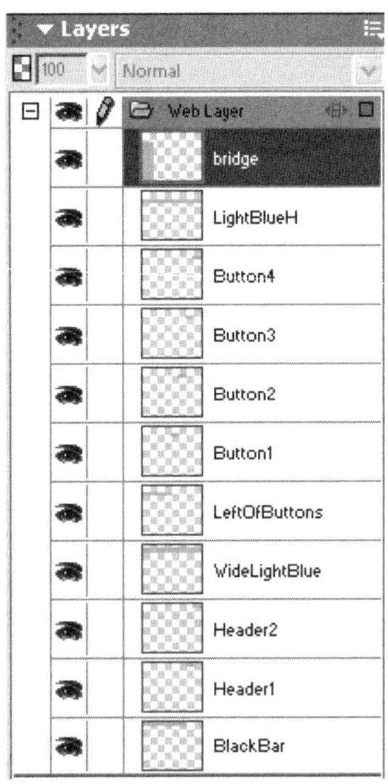

Fig. 6-46. New slice names within the Web layer.

6. Set the optimization setting for each slice.

TIP

File | Preview in Browser is a quick way to test your export settings in your primary and secondary browsers without having to export all slices on the canvas. Fireworks MX simply creates a temp file—a snapshot of sorts—of your current file and loads this preview into your web browser.

CAUTION

If you use Preview in Browser, be sure to remember that this is not your current export file. If you make changes to the document in Fireworks, you need to use Preview in Browser again to see a new version. Refreshing in your browser will not work for viewing updates.

a) Select Window | Optimize to open this panel if it is not already open. Select the *bridge* slice, and then select JPEG – Better Quality from the Setting field in the Optimize panel.
b) Click on the Preview tab to see the Optimization effects. Adjust the settings if necessary.
c) Select each image slice and apply optimization settings. In general, use JPEG for photographic images and GIF for images with fewer colors or less text. Click on the Preview tab to confirm your settings.

7. Now let's go ahead and export the file.
   a) Select File | Export.
   b) Within the *SaveWork* folder, create a folder named *HomePage*. Save the files in this folder.
   c) Name the file *HomePage.htm*.
   d) Fill in the following options.
      - *Save as Type:* HTML and Images
      - *HTML:* Export as HTML File
      - *Slices:* Export Slices
   e) Uncheck Include Areas without Slices.
   f) Check Put Images in Subfolder.
   g) Click on Save to export the files.
8. Use your computer's browse function to locate and open the *SaveWork* folder. Open the *HomePage* folder. Double click on the *HomePage.htm* file to view the exported file in your browser. See figure 6-47.

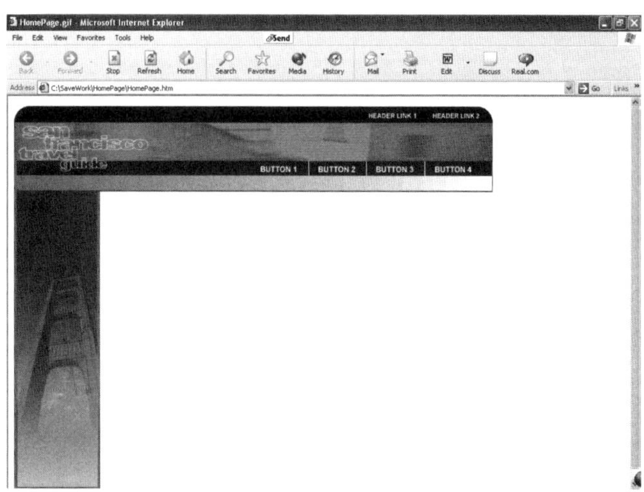

Fig. 6-47. Slices as viewed after export, through a browser.

9. Save the file.

CHAPTER 7

Graphic F/X

Chapter Topics:

- *Introduction*
- *Keys to Great Effects*
- *Practice Exercise 7-1: Fill Effects: Feathering, Opacity, and Textures*
- *Practice Exercise 7-2: Live Effects: Bevels, Embosses, Shadows, and Glows*
- *Image Manipulation: Photographic Images*
- *Practice Exercise 7-3: Photographic Effects: Color Effects and Blending*
- *Practice Exercise 7-4: Text Effects: Designing with Text*
- *Practice Exercise 7-5: Creating a Composite Illustration for the Home Page*

Introduction

Feathered edges, bevels, drop shadows, and color effects are just a few of the special effects that can be used to enhance artwork created in Fireworks MX. With the effects and filters that are built into Fireworks and a little practice, you will soon be able to add dimension and visual interest to any design. In addition, with the use of layers and text effects, you have unlimited possibilities for creating dynamic designs.

This chapter explores a variety of effects that can be applied to graphics. By the end of the chapter you will be able to:

- *Use the Effects settings to apply special effects to your graphics*
- *Create masks and work with color modes*
- *Create text along a path and within shapes*
- *Blend graphics across layers for special effects*

Keys to Great Effects

The sections that follow discuss combining effects across multiple layers, using opacity settings to blend images, and using blending modes to blend images.

Combining Effects Across Multiple Layers

As you begin working with special effects, it is important to first realize that these effects can be applied across multiple layers in your Fireworks document. Applying simple effects is easy enough, but for a truly spectacular rendering, you will need to combine effects. Often it is advantageous to spread the effects across multiple layers so that you have added control over how the effects overlap and mix. By analogy with traditional art media, this added control is similar to the blending of layers of oil paint on a canvas, or the gradual image buildup in a colored chalk drawing. In addition, the accumulative result of the effects from individual layers can combine to form a totally new effect that could not have been achieved without the use of layers.

Using Opacity Settings to Blend Images

As you will see in Practice Exercise 7-1, using adjustments in the opacity settings of objects can be an easy and effective way of creating blending effects. You can adjust the opacity of individual objects or adjust the opacity on an entire layer affecting all objects within that layer. This is a nice way of creating transparency effects that allow the textures and colors of other objects to blend. Keep in mind that this type of layering effect is often necessary, and that even though opacity is very simple, it is often extremely useful.

A simple way of changing the opacity of an object on a layer is to use the Opacity slider in the Layers panel. In figure 7-1, note that the Opacity slider is located in the upper left-hand corner (above the layer list) of the Layers panel. The slide can be adjusted from 0 to 100. 100 is the most opaque setting, which means there is no transparency. 0 is the least opaque setting, which means that the objects on the layer become completely transparent and disappear from view. To use this slider, simply select the layer you want to work with and move the slider to change the opacity.

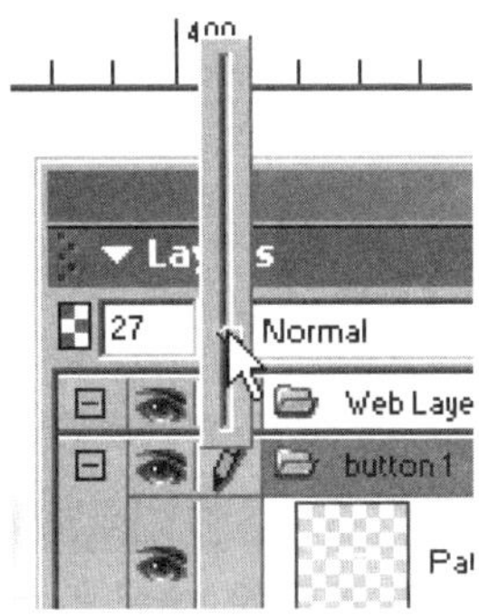

Fig. 7-1. Opacity slider in the Layers panel.

Using Blending Modes to Blend Images

Previously, you briefly used one of the blending mode settings when working with the bridge photograph in the sidebar on the home page design of our travel site. However, at that point, this function was not fully described. Blending modes can be set to objects or to layers, much like opacity. There are twelve blending modes available in the drop-down menu for the Blend Mode field, located in the upper right-hand corner of the Layers panel. (See figure 7-2.) These same modes are also available to be selected from the Blend Mode field in the Properties panel, as shown in figure 7-3. To access blending modes for objects in the Properties panel, you must first select the object on the canvas.

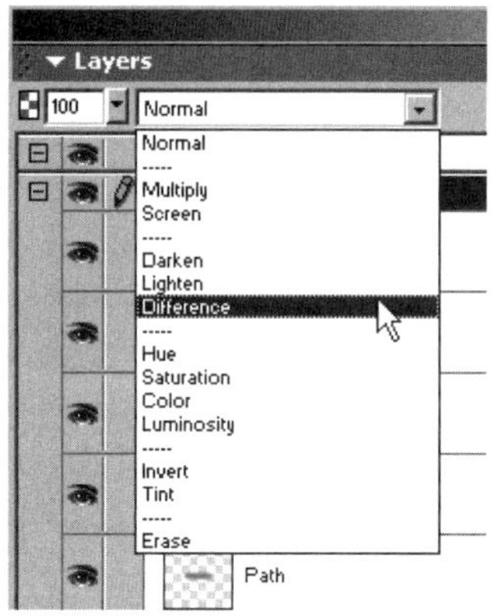

Fig. 7-2. Blending mode options in the Blend Mode field in the Layers panel.

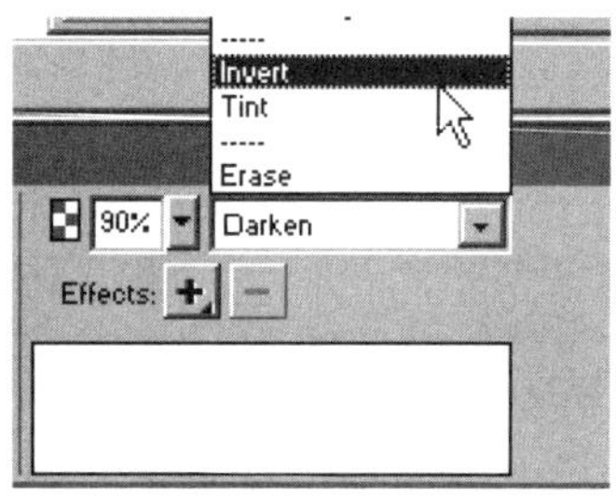

Fig. 7-3. Blending mode options in the Blend Mode field in the Properties panel.

TIP

A gel button is a translucent and reflective dimensional button. This style became popular when special effects filters evolved in Photoshop and Fireworks. You will create a gel button in Practice Exercise 7-1.

These modes will blend, in various ways, the colors of objects that overlap across layers. The manner of blend depends on the characteristics of each mode. Wherever objects overlap, the blending effect will be applied despite the fact that the objects are on separate layers. The easiest way to see the results is to pick an object and to experiment with the different settings. Later in this chapter, we will use blending modes to blend images with gradient colors across layers. This also works very well for blending multiple photographs. Throw in opacity settings and masks, and you have a full arsenal of tricks for applying special effects to images.

You will have the opportunity to practice these effects in the practice exercise that follows. You will design a button with a gel finish. To create this button you will start by drawing a button shape. You will then create five copies of the button, each on a separate layer. A specific effect will be applied to each copy, and the combined effect will result in the gel-like appearance of the button.

Practice Exercise 7-1: Fill Effects: Feathering, Opacity, and Textures

Description

This practice exercise examines applying fill properties to vector shapes, this time with more emphasis on using the Properties panel to create blending effects across layers. We will start by creating the dimensional surface of a gel button. By the end of this completed exercise you will be able to:

- *Create custom gradient fills*
- *Clone objects*
- *Apply feathered edge effects to vector shapes*
- *Create shadow effects*

Preview of Completed Exercise

Before beginning the exercise, let's take a look at the canvas in its completed state so that you can clearly see what it is you are about to build.

1. Use the menu option File | Open and locate the *Chapter 7* folder on the companion CD-ROM. Find the file named *Exercise7_1(complete).png*. Double click on this file to open it.
2. Take a look at the completed layout and make sure to also note the content of the Layers panel. Figure 7-4 shows you what the canvas will look like after completing this exercise.

Fig. 7-4. Canvas upon completion of the exercise.

Step-by-Step Instructions

1. Select File | New to open a blank file.
   a) Create a 500 x 500 canvas. Leave the Resolution set to 72 and the Canvas color set to white.
   b) Save the file in the *SaveWork* folder with the name *Exercise7_1.png*.
2. Create the basic shape for the gel button.
   a) Select the Ellipse tool from the Vector toolbox, shown in figure 7-5.

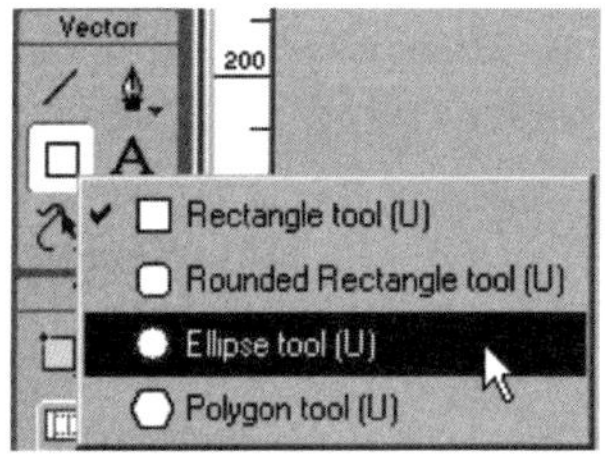

Fig. 7-5. Ellipse tool in the Vector toolbox.

b) Select a medium blue fill and a medium stroke from the Colors toolbox.

c) Draw a circle of any size on the canvas. Select the circle and change the following options in the Properties panel, shown in figure 7-6.

- *Width:* 50
- *Height:* 50
- *X:* 150
- *Y:* 225

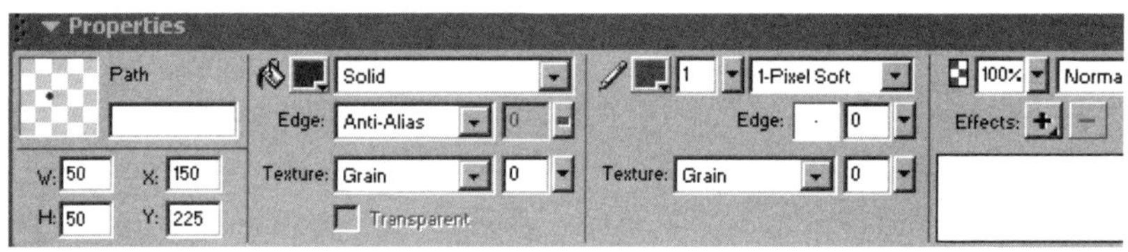

Fig. 7-6. Settings for the circle in the in Properties panel.

·TIP·

To sample a color, click on the Stroke or Fill icon in the Colors toolbox to display the Color palette. The cursor will turn to an eyedropper. Use this eyedropper to sample the color from any object on the canvas.

d) Select the Rectangle tool from the Vector toolbox, shown in figure 7-7.

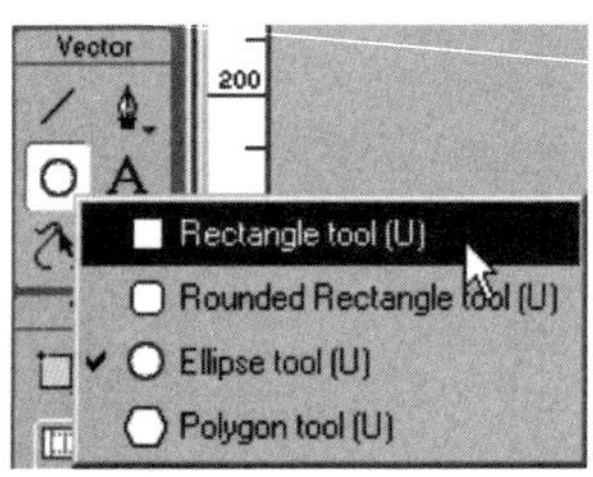

Fig. 7-7. Rectangle tool.

e) Draw a rectangle of any size, with same color and stroke as the circle, anywhere on the canvas.

f) Select the rectangle and change the following options in the Properties panel.

- *Width:* 150
- *Height:* 50
- *X:* 175
- *Y:* 225

g) Your screen should now look like that shown in figure 7-8.

Fig. 7-8. Combined circle and rectangle on the canvas.

h) Select the Ellipse tool from the Vector toolbox again. Draw a second circle, with the same color and stroke, on the canvas.

i) Select the circle and change the following options in the Properties panel.

- *Width:* 50
- *Height:* 50
- *X:* 300
- *Y:* 225

j) You should now see a pill button shape in the center of the canvas, similar to the object shown in figure 7-9.

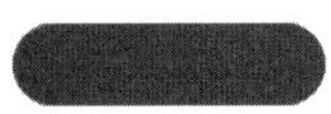

Fig. 7-9. Combination of three objects drawn on the canvas.

k) Select Select | Select All to select all three shapes on the canvas.

l) Select Modify | Combine Paths | Union. This command takes all three shapes and turns them into one shape. Note that the three shapes have been merged into a single path.

3. Next, let's create multiple copies of this shape to work with. We will create five copies of the button and apply different effects to each. Once combined, the shapes will create a beautiful translucent effect. We will use the Clone command to easily create copies.

a) Select the new path in *Layer 1*. Rename it *Button 1*.

b) Select Edit | Clone. Note that a second *Button 1* layer now appears in the Layers panel. It is the same graphic in the same location, but on a different sublayer. Change the name of this cloned *Button 1* sublayer to *Button 2*.

c) Select Edit | Clone three more times until you have five paths total. Change the name of each subsequent sublayer, respectively, to *Button*

Shortcut

The keyboard shortcut for Clone is:
PC: Ctrl + Shift + D
Mac: Cmd + Shift + D

3, *Button 4*, and *Button 5*. When you are finished, your Layers panel should look like that shown in figure 7-10.

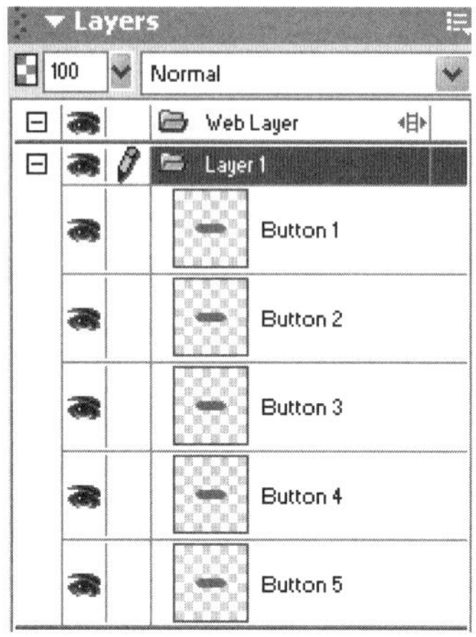

Fig. 7-10. Layer panel with five button sublayers.

d) Now let's change the stacking order of the sublayers so that they will be completely reversed from their current order. See figure 7-11.

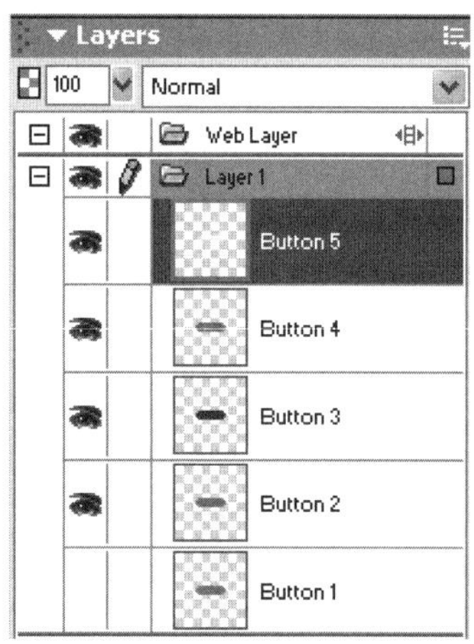

Fig. 7-11. Layer panel with the five sublayers in a new stacking order.

4. Now let's apply effects to the cloned buttons. First, we will create the base color for the button.
   a) Hide sublayers *Button 1*, *Button 2*, *Button 4*, and *Button 5* by clicking on the Eye icon next to each sublayer. Only the *Button 3* layer should be visible. It will be the only sublayer with an Eye icon next to it.

b) Using the Pointer tool, select the button shape on the canvas, and then establish the following settings in the Properties panel. See figure 7-12.

- *Fill Color:* #003399 (Select the Fill color swatch and type in the numbers at the top of the Color panel.)
- *Stroke:* No Color (From the Color panel, select the white swatch with a red diagonal strip through it.)
- *Opacity:* 50

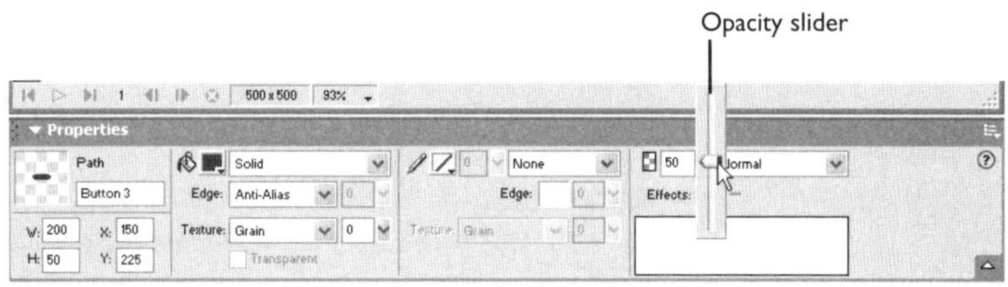

Fig. 7-12. Properties panel for the* Button 3 *sublayer.

5. Now we will create a bold highlight at the top of the shape. To create the translucent effect, we will adjust a series of highlights and shadows over the object. These next few steps will show you how to approximate these lighting effects.

   a) Select the *Button 5* sublayer to display it on the canvas. The Eye icon should be displayed. If it is not, click in the column to the left to display the icon and the sublayer.

·TIP·

Because we renamed the cloned sublayers, you can tell which one is selected by looking at the name in the Properties panel.

   b) Establish the following settings in the Properties panel.

   - *Width:* 185
   - *Height:* 30
   - *X:* 157
   - *Y:* 228
   - *Stroke:* No Color

·TIP·

You could also use the Transform tool to visually scale the button to roughly the same proportions without typing in width and height values.

   c) This should reduce the size of the shape and place it at the top center of the *Button 3* sublayer. See figure 7-13.

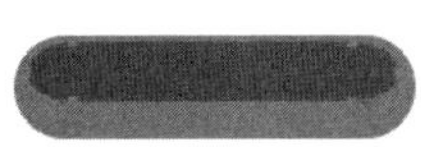

Fig. 7-13.* Button 5 *sublayer on top of* Button 3 *sublayer on the canvas.

   d) Now we need to set the color of the *Button 5* sublayer. The top highlight of the finished gel button should have a hard edge that defines the brightest point of the reflection. We will create this effect using a gradient.

e) Select the *Button 5* object. In the Properties panel, select Linear in the Fill Category option for the shape and click on the Fill color swatch to enter the gradient editing panel, shown in figure 7-14.

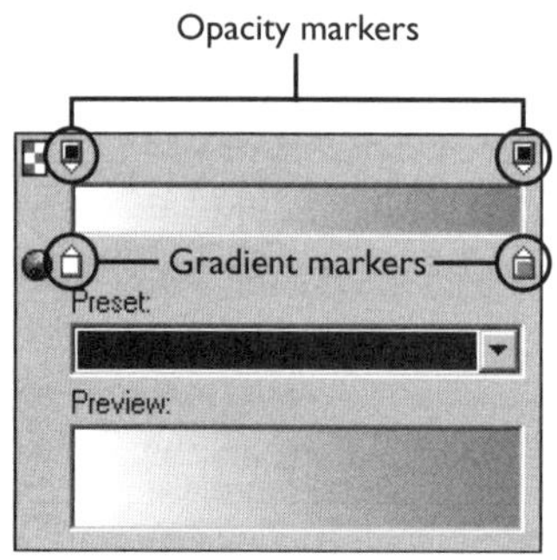

Fig. 7-14. Linear Gradient editing panel available within the Properties panel.

f) Click on each gradient marker and use the color palette that opens to change them both to white, so that the gradient is white to white. See figure 7-15.

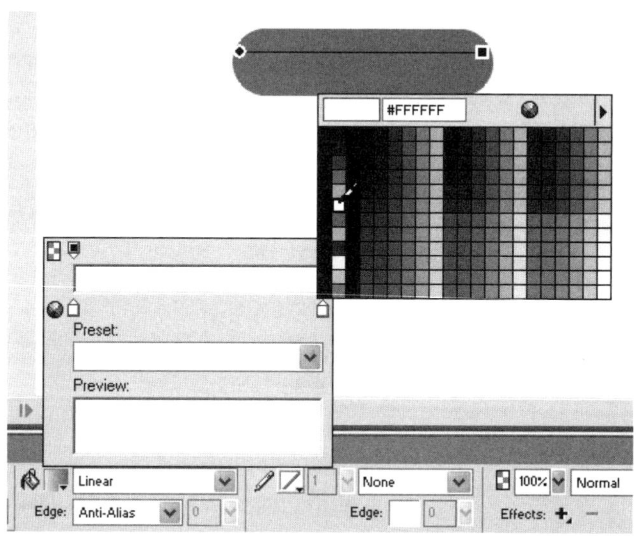

Fig. 7-15. Color palette opening from each gradient marker.

g) A second set of markers above the gradient preview allows you to change opacity. Click on the right-hand opacity marker. (See figure 7-15.)

h) A slider window now opens (see figure 7-16) to allow you to set the opacity for the right-hand marker. Set it to 0. This creates a white-to-transparent gradient.

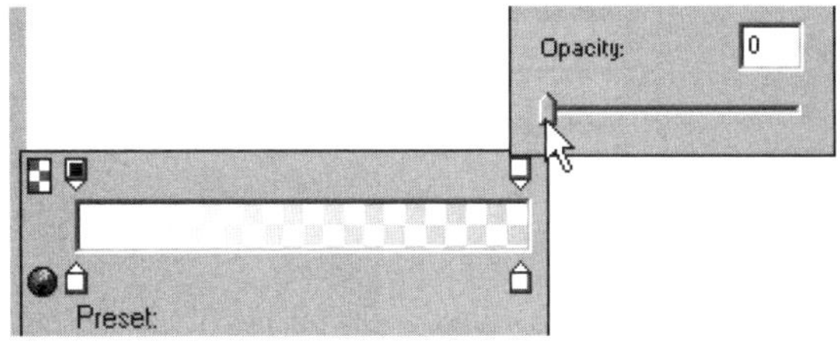

Fig. 7-16. Opacity slider for right-hand opacity marker.

i) When selected, *Button 5* on the canvas shows the gradient with a black line running horizontally. At the end of the lines are two handles. These handles allow the gradient to be adjusted. Click on and drag the gradient handles to move the gradient so that it runs vertically (top to bottom) in the shape, with the white at the top. See figure 7-17.

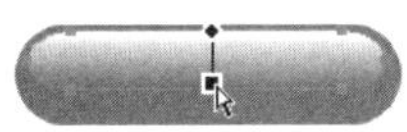

Fig. 7-17. Gradient adjusted to run vertically, with white at top.

6. At this point, you can already start to see the reflection. We will add one more highlight to the top, and then move on to the button shadows.
   a) Select the *Button 4* sublayer to display it on the canvas. The Eye icon should be displayed. If it is not, click in the column to the left to display the icon and the sublayer.
   b) With the *Button 4* shape selected, establish the following settings in the Properties panel.
      - *Width:* 168
      - *Height:* 40
      - *X:* 166
      - *Y:* 250
      - *Stroke:* No Color
   c) This should reduce the size of the shape and place it at bottom center in the button, as shown in figure 7-18.

Fig. 7-18. **Button 4** *location and size on the canvas.*

d) Now let's add a gradient to the *Button 4* object to create a highlight. However, this highlight will be a little more subtle, with no hard edges. In fact, we are actually going to create a soft glow with this effect, which will represent refracted light.

e) In the Properties panel, set Fill Category to Linear for the *Button 4* object.

f) Click on the Fill swatch and change the color of both markers to white. Click in the center of the gradient to add a third marker. See figure 7-19.

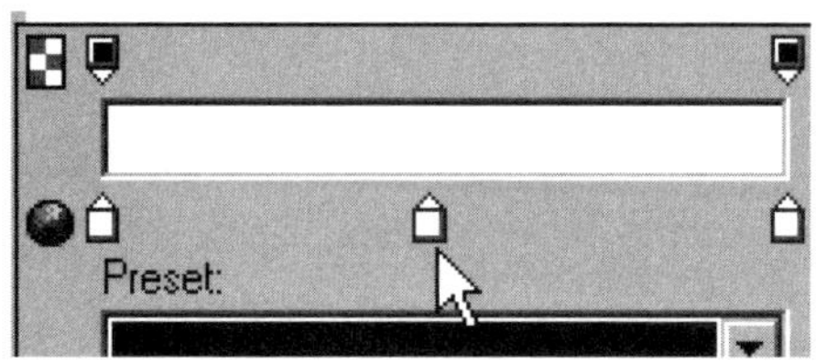

Fig. 7-19. Third gradient marker added by clicking below the gradient window.

g) Click to add an opacity marker above the middle gradient marker. Set the value for the outer opacity markers to 0 (leaving the Opacity setting at 100 for the center marker). Click on the canvas to close the gradient editing window.

h) On the canvas, adjust the gradient handles so that they are vertical and the white glow is horizontal along the lower edge of the button, as shown in figure 7-20.

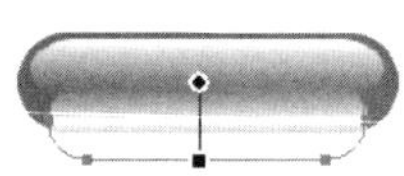

Fig. 7-20. Gradient handles adjusted for the* Button 4 *object.

i) To remove the hard edges of this gradient, we will change the fill to a feathered edge.

j) In the Properties panel, set the Fill Edge option to Feather, and adjust the size slider to 12, as shown in figure 7-21. Note that the object now has a nice feathered edge and resembles a glow effect.

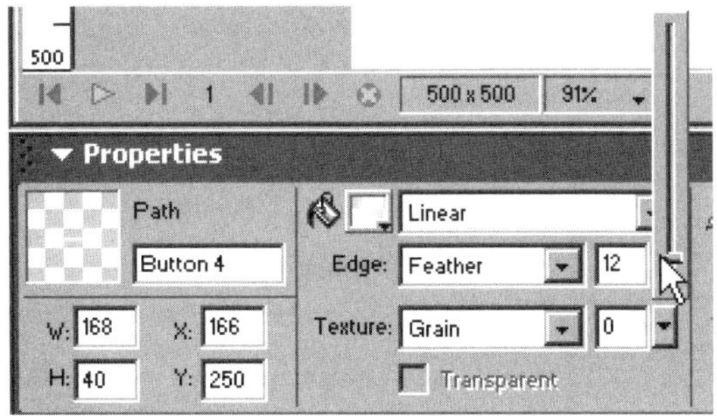

Fig. 7-21. Fill Edge set to Feather, 12-point.

k) In the Properties panel, set the opacity slider to 80. See figure 7-22.

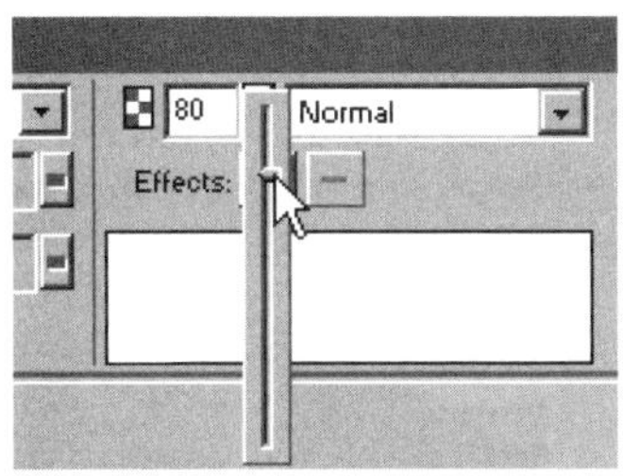

Fig. 7-22. Opacity slider in the Properties panel for the Button 4 object.

7. To finish the gel button, we will practice applying a shadow.
   a) Select the *Button 1* sublayer to display it on the canvas. The Eye icon should be displayed. If it is not, click in the column to the left to display the icon and the sublayer.
   b) With the *Button 1* shape selected, establish the following settings in the Properties panel. See figure 7-23.

      - *X:* 155
      - *Y:* 235
      - *Fill Color:* #999999
      - *Edge:* Feather 16-pt
      - *Stroke:* No Color
      - *Opacity:* 75

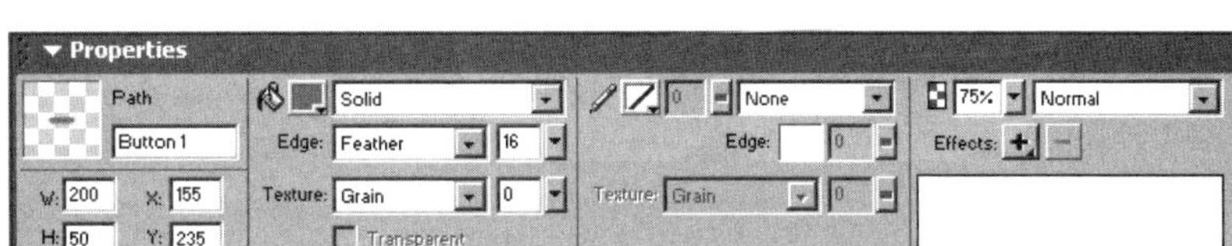

Fig. 7-23. Properties panel settings for the Button 1 object.

·T/P·

Feather adjustments on the fill color work well for both glows and shadows. In the third guided tour of this chapter, feathered edges will also be used to easily create soft-edged effects on photographs.

c) Your gel button and shadow should now look like that shown in figure 7-24.

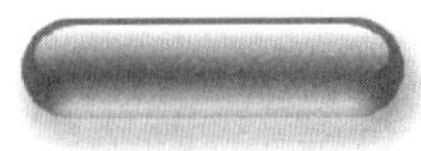

Fig. 7-24. Gel button with shadow.

8. One last detail remains before we wrap it up. We will use the remaining path shape (sublayer) to create a subtle outer glow. This will pop the button off the shadow by creating the illusion of reflected light on the edge of the shadow.
   a) Select the *Button 2* sublayer to display it on the canvas. The Eye icon should be displayed. If it is not, click in the column to the left to display the icon and the sublayer.
   b) With the *Button 2* shape selected, establish the following settings in the Properties panel.
      - *Fill Color:* No Color
      - *Stroke Color:* White
      - *Stroke Size:* 8-pt, 1-Pixel Soft
      - *Stroke Edge:* 100
      - *Opacity:* 50
   c) You should now see a soft glow surrounding the button edge.
9. Save this file in your *SaveWork* folder.

Gradients and feathered effects are terrific tools for creating dimensional effects with shapes on your canvas. In Practice Exercise 7-2 you will be introduced to Live Effects options in the Properties panel that provide even more opportunities for applying interesting effects to your artwork.

Practice Exercise 7-2: Live Effects: Bevels, Embosses, Shadows, and Glows

Description

Now that you can layer shapes to produce effects such as highlights, shadows, and glows, we will explore how you can also create these effects using the Live Effects feature in the Properties panel. The benefits of "live effects" are that they are editable from the Properties panel, can be turned on or off, and can even be saved as custom effects you create yourself. Live effects are also much faster to apply and customize than the manual effects learned in Practice Exercise 7-1. By the end of this exercise you will be able to:

- *Use the Effects menu in the Properties panel*
- *Create a metallic surface texture*
- *Apply a bevel effect*
- *Apply a glow effect*
- *Insert and emboss text*

Preview of Completed Exercise

Before beginning the exercise, let's take a look at the canvas in its completed state so that you can clearly see what it is you are about to build.

1. Use the menu option File | Open and locate the *Chapter 7* folder on the companion CD-ROM. Find the file named *Exercise7_2.png*. Double click on this file to open it.
2. Take a look at the completed layout and make sure to note the content of the Layers panel. Figure 7-25 shows you what the canvas will look like after completing this exercise.

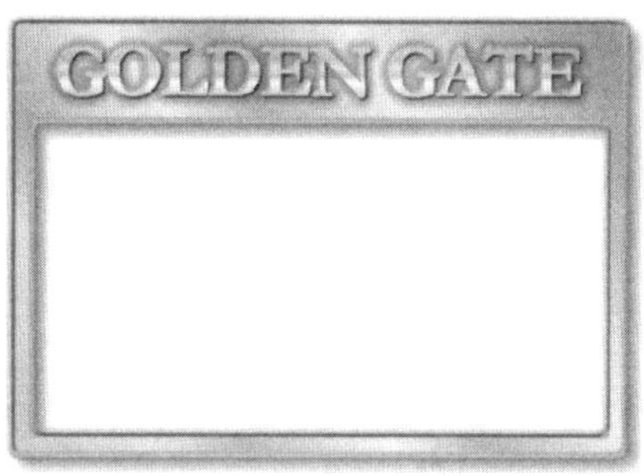

Fig. 7-25. Canvas when the exercise is completed.

Step-by-Step Instructions

1. Select File | New to open a blank file.
   a) Create a 500 x 500 canvas. Leave the Resolution setting at 72, and the Canvas color set to white.
   b) Save the file in the *SaveWork* folder with the name *Exercise7_2(complete).png*.
2. Select the Rectangle tool in the Vector toolbox and draw a rectangle anywhere on the canvas.

3. With the rectangle selected, take a look at the Properties panel. In particular, look at the right-hand side and click on the Plus (+) icon next to the Effects field. Examine the Live Effects options available to you, as shown in figure 7-26.

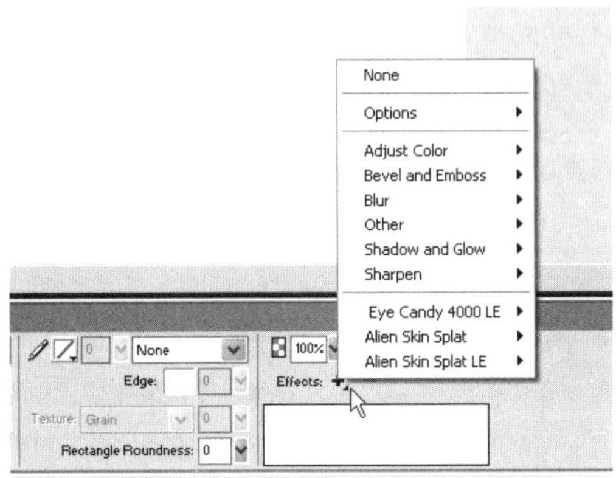

Fig. 7-26. Effects menu in the Properties panel.

4. Each of these Live Effects options applies a custom setting that simulates such effects as beveled edges, shadows, and glows. These effects can be adjusted after their application. In addition, other effects can be added to this menu by downloading effects through the Extensions Manager.
   a) Try a couple of these effects.
   b) Once you are done, delete the rectangle from your canvas.
5. Now let's look more closely at these features and learn how to create a metallic effect.
   a) Select the Rectangle tool and draw a new rectangle on the canvas. With the rectangle still selected, establish the following settings in the Properties panel.
      - *W:* 450
      - *H:* 315
      - *X:* 25
      - *Y:* 48
      - *Fill:* #CCCCCC
      - *Texture:* Crosshatch 1, 10%
      - *Stroke:* #999999
      - *Stroke Width:* 4-Pt, 1-Pixel Soft
      - *Rectangle Roundness:* 4

b) Next, we will apply a gradient to give the appearance of a reflective metal surface. In the Properties panel, set the Fill Category option to Linear, and click on the Fill Color swatch to access the gradient editor.

c) From the preset menu in the middle of the window, select the Silver option and edit the markers to lighten the color. Click on the darkest color marker and replace it with a lighter gray. Add a few other midrange color markers to create a nice blend of grays alternating between lighter and darker. Your gradient may not look like what we have created; take artistic license. See figure 7-27.

TIP

When creating gradients that represent a metallic surface, it is often wise to exclude the darkest and lightest colors so that the gradient does not become overwhelming. This is especially true if designing for an interface.

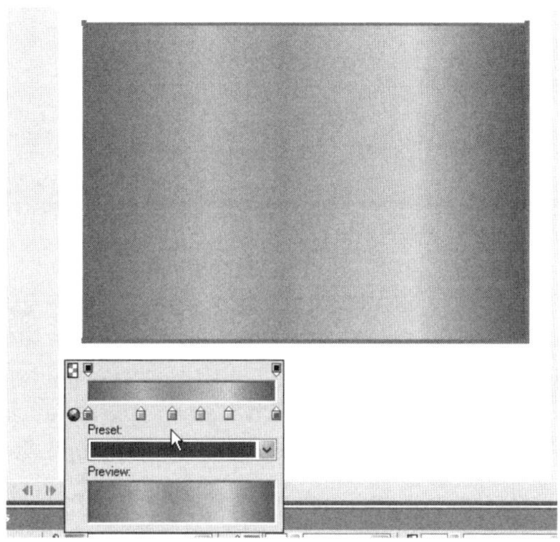

Fig. 7-27. Metallic gradient set in editor.

d) Select the Pointer tool and drag the gradient handles on the canvas to set the angle of the gradient on a diagonal to create a nice visual flow for the reflection, from upper left to lower right, as shown in figure 7-28.

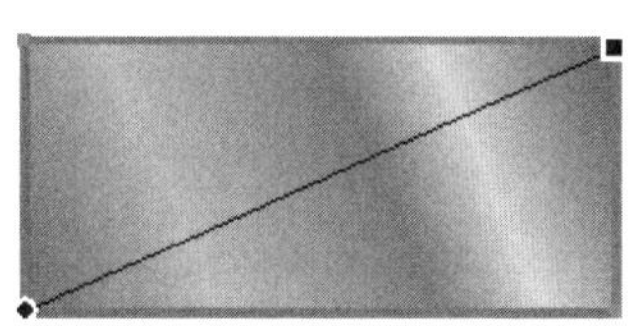

Fig. 7-28. Metallic gradient set at diagonal.

6. Now that we have a usable base shape, we can apply effects to it to make it more 3D. Let's start by adding a color effect called Levels. The Levels effect adjusts the midtones, highlights, and shadows of an image. In this instance, we will use it to lighten or darken the gradient.

a) With the rectangle shape still selected, in the Properties panel click on the Plus (+) icon next to the Effects field and select Adjust Color | Levels. The Levels window, shown in figure 7-29, appears.

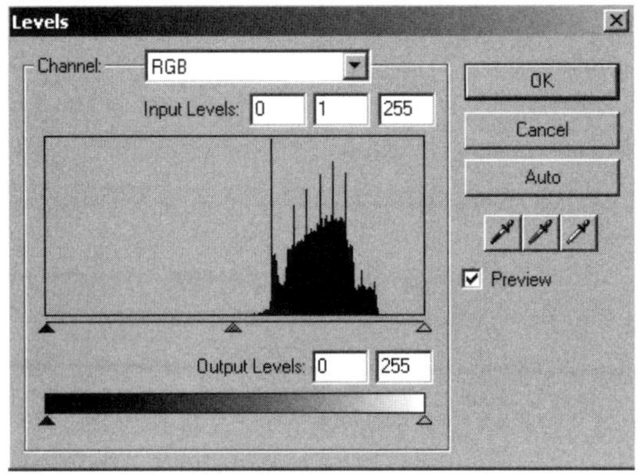

Fig. 7-29. Levels window.

b) The Levels window displays a histogram view of the graphic. Note the three markers below it. Select the marker in the middle and drag it slightly to the left to lighten the midtones in the image.

c) Click on the OK button and note that *Levels* has been added to the Effects list in the Properties panel. See figure 7-30.

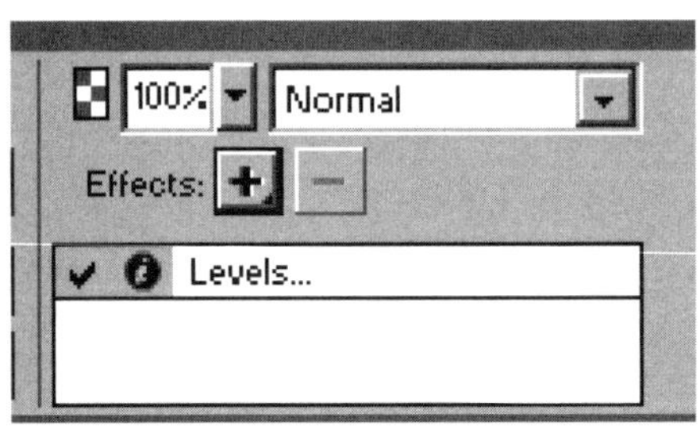

Fig. 7-30.* Levels *in the Effects list.

7. Next, let's apply a Bevel effect.

   a) With the rectangle shape still selected, click on the Plus (+) icon next to the Effects field in the Properties panel, and then select Bevel and Emboss | Inner Bevel. The Inner Bevel settings pop-up window appears above the Effects menu in the Properties panel, as shown in figure 7-31.

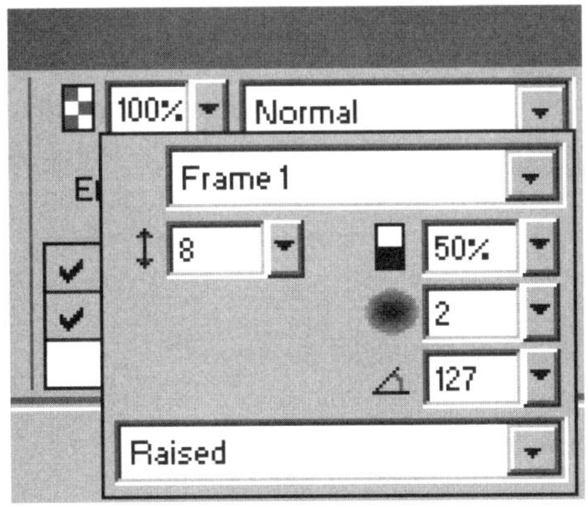

Fig. 7-31. Inner Bevel pop-up window.

b) Establish the following settings in the Inner Bevel pop-up window.

- *Bevel Edge Shape:* Frame 1
- *Width:* 8
- *Contrast:* 50%
- *Softness:* 2
- *Angle:* 127
- *Button Preset:* Raised

c) Click on the canvas to close the window. The bevel as applied should look like that shown in figure 7-32.

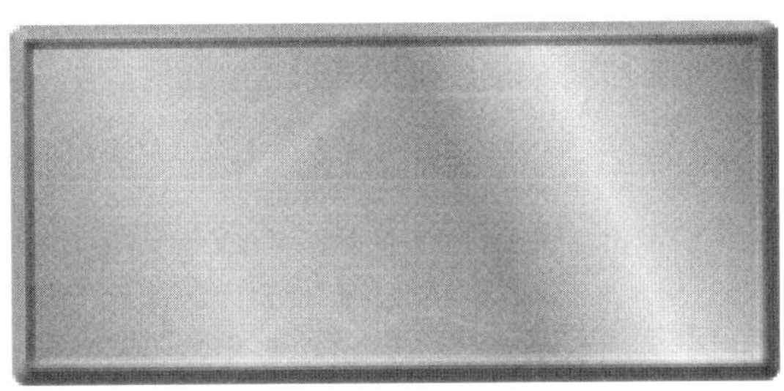

Fig. 7-32. Inner bevel applied to rectangle.

8. Let's refine that bevel edge a bit more by adding a Glow and Inner Glow effect. Note that the order of the effects (in the Effects list) within the Properties panel determines how the effects will blend. By changing the order of effects, you can change the look of an object. We will want these two new effects to appear above the Inner Bevel effect, so we will need to move them in the stacking order after we add them.

a) With the rectangle shape still selected, click on the Plus (+) icon next to the Effects field in the Properties panel and select Shadow and Glow | Glow. The Glow settings pop-up window appears above the Properties panel, just as the Inner Bevel pop-up window did previously. Establish the following settings, as shown in figure 7-33. Click on the canvas to close the window.

- *Color Fill:* #FFFFFF (white)
- *Width:* 2
- *Opacity:* 50
- *Softness:* 3
- *Offset:* 0

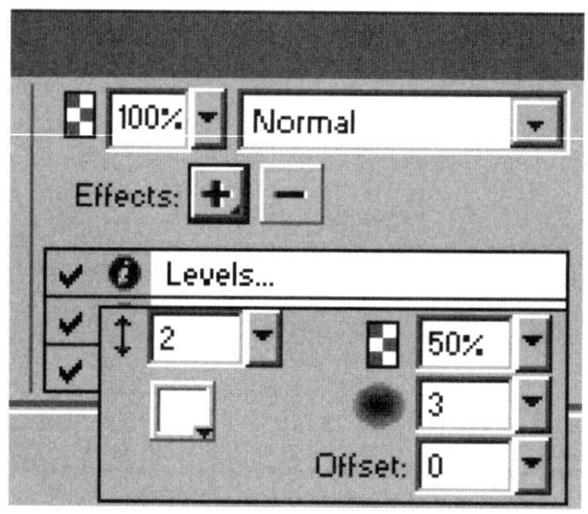

Fig. 7-33. Glow settings.

b) In the Effects list (within the Properties panel), click and drag the Glow effect above the Inner Bevel Effect in the list. Note that the bevel edge softens.

c) Now let's add an inner glow by clicking on the Plus (+) icon next to the Effects field and selecting Shadow and Glow | Inner Glow. The Inner Glow settings pop-up window appears above the Properties panel. Establish the following settings.

- *Color Fill:* #000000 (black)
- *Width:* 4
- *Opacity:* 50
- *Softness:* 4
- *Offset:* 0

d) Drag the Inner Glow effect directly above the Inner Bevel effect in the Effects list (within the Properties panel). Note that the bevel edge becomes more defined. See figure 7-34.

·TIP·

This is just one approach to creating bevels. You might want to experiment with combining this approach with other bevel effects. You can even use multiple instances of the same effect type, such as adding another inner bevel on top the current setup.

Fig. 7-34. Canvas in progress.

9. We will now add a drop shadow to finish the effect.
   a) With the shape still selected, click on the Plus (+) icon next to the Effects field and select Shadow and Glow | Drop Shadow.
   b) The Shadow settings pop-up window appears above the Properties panel. Establish the following settings.
      - *Distance:* 10
      - *Color Fill:* #999999 (gray)
      - *Opacity:* 65
      - *Softness:* 6
      - *Angle:* 315

·TIP·

If you need to adjust any effects applied to an object, simply double click on the name in the Effects listing in the Properties panel.

10. The metal shape looks pretty good at this point. Let's try cutting a panel out of it and see how the effects behave.
    a) Select the Rectangle tool and draw a rectangle on the canvas. Establish the following settings in the Properties panel.
       - *W:* 430
       - *H:* 230
       - *X:* 35
       - *Y:* 120
       - *Fill Category:* Solid

- *Fill Color:* White
- *Stroke:* None
- *Rectangle Roundness:* 4

b) Make sure the new rectangle is above the metal rectangle, and then select Select | Select All to select both rectangles.

c) Select Modify | Combine Paths | Punch.This command causes the top rectangle to punch out, in the metal rectangle, a hole the same size and shape as the the top rectangle. Note that the effects are now applied to the punched-out rectangle. See figure 7-35.

Fig. 7-35. Effects applied to punched-out rectangle.

11. Now let's add some chiseled-looking type.

a) Select the Text tool in the Vector toolbox.

b) Click anywhere on the canvas and type in the text *GOLDEN GATE* in all caps. Select the text box with the Pointer tool and establish the following settings for the text options in the Properties panel.

- *Font:* Garamond (or other serif font)
- *Color:* #999999 (middle gray)
- *Size:* 55
- *Style:* Bold
- *Kerning:* -3

c) Move the text box so that it is centered in the top metal area of the rectangle. See figure 7-36.

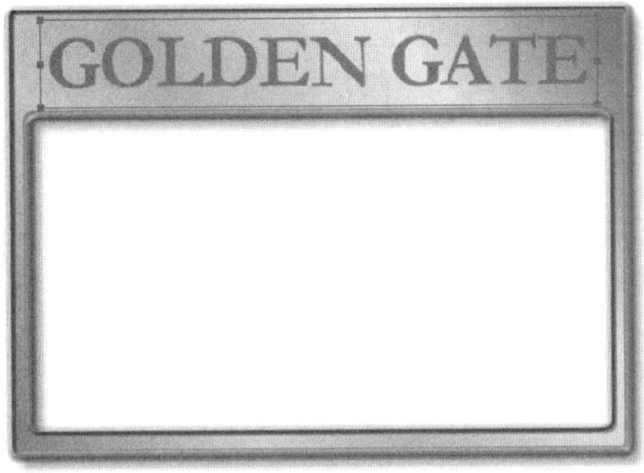

Fig. 7-36. Text centered in top area.

d) Now we will apply effects to get the type to blend with the metal background. With the text still selected, click on the Plus (+) icon next to the Effects field and then select Bevel and Emboss | Inset Emboss.
e) Establish the following settings in the Inset Emboss pop-up window.
   - *Width:* 2
   - *Contrast:* 60%
   - *Softness:* 1
   - *Angle:* 135
f) Click on the canvas to close the window. Now add another effect to the text box by clicking on the Plus (+) icon next to the Effects field and selecting Shadow and Glow | Glow.
g) Establish the following settings in the Glow pop-up window.
   - *Distance:* 2
   - *Color:* #FFFFFF (white)
   - *Opacity:* 25%
   - *Softness:* 4
   - *Offset:* 0
h) Close the Glow window. The letters now have a basic chiseled effect. See figure 7-37.

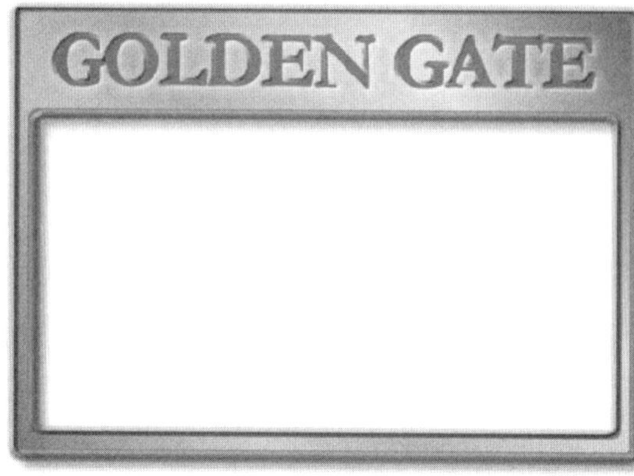

Fig. 7-37. Text with applied effects.

12. With a few more effects, we can make the chiseled text look a little more realistic.
    a) Using the Pointer tool, select the Golden Gate text box.
    b) In the Properties panel, click on the Plus (+) icon next to the Effects field and select Adjust Color | Color Fill from the Effects menu.
    c) Establish the following settings in the Color Fill pop-up window.
        - *Color:* #CCCCCC (light gray)
        - *Blending Mode:* Invert
        - *Opacity:* 100
    d) Close the pop-up window. The Invert mode creates a darker effect over the text and all previously applied effects.
    e) To lighten up the effect, double click on the Glow effect in the list and change the fill color to #CCCCCC.
    f) Your canvas should look similar to that shown in figure 7-38.

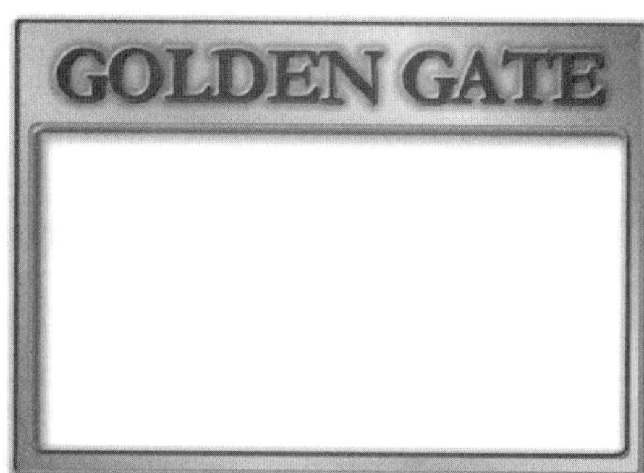

Fig. 7-38. Text in progress.

13. Finally, we will finish the type effect by creating a nice metallic gradient blend.
    a) With the Pointer tool, select the text object and then press the key combination Ctrl + Shift + D (Mac: Cmd + Shift + D) to clone the box. This creates a duplicate of the text.
    b) Select the duplicate of the text in the Layers panel and rename it *Text 2*. It should be the sublayer on top.
    c) With the duplicate type selected, turn off all effects that were copied with it. Click on the Plus (+) icon next to the Effects field and select Options | All Off.
    d) In the Properties panel, click on the text fill color. In the Color palette that appears, click on the Fill Options button at the bottom of the palette. In the Fill Options window, change the fill setting from Solid to Linear and select the Silver gradient preset.
    e) Move the gradient handles on the canvas so that they are vertical and so that the gradient goes from top to bottom within the letters. See figure 7-39.

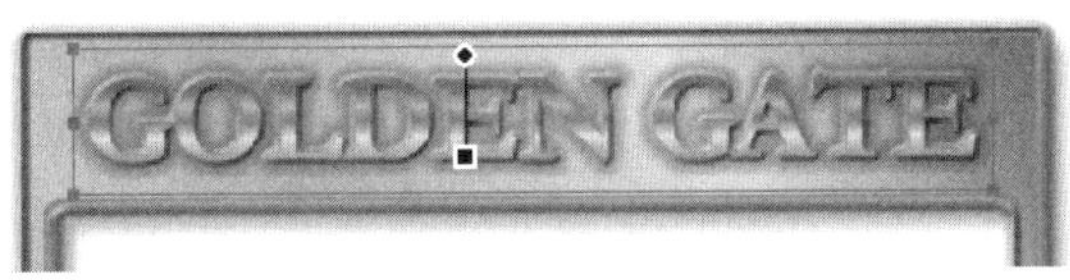

Fig. 7-39. Gradient handles rotated so that they are vertical within the letters.

    f) In the Properties panel, in the Blend Mode field, change the setting from Normal to Screen, as shown in figure 7-40.

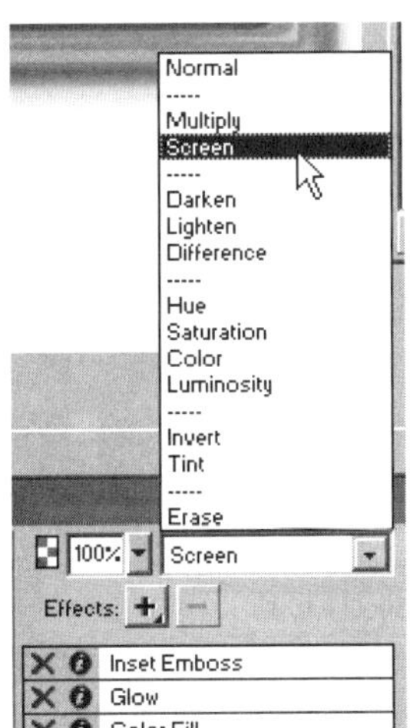

Fig. 7-40. Blend Mode field with Screen option selected.

g) The effect is now complete! Your screen should look similar to that shown in figure 7-41. Save this file in your *SaveWork* folder.

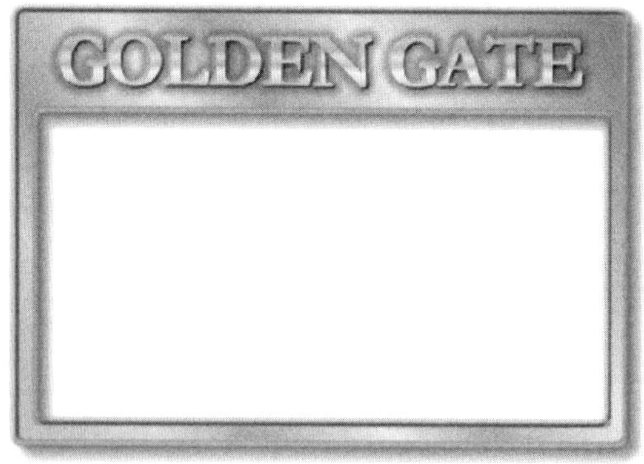

Fig. 7-41. Canvas with completed exercise.

Image Manipulation: Photographic Images

Color Effects

Color effects range from image touch-ups (such as lightening image colors, adding more color saturation, and removing scratches) to completely changing image color into grayscales or duotones. Because we will experiment with only a handful of color effects in this chapter, Table 7-1 outlines all Fireworks color correction options available from the Filters menu or Effects menu in the Properties panel.

Effect Name	Description
Auto Levels	Automatically adjusts the highlights, midtones, and shadow ranges of an image.
Brightness/Contrast	Adjusts the brightness and contrast of an image.
Curves	Allows you to adjust the level of a color within an image without adjusting the other colors. Can be used subtly, or for more intense effects (such as posterization).
Hue/Saturation	Adjusts the color in an image and the amount of saturation of that color. Can be used to create tints and colorized images.
Invert	Changes each pixel in an image to its exact opposite color.
Levels	Adjusts the tonal range (highlights, midtones, shadows) of an image. Used to lighten and darken an image.
Blur	Blurs pixels together for a softer effect. Often used to cover up imperfections or soften the focus of an image.
Blur More	Same as Blur but affects a wider range of pixels.
Gaussian Blur	Allows you to specify the amount of blur.
Sharpen	Sharpens the focus in an image by creating greater contrast between pixels. Used to create a crisper image.
Sharpen More	Same as Sharpen but affects a wider range of pixels.
Unsharp Mask	Allows for more control over which pixels are sharpened by adjusting the image in a grayscale mask.

Table 7-1: Fireworks MX Color Correction Options

Blending Effects

Blending effects are usually achieved with blend modes, masks, and opacity controls. Blending is simply a way of getting multiple images to blend into one effect. Much like the process in the earlier chapters, we will use graphics on multiple layers to render blending effects.

In Practice Exercise 7-3 we are going to shift gears a bit. Instead of rendering effects on graphics we created, we are going to work with imported photos and practice using color and blending effects to manipulate photographic images.

Practice Exercise 7-3: Photographic Effects: Color Effects and Blending

Description

This practice exercise involves applying two types of photographic effects: color effects and image blending effects. By the end of this practice exercise you will be able to:

- *Apply filters such as brightness/contrast and hue/saturation*
- *Make selections with the Lasso tool*
- *Apply masks*

Preview of Completed Exercise

Before beginning the exercise, let's take a look at the canvas in its completed state so that you can clearly see what it is you are about to build.

1. Use the menu option File | Open and locate the *Chapter 7* folder on the companion CD-ROM. Find the file named *Exercise7_3(complete).png*. Double click on this file to open it.
2. Take a look at the completed layout and make sure to note the content of the Layers panel. Figure 7-42 shows you what the canvas will look like after completing this exercise.

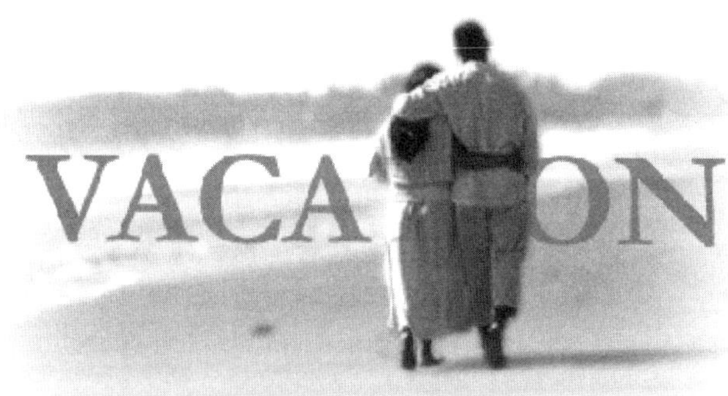

Fig. 7-42. Canvas upon completion of the exercise.

Step-by-Step Instructions

First, let's explore both color correction and image blending by creating a photographic illustration. We will use one photo, but will make edits across multiple layers.

1. Select File | New to open a blank file.
   a) Create a 500 x 500 canvas. Leave the Resolution setting at 72, and the Canvas color set to white.
   b) Save the file into the *SaveWork* folder with the name *Exercise7_3.png*.
2. Let's import the image we will be working with.
   a) Select File | Import and browse in the *Chapter 7* folder on the companion CD-ROM. Select the *walking.png* image from the *Chapter 7* folder.
   b) Click on Open and click the cursor on the canvas to place the image of a couple walking along a beach roughly in the center of the canvas. Our goal will be to create an image in which the background is out of focus, with the image of the couple sharpened. We will also incorporate some text in the effect.
3. To adjust the color range of the imported image, we will use the Brightness and Contrast filter to add more contrast to the image, particularly the people.
   a) Using the Pointer tool, select the imported bitmap, and then select Filters | Adjust Color | Brightness and Contrast. In the window that opens, set the Contrast slider to a value of 15, and the Brightness slider to a value of 0. See figure 7-43.

TIP: We will use the Filters menu and the Color Effects menu from the Properties panel to adjust this image. Note that both menus have the same set of controls. The difference is that the Filters menu applies nonadjustable color corrections, whereas the Color Effects menu adds editable live effects that can be changed or removed at any time.

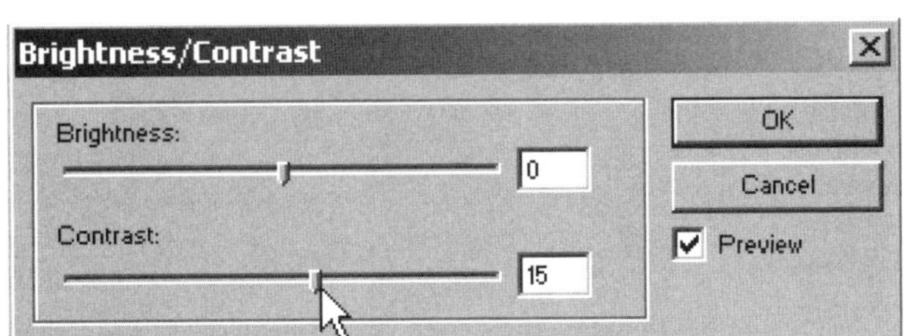

Fig. 7-43. Brightness and Contrast slider settings.

   b) Click on the OK button. The image now has a slightly higher contrast.

TIP: If Preview is selected, you should see the image update on the canvas.

4. Next, create the separation between the background and the people so that we can perform the focus effect. We will do this by cloning the photo, adding a mask over the area of the image of the couple to protect it. This will then allow us to blur the rest of the image without affecting the couple.

a) Using the Pointer tool, select the photo and clone it to create a duplicate. Use the keyboard command Ctrl + Shift + D (Mac: Cmd + Shift + D) to clone the image.

b) Select the Polygon Lasso tool in the Bitmap toolbox, shown in figure 7-44.

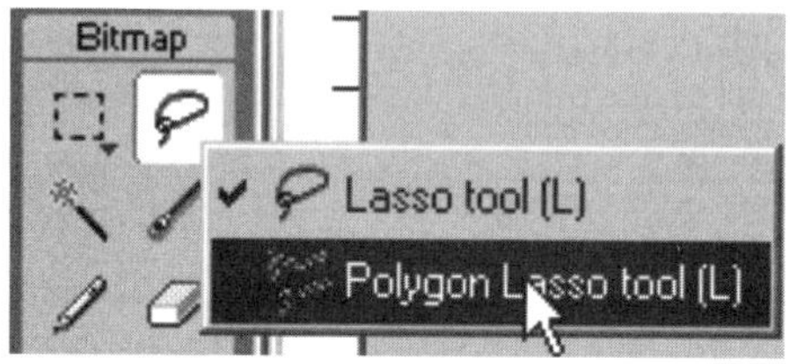

Fig. 7-44. Polygon Lasso tool in the Bitmap toolbox.

c) With the Polygon Lasso tool, click around the people on the canvas until you have drawn a selection that completely surrounds them. Get as close to the edge as possible, but do not worry about being too precise. You can use the Zoom tool to get closer to the image to see in better detail.

d) Once you have finished drawing the selection, make sure to click on the first anchor point you created when you started drawing the selection, in order to close the selection. A crawling marquee will appear around the couple when it is closed. See figure 7-45.

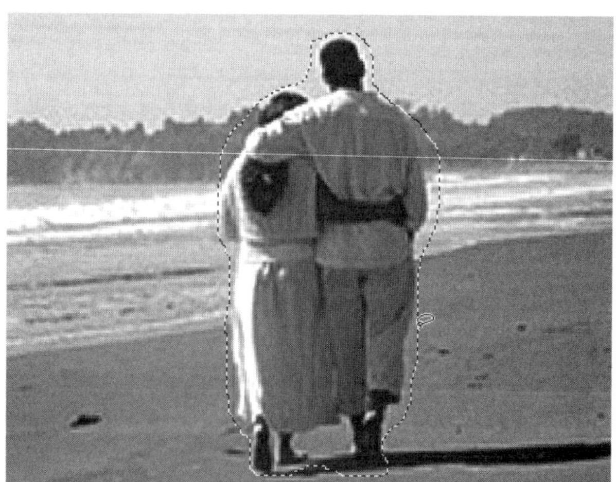

Fig. 7-45. Polygon Lasso tool outlining the magnified view of the couple.

Shortcut

You can use the regular Lasso tool like the Polygon Lasso if you hold down the Alt (Mac: Option) button on the keyboard. This allows you to draw a selection in either free-form or point-by-point mode.

e) Select Select | Feather and in the pop-up window that opens type *4* (pixels) as the Feather amount. This will ensure that there are no hard edges in the mask you are about to create. Click on the OK button to close the window.

f) Select Modify | Mask | Reveal Selection. A mask icon appears in the Layer panel, next to the new *Bitmap* sublayer. See figure 7-46.

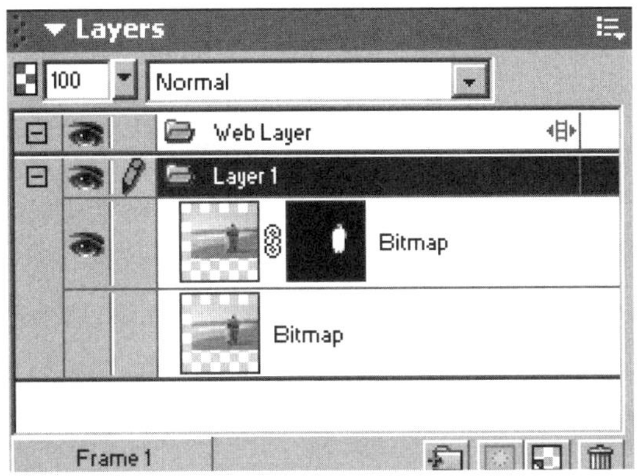

Fig. 7-46. Mask icon in the Layers panel.

g) We can see the mask by hiding the bottom image in the Layers panel. Select the bottom Bitmap sublayer (the one without the mask icon) and then click on the Eye icon to hide this sublayer. You now should see the effect of the mask. Only the couple is visible. See figure 7-47.

Shortcut

You can use the Quick Mask icon on the bottom of the Layer panel to achieve the same effect as Reveal Selection.

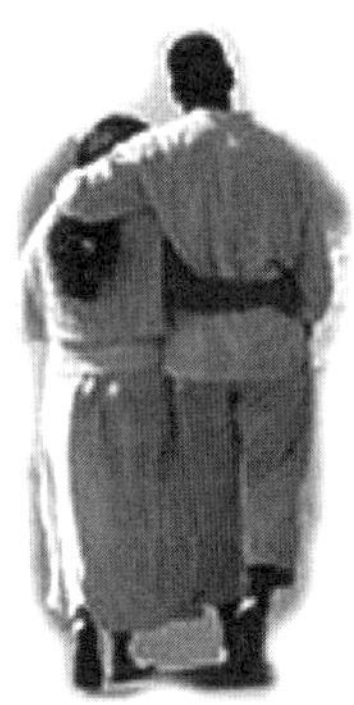

Fig. 7-47. Mask sublayer displayed on canvas.

·TIP·

You can remove a mask from an object by selecting the Mask icon in the layer stack and dragging it to the Trash Can icon at the bottom of the Layers panel.

CAUTION

Applying masks this way only works with bitmap images. Later we will look at other ways to mask vectors.

5. Next, let's add the blur effect to the bottom image to adjust the focus.
   a) Reveal the *Bitmap* sublayer (without the mask) by clicking in the column to reveal the Eye icon and the image on the canvas.
   b) This time, we will use a color effect instead of a filter. This way, we can make adjustments on the effect later, once all of the pieces are in place.
   c) With the Pointer tool, select the full image on the canvas. In the Properties panel, click on the Plus (+) icon next to the Effects field and then select Blur | Gaussian Blur. Gaussian Blur allows you to adjust the amount of blurring added to the image. In the window that appears, move the slider to 2. Click on the OK button. The background image is now blurred, but the masked area is still in focus. See figure 7-48.

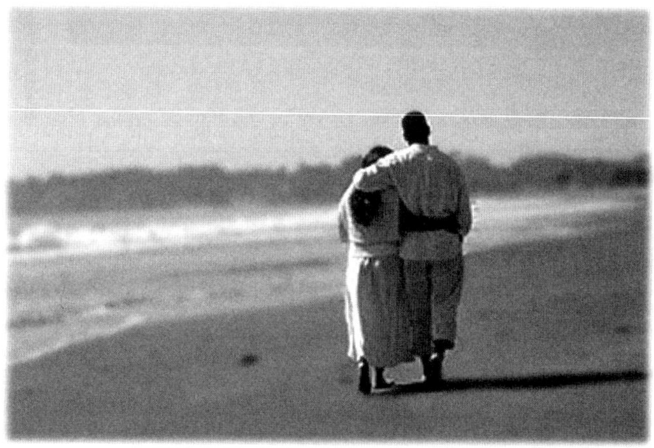

Fig. 7-48. Couple in the* Mask *sublayer is sharply focused, whereas the background has been blurred.

   d) Let's also add a Levels effect to lighten the background bitmap. Click on the Plus (+) icon next to the Effects field and then select Adjust Color | Levels.
   e) In the Levels window that appears, move the midtone slider (the one in the middle) to the left until the midtone value reads about 1.45. Move the highlight slider (the one on the right) until it reads about 220. (See figure 7-49.) Click on the OK button to close the window.

·T/P·

Using the editable color effects from the Properties panel allows you to make adjustments later as the illustration evolves. For example, you may want to adjust the blur or the lightness in the levels. With Properties panel effects, these settings can be adjusted by double clicking on the effect, whereas the first contrast setting cannot be adjusted.

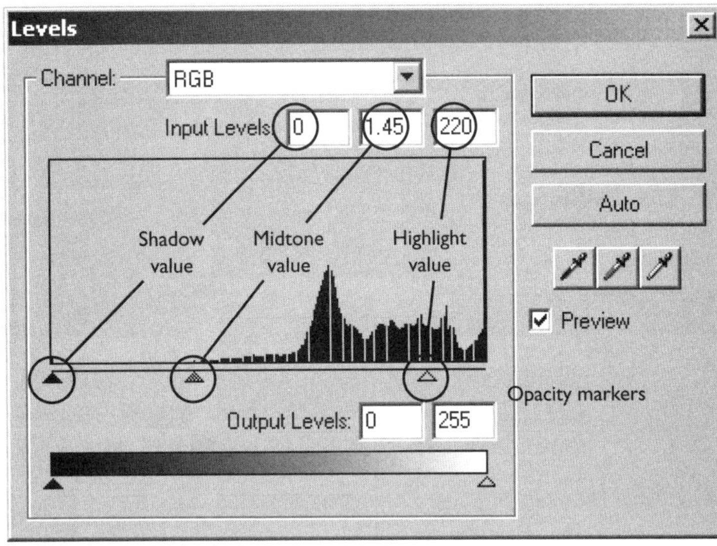

Fig. 7-49. Adjusted values within the Levels window.

·T/P·

When creating shapes to be used as a mask, as for this rectangle, make sure the fill color is white. Fireworks will interpret a white color as a visible area and a black color as a nonvisible area.

6. We will use a different masking method to fade the edges of the blurred bitmap.
   a) Select the Rectangle tool and draw a rectangle roughly 330 by 200 pixels. Turn off the stroke color and make sure the Fill Color is set to white. Set Fill Edge to Feather and Feather Size to 60 in the Properties panel.
   b) Position the rectangle roughly in the center of the blurred bitmap.
   c) Select both the rectangle and the blurred bitmap, and then select Modify | Mask | Group as Mask.
   d) You should see a Mask icon appear in the sublayer stack next to the bitmap, and the edges of the blurred image should now be faded, as shown in figure 7-50. If the rectangle was not lined up correctly, select Edit | Undo and reapply the effect.

·TIP·

This second masking effect we have used will work on vectors as well as bitmaps.

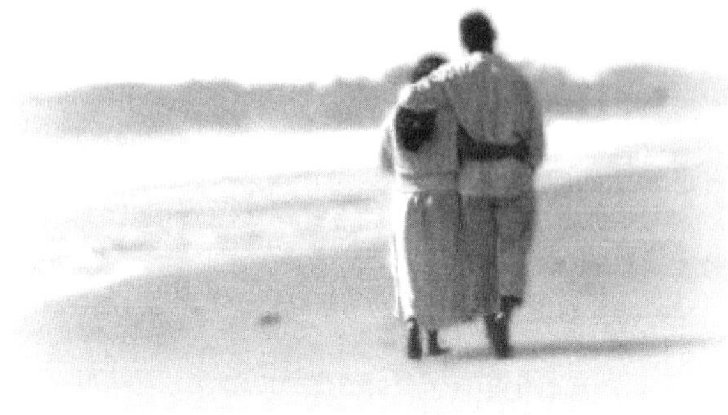

Fig. 7-50. Mask applied to feathered edges of the photo.

7. Next, let's add some text to complete the effect. We will add the word *VACATION* between the two bitmap layers.
   a) Select the Text tool from the Vector toolbox. Click on the canvas and type the word *VACATION* in all caps. Using the Pointer tool, select the text object, and then establish the following settings in the Properties panel.
      - *Font:* Garamond (or other serif font)
      - *Style:* Bold
      - *Size:* 72
      - *Kerning:* -2
      - *Color:* #999999 (light gray)
      - *Opacity:* 75%
   b) Position the text so that it sits roughly in the center of the blurred bitmap.
   c) Move the *Text* sublayer to between the two bitmaps in the layer stack. Your finished canvas should now look similar to that shown in figure 7-51. Save this file.

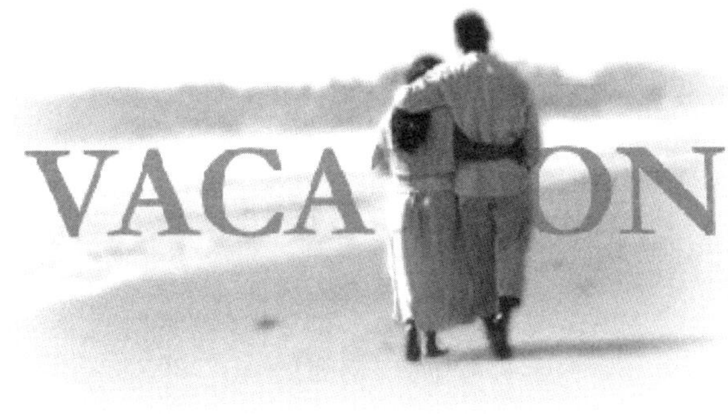

Fig. 7-51. Finished canvas.

As you just saw, moving the *Text* sublayer between the two bitmap layers creates a blending effect that draws the viewer into the image. This is just one example of interesting text effects that can be achieved using layers. In Practice Exercise 7-4 you will work exclusively with text effects to create an interesting design using text.

Practice Exercise 7-4: Text Effects: Designing with Text

Description

Using text in Fireworks is very different from typing text in a word processing program. In Fireworks, text can become an important part of your graphic design and can be manipulated in a manner similar to bitmaps and other vector graphics. Fireworks MX also has built-in tools that allow you to run text along a path, as well as to mask images and textures for special text fills.

In this exercise, we will look closely at some of the less obvious (but creative) tricks in working with text. We will explore working with text along a path, detaching text to create regular paths, and working with text across multiple layers for enhanced effects.

Preview of Completed Exercise

Before beginning the exercise, let's take a look at the canvas in its completed state so that you can clearly see what it is you are about to build.

1. Use the menu option File | Open and locate the *Chapter 7* folder on the companion CD-ROM. Find the file named *Exercise7_4(complete).png*. Double click on this file to open it.
2. Take a look at the completed layout and make sure to note the content of the Layers panel. Figure 7-52 shows you what the canvas will look like after completing this exercise.

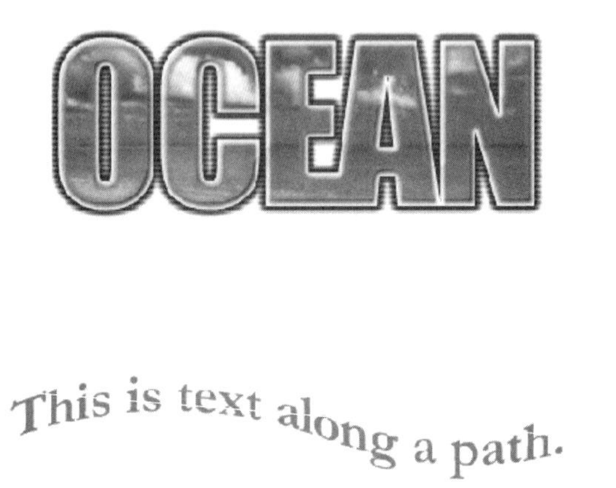

Fig. 7-52. Completed canvas.

Step-by-Step Instructions

1. Select File | New to open a blank file.
   a) Create a 500 x 500 canvas. Leave the Resolution setting at 72 and the Canvas color set to white.
   b) Save the file into the *SaveWork* folder with the name *Exercise7_4.png*.
2. Let's create the text and the path to use for the experiment.
   a) Select the Text tool and type *This is text along a path.* (including the period) on the canvas. Select the text object and establish the following settings in the Properties panel.
      - *Font:* Garamond (or other font of your choice)
      - *Size:* 40
      - *Style:* Bold
      - *Color:* #666666 (medium gray)
   b) Next, select the Pen tool and add three points: one on the left edge of the canvas, one in the middle, and one on the right edge. Hold down the Shift key as you do this, to constrain to a horizontal line.

c) With the Pen tool, click and drag on the middle point to pull out the bezier handles and curve the line. Drag the handles out until you have a nice smooth curve, as shown in figure 7-53.

TIP

We are using a simple curve for our path, but you could use a circle or any other shape as a path.

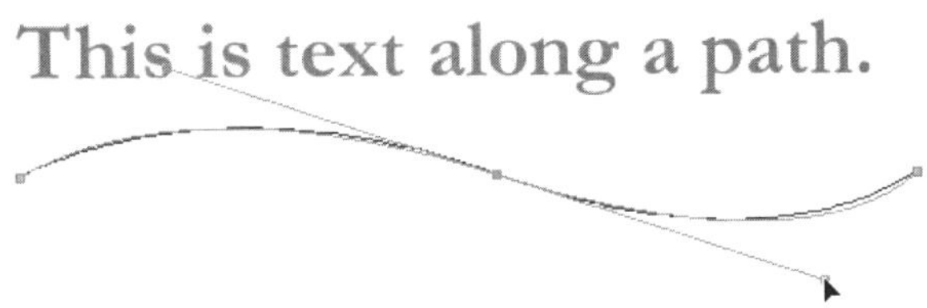

Fig. 7-53. Curved path created with the Pen tool.

3. Now we will attach the text to the curved path.
   a) Select both the text and the line path by holding down the Shift key and clicking on both objects with the Pointer tool.
   b) Select Text | Attach to Path. The text has now been attached to the curved line, as shown in figure 7-54.

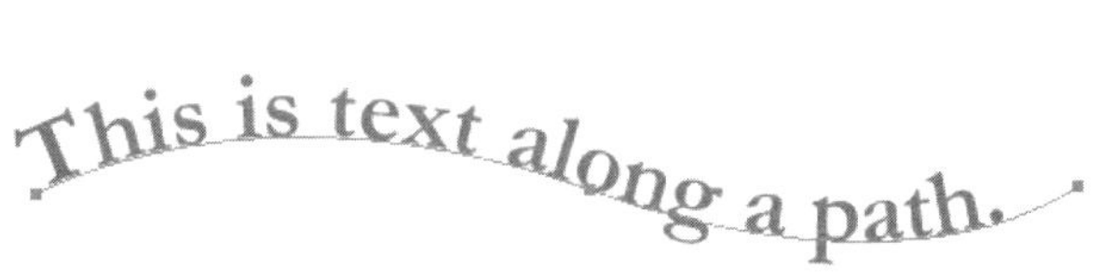

Fig. 7-54. Text attached to the path.

TIP

The Orientation commands for text allow you to correctly position text along curved or odd-shaped paths.

4. There are several ways to edit text attached to a path.
   a) To change the way the letters rest on the path, select Text | Orientation | Skew Vertical. Note that the orientation of the text has changed slightly to appear vertical.
   b) Select Text | Reverse Direction to see the text switch direction along the path, as shown in figure 7-55. This is a great command to use when using circle paths.

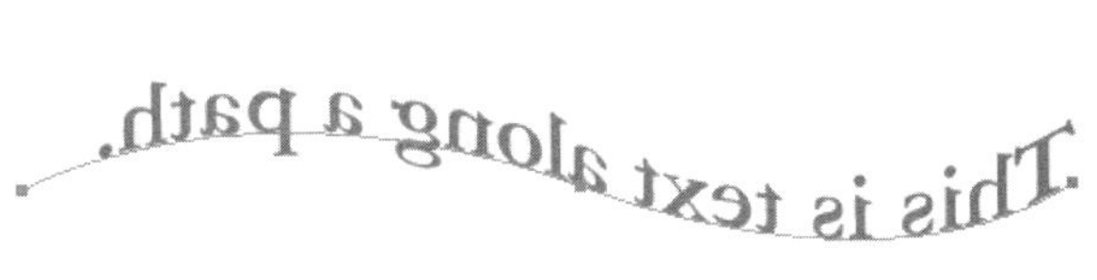

Fig. 7-55. Text reversed along a path.

   c) To detach the text from the path, select Text | Detach from Path. This returns the two objects to their original separate positions.

·TIP·

You can change the size, color, spelling, font, and alignment of text (and edit text in other typical ways) while it is attached to the path.

d) Delete both the text and the line path. We will now work on a different text effect. You should now have an empty canvas.

5. A more complex text effect is to use text as a mask in order to create a custom fill effect. Next, we are going to use the word *OCEAN* as a mask and import an ocean photo to use as the fill for the text. Start by importing the ocean image.

6. Select File | Import and browse for the *Chapter 7* folder on the companion CD-ROM. Select the *ocean.png* image and click on Open.

7. Click the cursor on the canvas to place the image roughly in the center of the screen.

8. Now, add the text that will become the basis for the effect.

   a) Select the Text tool and click anywhere on the canvas. Type the word *OCEAN* in all caps. Using the Pointer tool, select the text object, and then establish the following settings in the Properties panel.

      - *Font:* Impact
      - *Size:* 150 (You will need to type in this number, because the slider does not go this high.)
      - *Style:* Bold
      - *Color:* #FFFFFF (white)
      - *Kerning:* -4

   b) Position the text so that it sits on top of the ocean photo. See figure 7-56.

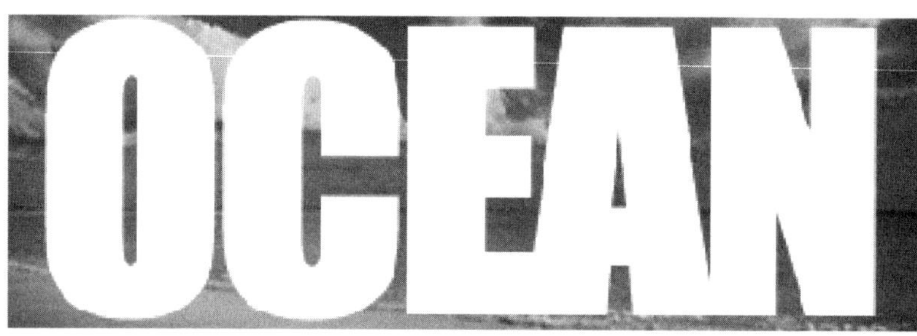

Fig. 7-56. White text on top of the ocean bitmap.

Shortcut

The keyboard command for Convert to Paths is:

PC: Ctrl + Shift + P
Mac: Cmd + Shift + P

CAUTION

Converting text to paths is often a nice thing to be able to do when creating text effects. However, be aware that you can no longer edit the text after you do this. It is a good idea to create a backup copy of the text before you convert it.

9. Next, we are going to convert the text object to vector paths so that we can manipulate the letters not as text but as graphics. Once converted to paths, the letters can no longer be edited as text.
   a) With the Pointer tool, select the *OCEAN* text object and then select Text | Convert to Paths.
   b) Note that in the Layers panel, the *Text* sublayer has now been renamed *Group: 5 Objects*. This means that the word *OCEAN* is a group consisting of five different paths—one for each letter. Let's make them one combined path.
   c) Ungroup the word *OCEAN* by selecting Modify | Ungroup. Each letter is now an independent path. Note the change in the sublayers in the Layers panel.
   d) Select all letters, and then select Modify | Combine Paths | Union. The letters are now combined to form one composite path. Now we can treat the letters as one object. This is different from grouping the letters because groups consist of multiple objects.
   e) Clone the new composite path by selecting Edit | Clone. This creates a copy of the *OCEAN* path. Rename the cloned sublayer *Ocean 2*. (It should be the topmost sublayer.) Hide the *Ocean 2* sublayer in the Layers panel.
10. Now let's create a mask using the text *OCEAN*.
   a) Select the text *OCEAN* (*Composite Path* sublayer) and the ocean image (*Bitmap* sublayer) by holding down the Shift key and clicking on both objects.
   b) Select Modify | Mask | Group as Mask.
   c) The text has masked the ocean image so that only the parts of the image covered by the "text" appear. The text appears to be filled by the ocean photograph, as shown in figure 7-57.

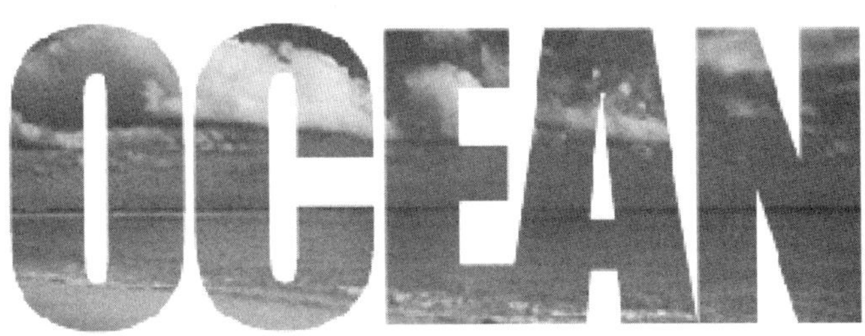

Fig. 7-57. Ocean text masking the ocean photo.

11. We will use the cloned text to add some stroke effects to the text mask. We have to do this on a separate layer, because the text mask is

actually the bitmap image with a mask over it, and the bitmap layer has no stroke properties.

a) Show the *Ocean 2* sublayer by clicking on it in the layer stack. Both the Eye icon and the outline of the image should now appear.

b) Establish the following settings in the Properties panel.

- *Fill:* None
- *Stroke Color:* #003366
- *Stroke Size:* 6, Soft Rounded
- *Edge:* 100%
- *Stroke Texture:* Line-Horiz3
- *Texture Amount:* 50%

12. Let's add one more stroke, for more contrast.

a) Select the *Ocean 2* sublayer and then select Edit | Clone.

b) Select the new cloned layer (top layer) and rename it *Ocean 3*.

c) In the Properties panel, establish the following *Ocean 3* settings.

- *Stroke Color:* #FFFFFF (white)
- *Stroke Size:* 4, Soft Rounded
- *Edge:* 100%
- *Stroke Texture:* Line-Horiz3
- *Texture Amount:* 0%

d) This creates a white stroke. However, note that at this point the white stroke covers the blue stroke. Let's make an adjustment to the path.

e) In the Properties panel, select Stroke Category | Stroke Options, as shown in figure 7-58.

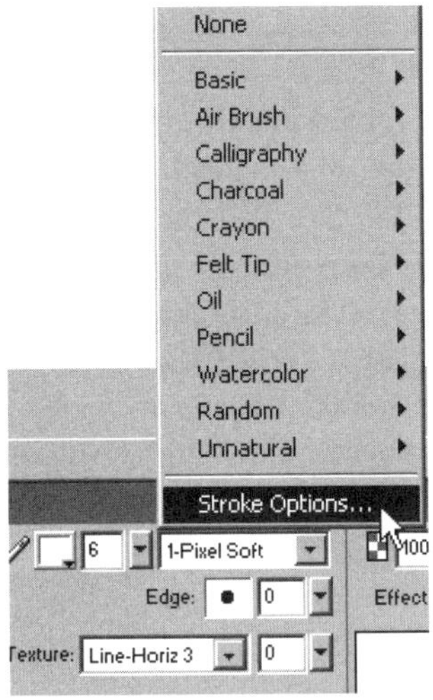

Fig. 7-58. Stroke Category menu with Stroke Options highlighted.

f) In the Stroke Options pop-up window, change the stroke orientation from Outside Path to Inside Path. (See figure 7-59.) Click on the canvas to close the window.

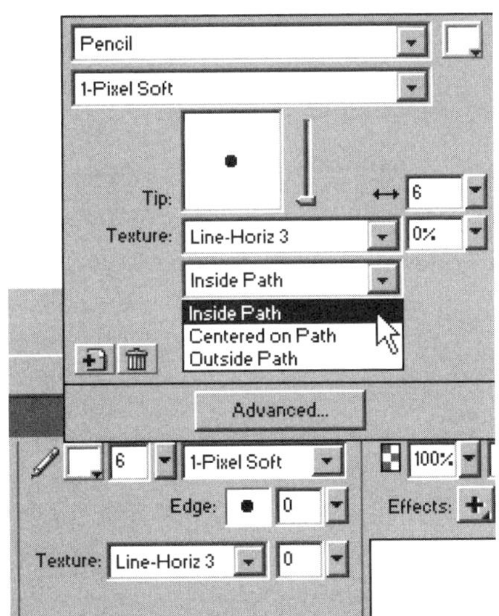

Fig. 7-59. Inside Path in the Stroke Options window.

g) Note that the white stroke now sits inside the path and thus part of the blue stroke underneath is revealed.

13. We are almost finished with the ocean graphic, but let's add some other effects to the ocean bitmap to make it a little more interesting.
    a) Select the ocean bitmap sublayer and then click on the Plus (+) icon next to the Effects field. In the menu that opens, select Blur | Gaussian Blur. Set Blur Radius to 0.8
    b) With the ocean bitmap still selected, click on the Plus (+) icon next to the Effects field, and then select Adjust Color | Brightness and Contrast. Set Contrast to 20. Click on the OK button to close the window.
    c) Click on the Plus (+) icon next to the Effects field and in the menu that opens, select Shadow and Glow | Inner Glow. Establish the following settings.
        - *Width:* 9
        - *Color:* #00CCFF
        - *Opacity:* 65%
        - *Softness:* 3
    d) Click on the Plus (+) icon next to the Effects field and in the menu that opens, select Bevel and Emboss | Inner Bevel. Establish the following property settings.
        - *Bevel Edge Shape:* Flat
        - *Width:* 7
        - *Contrast:* 60%
        - *Softness:* 5
    e) Your graphic should now look similar to that shown in figure 7-60. Note that the effects we just applied adhere to the shape of the mask within the bitmap.

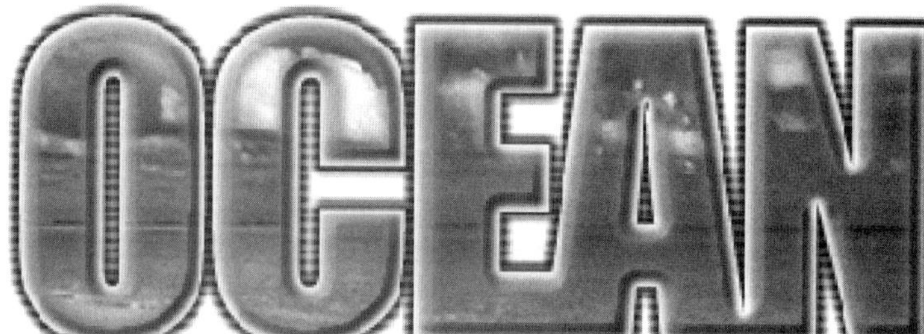

Fig. 7-60. Completed ocean graphic.

Now that you have learned how to work with text, masking, and many Fireworks MX special effects, we will turn back to the San Francisco Travel Guide web site. In Practice Exercise 7-5 you will apply some of these techniques to create an illustration for the home page of the web site.

Practice Exercise 7-5: Creating a Composite Illustration for the Home Page

Description

In this exercise, we will apply some of the techniques we have learned in the last few exercises to create an illustration for the home page of the San Francisco Travel Guide web site. The illustration will consist of blended images and a mixture of special effects.

Preview of Completed Exercise

Before beginning the exercise, let's take a look at the canvas in its completed state so that you can clearly see what it is you are about to build.

1. Use the menu option File | Open and locate the *Chapter 7* folder on the companion CD-ROM. Find the file named *Exercise7_5(complete).png*. Double click on this file to open it.
2. Take a look at the completed layout and make sure to note the content of the Layers panel. Figure 7-61 shows you what the canvas will look like after completing this exercise.

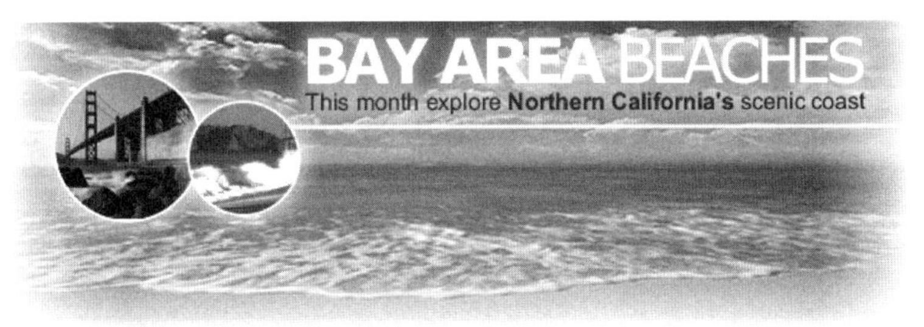

Fig. 7-61. Completed canvas.

Step-by-Step Instructions

1. Use the menu option File | New and create a file with a 660- x 250-pixel canvas. Set the Background color option to White, and leave the

Resolution setting at 72. Save the file into the *SaveWork* folder with the name of *Exercise7_5.png*.

2. Let's now create a background color we can use for blending and texture effects.
   a) In the Layer panel, double click on *Layer 1* and rename it *Background*.
   b) Select the Rectangle tool from the Vector toolbox, and draw a rectangle on the canvas. Establish the following settings in the Properties panel.
      - *W:* 640
      - *H:* 200
      - *X:* 10
      - *Y:* 10
      - *Fill Color:* #CCCCFF
      - *Stroke Color:* None
   c) A light blue/purple rectangle now covers most of the canvas.
3. Now let's import a cloud image and blend it into the background with a mask.
   a) Select File | Import and browse in the *Chapter 7* folder. Select the *clouds.png* file and click on Open.
   b) Click the cursor to place the image at the top left of the rectangle, and then establish the following settings in the Properties panel.
      - *W:* 640
      - *H:* 105
      - *X:* 10
      - *Y:* 10
   c) The clouds now stretch over the top part of the rectangle, as shown in figure 7-62.
   d) Rename the new *Bitmap* sublayer *Clouds*.

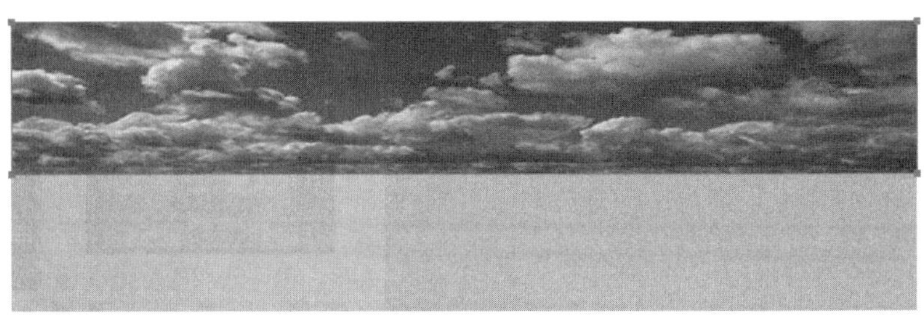

Fig. 7-62. Cloud image placed on the rectangle.

e) Select the Rectangle tool and draw a rectangle over the clouds image so that the rectangle is slightly larger than the clouds. Deselect the rectangle.

f) Select the Gradient tool in the Bitmap toolbox. See figure 7-63.

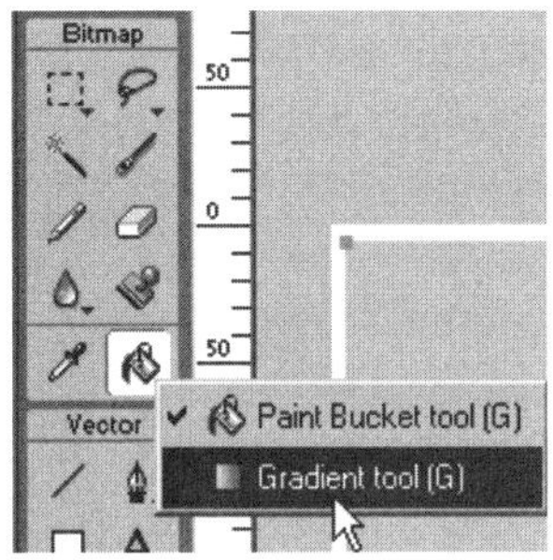

Fig. 7-63. Gradient tool in the Bitmap toolbox.

g) With the new rectangle still selected, in the Properties panel, click on the Fill swatch. Select Black, White from the preset gradient list. Close the window.

h) Using the Gradient tool, click and drag the bottom of the recently drawn rectangle. Drag upward until about 1/4 of the way from the top and then release. (If you hold the Shift key down as you drag, you will get a straight line for the gradient.)

i) The rectangle will fill with the black-to-white gradient, with the white at the top, as shown in figure 7-64. In a mask effect, white marks the visible area. This will be important in the next step.

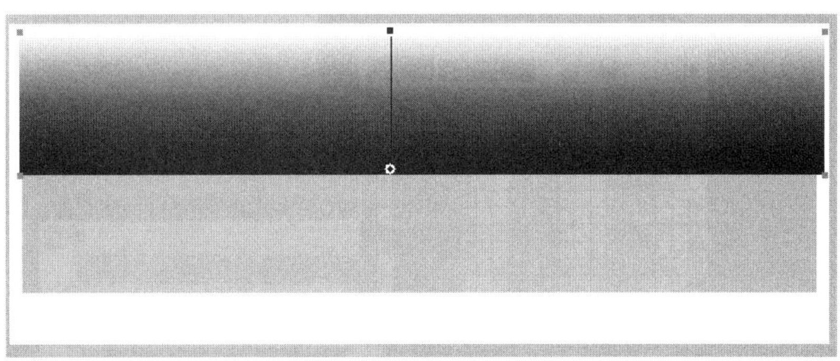

Fig. 7-64. Gradient fill applied to the rectangle.

j) Select the Pointer tool and in the Layers panel select the *Clouds* sublayer and the rectangle you just drew by holding down the Shift key and clicking on each sublayer.

k) Select Modify | Mask | Group as Mask. You should see that the clouds have been masked and blended into the light blue/purple background, as shown in figure 7-65. Note that the pure white part of the gradient completely shows the image when applied as a mask, and the pure black part of the gradient completely hides the image when applied as a mask. As the gradient fades from white to black, the corresponding cloud image fades to transparent.

Fig. 7-65. Cloud masking.

l) To finish the clouds, a few color effects will refine the image. With the *Cloud* bitmap selected, in the Properties panel click on the Plus (+) icon next to the Effects field, and then select Adjust Color | Hue and Saturation. Establish the following settings.

- *Hue:* 0
- *Saturation:* 44
- *Lightness:* 0

m) Click on the OK button to close the window. In the Properties panel, click on the Plus (+) icon next to the Effects field and then select Sharpen | Sharpen to apply focus to the pixels within the cloud image.

4. Now let's import the seashore image and blend it with a mask.

a) Select File | Import and browse in the *Chapter 7* folder on the companion CD-ROM. Double click on the *seashore.png* image to import it.

b) Click the cursor on the canvas to place the *seashore.png* image in the middle-left of the rectangle. Rename this sublayer *Seashore*. Establish the following settings in the Properties panel.

- *W:* 640
- *H:* 150
- *X:* 10
- *Y:* 88

c) You should now see the seashore image stretch to match the width of the other objects on the canvas. Photo magic! Using photo elements, you have just created a photo that looks realistic. (See figure 7-66.) However, we are not done yet.

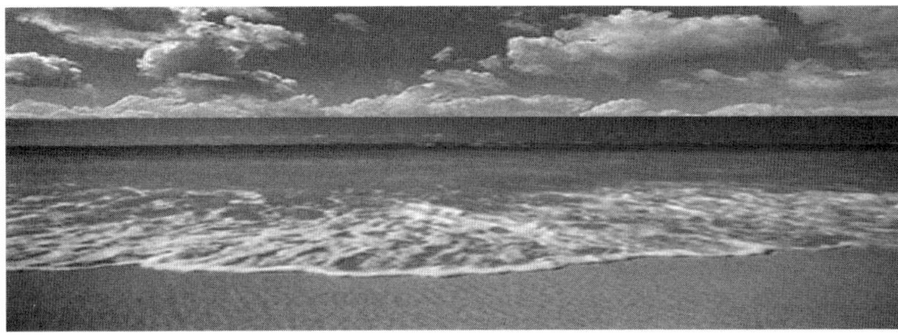

Fig. 7-66. Photo elements combined to create a new image.

d) Select the Marquee tool in the Bitmap toolbox. In the Properties panel, make sure Edge is set to Anti-Alias. In the Layer panel, make sure the *Seashore* sublayer (bitmap) is still selected.

e) Using the Marquee tool, draw a selection around the *Seashore* bitmap. Start the selection just above the dark horizon line in the image and end the selection just above the bottom of the canvas. Make sure to include the entire width of the bitmap. See figure 7-67.

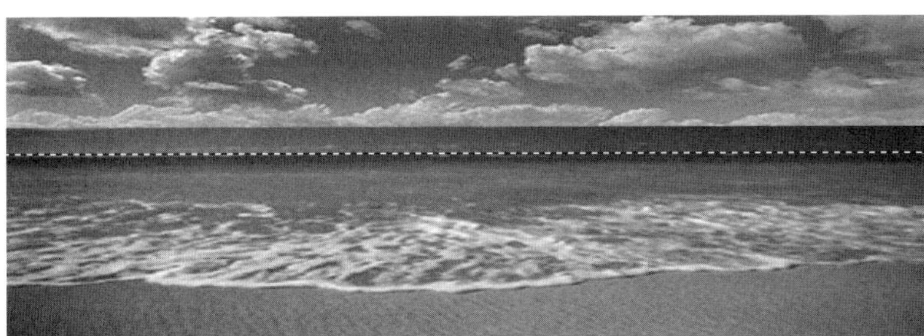

Fig. 7-67. Seashore masking in progress.

f) We are going to apply this selection as a mask, but feather the edge first so that we get a nice smooth blend. Select Select | Feather and set the amount to 16. Click on the OK button to close the window.

g) Select Modify | Mask | Reveal Selection to activate the selection as a mask.

h) Note that the images relatively blend together at this point. The images look pretty good, but let's add a saturation effect to the seashore to make it match the clouds a little better.

i) With the *Seashore* sublayer (bitmap) selected, click on the Plus (+) icon next to the Effects field and then select Adjust Color | Hue and Saturation. Establish the following settings.

- *Hue:* 17
- *Saturation:* 10
- *Lightness:* 18

j) Click on the OK button to close the window and see the completed effect.

5. The background needs a little more work to be a convincing beach scene. We will use some white gradients with transparent fades to create the edge transitions.

a) On the bottom of the Layers panel, click on the Folder icon to create a new layer. Name this layer *Gradients*.

b) Using the Rectangle tool, draw a rectangle over the bottom quarter of the image.

c) Select the Gradient tool and click on the Fill swatch in the Properties panel, to change the gradient colors. In the gradient window that opens, set both gradient markers to white. You should now have a white-to-white gradient.

d) Set the opacity marker on the far right to 0. See figure 7-68.

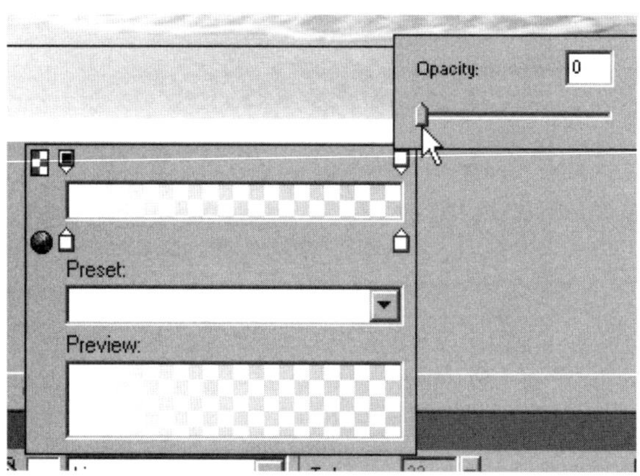

Fig. 7-68. Opacity marker set to 0.

e) Using the Gradient tool, click at the bottom of the rectangle and drag upward, stopping just before the top of the rectangle. You should see the beach image gradient blend to white. See figure 7-69.

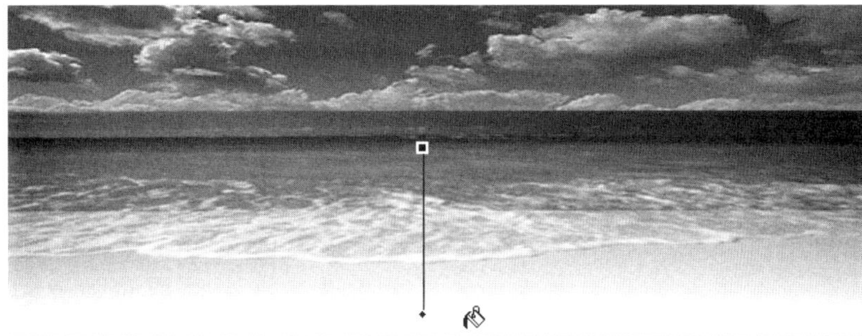

Fig. 7-69. Beach image fading to white at the bottom of the image.

f) Using the Rectangle tool, draw a rectangle over the entire left side of the image, and another over the entire right side of the image.

g) Fill the rectangles with the gradient tool to complete the edge fades. You will need to drag from left to right for the left rectangle. Drag from right to left for the right rectangle. Adjust the gradient until the desired effect is achieved. See figure 7-70 as an example.

TIP

Using gradients with transparency for edge fades is often advantageous, because the fades can be edited and moved very easily.

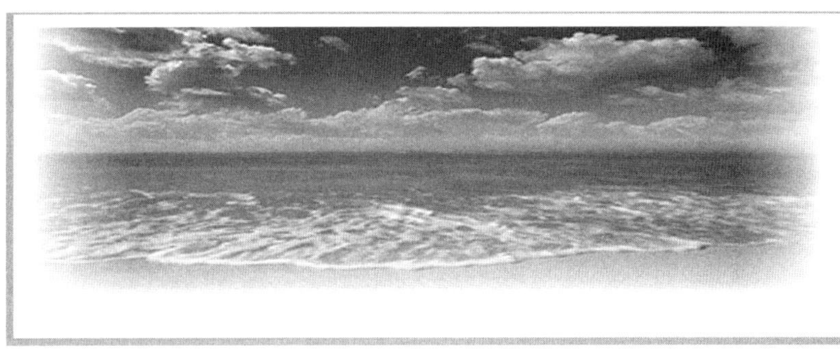

Fig. 7-70. Gradients applied to the image edges.

6. Now let's import the text logo for the image.
   a) In the Layer panel, create a new layer named *Logo*.
   b) Select File | Import and browse in the *Chapter 7* folder. Double click on the *illus_logo.png* image to import it.
   c) Click the cursor on the canvas to place the image near the middle. In the Properties panel, establish the following settings.
      - *X:* 218
      - *Y:* 18
   d) Let's add a glow effect to the logo. Using the Pointer tool, select the logo. In the Properties panel, click on the Plus (+) icon next to the

Effects field and then select Shadow and Glow | Glow. Establish the following settings.

- *Width:* 5
- *Color:* #FFFFFF (white)
- *Opacity:* 50%
- *Softness:* 12

e) You should now see a slight glow around the logo. See figure 7-71.

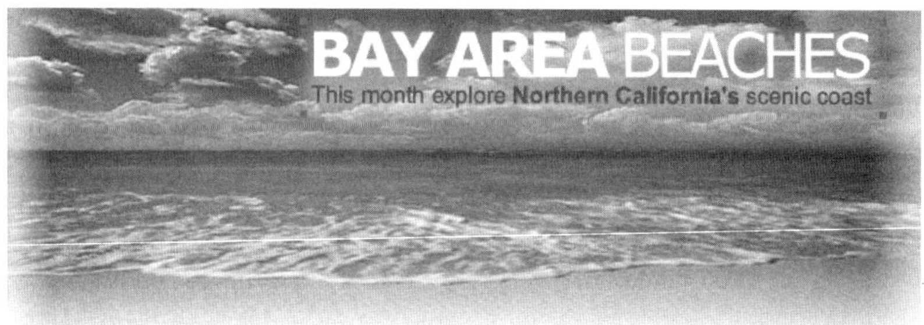

Fig. 7-71. Glow effect applied to the text logo.

7. To finish up the illustration, we will import two more images and mask them into a simple layout to the left of the logo.
   a) In the Layers panel, create a new layer named *Circle Images.*
   b) Select the Line tool in the Vector toolbox. In the Properties panel, establish the following settings.

      - *Stroke Color:* White
      - *Stroke Size:* 2, 1-Pixel Soft

   c) Draw a horizontal line all the way across the canvas. Hold down the Shift key as you draw to create a perfectly straight line.
   d) With the line selected, adjust the Y coordinate setting to 82.
   e) Using the Ellipse tool, draw a circle. Establish the following settings.

      - *W:* 100
      - *H:* 100
      - *X:* 47
      - *Y:* 44
      - *Fill Color:* #CCCCCC (light gray)
      - *Edge:* Hard
      - *Stroke Color:* #FFFFFF (white)
      - *Stroke Width:* 3, 1-Pixel Soft

f) With the circle selected, in the Properties panel, click on the Plus (+) icon next to the Effects field and then select Shadow and Glow | Glow. Establish the following settings.

- *Width:* 5
- *Color:* #FFFFFF (white)
- *Opacity:* 65%
- *Softness:* 12

g) Select the circle and then press Ctrl + C (Mac: Cmd + C) to copy it. We will need it in memory so that we can paste it as a mask.

h) Next, let's import the image that will be masked in the circle. Select File | Import and browse for *coast1.png* in the *Chapter* 7 folder. Double click on *coast1.png* to import it.

i) Click to place the image on the canvas. In the Properties panel, establish the following settings (to move the image per these coordinates).

- *X:* -8
- *Y:* 41

j) Select the bitmap you just imported, and then select Edit | Paste as Mask. The image is now masked to fit within the white outline. See figure 7-72.

CAUTION

If you do not select Ctrl + C (Mac: Cmd + C) to copy the circle, the mask will not be applied. You must always paste the copy to the clipboard. It is the circle that is being pasted as a mask over the image, not the photo.

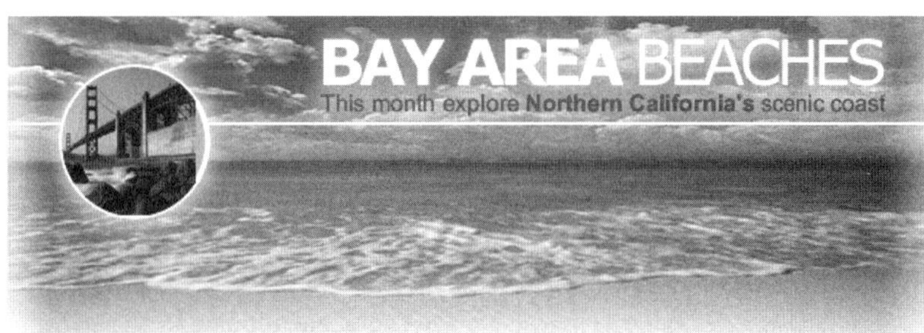

Fig. 7-72. Bitmap masked within the circle.

k) Notice that a small amount of the gray fill in the circle is still showing (in the right-hand portion of the circle). Adjust the position of the image inside the circle by selecting the image with the Pointer tool. Click and drag the four-arrowed center point to the right to move the image inside the mask.

l) Draw another circle so that you can repeat the process. Establish the following settings.

- *W:* 75
- *H:* 75
- *X:* 140
- *Y:* 65
- *Fill Color:* #CCCCCC
- *Stroke Color:* #FFFFFF (white)
- *Stroke Width:* 3, 1-Pixel Soft

m) With the circle selected, in the Properties panel, click on the Plus (+) icon next to the Effects field and then select Shadow and Glow | Glow. Establish the following settings.

- *Width:* 5
- *Color:* #FFFFFF (white)
- *Opacity:* 65%
- *Softness:* 12

n) Select the circle and press Ctrl + C (Mac: Cmd + C) to copy it.

o) Let's import the image that will be masked in the circle. Select File | Import and browse for *coast2.png* in *Chapter 7* folder. Double click on *coast2.png* to import it.

p) Place the image on the canvas. Establish the following settings (to move the image per these coordinates).

- *X:* 138
- *Y:* 28

q) Select the bitmap, and then select Edit | Paste as Mask.

r) Click on the work area and then click again on the image you just masked within the second circle. Click and drag the four-arrowed center point to the right to move the image inside the mask, to where you would like it. See figure 7-73.

s) Save the file.

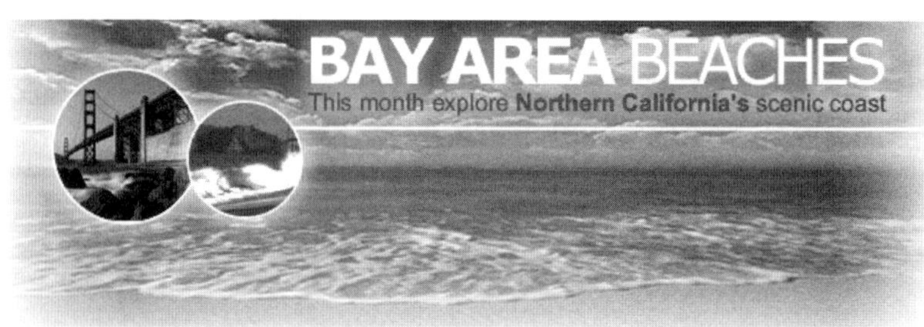

Fig. 7-73. Completed exercise on the canvas.

CHAPTER 8

Animation Techniques

Chapter Topics:

- *Introduction*
- *Guided Tour 8A: The Frames Panel*
- *Guided Tour 8B: The Library Panel and Animation Symbols*
- *Guided Tour 8C: Animation Settings*
- *Practice Exercise 8-1: Creating an Animated Banner for the Home Page*

Introduction

In just the past five years, web-based animation has become a popular and exciting medium for designers using desktop computers. With tools such as Flash, Director, and Dynamic HTML (DHTML), developers have many options for content delivery. However, as exceptional as these tools are, they do come at a cost. Flash and Director are dependent on browser plug-ins, and DHTML relies on features only available in the latest and most popular browsers. For simple animation that is easy to learn and accessible to everyone, the time-tested animated GIF file is the way to go.

An animated GIF is a file containing a series of GIF images shown one after another, in a manner similar to the playback of a flipbook animation. With Fireworks MX, playback speed can be controlled, and looping controls can be set for creating continuous displays. GIF animation is ideal for ad banners, animated logos, text blurbs, and animated bullets. With Fireworks MX tools, animated GIF files can be easily created using any of your designs.

In this chapter, we will explore three methods for producing Fireworks animations. By the end of the chapter you will be able to:

- *Describe the general capabilities and properties of the Fireworks animation tools*
- *Create a frame-by-frame animation*
- *Develop an animation using animation symbols*
- *Use symbol tweening to create an animation with special effects*

Getting started with animation in Fireworks MX means you must first take a closer look at the Frames panel. In Guided Tour 8A, you will explore the features of the Frames panel and will be shown how to use frames to construct animated sequences from your original designs.

Guided Tour 8A: The Frames Panel

The Frames panel allows you to control the display and placement of graphics across a series of frames. To understand this concept, let's return to the flipbook analogy mentioned in the introduction to this chapter. Many of you probably created your own flipbooks or played with flipbooks as children. You might have created one yourself, drawing a stick figure on many pages in a book, with the arm and hand position slightly different on each page. Once the figure is drawn on each page, and you flip the pages of the book, you create the illusion of movement, such as the figure appearing to wave arm and hand.

When working with the Frames panel, try to think of each frame added to your document as a page in a digital flipbook. An animated GIF is a series of images drawn on different frames shown one after another, like a flipbook animation. As your GIF animation plays, the frames that make up the animation are shown sequentially, just as each page in the flipbook. Creating individual frames with incremental changes is called frame-by-frame animation.

In Fireworks MX, each file starts with only one frame. You may have noticed that in all the exercises we worked with in previous chapters, the artwork had just one frame. This was all we needed because we were not trying to create any movement. For animated effects, we will need to add more frames to our documents to create the illusion of movement. To get started with animation effects, let's take a look at the Frames panel.

1. Start by opening a new file. Select File | New. Set the Width to 468 pixels and the Height to 60 pixels. This is the standard size for an ad banner. We will be using these dimensions throughout this chapter. Leave the canvas color as white and the resolution set at 72.
2. Select Window | Frames to open the Frames panel. By default, the Frames panel is grouped with the History panel and should be located in the lower right-hand corner of your screen. However, as you work with panels in Fireworks, you can create your own panel groupings and place them wherever you want.
3. During the process of animating, you will be working with the Frames and Layers panels extensively. If you like, go ahead and group these two panels together.
   a) Look at the upper right-hand corner of the Frames and History panel. You should see an icon you have seen before, in the Layers panel. The Panel Menu icon indicates that there is an Options menu available. See figure 8-1.

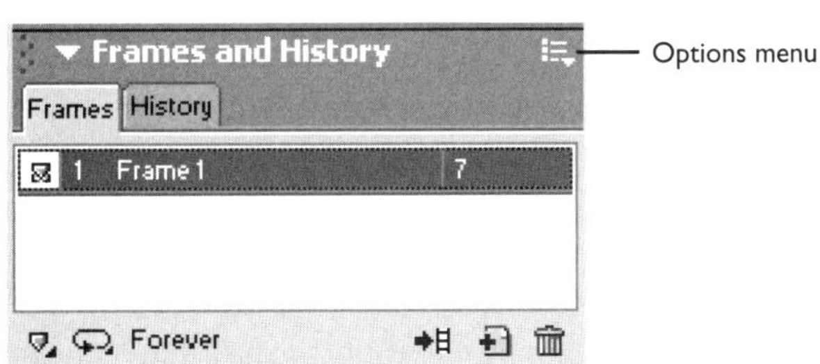

Fig. 8-1. Options menu on the Frames and History panel.

   b) Go ahead and click on this icon to open the Options menu.
   c) From the Frames Option menu, select Group Frames with | Layers to place these panels side by side.

d) You should now be able to see the newly combined Layers and Frames panel in the upper right-hand corner of your screen. See figure 8-2.

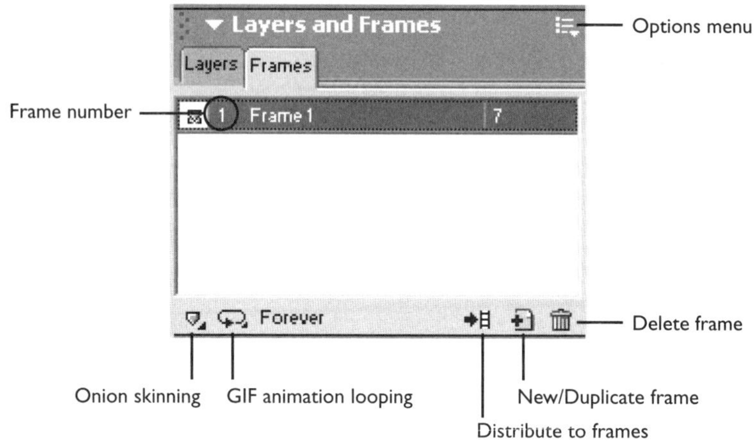

Fig. 8-2. Newly combined Layers and Frames panel.

4. Examine the Frames panel on your screen, or that shown in figure 8-2. Note that the new file was created with only one frame. This frame is highlighted in blue because it is the active frame at this point.

5. Now look at the bottom of the Frames panel, both the left and right corners. You should see five icons. (See figure 8-2.) These icons will be your primary means of manipulating frame settings. The icons are, from left to right on the panel, as follows.

   - *Onion Skinning:* Onion skinning is a feature that allows you to see the content of multiple frames at the same time, as if they were on translucent (onion skin) paper in a stack. This feature allows you to choose which frames are visible along with the current frame, and whether those additional frames are editable or not.
   - *GIF Animation Looping:* Loop sets the number of times the GIF animation will play through the series of frames. The default setting is Forever. Whatever setting you select is displayed immediately to the right of this button. Note that in figure 8-2 you can see that the word Forever is displayed to right of the GIF Animation Looping control button. Looping can be turned off or set to however many times you want the animation to repeat.
   - *Distribute to Frames:* If you have a series of objects selected on a frame, Distribute to Frames will distribute each object to a separate frame, starting at the current frame location.

- *New/Duplicate Frames:* Clicking on this button will create a new frame directly after the current frame. Dragging the current frame over this icon will duplicate the current frame and place the duplicate frame directly after the original.
- *Delete Frames:* Clicking on this button deletes selected frames. You can also drag frames over this icon to delete them.

6. You have now had a brief overview of the frame controls. Now let's add a graphic to *Layer 1*, along with a second frame to see the effect this has on the Frames panel.
   a) Click on the Layers tab to bring the Layers panel to the front.
   b) Select the Rectangle tool and draw a red square and place it on the left-hand side of the canvas. Note that a new sublayer named *Rectangle* was added below *Layer 1*.
   c) Rename the Rectangle sublayer *Square*.
   d) Click on the Frames tab to bring the *Frames* layer to the front.
   e) Click on the New/Duplicate Frames icon in the Frames panel to add *Frame 2*. Note that *Frame 2* is now highlighted blue because it is the current frame. (See figure 8-3.) Also note that the red square is no longer visible on the canvas because the canvas now displays *Frame 2*.

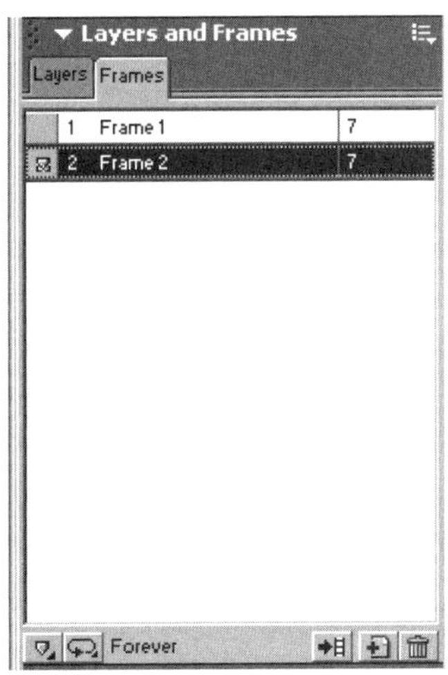

Fig. 8-3.* Frame 2 *added and highlighted.

   f) Click on *Frame 1* in the Frames panel. The red square is now visible on the canvas again. The red square exists only in *Frame 1*. By clicking on *Frame 1*, we see the graphic we initially added to that frame.

7. Next, let's add a graphic to *Frame 2*.

a) Click on *Frame 2* in the Frames panel. The red square should disappear from the canvas.
b) Draw a blue circle on the right-hand side of the canvas.
c) Click back and forth between *Frame 1* and *Frame 2* in the Frames panel. Note that the square disappears in *Frame 2* and the circle disappears in *Frame 1*. As this exercise illustrates, objects only appear in the frame they were created in or are copied to.

8. Using the Pointer tool, select the red square on the canvas in *Frame 1*. Take a closer look at *Frame 1* in the Frames panel. When you select an object, a blue square (selection icon) appears on the right-hand side of the frame holding the object. See figure 8-4.

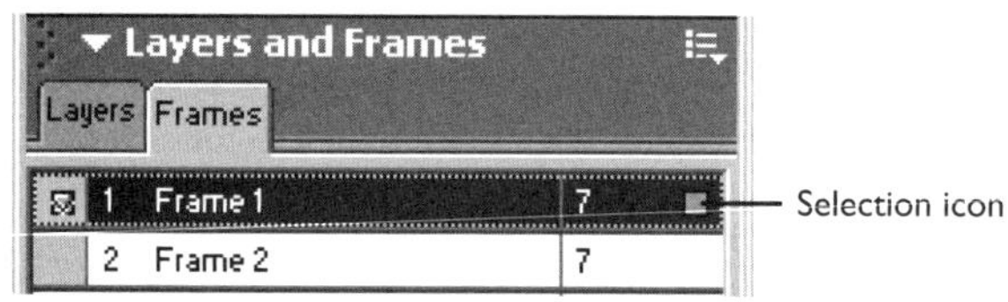

Fig. 8-4. Blue square in the Frames panel.

a) Click the cursor on the blue selection icon in *Frame 1* and drag it to *Frame 2*. Note that now the red square and blue circle are both in *Frame 2*.
b) Click on *Frame 1*. What? Nothing is there. By clicking and dragging the blue selection icon from one frame to another, you moved the red square from *Frame 1* into *Frame 2*.
c) Click on *Frame 2* and select both objects. Drag the blue selection icon in *Frame 2* to the New/Duplicate Frame icon. See figure 8-2.
d) Look at the Frames panel and note that you are currently looking at the red square and blue circle in *Frame 3*.
e) Click on *Frame 2*. A red square and blue circle are also in *Frame 2*. By selecting objects in a frame and then dragging the selection icon for that frame over the New/Duplicate Frame icon, you are really doing two things: creating a new frame and copying the selected objects into that new frame.
f) Select *Frame 3* and click on the Delete Frame icon (see figure 8-2) to get rid of this frame.
g) Select the red square in *Frame 2*. Drag the blue selection icon in *Frame 2* into *Frame 1*.
h) You should now be looking at the red square in *Frame 1*. Click on *Frame 2*, and note that you see only the blue circle in *Frame 2*. By selecting the red square only, and then dragging the blue selection icon from *Frame 2* into *Frame 1*, you moved only the red square into *Frame 1*, leaving the unselected blue circle in *Frame 2*.

Now that you have seen some of the basics of how the Frames panel works, let's move on to see how the animation controls work.

Animation Playback Controls

Using the animation playback controls is another way of viewing the content of each frame, rather than clicking back and forth between frames (as we have previously been doing). The animation playback controls are located in the lower left of each Document window, as shown in figure 8-5. These VCR-style controls, outlined in the following, are used as a convenient means of playing through or stepping forward/backward through the frames to review the animation.

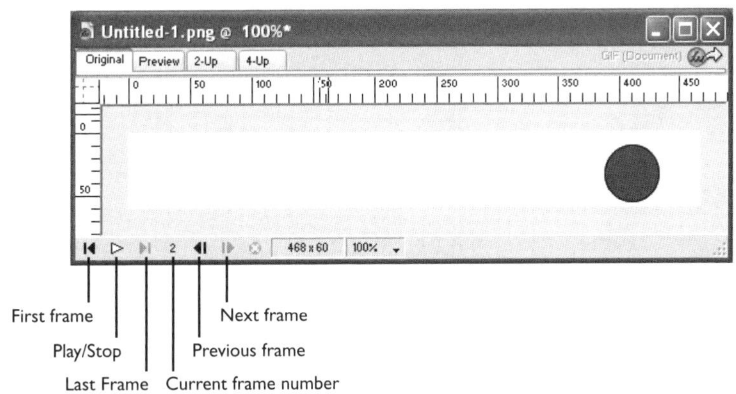

Fig. 8-5. Animation playback controls.

1. Let's take a look at the Animation Playback Controls, starting from left to right. See figure 8-5.
   - *First Frame:* Rewinds the animation to Frame 1.
   - *Play/Stop:* Toggles between the Play and Stop functions.
   - *Last Frame:* Jumps forward to the last frame.
   - *Current Frame Number:* Shows the number of the current frame.
   - *Previous Frame:* Steps backward to the previous frame.
   - *Next Frame:* Steps forward to the next frame.
2. Click on the Play button to automatically play through the two frames in the Frames panel. The default looping option is set to Forever, so it will continue to loop until stopped.
3. Click on the Stop button to cease the looping.
4. Click on the Looping icon located in the lower left-hand corner of the Frames panel. Set the number to 2. The Looping option sets the number

of times the GIF animation will play through its frames. You should now be able to see that a 2 is displayed to the right of the Looping control button. To view a file with it's looping setting, select File | Export Preview and use the controls at the bottom of the window, or export the file and view the GIF in a browser. We will use the first method.

a) Select File | Export Preview. The Export Preview window now opens. See figure 8-6.

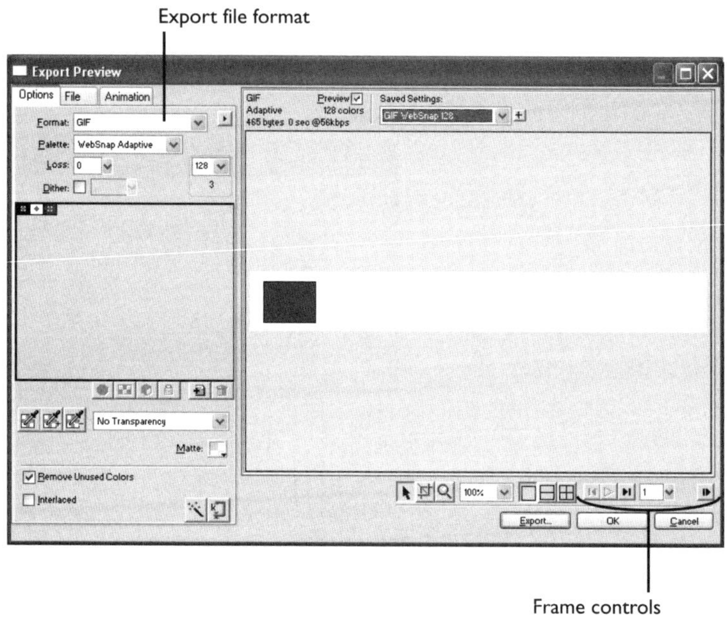

Fig. 8-6. Export Preview window.

b) In the window that has now opened, locate the Export File Format field (see figure 8-6) and then select the Animated GIF option.

c) In the lower right-hand side of the window, locate the frame control buttons. Click on the Play button. The animation should have looped through the frames twice.

d) Click on the Cancel button to close this window.

·TIP·

The animation playback controls also exist in the Export Preview window. Select File | Export Preview to use the playback and optimization controls in one location.

Frames Options

Let's wrap up our overview of the Frames panel by taking a look at the frames options. You will use these options quite a bit in the guided tours and practice exercises that follow.

1. Click on the Options menu icon, located in the upper right-hand corner of the Frames panel. The Frames Options menu should now be open. (See figure 8-7.) The available options are as follows.

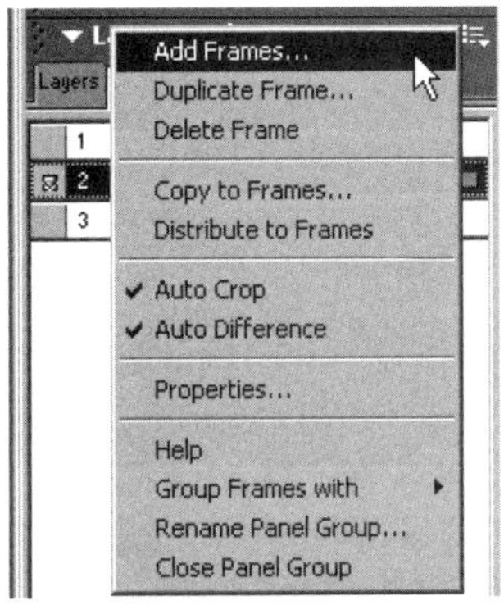

Fig. 8-7. Frame Options menu.

- *Add Frame:* Adds new frames to the Frames panel.
- *Duplicate Frames:* Copies the current frame one or more times and places these copies at a specific location in the Frames panel.
- *Delete Frame:* Deletes selected frame.
- *Copy to Frames:* Adds one or more copies of a selected graphic to a specific frame or frame range. Note that this option copies selected objects within a frame, whereas the Duplicate Frame option copies the entire frame with all content.
- *Distribute to Frames:* If a series of objects is selected on a frame, this option will distribute each object to a separate frame, starting at the current frame location.
- *Auto Crop:* This optimization setting reduces the file size by comparing each frame and then cropping the resulting frames to a pixel area that contains only the changes from one frame to another.
- *Auto Difference:* This optimization setting reduces file size by converting unchanged pixels to transparent pixels within each auto-cropped area.

  Properties: Allows you to set the frame delay settings for playback.

2. Save this file in the *SaveWork* folder. Name the file *Tour_8A.png*.

Now that you have been introduced to the Frames panel and the concept of frame-by-frame animation, in Guided Tour 8B you will work with other types of animated effects, which allow for more subtle transitions between frames.

Guided Tour 8B: The Library Panel and Animation Symbols

You have just seen how frame-by-frame animation can be a fairly easy and effective way of creating basic GIF animations. Over time you may find this frame-by-frame process tedious if you need to create movement or effects such as text fades and object scaling. To answer more advanced needs, Fireworks MX offers animation symbols as a means of creating more subtle animated effects.

Animation symbols are created using the Library panel. The Library panel acts as a storage area for reusable objects such as graphics, buttons, and multi-frame animations. You can think of the Library panel as an electronic library in which instead of books you check out copies of objects. Objects stored in the library are referred to as *symbols*. These objects can be "checked out" from the library and placed repeatedly on the canvas on any layer and any frame. The object or symbol physically exists in only one place, the Library panel. As you will see in material to follow, symbols are created separately from the main canvas and have their own editing area.

Each time you take a copy of a symbol and place it on the canvas, it is referred to as an *instance* of that symbol. The instance actually only references (and reuses) the original symbol stored in the library. In this way, library symbols can be reused many times, helping the development process become much more efficient, organized, and streamlined.

A collection of symbols in the Library can be exported as a PNG file so that other Fireworks documents can import them and use them as symbols. By importing and exporting a common symbols PNG file, you can, in effect, share symbols between documents for greater consistency. We will explore these functions in greater detail later in this chapter. First, let's take a closer look at the Library panel and the animation symbol.

1. Start by opening a new file. Set the Width to 468 pixels and the Height to 60 pixels. Leave the canvas color as white and the resolution set at 72.
2. Select Window | Library to open the Library panel. The Library panel is set up to create, maintain, and manage symbols. You will use a simple set of controls to add and edit objects stored in the library.
   a) Note that the library is grouped in the Assets panel, along with the Styles and URL panels. See figure 8-8.

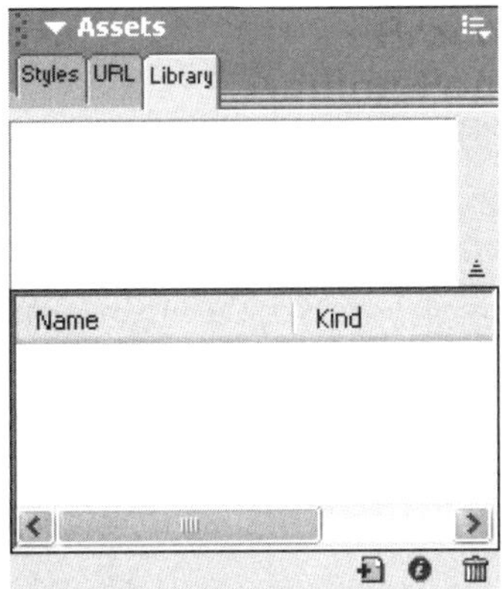

Fig. 8-8. Library panel grouped with the Styles and URL panels.

b) Let's ungroup this panel. Select the Options menu, located in the upper right-hand corner of the current panel.

c) In the Options menu that now opens, select Group Library with | New Panel Group. This action now separates the Library panel from all other panels. See figure 8-9.

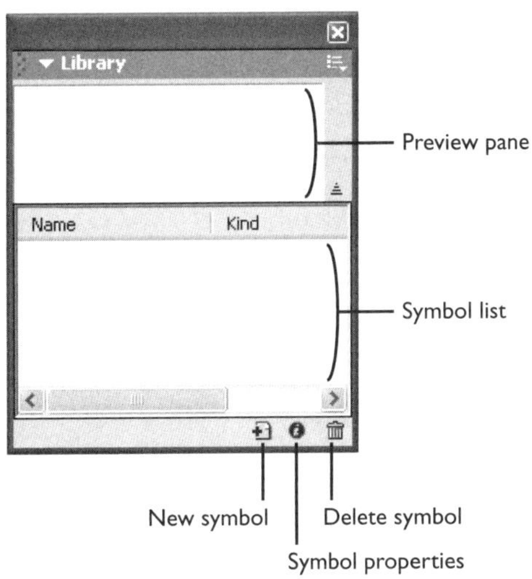

Fig. 8-9. Library panel by itself.

d) Note that the Library panel is now a panel by itself, and can be placed anywhere. The Library panel appears to be split horizontally. The library is currently empty, but when content is added to it, the top portion will display a preview of a selected symbol, and the bottom portion will display a complete list of symbols associated with the open document.

e) Look at the bottom right of the panel to see the three icons associated with the library. (See figure 8-9.) From left to right, the icons are as follows.

- *New Symbol:* Creates a new symbol in the library and immediately launches into symbol editing mode.
- *Symbol Properties:* Opens the window for defining the symbol name and type.
- *Delete Symbol:* Deletes any selected symbols.

Creating Animated Symbols

Now that you have a general sense of the Library panel and its icons, let's walk through the procedure for creating an animated symbol. There are two methods you can employ to accomplish this. In this tour, we will focus on the first method, by creating a new symbol from scratch, using library editing mode.

Shortcut

The keyboard shortcut for New Symbol is Ctrl + F8 (Mac: Cmd + F8).

1. Click on the New Symbol icon on the Library panel. See figure 8-9.
2. The Symbol Properties window has now opened. See figure 8-10.

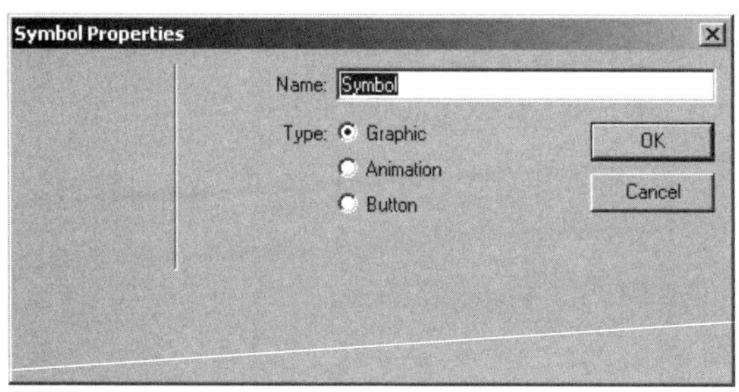

Fig. 8-10. Symbol Properties window.

3. The Symbol Properties window asks for two pieces of information that will be used to define your symbol and it's behavior. The fields are as follows.
   - *Name:* A unique name for this symbol.
   - *Type:* Select one of the following three types of symbols, each with a different behavior.
     - *Graphic:* Creates a simple reusable object with its own editing area.
     - *Animation:* Creates a reusable object with its own editing area and animation properties.
     - *Button:* Creates a button capable of holding complex graphic states.

4. Let's complete this information.
   a) Name this symbol *Anim01*.
   b) Set Type to Animation.
   c) Click on the OK button to close the window.

Symbol Editing Mode

A new window, named *Symbol : Anim01*, has now opened. See figure 8-11.

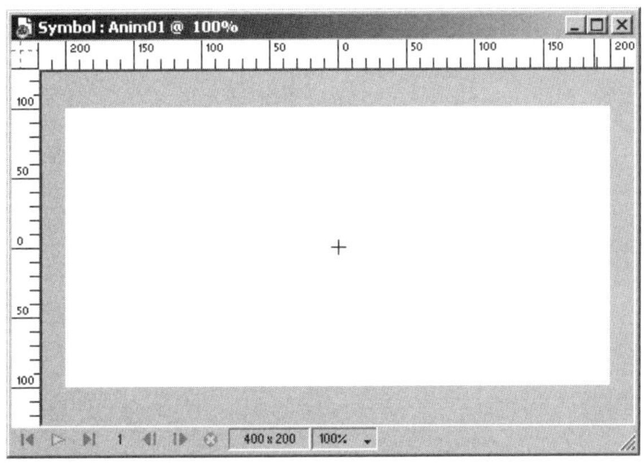

***Fig. 8-11. Symbol editing mode for* Anim01.**

·TIP·

Animation symbols can have their own layers in symbol editing mode, and contain their own frames and animations.

This is a separate symbol editing area to be used with the *Anim01* symbol. You work within this window just as you would work on the main canvas. You can use layers and any of the tools. Think of this as a separate canvas specifically for a selected symbol.

1. Let's take a quick look at how symbol editing mode works.
   a) Select the Rectangle tool and draw a green rectangle on the canvas.
   b) Use the Pointer tool to position the rectangle on the center of this canvas. Note that the crosshair present on the Symbol Editing Mode canvas shows the exact center of the area. (See figure 8-11.) The crosshair is displayed to help you with alignment.
2. Close the *Symbol :Anim01* window by clicking on the X in the upper right-hand corner of the window.
3. Note the new symbol in the Library panel.
4. Click on the *Anim01* symbol in the Library and note that a preview of the rectangle you drew is now displayed in the Preview pane. See figure 8-12.

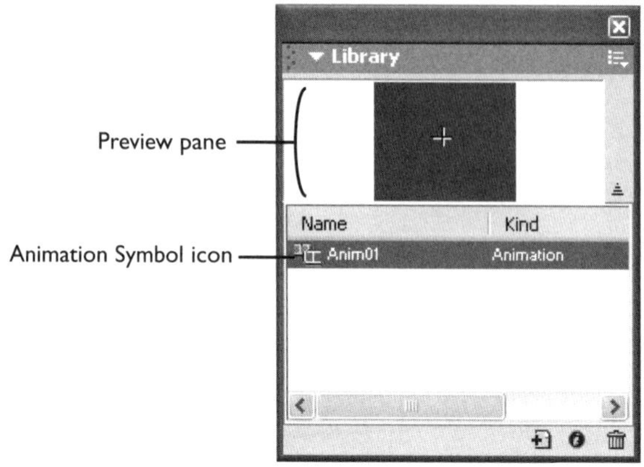

Fig. 8-12.* Anim01 *symbol and preview in the Library panel.

5. Undoubtedly you will need to make updates or changes to symbols at some point. This is an easy task. Let's try it.
   a) Double click on the symbol in the Preview pane, or double click on the Animation Symbol icon (not on the Symbol name) in the Library list.
   b) The Symbol Editing Mode window for *Symbol : Anim01* should now be open.
   c) Change the rectangle from green to black.
   d) Close the *Symbol : Anim01* window. The symbol should now be black, as it has been updated.
6. Save this file as *Tour_8B.png*. We will use this graphic in the next tour to explore animation settings.

As you can see, it is easy to create animation symbols and store them in the library. However, at this point there are no graphics on the canvas and nothing has been animated. Until we add an instance (or copy) of this symbol to the canvas and adjust its animation properties, the symbol only exists in the library. In Guided Tour 8C you will adjust the animation settings of our *Anim01* symbol and learn how to use it in the document.

Guided Tour 8C: Animation Settings

Now that you are familiar with the Library panel and the basics of creating animation symbols, it is time to experiment with some animation properties. By using the animation settings and the controls in the Objects panel, you can direct instances of animation symbols as to how to animate over time by using directional movement, rotation, scale, and opacity.

1. Start by opening the *Tour_8B.png* file used in the last guided tour, if it is not already open.

First, we are going to create a new animation symbol to illustrate the concept of animation properties. This time we will start by drawing a new graphic on the canvas and converting it into a symbol instead of creating a blank symbol, as in the last guided tour. This is a much more common route for creating animation symbols because it creates an instance of the symbol on the canvas immediately.

Shortcut

The shortcut for Convert to Symbol is F8.

2. Draw a purple oval on the left-hand side of the main canvas.
   a) Using the Pointer tool, select the oval.
   b) Select Modify | Symbol | Convert to Symbol. The Symbol Properties window opens (you first saw this window in the last guided tour).
   c) In the Symbol Properties window, set the following properties and then click on the OK button to close it.
      - *Name:* Anim02
      - *Type:* Animation

3. This time, instead of opening the Symbol Editing Mode window (as was the case in the last guided tour), Fireworks displays the Animate (settings) window. See figure 8-13.

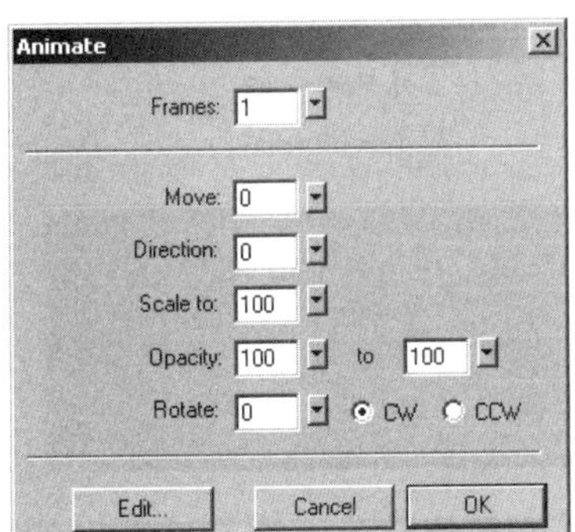

Fig. 8-13. Animate (settings) window.

4. As soon as the oval was converted into a symbol and added to the library, the graphic on the stage became an instance (copy) of that symbol. Because we are starting with an instance on the stage, we are presented with the animation property settings for that instance. Let's take a look at these settings. Starting from the top of this window, the settings are as follows.
   - *Frames:* Specifies the duration of the animation in frames.
   - *Move:* Specifies how many (if any) pixels the instance will move.

- *Direction:* Specifies the direction in which the instance will move. The default setting of 0 moves horizontally from left to right. Clicking on an area of the "directional circle" will specify an angle from which to move.
- *Scale to:* Specifies the change in object size (if any) from the starting point to the finishing point. This field will accept a percentage value between 0 and 250.
- *Opacity:* Specifies the change in transparency (if any). Both the starting point and the ending point of the animation may be set to a percentage value between 0 and 100.
- *Rotate:* Specifies the rotation (if any) from the starting point to the ending point of the animation. This property can be set to rotate either clockwise or counterclockwise.
- *Edit button:* Allows you to open, in symbol editing mode, the symbol in the library for the purpose of making changes.

5. Enter the following values in the Animate (settings) window. Leave the fields that are not listed in the following at their default settings. You can adjust any or all of the properties at any time. Click on the OK button after establishing the following settings.
   - *Frames: 5*
   - *Move: 200*
   - *Scale: 50*
6. Note that a pop-up warning window has now appeared to ask if you want to automatically add new frames. Because we specified five (5) frames in the Animate (settings) window, click on OK to add these additional frames.
7. Examine the Frames panel. As you can see, there are now five frames. See figure 8-14.

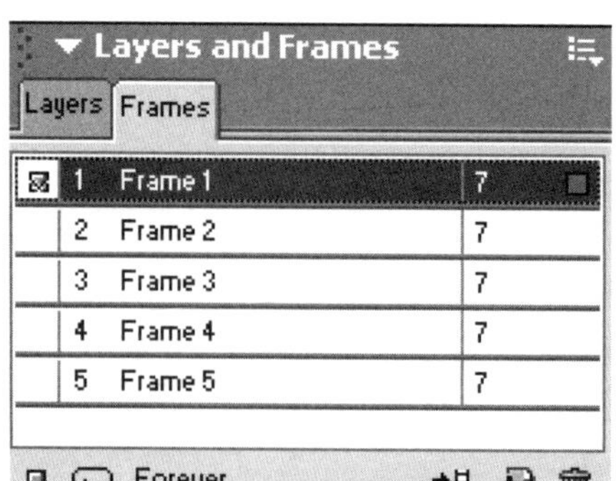

Fig. 8-14. Frames panel showing the newly added frames.

8. Examine the main canvas. You should see the purple oval and a line with four dots extending to the right. See figure 8-15.

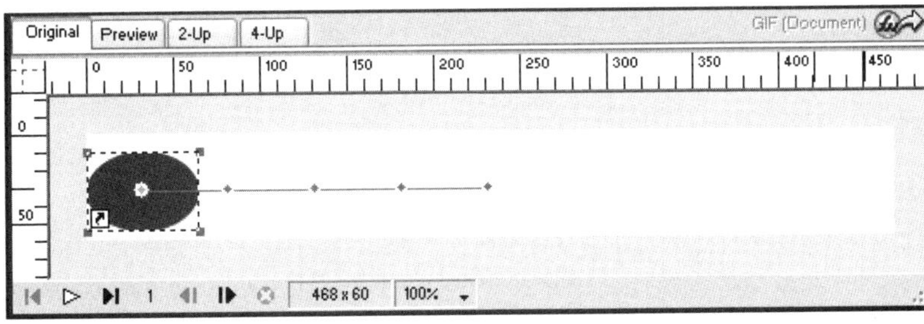

Fig. 8-15. Main canvas showing the oval and line extending to the right.

9. In the Frames panel, click on *Frame 2*. Click on *Frame 3*, *Frame 4*, and *Frame 5*. As you have just seen, the settings you selected in the Animate window created four new frames, and in each of these frames automatically created a copy of the oval. However, in each case the oval was moved to the right and each instance was made smaller than the immediately preceding instance. See figure 8-16.

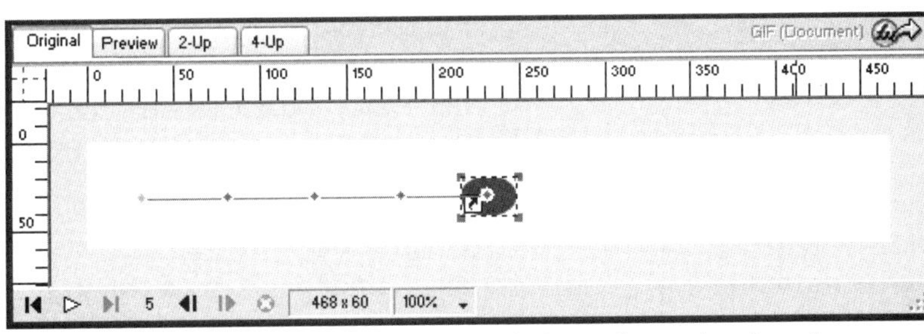

Fig. 8-16. Main canvas showing* Frame 5 *with the oval moved and smaller.

10. Examine the Library panel. The purple oval graphic on the canvas has become an instance (copy) of the *Anim02* symbol, and this symbol has been added to the library's symbol list.
11. Click on *Frame 1* (so that we can examine a larger instance). Examine the main canvas. With the oval selected, note the dotted line around the instance on the canvas, along with an arrow (Symbol Editing Mode icon) located in the lower left. See figure 8-17.

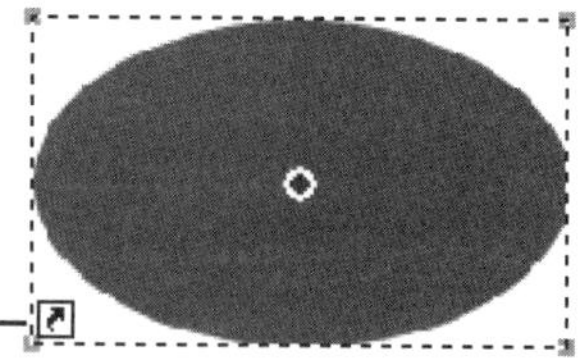

Fig. 8-17.* Anim02 *instance selected on the main canvas.

This arrow indicates that the object can be edited. To edit the symbol, you can either double click on this icon or you can double click on the instance on the canvas. Either method will result in opening symbol editing mode for that instance. If you have opened the Symbol Editing Mode window, close it.

12. Now back to the oval on the canvas. Note the presence of a circle in the middle of the oval. This circle denotes the center point of the instance. This center point can be adjusted in the Symbol Editing Mode window.
13. Now let's try playing the animation.
    a) Click on the Play button at the bottom of the Document window to watch the oval move across the canvas. Click on the Stop button to halt the animation at any time.
    b) Click on the Previous frame and Next frame buttons to step through the frames in the animation, one frame at a time.
14. There are two methods for editing the Animate settings for this instance. First, let's try using the Modify menu.
    a) Bring the animation back to *Frame 1* and using the Pointer tool, select the instance on the main canvas.
    b) Select Modify | Animation | Settings. This reopens the Animate (settings) window.
    c) Establish the following settings.
       - *Scale:* 100
       - *Opacity:* 0 to 100

       Click on the OK button.
    d) Click on the Play button to see the effects of these changes. Click on the Stop button to halt the animation.
15. You can also use the Properties panel to modify the animation settings of an instance.
    a) Select a frame where you can see the oval on the canvas. Using the Pointer tool, select this instance on the canvas.

TIP

The Animate (settings) window can also be opened by right-clicking (Mac: Ctrl + clicking) on the instance and selecting Animation | Settings from the pop-up menu that appears.

b) The Properties panel reflects the settings that have been applied to the animation. (See figure 8-18.) Enter *200* in the *Scale to* field. Press the Enter/Return key.

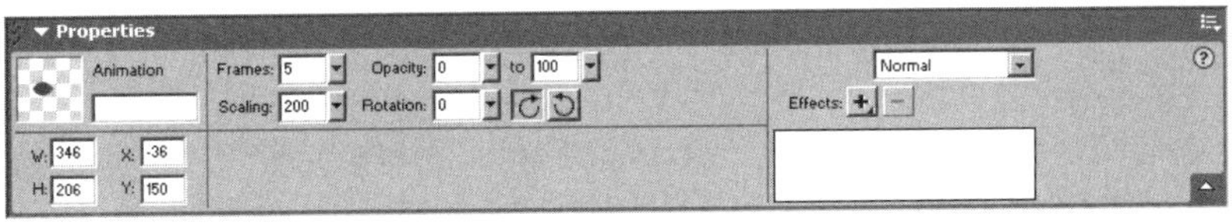

Fig. 8-18. Properties panel for the animation.

c) Press the Play button to see the update. Stop the animation when you are finished.

16. Let's remove the animation settings that have been applied to this instance of the symbol.
    a) Select the instance on the main canvas.
    b) Select Modify | Animation | Remove Animation. This clears all animation settings but leaves the instance on the canvas in *Frame 1*.

Removing the animation does not delete any additional frames that have been added, although the content on them will be removed along with the animation settings. To delete frames, you must use the Trash Can icon in the Frames panel.

17. Save this file as *Tour_8C* in the *SaveWork* folder.

As you can see, animating objects is a simple procedure in Fireworks MX. Practice Exercise 8-1 takes you step by step through the process of creating a very practical project: an animated advertisement for a web page. We will apply what you have already learned about converting graphics to symbols, and then apply animation settings to create a banner that will be added to the home page of the *San Francisco Travel Guide* web site we have been working on in each chapter.

Practice Exercise 8-1: Creating an Animated Banner for the Home Page

Description

In this exercise, we will apply the animation techniques from the previous guided tours to create an ad banner with a GIF animation. The first step will be to start with a frame-by-frame animation for an airline ad. We will then add animation symbols and effects to apply the finishing touches.

Preview of Completed Exercise

Before beginning the exercise, let's take a look at the banner in its completed state so that you can clearly see what it is you are about to build.

·TIP·

As we set up the graphics for the ad banner, note that we are using a very limited range of colors and frames. Often when creating ad banners for the Web, you will have a specific size limitation of 8K to 10K or larger, depending on the site. Keeping the colors and number of frames down will allow you to stay within these specifications more easily. Often, the more complicated the animation and image, the larger the file size.

1. Use the menu option File | Open and locate the *Chapter 8* folder on the companion CD-ROM. Find the file named *Exercise8_1(complete).png*. Double click on this file to open it.
2. Click on the Play button at the bottom of the Document window to play through the completed animation. There is a time delay, so that each message is displayed for a few seconds before changing to the next message. Figures 8-19 through 8-22 show you the completed frames in the ad banner.

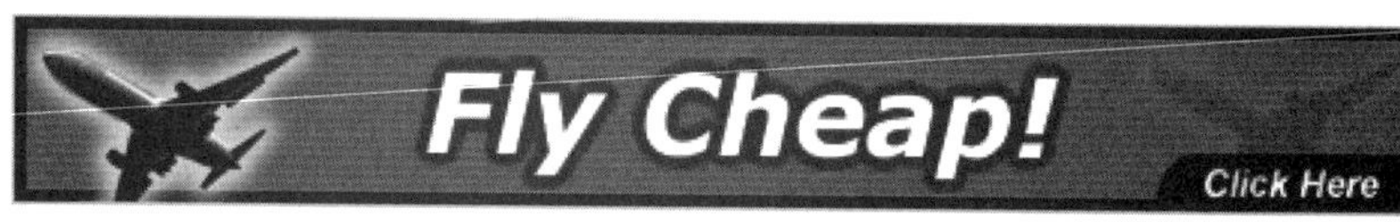

Fig. 8-19. Frame 1.

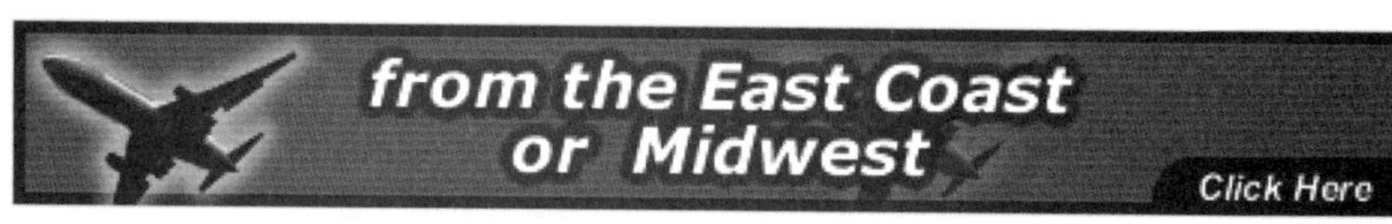

Fig. 8-20. Frame 2.

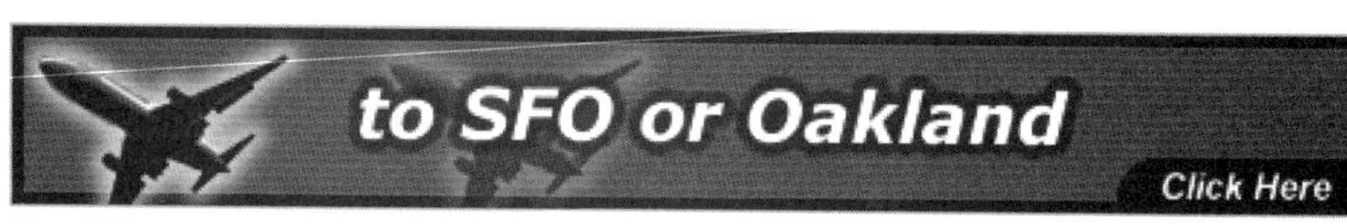

Fig. 8-21. Frame 3.

Fig. 8-22. Frame 4.

Step-by-Step Instructions

1. Select File | New to create a blank file. Set the canvas to 468 x 60 pixels but do not close the window.
   a) Set the resolution to 72.

b) Select Custom as the background color setting. Click on the color swatch and set the color to #000066 by typing this number into the Hexadecimal Color field at the top of the color palette that opens. Press the Enter/Return key to close the color palette.

c) Click on the OK button to close New Document window.

d) Save this file in the *SaveWork* folder. Give it the file name *Exercise8_1png*.

2. Let's import the background graphic for the animation.

a) Select File | Import and browse for the *Background.png* file in the *Chapter 8* folder on the companion CD-ROM.

b) Click to place the graphic in the upper left-hand corner. Use the Properties panel to adjust the placement to X = 4 and Y = 4. Your canvas should now look like that shown in figure 8-23.

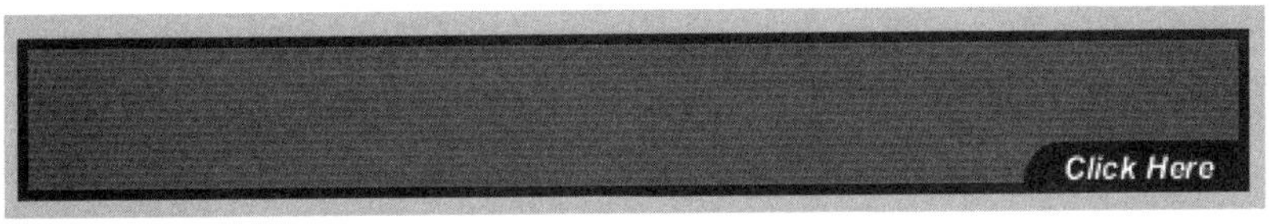

Fig. 8-23. Canvas with the background image inserted.

c) In the Layers panel, rename *Layer 1* as *Background*.

·TIP·

Note the *Click Here* text in the lower right of the imported image. We will not add a hotspot link to this area. Instead, the entire image will be used as a link so that no matter where the user clicks, it will link to the appropriate web site.

3. Next, let's import the jet image.

a) In the Layers panel, insert a new layer above the *Background* layer and name it *Airliner*.

b) Select File | Import and browse for the *Masked_airliner.png* file in the *Chapter 8* folder on the companion CD-ROM. Click to place the image on the left of the canvas.

c) The image is too large for the canvas, so we need to adjust the dimensions and the placement of the image on the canvas. Select the image and establish the following settings in the Properties panel.

- *W:* 95
- *H:* 78
- *X:* 3
- *Y:* 0

d) Let's add a glow effect to the jet graphic to make it visually pop out from the background. Select the jet and in the Properties panel select the Effects + icon and then select Shadow and Glow | Glow. Enter the following properties:

- *Width:* 3
- *Color:* #FFFFFF (white)

- *Opacity:* 75%
- *Softness:* 6

A nice white glow now appears around the jet image. See figure 8-24.

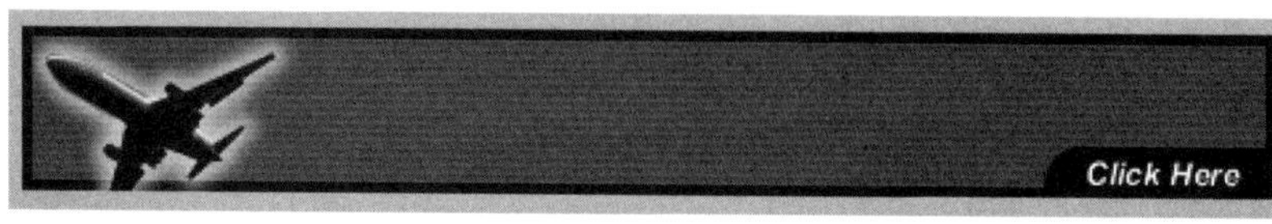

Fig. 8-24. Glow around the jet image.

4. After setting up the background and jet image, we now need to add text and set up the animation in different frames. For the first part of the animation, we will create a simple frame-by-frame animation of text changing, almost like a slideshow effect. First, we will set the *Background* and *Airliner* layers to be shared across frames so that these images appear in every frame of the animation, not just the first frame.
   a) Double click on the *Background* layer. Instead of changing the layer name, as we have used this window before, look at the lower left-hand corner of the window. Check the Share Across Frames option. Press Enter/Return to close the window.
   b) Double click on the *Airliner* layer. Check the Share Across Frames option. Press Enter/Return to close the window.
   c) Add a new layer above the *Airliner* layer and name it *Text*.
   d) In the *Text* layer, select the Text tool and type the text *Fly Cheap!*. Establish the following text settings in the Properties panel.
      - *Font:* Verdana (or other sans serif font, such as Arial or Helvetica)
      - *Style:* Bold, Italic
      - *Size:* 36
      - *Color:* #FFFFFF (white)
   e) Place the text in the center of the canvas. This can be done visually and does not have to be exact. Use the arrow keys to nudge the text box in small increments.
   f) Add a glow effect to visually separate the text from the background. In the Properties panel, select the Effects + icon and then select Shadow and Glow | Glow. Establish the following property settings.
      - *Width:* 3
      - *Color:* #000066
      - *Opacity:* 65%
      - *Softness:* 1

Shortcut

You can move between frames without opening the Frames panel by using the Frames menu on the bottom left of the Layers panel. Click on Frame 1 to use the menu to toggle between each frame.

TIP

By copying text from frame to frame you do not have to reset all text properties or effects in each frame.

g) Select the Frames panel. Open the Options menu in the upper right-hand corner and select Add Frames. Add three frames after the current frame. Click on the OK button.

h) You should now have a total of four frames in the Frames panel, and you should now be looking at *Frame 2*. The text we just created has disappeared in this frame because the *Text* layer is not shared across frames. Click on *Frame 1* and return to the Layers panel.

i) Using the Pointer tool, select the text *Fly Cheap!*, and then select Edit | Copy to copy the text into the buffer.

j) In the Frames panel, select *Frame 2* and paste the copied text by selecting Edit | Paste.

k) Let's change the text pasted in *Frame 2*. First make sure the text object is selected and then change the following settings in the Properties panel.

- *Size:* 21
- *Alignment:* center

l) Select the Text tool and highlight the text *Fly Cheap!*. Replace this text with - *from the East Coast or Midwest*.

m) Center the text on the canvas and use the Pointer tool to drag the right side of the text box toward the center to make it narrower, so that the text wraps into two lines, as shown in figure 8-25.

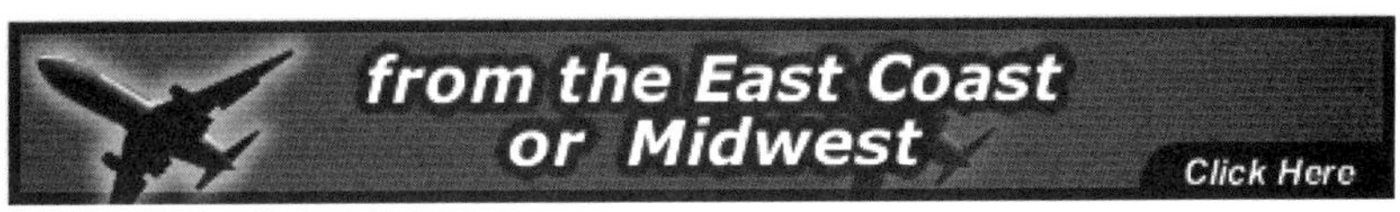

***Fig. 8-25.* Frame 2 text.**

n) Copy the text from *Frame 2* and paste it into *Frame 3*.

o) Change the text to read *to SFO or Oakland*. Change the size to 24 in the Properties panel and center the text on the canvas, as shown in figure 8-26.

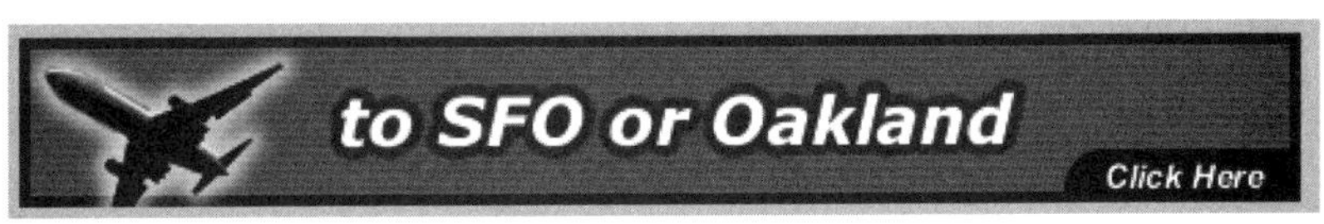

***Fig. 8-26.* Frame 3 text.**

5. In the Frames panel, let's now set the frame delay for each frame. The frame delay is the rate at which the frames progress through the animation. Not every frame has to have the same speed, but in this case we

want to set all frames to the same speed, for a nice steady progression of frames to achieve the slideshow effect of this banner ad.

a) In the Frames panel, note the default frame delay setting of 7 next to the Frame label, as shown in figure 8-27.

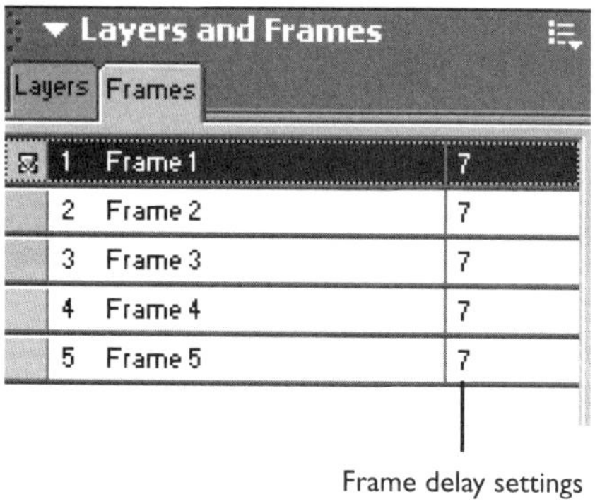

Fig. 8-27. Frame delay settings.

b) In *Frame 1*, double click on the default frame delay of 7 and change it to 300. The higher the number in the frame delay, the longer the delay. Make sure to click on the number 7 or you might accidentally rename the frame instead of changing the delay timing. Leave *Include when Exporting field* checked. Press Enter/Return to close this window.

c) Repeat step a for frames 2 through 4. The last frame does not have any text in it. It will be used as a pause before restarting the looping animation.

d) Leave the Loop setting at the bottom of the Frames panel set to Forever. See figure 8-28.

e) Save this file.

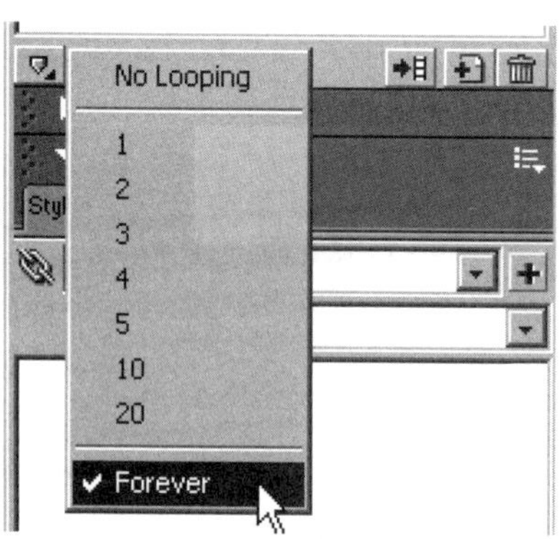

Fig. 8-28. Loop setting.

6. Now let's preview the animation.
   a) Click on the Preview tab in the upper left-hand corner of the Document window. Click on the First Frame button to return to *Frame 1*.
   b) Click on the Play button and watch as the image cycles through the frames. Remember, there is a noticeable delay between frames, so you will have to wait a few seconds before each frame progresses.
7. Next, we will export the file as a GIF animation in order to insert it into a web page.
   a) Select File | Export Preview. A window opens with a preview of *Frame 1* on the right-hand side of the window, and the optimization settings on the left. Note the Options, File, and Animation tabs at the top left of the window.
   b) The Options tab should be currently selected. Set the Format option to Animated GIF and the number of colors to 16. This drops our file size down to about 9K, which is an acceptable size for an ad banner. See figure 8-29.

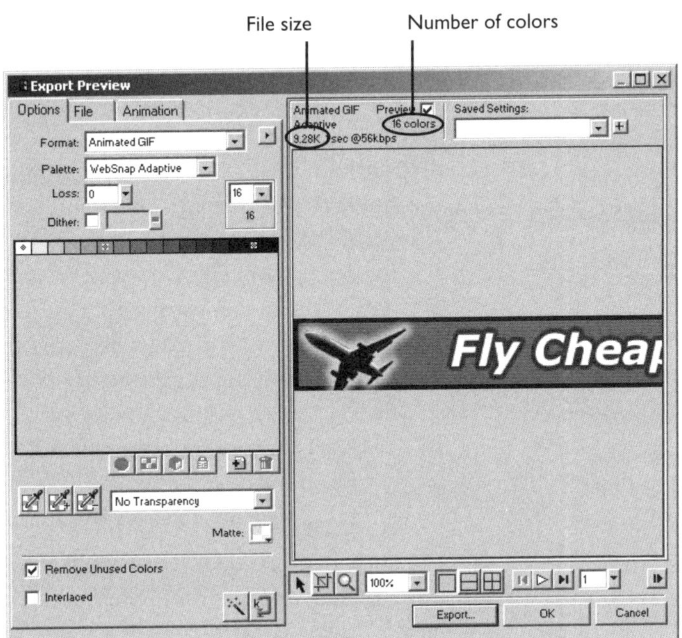

Fig. 8-29. Export Preview window with the Options tab selected.

   c) Click on the Animation tab and look over the options available, shown in figure 8-30. Make sure Auto Crop and Auto Difference are checked, which will decrease the file size.

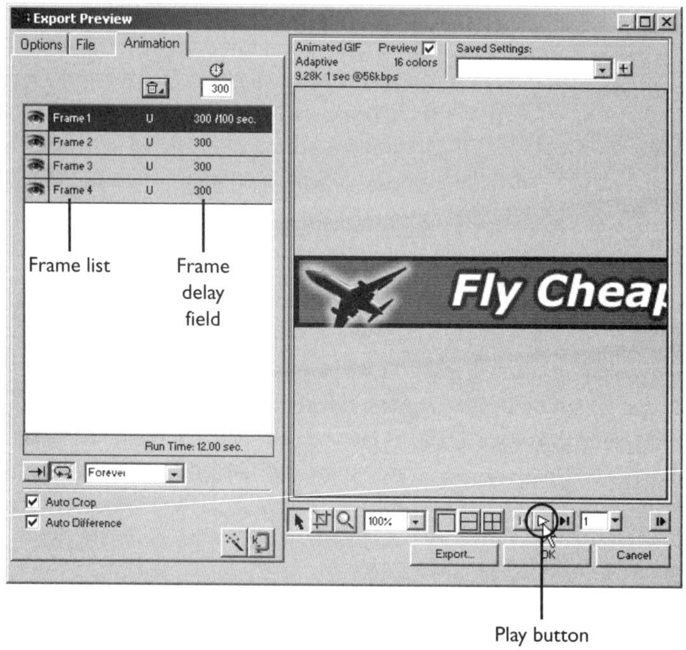

Fig. 8-30 Export Preview window with the Animation tab selected.

d) Click on the Play button underneath the preview (as shown in figure 8-30) to play through the animation and preview it in the Preview pane. The you can make the Preview pane larger by using the double-headed arrow cursor to click on and drag the window edge.

e) You can also click on each frame to preview them individually. Note that frame delay can also be set in the Export Preview window. Just click on each frame and change the frame delay in the Frame Delay field at the top of the Frames list.

f) Click on the Export button at the bottom of the window, and save the file in the *SaveWork* folder with the name *Airline_banner.gif*. Select Images Only from the Save as Type option.

8. Minimize Fireworks for a moment and locate the *SaveWork* folder on your hard drive. Open this folder and you should see the file *Airline_banner.gif*. Double click on this file and use the controls to play it. When finished, close the window and return to Fireworks.

Animation Symbols

When file size is an issue in your design, you might want to stick with simple frame-by-frame animation. If you have a little more flexibility in the file size, working with animation symbols can be beneficial. Let's work with some symbols and add a subtle version of the jet animating in the background.

1. Let's turn the jet bitmap into an animation symbol.
   a) Click on the Original tab in the upper left-hand corner of the Document window.
   b) Select the jet bitmap and then select Modify | Symbol | Convert to Symbol.
   c) In the window that opens, enter the name *Airliner* (static) and leave the Type setting as Graphic.
   d) Click on OK. You should see the symbol appear in the Library panel, and a new set of selection handles surrounding the instance on the stage.
2. Next, we will set up an animation using the new *Airliner* symbol on another layer.
   a) Copy the instance of the jet image you just created by pressing the Ctrl (Cmd) + C keys.
   b) In the Layers panel, in the column to the right of the Eye icon in the *Airliner* layer, click to change the Pencil to a Lock icon, so that you cannot make changes to this sublayer.
   c) Create a new layer and drag it directly above the *Airliner* layer. Name the new layer *Jet Animation*.
   d) Press Ctrl + V (Mac: Cmd + V) to paste a new instance (copy) of the jet into the new layer.
   e) Drag this instance of the jet to the right side of the canvas, over the *Click Here* text, as shown in figure 8-31.

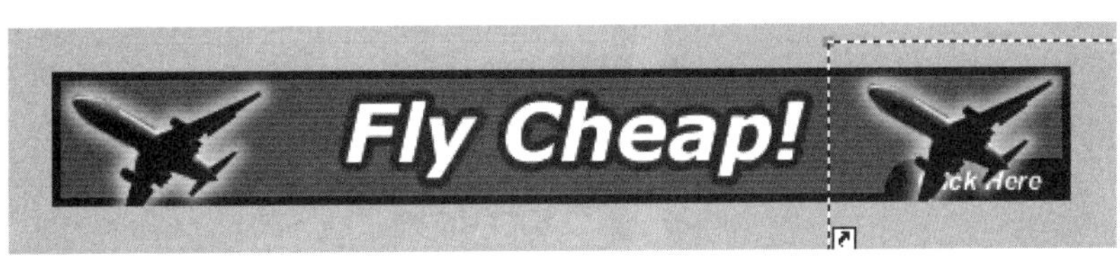

Fig. 8-31. Jet placed over the* Click Here *text.

   f) Select the Frames panel and make sure *Frame 1* is selected. Select the instance and then select Modify | Animation | Animate Selection. This will convert the graphic symbol instance into an animation symbol instance.
   g) The Animate window opens. Establish the following settings.
      - *Frames:* 4
      - *Move:* 370

- *Direction:* 180
- *Opacity:* 10 to 60

Click on the OK button.

h) Note that on the main canvas you now see a line with four dots, representing the animation sequence through the four frames. See figure 8-32.

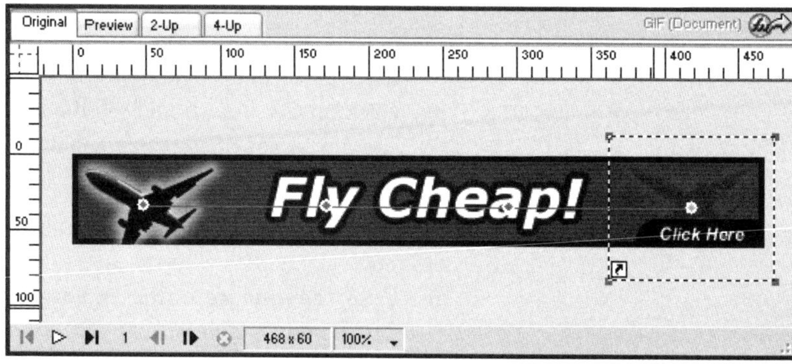

Fig. 8-32. Animation symbol indicating the path over four frames.

i) In the Frames panel, click on *Frame 4* and use the arrow keys to move the selected animation symbol of the jet so that it perfectly lines up with the graphic instance of the jet on the locked *Airliner* layer. The placement of the jet animation symbol in *Frame 4* determines where the animation will end up during the transition between *Frame 1* and *Frame 4*. We do not need to worry about the placement of the animation symbol in *Frame 2* and *Frame 3* because Fireworks calculates the movement between *Frame 1* and *Frame 4* for you.

j) Preview the animation using the controller in the Document window. As the plane moves behind the text, the opacity of the jet increases because we specified that the opacity should go from 10 to 60. 100 is the highest degree of opacity. 0 is completely transparent.

Symbol Tweening

To finish, let's try a slightly different way of producing the same jet animation. This time we will use an effect called *symbol tweening* to create the animation. Symbol tweening provides greater control over the animated effect than the animation symbol. Not only will we create movement and opacity effects, as we did with the animation symbol, but we will also fade the glow effect out while the animation occurs. This type of control over effects is not possible with an animation symbol.

·T/P·

When using symbol tweening, you have to use two or more instances of the same symbol. Furthermore, if you want to tween an effect such as Glow, it must be the same effect applied to both instances of the symbol.

1. First let's set up the symbol tween.
   a) Delete the *Jet Animation* layer by selecting it in the Layers panel and then clicking on the Trash Can icon. You have just deleted the previous animation.
   b) Add a new layer above the *Airliner* layer and name it *Jet Tween*.
   c) Click on the Padlock icon next to the *Airliner* layer to unlock this layer.
   d) Double click on the jet on the canvas to open the Symbol Editing Mode window, in order to delete the Glow effect. Currently, the Glow effect resides inside the symbol. Because anything inside the original symbol is applied to all instances of this symbol, we need to delete anything that will not be applied to every instance (copy) of the symbol on the canvas.
   e) Click on the Glow effect in the Properties panel. Click on the Effects icon to delete the Glow effect. Close the Symbol Editing window.
   f) Now that we are no longer editing the symbol stored in the library, we will instead add the Glow effect to the instance (copy) on the canvas. Select the jet instance on the main canvas and in the Properties panel click on the Effects + icon and then select Shadow and Glow | Glow. Establish the following property settings.
      - *Width:* 3
      - *Color:* #FFFFFF (white)
      - *Opacity:* 65%
      - *Softness:* 6
   g) Press Ctrl + C (Mac: Cmd + C) to copy the jet instance on the *Airliner* layer. Click on the Eye icon next to the *Airliner* layer to hide the content of this layer.
   h) Select the *Jet Tween* layer and use the keyboard command Ctrl + V (Mac: Cmd + V) to paste an instance into the *Jet Tween* layer. Using the Properties pane, set the values for the jet to X = 0 and Y = 0.
   i) In the Properties panel, double click on the Glow effect and change the Opacity setting to 0%.
   j) The following is a quick way of creating another copy of the jet instance. Hold down the Alt key (Mac: Option key) and drag the instance over the *Click Here* text and release the mouse to place the copy in this location.
   k) Select the instance on the right, double click on the Glow effect in the Properties panel, and change the Opacity setting to 65%.
   l) Now let's reduce the opacity of the jet itself. With the instance on the right still selected, in the Properties panel, use the Opacity slider

above the Effects list in the Properties panel to change the opacity of the jet to 15%. See figure 8-33.

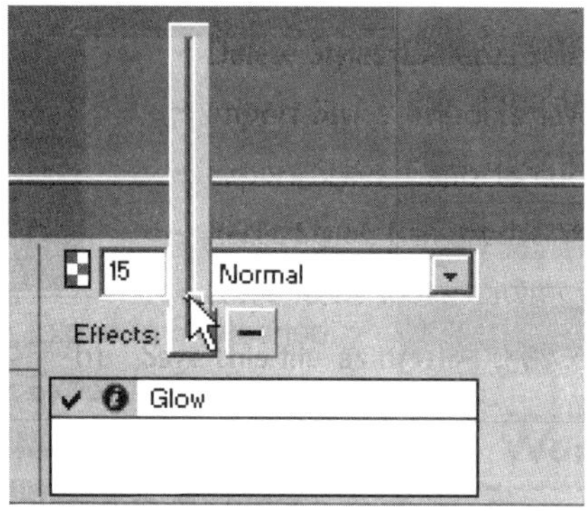

Fig. 8-33. Opacity slider for the **Background** *layer in the Properties panel.*

m) In the Layers panel, drag the sublayer with the jet instance (on the right) below the sublayer with the jet instance on the left of the canvas. This will ensure that the animation plays right to left and not vice versa.

n) The two instances combined make up the completed animation. Press the Shift key, click to select both instances of the jet animation in Layers panel, and select Modify | Symbol | Tween Instances. Establish the following settings in the Tween Instances window that appears.

- *Steps:* 2
- *Distribute to frames:* checked

TIP

If you choose not to use the Distribute to Frames option, you can create a trailing effect of multiple graphics on one frame.

o) Click on OK. You should now see the instance only on the right, at *Frame 1*.

p) Click on the Eye icon next to the *Airliner* layer, to display the content on this layer.

q) Preview the animation using the controller in the Document window. By using the tweening effect, we were able to create the animation and fade the glow so that it does not double up when the animation stops under the static jet on the left.

2. Save the file.
3. Select File | Export Preview to finalize your optimization settings and export the graphic. Note that the tweened animation added some file size, but surprisingly not a lot. Keeping the number of colors and the frame count down helped counter the effects of tweening.

CHAPTER 9

Working with JavaScript Behaviors

Chapter Topics:

- *Introduction*
- *Guided Tour 9A: The Behaviors Panel*
- *Practice Exercise 9-1: Building a Menu Using Swap Image Behaviors*
- *Practice Exercise 9-2: Adding Status Text to a Button*

Introduction

In Chapter 6 you learned how to export HTML code along with sliced graphics in order to create a web page with the same layout as your original Fireworks MX document. Along with HTML code, Fireworks can also export JavaScript behaviors that are automatically incorporated into the HTML coding. For those who are not familiar with coding, JavaScript is a scripting language that allows you to control how elements of a web page behave, often based on the actions of the user. These behaviors are probably familiar to anyone who surfs the Web, although you may not have been aware that it was a JavaScript behavior responsible for what you saw or heard on screen.

One familiar example of a JavaScript behavior is a button rollover effect. The effect occurs when the mouse cursor is positioned over (or rolls over) the button and results in the button changing appearance. The button may appear to glow or change color. Other uses of JavaScript include automatically redirecting a user to a new URL, controlling the display of a browser status bar, and creating pop-up windows. Again, these are just a few of the many examples of how JavaScript can be used on web pages.

In Fireworks MX, you can apply JavaScript behaviors to slices and hotspots on your *Web* layer by using the Behaviors panel (another panel you will work with in the material that follows). Behaviors are prewritten, self-contained bits of "programming code" built into Fireworks MX to perform specific functions. Behaviors consist of two parts: an event that triggers the code to start, and the action that results from the event being triggered. In the example cited in the previous paragraph, the event is the mouse cursor moving over the button. The action is the change in appearance of the button.

Using the Behaviors panel, you can customize and apply these behaviors without ever needing to know how to actually write the programming code. When the files are exported, you can then choose to export the HTML and JavaScript code, just as you did when working with slices. In this chapter, we will cover the basics of working with behaviors. By the end of the chapter you will be able to:

- *Identify and list the behaviors available in the Behaviors panel*
- *Work with hotspots, the* Web *layer, and the Properties panel for event control*
- *Manipulate frames and the Swap Image behavior to create rollovers*
- *Control the status bar on rollovers by using the Status behavior*

Guided Tour 9A: The Behaviors Panel and Behavior Types

JavaScript behaviors are simply prebuilt JavaScript commands that add functionality to your Fireworks designs by adding one or more behaviors to a slice or hotspot object. To add, remove, and edit behaviors, you will need to work with the Behaviors panel. Adding behaviors is a simple process that does not require knowledge of programming. In this guided tour, you will open a sample file and learn how to apply and customize behaviors.

Behavior Basics

1. Select File | Open and browse in the *Chapter 9* folder on the companion CD-ROM. Double click on the file *Tour_9A.png* to open the file in Fireworks.

To attach a behavior to part of your image, you will first need to define areas of your document with a hotspot or slice. The file you just opened already has slices created for you over the buttons on the canvas. As you probably remember from Chapter 6, you normally add slices by selecting the Slice tool and drawing a selection around the target graphic. The slices are automatically created on sublayers in the *Web* layer. You may want to review Chapter 6 if your memory of "slices" recalls oranges or golf swings rather than web graphics.

2. Let's take a look at the slices that have already been inserted in the *Tour_9A.png* file.
   a) You can display the *Web* layer either by clicking on the Show Slices and Hotspots button in the Web toolbox (shown in figure 9-1) or by clicking on the Eye icon next to the *Web* layer in the Layers panel (shown in figure 9-2).

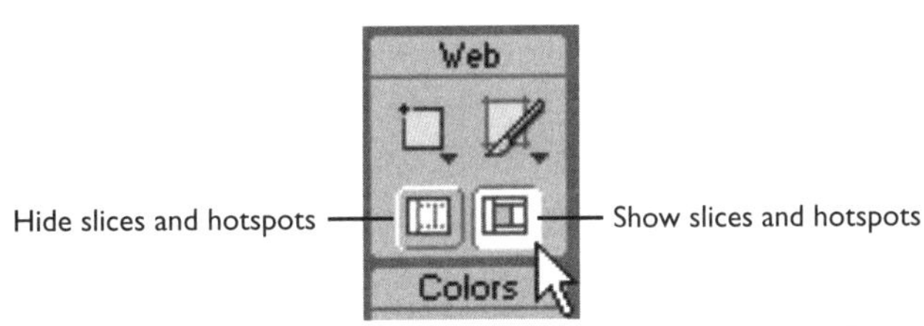

Fig. 9-1. Show/Hide Slices and Hotspots button in Web toolbox.

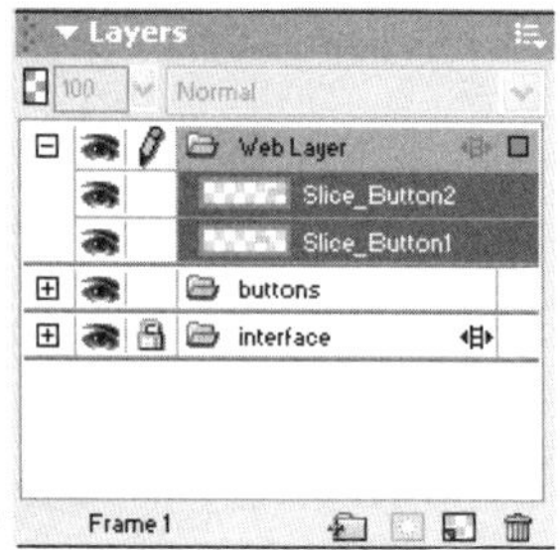

Fig. 9-2. Eye icon next to **Web** *layer in the Layers panel.*

> **TIP**
>
> As you learned in Chapter 1, panels can be opened and closed independently, or you can create custom group panels based on whatever panels you would like to put together. Once you have created a custom group panel, the group panel will open as you have defined it each time you open Fireworks MX.

b) Two slices are revealed on the canvas completely covering each button. (See figure 9-3.) These slices will eventually trigger a button rollover behavior, and therefore the slices have been drawn to completely cover the intended active area.

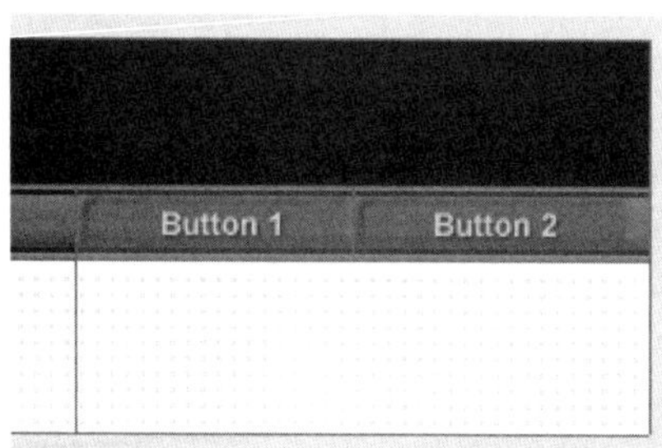

Fig. 9-3. Green slices on canvas over **Button 1** *and over* **Button 2.**

c) Select the Pointer tool and then click on *Button 1* on the canvas. Look in the Layers panel, under the *Web* layer. As you can see, the slice for *Button 1* is highlighted.

d) Click on *Button 2* on the canvas. In the Layers panel, you can now see that the slice for *Button 2* is highlighted.

Rollover Behaviors

As you continue in this guided tour, you will learn to create a simple rollover behavior. Essentially, a rollover is triggered when a user places the mouse cursor over a graphic, such as a button, on a web page. The JavaScript attached to this button responds to the user's mouse placement by swapping out the original image with a second (rollover) graphic. The original image is often called the Up state of the button. The image that appears when the user rolls over the Up state is called the Over state.

Most button rollovers return the button to the Up state when the user moves the mouse cursor outside the area of the graphic. Because you have two graphics that are swapped in and out, an easy way to create this effect is to use two frames in Fireworks MX. This means that the Up state (the default graphic) is created on *Frame 1* and the rollover graphic is created on *Frame 2*. Once we insert a slice over the button, we can then attach a JavaScript behavior that swaps the images in and out based on a user's actions.

1. Let's take a closer look at the buttons and frames in the *Tour_9A.png* file.
   a) Hide the *Web* layer by clicking on the Hide Slices and Hotspots button in the Web toolbox (or by clicking on the Eye icon next to the *Web* layer) so that you can get a better look at the graphics. As you work with slices in Fireworks, you will discover that frequently showing and hiding the *Web* layer is a very common task when setting up graphics and interactivity.
   b) The Layers panel and Frames and History panel group are probably already open (take a look in the lower portion of the panel groupings on the right side of your screen). If the Frames panel is not already open, go ahead and open it now (Window | Frames). If the Frames and History panel group is on screen, you may need to click on the triangle in order to expand the panel group to view the Frames and History tabs. Now you may need to click on the Frames tab to bring the Frames panel to the front (if it is not already).
   c) You should see that there are two frames in the Frames panel. Click on each frame and take a look at the content of each on the canvas. The only noticeable difference between the content of *Frame 1* and *Frame 2* is the color of the button and button text. In *Frame 2* the Up state button colors are replaced with the Over state button colors, which are a darker blue button background and yellow button text. Once we apply a rollover behavior to the slice covering each button, this will constitute our basic design for a simple rollover effect that switches the graphics from *Frame 1* to *Frame 2* when the user's mouse rolls over the button. The rest of the design is the same in both frames and will not have any behaviors attached.
   d) As a quick side note, you can also look at the content of frames from the Layers panel. Click on the Layers tab to open that panel. Use the Frame menu located in the lower left-hand corner of the Layers panel to toggle between *Frame 1* and *Frame 2*. See figure 9-4.

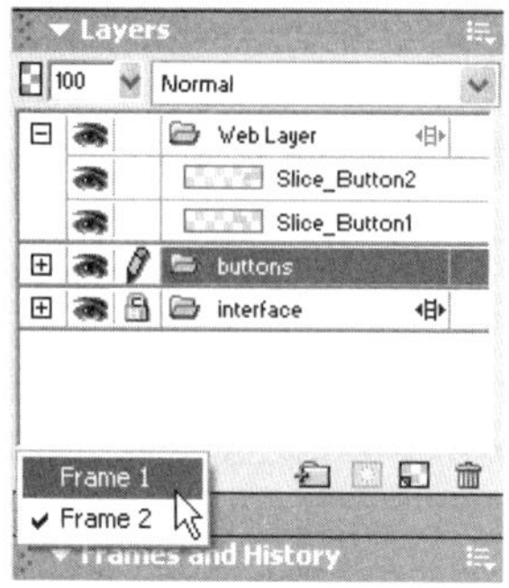

Fig. 9-4. Frame menu in the Layers panel.

e) Take a look at the *Interface* layer and note the Share Across Frames symbol to the right of the layer name. (See figure 9-5.) This symbol indicates that the content of the layer (all sublayers) will be visible across each frame in the document. Note that the *buttons* layer does not have this symbol because the text and button color in this layer will change in *Frame 2*.

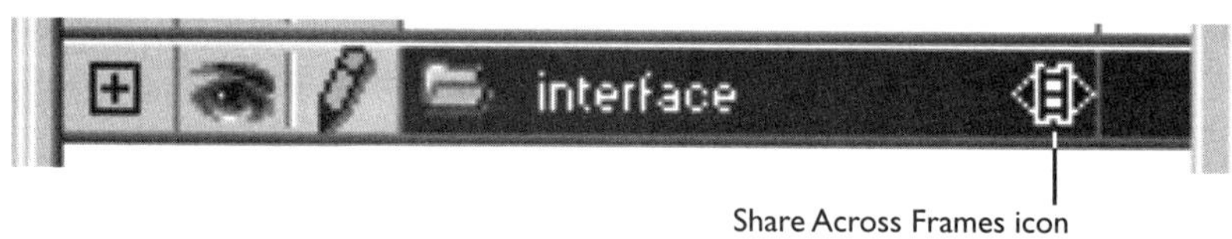

Fig. 9-5. Share Across Frames symbol.

TIP

The *Web* layer is always shared across all frames. This means that the slices and hotspots you create on the *Web* layer are applied to all graphic states across all frames in the document.

2. Toggle back to *Frame 1* using the Frame menu in the Layers panel. We will now explore a very simple way of applying behaviors to slices before learning more about the Behaviors panel.
   a) Show the slices on the *Web* layer using either of the methods presented in step 2a of the previous section.
   b) Using the Pointer tool, on the canvas click on the slice covering *Button 1*.
   c) A circular icon now appears in the center of the slice.
   d) Click on this circle in the center of the slice. A slice menu now appears. See figure 9-6.

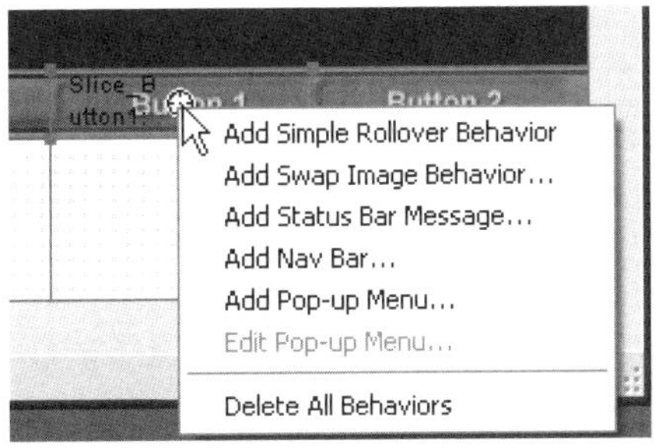

Fig. 9-6. Slice menu containing options.

e) This menu represents the simplest means of adding basic behaviors to a slice.

f) Let's take a closer look. Click on the Add Swap Image Behavior option. As you release the mouse, you will see an options panel appear that allows you to customize the effects of this behavior. Click on the Cancel button in the open window.

g) Click on the circle in the center of the slice again. A slice menu appears.

h) There are additional settings for each of these main options except for Simple Rollover, which has no options.

i) Note that on the very bottom of this menu, you also have the option to delete all behaviors from a slice. Go ahead and select this option, just in case you accidentally added a behavior as we were looking around.

You have now seen one method of adding prebuilt behaviors to slices within Fireworks MX. Let's move on.

The Behaviors Panel and Controls

An alternate method of adding, removing, or editing behaviors attached to a slice is to use the Pointer tool to select the slice on the canvas and then use the Behaviors panel. This second method is often preferred, especially if you need to edit or remove single behaviors after they have been applied, or if you would like to choose from a more extensive list of behaviors. In the next part of this guided tour, you will learn about the components of the Behaviors panel.

1. Open the Behaviors panel by selecting Window | Behaviors.

   a) The Behaviors panel should now appear on screen. See figure 9-7.

As you look at figure 9-7, note the first two columns – Events and Actions. A Behavior is composed of two parts, the Event and the resulting Action. The Event is the trigger or situation that activates the Behavior. Common Events include the mouse clicking on an object or the mouse cursor moving over an object. The Action is whatever happens as a result of the Event. Common

Actions include, swapping one image for another or restoring the original image. The third column, Info, displays additional information about the Behavior that is listed.

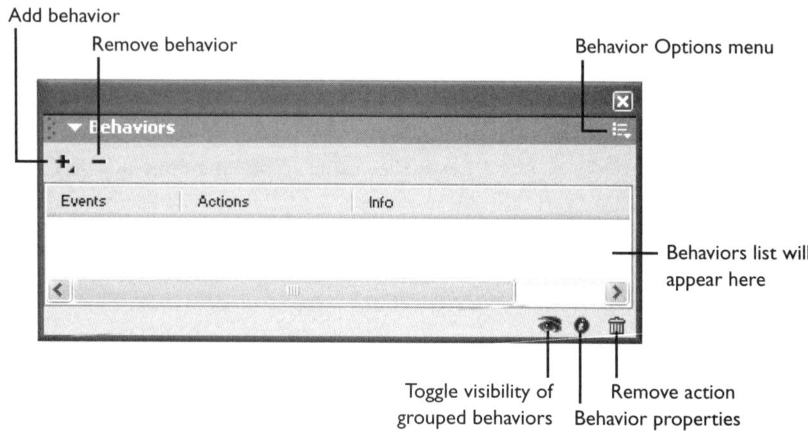

Fig. 9-7. Behaviors panel and its panel controls.

   b) Using the Pointer tool, select the *Button 1* slice on the canvas.

2. Now let's take a closer look at the panel controls, shown in figure 9-7.
   - *Add Behavior (+):* Go ahead and click on the Add Behavior button (Plus icon). You should now see a menu that allows you to select from a list of behaviors to add to a slice or hotspot. See figure 9-8.

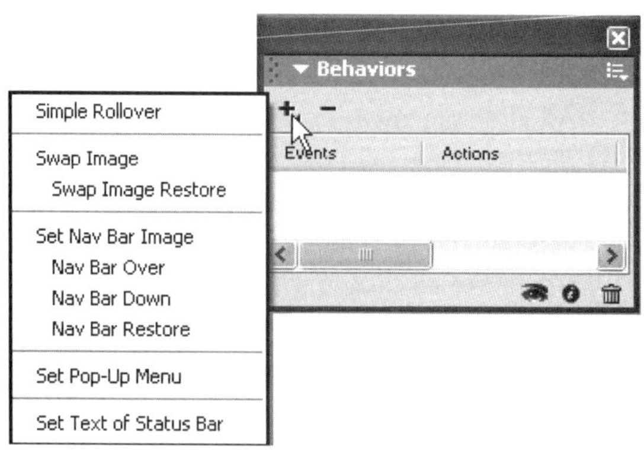

Fig. 9-8. Add Behavior icon with its menu of options.

   - *Remove Behavior (-):* Clicking on the Remove Behavior button (Minus icon) allows you to remove a selected behavior from a slice or hotspot.

- *Behaviors List:* The center section of the Behaviors panel is split into three columns that list each component of the behavior already attached to a slice or hotspot. You may need to either use your mouse to make the Behaviors panel wider or use the scroll bar at the bottom of the panel to scroll to the right to see all columns. The first column, Events, displays the mouse event that triggers the behavior. The second column, Actions, lists the thing that is actually done by the behavior. Events and actions are explored further later in this chapter. The third column, Info, provides additional information about how the slice or hotspot has been customized.
- *Toggle Visibility of Grouped Behaviors (Eye icon):* Some behaviors actually contain multiple behaviors that work together to achieve a certain effect. For example, the Swap Image behavior automatically includes both the Swap Image and the Swap Image Restore behaviors. This second command restores the original image based on a user action. The Toggle Visibility button will show and hide the grouping of actions within a behavior.
- *Behavior Properties (i icon):* Launches the Properties window for a selected behavior. This is the same as double clicking on the action of a behavior in the Behaviors list.
- *Remove Action (trash can icon):* Removes a selected behavior from the Behaviors list.

3. Now let's take a closer look at the Options menu of the Behaviors panel. Click in the upper right-hand corner of the Behaviors panel to access the Options menu. See figure 9-9.

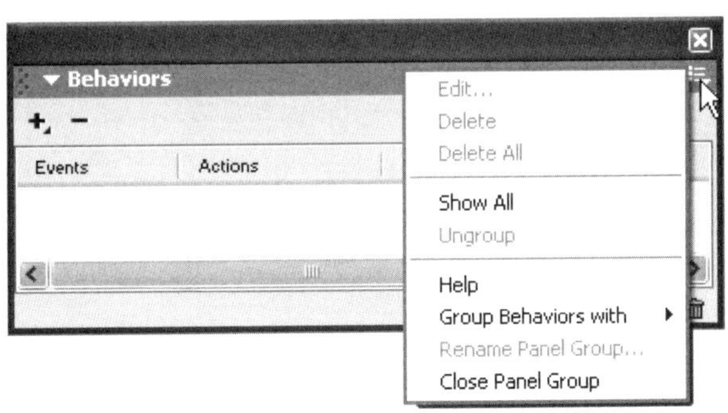

Fig. 9-9. Options menu of the Behaviors panel.

- *Edit:* Allows you to edit the properties for a selected behavior.
- *Delete:* Allows you to delete a selected behavior.
- *Delete All:* Deletes all behaviors attached to a slice or hotspot.

·TIP·

The last four menu choices listed here reference global panel settings that are not specific to Behaviors but are listed in the menu as a matter of conveniece.

- *Show All:* Same as Toggle Visibility. Will show the groupings of actions within a behavior.
- *Ungroup:* Will ungroup actions within a behavior so that each component can be configured.
- *Help:* Opens a help window with content listings, index, search functionality, and favorite capabilities selections, especially for behaviors.
- *Group Behaviors With:* Opens a menu that allows you to group the Behaviors panel with a number of other panels.
- *Rename Panel Group:* Allows you to provide another name for the custom panel group you have created.
- *Close Panel Group:* Closes the currently open panel group containing the Behaviors panel.

4. Now let's add a behavior to the *Button 1* slice.
   a) Click with the Pointer tool to select *Button 1* on the canvas, if it is not already selected.
   b) Click on the Add Behavior (+ icon) button in the Behaviors panel.
   c) Select the Swap Image behavior from the Options menu. The Swap Image window appears. (See figure 9-10.) Read the description of this behavior at the bottom of this window. For now, click on the OK button in this window to use the default settings. We will return to this window later in this chapter.

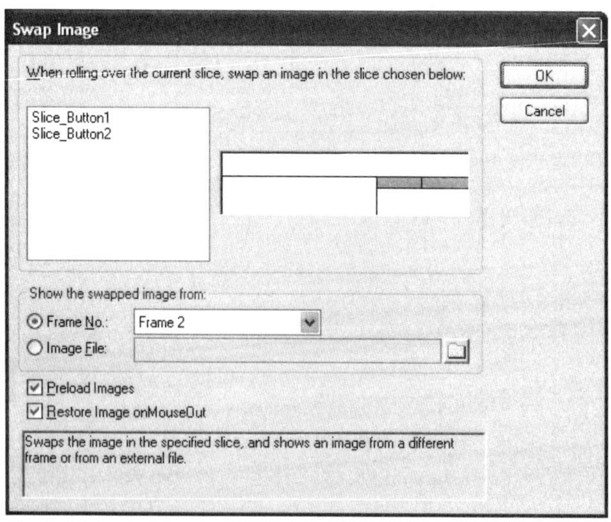

Fig. 9-10. Swap Image window after selecting the Swap Image behavior.

d) Note that the Swap Image behavior now appears, with an event and an action, in the Behaviors list of the Behaviors panel, as shown in figure 9-11.

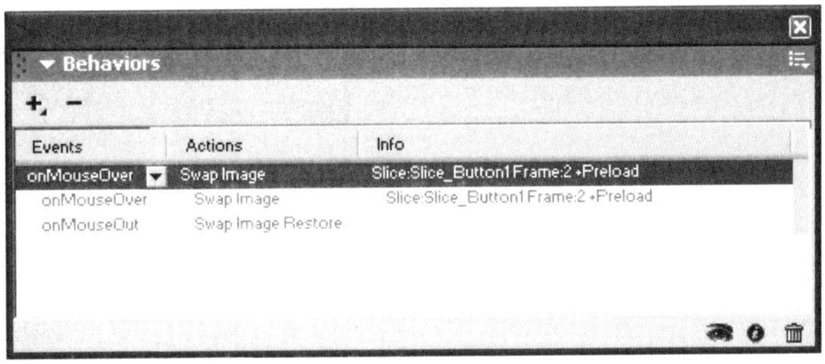

Fig. 9-11. Behaviors panel with newly added Swap Image behavior.

5. Take a closer look at this newly added behavior in the Behaviors panel.
   a) Click on the Toggle Visibility of Grouped Behaviors button, located in the lower right-hand corner of the Behaviors panel (the Eye icon). Note that the Swap Image behavior is actually two actions combined: Swap Image and Swap Image Restore (both are indented below the initial Swap Image behavior).
   b) Note the first indented action, Swap Image. The default event for the Swap Image action is *onMouseOver*. This event setting signals that when the user "mouses over" or moves the mouse cursor over the button, the JavaScript behavior is triggered. The default settings tell Fireworks to replace the image in *Frame 1* with the image in *Frame 2* when the mouse cursor "mouses over" this first button.
   c) Click on the Triangle icon next to the *onMouseOver* text to display the Event menu, shown in figure 9-12.

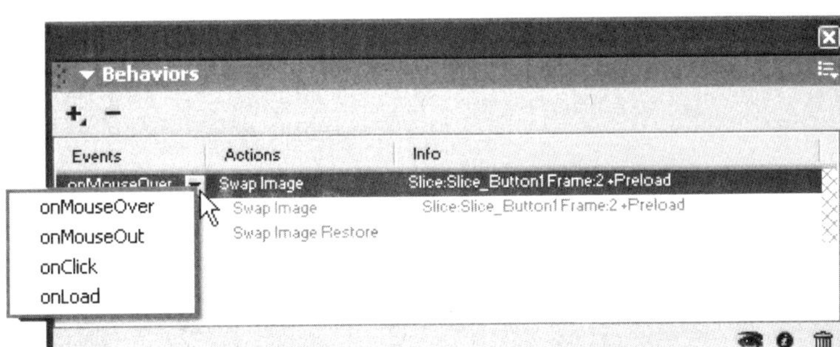

Fig. 9-12. Event menu opened by clicking on the Triangle icon.

You can select any of these options from the menu to control how your file behaves. The event options are as follows.

- *onMouseOver:* Triggers the action when the mouse cursor rolls over the slice or hotspot.
- *onMouseOut:* Triggers the action when the mouse cursor moves off the slice or hotspot.
- *onClick:* Triggers the action when the user clicks the mouse on a slice or hotspot.
- *onLoad:* Triggers the action when the page loads.

d) Click on the gray blank area or empty canvas to close the window.

e) Examine the second indented action, *Swap Image Restore*. The default event for this action is *onMouseOut*. This action tells Fireworks to restore the original image when the mouse cursor leaves the *Button 1* area.

6. Once you have applied a behavior, you might want to edit the behavior properties.

   a) To return to the action properties for a behavior, double click on the Swap Image action in the Behaviors panel. Make sure to double click directly on Swap Image in the Actions column in order to open the Swap Image settings window.

   b) These window settings will change depending on the behavior you have selected. In this example, the Swap Image window allows you to designate which slice is swapped out, along with what image file and frame is used. We will look at this window in greater detail in material to follow.

   c) Click on the Cancel button to close this window.

   d) You can also edit a behavior displayed in the Behaviors panel by first selecting it in the panel and then clicking on the Behavior Properties button (the *i* icon located in the lower right-hand corner of the Behaviors panel). This opens the same Swap Image window you just saw. If you opened this window, go ahead and close it.

7. Removing a behavior is a very simple procedure. To delete the Swap Image action from the Behaviors panel, select the Swap Image action from the Behaviors panel and then perform one of the following.

   - *Click on the Remove Behavior (Minus icon) button*
   - *Click on the Remove Action button (Trash Can icon) at the bottom right of the panel*
   - *Select Delete or Delete All from the Options menu in the Behaviors panel*

Shortcut

You can remove multiple behaviors attached to an object at one time by selecting Delete All from the Options menu.

Behavior Types

There are five basic behavior types available in Fireworks MX. Some of these behaviors are actually groups of actions that perform a task. Click on the Add Behavior (+ icon) to open the Options menu. Note that this window is divided by horizontal lines into five categories. These are the basic behavior types. See figure 9-13.

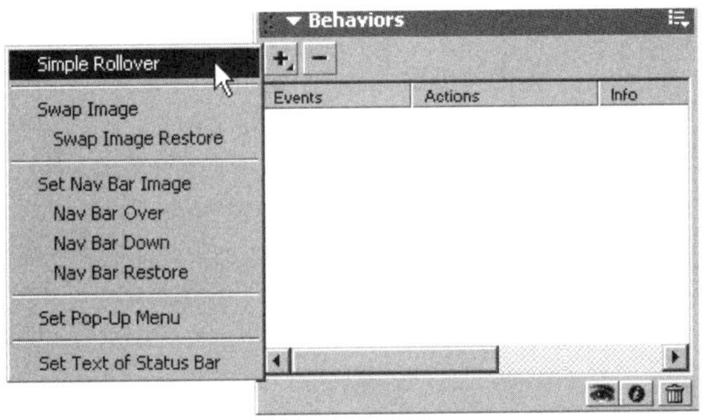

Fig. 9-13. Five categories of behaviors in the Options menu, separated by horizontal lines.

Simple Rollover

First, let's examine the Simple Rollover behavior.

1. Simple Rollover generates a simple highlight state (rollover) when the user moves the cursor over a button. Simple Rollover creates a rollover effect between the graphic on the first frame and the graphic on the second frame. Simple Rollover is similar to the Swap Image behavior; the difference is that it does not have any options, as does the Swap Image behavior. Options within the Swap Image settings window allow you to customize which slices and frames will swap.
   a) Using the Pointer tool, select the *Button 1* slice on the canvas.
   b) Click on the Add Behavior button (+ icon) on the Behaviors panel.
   c) Select Simple Rollover from the list.
   d) Note that no window appears. Instead, the Simple Rollover action is applied directly to the behavior list for the *Button 1* slice. This is all that needs to be done to set up this behavior.
   e) Note that Simple Rollover is actually two actions combined: Swap Image and Swap Image Restore. (Click on the Toggle Visibility of Grouped Behaviors button, if you need to). These are the same actions you saw in step 5a above.

CAUTION

Simple Rollover requires the equivalent of two graphics frames in the same slice area to work correctly.

f) To preview the Simple Rollover behavior, select the Preview tab on the Document window. Now move your cursor over the *Button 1* image. You should see that the button reads *Over state* and remains on screen as long as you keep the mouse over *Button 1*.

g) Select the Original tab to exit preview mode.

Swap Image

Next, let's take a closer look at the Swap Image behavior.

1. As we just saw, the Simple Rollover behavior was actually a Swap Image function without any adjustable properties. It only works between *Frame 1* and *Frame 2* within a single slice. Swap Image, on the other hand, will perform a similar task, but will also allow you to create additional rollover effects where a mouseover event can trigger a swap image on other slices and graphics across multiple frames.
   a) Using the Pointer tool, select the *Button 2* slice.
   b) Click on the Add Behavior button (+ icon) on the Behaviors panel.
   c) Select Swap Image from the list.
   d) This time a Swap Image window appears with the adjustable properties for the Swap Image behavior. Let's take a closer look. See figure 9-14.

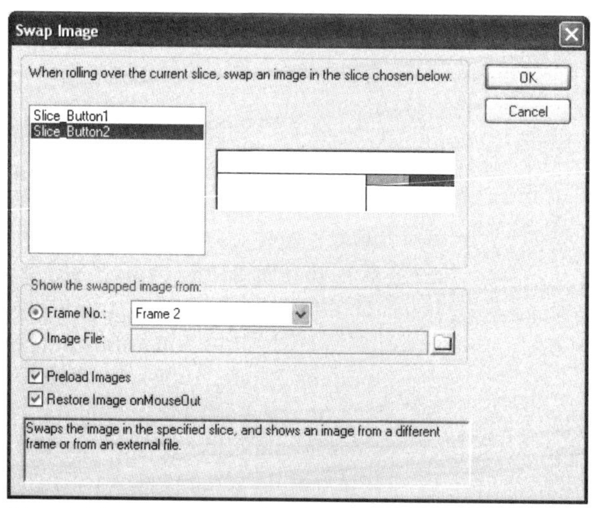

***Fig. 9-14. Swap Image window for* Button 2.**

- *Choose Slice for the Image Swap:* The top section of the Swap Image window is dedicated to selecting the slice that will be replaced – in other words, what is originally on screen. You can select a slice either by clicking on the slice name on the left or by clicking on the slice in the graphic preview located on the right.

·TIP·

Preload Images and Restore Image onMouseOut are included by default when using the Simple Rollover behavior. They are optional when using the Swap Image behavior.

- *Show the Swapped Image from:* In the bottom section of the Swap Image window, either select a frame number or select an external image file to link to and load it into the slice.
- *Preload Images:* Preload the images to be "swapped in," as well as the default images when the page loads. Preload Images is selected by default so that the swapped-in graphics are downloaded immediately to the browser cache as the page loads (so that there is no delay in the rollover effect).
- *Restore Image onMouseOut:* Restores the original image when the cursor leaves the slice that triggered the action.

e) Make sure the *Button 2* slice is selected in the Swap Image window and that the frame number is *Frame 2*. Click on the OK button.

f) In the Behaviors panel, make sure Toggle Visibility of Grouped Behaviors is on. If it is not, click on this button at the bottom of the Behaviors panel. Note that the two grouped actions for the Swap Image behavior are the same as those for the Simple Rollover behavior.

g) To preview the Swap Image behavior, select the Preview tab on the Document window. Move the cursor over the *Button 1* and *Button 2* images. Note that exactly the same rollover effect has been accomplished even though different behaviors are attached to these images. Let's try editing the properties of the Swap Image behavior to examine one of the differences between the Simple Rollover behavior and the Swap Image behavior.

h) To exit preview mode, select the Original tab.

i) Select the *Button 1* slice on the canvas. Click on the Trash Can icon to delete the Simple Rollover behavior.

j) Select the *Button 2* slice on the canvas. In the Behaviors panel, double click on the Swap Image behavior in the Actions column. The Swap Image window opens.

k) In the Swap Image window, in the top section of the window, select the *Button 1* slice name from the list or click on the *Button 1* preview drawing. (See figure 9-15.) Leave the frame number set to *Frame 2*. Click on the OK button.

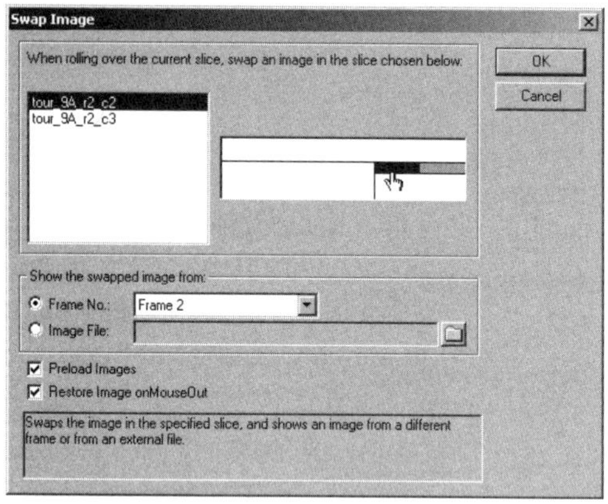

Fig. 9-15. **Button 1** *slice selected.*

l) To preview the changes to the Swap Image behavior, select the Preview tab on the Document window. Now move your cursor over the *Button 2* image. Note that by changing the slice to *Button 1*, we can now have the *Button 1* image swap when we mouse over *Button 2*. With the Simple Rollover behavior, this effect is not possible.

m) Select the Original tab. Delete the Swap Image effect from the *Button 2* slice.

n) Close this file without saving it.

Set Nav Bar Image

So far we have seen two ways of working with buttons using the Simple Rollover behavior and the Swap Image behavior – as you would normally and then with disjointed rollovers. The Set Nav Bar behavior also allow you to create button effects. A Set Nav Bar behavior can have a rollover state, a down state (appearance as it is clicked on), and a "restore to the original button" state. The extra button state (down) is not the only advantage to this behavior, as it also creates a grouping of buttons that react together. With a Set Nav Bar behavior, when you click on a button it is depressed or switches to its down state. It remains depressed until another button is clicked. Then it returns to the default image when the new selection is depressed.

As an analogy, you might think of a kitchen blender that has push-button controls. Before starting, the Off button is pressed down and stays down until you press another button. When you press the Low speed button, it goes down as the Off button comes back up, and so on. The Set Nav Bar behavior must have at least three frames in order to switch between these different states. Usually, the Set Nav Bar behavior is used with frame sets in HTML. The Set Nav Bar behavior needs to be downloaded only once, and will reflect the state of the currently selected buttons on the download page.

1. Let's try adding a Set Nav Bar behavior.
   a) Select File | Open and browse in the *Chapter 9* folder on the companion CD-ROM. Select and open the *Tour_9A_navbar.png* file. On the canvas, this file looks the same as the *Tour_9A.png* file you worked with in the previous guided tour.
   b) Examine the Frames panel, and note that this file has four frames. The third frame is the *Down* frame we will use in the Set Nav Bar behavior. The fourth frame is the *Over While Down* frame (more on this button state in the descriptions in step f).
   c) Select the *Button 1* slice on the canvas.
   d) Click on the Add Behavior button (+ icon) on the Behaviors panel.
   e) Select the *Set Nav Bar Image* action from the list.
   f) A window appears with the adjustable properties for Set Nav Bar, as shown in figure 9-16. The properties available in this window are outlined in the following.

TIP

All button slices within the group of frames must have this behavior attached to them in order to work correctly. This behavior is actually a group of behaviors, including Nav Bar Over, Nav Bar Down, and Restore Nav bar.

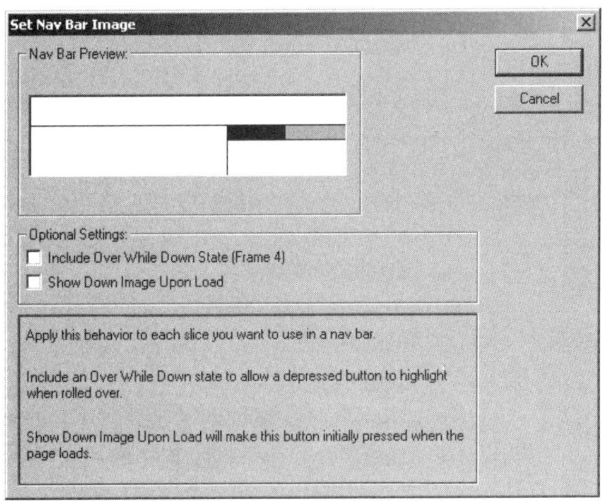

Fig. 9-16. Set Nav Bar Image window.

- *Include Over While Down State (Frame 4):* This effect requires button state graphics to be built across three or four frames. Frame 1 holds the default (or normal) Up button. Frame 2 holds the Rollover button. Frame 3 holds the Down button. Frame 4 is optional and can hold the Over While Down button. Check this option if you would like a rollover state for the button that is currently depressed.
- *Show Down Image Upon Load:* This will show the Down state of a button within the group as the selected page loads.

g) For now, leave the default settings and click on the OK button. Note that there are now three indented items that are part of this behavior. See figure 9-17.

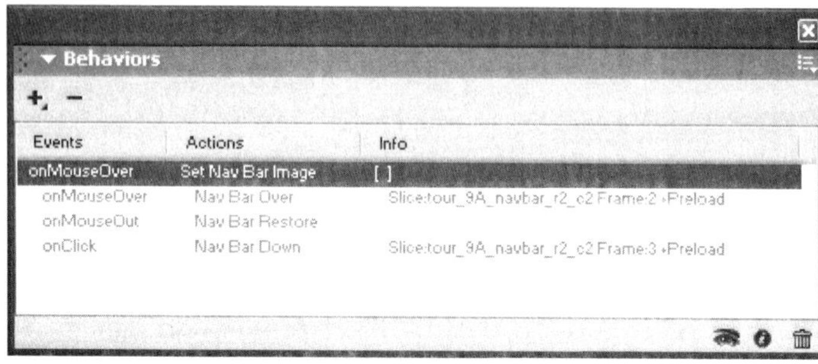

Fig. 9-17. Three aspects of the Set Nav Bar behavior.

h) Select the *Button 2* slice on canvas.
i) Click on the Add Behavior button (+ icon) on the Behaviors panel.
j) Select the Set Nav Bar Image action from the list.
k) A window appears with the adjustable properties for the Set Nav Bar Image behavior.
l) Click on the OK button to accept the default properties.

2. Now let's take a look at what we just accomplished.
   a) To preview the Set Nav Bar Image behavior, select the Preview tab on the Document window.
   b) Hide the *Web* layer in order to see the buttons more clearly.
   c) Move the cursor over the *Button 1* image. The Over state in *Frame 2* appears.
   d) Click on the *Button 1* image. When you click on the button, *Frame 3* (the Down state for *Button 1*) appears.
   e) Move the cursor over the *Button 2* image to display the Over state (*Frame 2*).
   f) Click on *Button 2*. The Down state for *Button 2* appears, and *Button 1* automatically switches back to *Frame 1*, the original state. Cool!
3. Next, take a look at how you can modify these other button states.
   a) Click on the Original tab and make the *Web* layer visible again.
   b) Click on *Button 1* on the canvas.
   c) Click on the Add Behavior (+ icon) button and select the Nav Bar Over behavior. Take a look at the window that opens. This behavior allows you to specify the *Over* state graphic for the selected button. You can specify a graphic on a frame or an external file. When you are finished looking around, click on the Cancel button.

d) Click on the Add Behavior button and select the Nav Bar Down behavior. Take a look at the window that opens. This behavior allows you to specify the *down* graphic for this button in the nav bar group. You can specify a graphic on a frame or an external file. When you are finished looking around, click on the Cancel button.

e) Click on the Add Behavior button and select the Nav Bar Restore behavior. Note that no window appears, but look at the last line that was just added to the Behaviors panel. This behavior restores all other slices on the canvas to their respective default state.

f) Select Edit | Undo Add Behavior.

4. For the final step, let's add the Over While Down state in *Frame 4* for *Button 1*.

a) In the Layers panel, make sure the *Web* layer is displayed (Eye icon is present).

b) Select the *Button 1* slice. Double click on the Set Nav Bar Image action in the Behaviors panel to open the Set Nav Bar properties window.

c) Select the Include Over While Down State (*Frame 4*) check box in the middle of the currently open window. (See figure 9-18.) Click on the OK button.

TIP

If you add a frame, for a total of four frames in the Frames panel, this will allow you to set an Over While Down state. This is the same effect as the Over state. However, it is only triggered when the navigation bar is in the Down state.

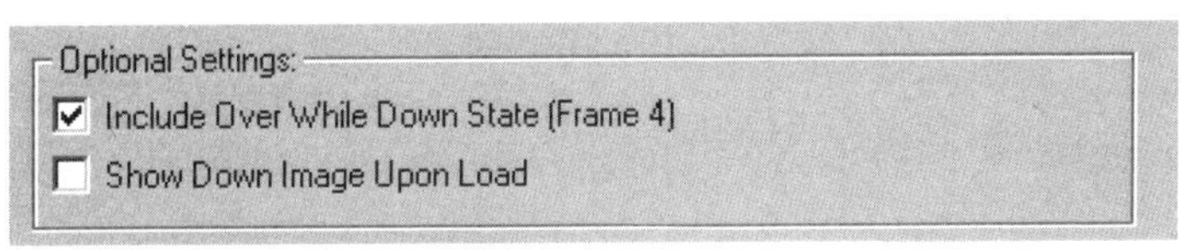

Fig. 9-18. Place a check mark in the Over While Down State* (Frame 4) *check box.

d) Select the *Button 2* slice. Double click on the Set Nav Bar Image action in the Behaviors panel to open the Set Nav Bar properties window.

e) Select the Include Over While Down State (*Frame 4*) check box. Click on the OK button.

f) To preview the Set Nav Bar Image behavior, select the Preview tab in the Document window.

g) Hide the *Web* layer in order to see the buttons more clearly.

h) Move the cursor over the *Button 1* image. The Over state in *Frame 2* appears.

i) Click on the *Button 1* image. When you click on the button, *Frame 3* (the Down state) appears.

j) Move your cursor over the *Button 2* image to display the Over state (*Frame 2*).

k) Move the cursor back over the *Button 1* image to display the Over While Down state (*Frame 4*). This frame displays an Over state while the button is depressed.

l) Click on *Button 2*. The Down state for *Button 2* appears, and *Button 1* automatically switches back to *Frame1*, the original state.

m) Select the Original tab. Delete the Set Nav Bar Image behavior from the *Button 1* and *Button 2* slices.

n) To exit preview mode, click on the Original tab.

Shortcut

Building buttons inside of button symbols automatically adds the Set Nav Bar Image behavior code for you. This technique is used in the practice exercises that follow this guided tour.

Set Pop-Up Menu

The next behavior is Set Pop-Up Menu. This feature has been greatly enhanced in Fireworks MX in order to give you greater control over the display of menus. In the Pop-Up Menu editor, you can easily set the text, links, size, colors, look, and position of menu fields.

1. Let's add the Pop-Up Menu behavior to a slice. Make sure the *Web* layer is currently displayed.
   a) Select the *Button 1* slice.
   b) Click on the Add Behavior button on the Behaviors panel.
   c) Select the Set Pop-Up Menu option from the list.
   d) The Pop-Up Menu editor appears. Note that there are four tabs in this editor. The Content tab should be on top by default (if not, select the Content tab). Let's take a look at the adjustable properties found on this tab. See figure 9-19.

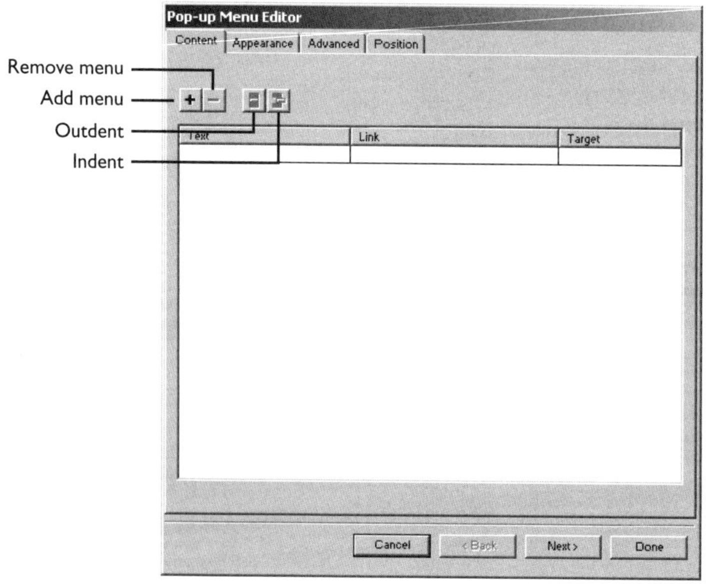

Fig. 9-19. The Content tab with button controls.

- *Add Menu (+ icon):* Adds a menu item to the list.
- *Remove Menu (- icon):* Removes a menu item from the list.
- *Outdent/Indent:* Adds or removes the selected menu line as a submenu for the item above it.
- *Text Column:* Adds the text label for the menu item.
- *Link Column:* Adds the link for each text label.
- *Target Column:* Adds a target if working with a frame set or using a standard target link (_blank, _parent, _top, _self, and so on).

e) Double click on the first line in the Text column, and in the entry window that opens type *Text Link 1*. Press the Enter/Return key.

f) An entry window should have opened on the next line of the Text column (if not, click on the Add Menu button to add another link to the menu and double click on the second line).

g) In the entry window that opens, type *Text Link 2*. Press the Enter/Return key.

h) An entry window should have opened on the next text line (if not, click on the Add Menu button to add another link to the menu and double click on the second line).

i) In the entry window that opens, type *Text Link 3*.

j) Click on the Next button in the lower right-hand corner of the window, or click on the Appearance tab at the top of the window. You should now be looking at the Appearance tab. Let's take a look at the adjustable properties found on this tab. See figure 9-20.

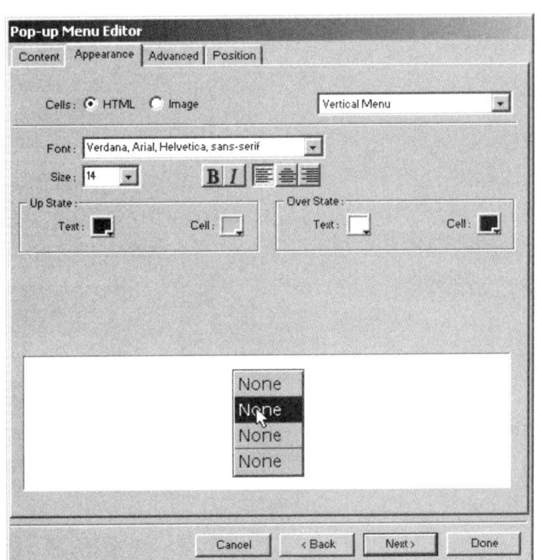

Fig. 9-20. Appearance tab.

- *Cells:* Use either HTML- or image-based graphics to fill the cells of the menu. The selection will update in the preview.
- *Alignment:* Choose either a vertical or horizontal setting for the menu.
- *Font Settings:* Choose a font face, size, style, and justification.
- *Up State:* Choose the text color and cell color for the default state of the menu button cells. If you selected Image in the Cells field, the options listed here will be different and you will see image style previews.
- *Over State:* Choose the text color and cell color for the Over state of the menu button cells. If you selected Image in the Cells field, the options listed here will be different and you will see image style previews.
- *Preview window:* Shows a live preview of all appearance changes made to the menu.

k) Select a font and colors from the Appearance menu.

l) Click on the Next button in the lower right-hand corner of the window, or click on the Advanced tab at the top of the window. You should now be looking at the Advanced tab. Let's take a look at the adjustable properties found on this tab. See figure 9-21.

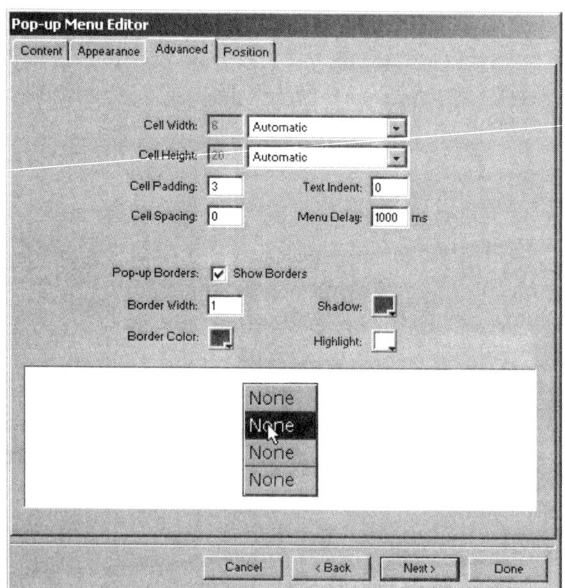

Fig. 9-21. Advanced tab.

- *Cell Width:* Set the width to automatically adjust to the length of the text you have entered, or set the width to a specific pixel number.
- *Cell Height:* Set the height to automatically adjust to the height of the text you have entered, or set the height to a specific pixel number.
- *Cell Padding:* Padding within each table cell affects spacing between the button edge and the text content.
- *Cell Spacing:* Spacing between table cells affects distance between buttons.
- *Text Indent:* Indent space affects distance between text and the button edge.
- *Delay:* Affects the delay time in milliseconds for the menu to close after the cursor has left the active area.
- *Pop-Up Borders:* Controls the width and highlight shadow colors of the menu borders or turns off the borders completely.

m) Select whatever options you would like to on the Advanced tab.

n) Click on the Next button, or click on the Position tab at the top of the window. You should now be looking at the Position tab. Let's take a look at the adjustable properties found on this tab. See figure 9-22.

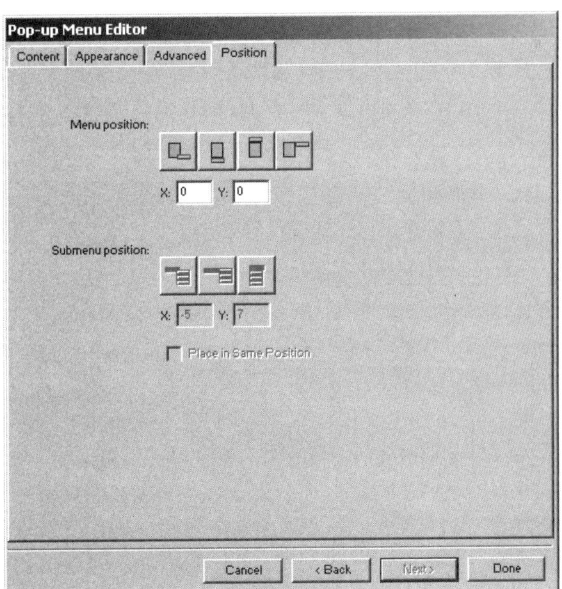

Fig. 9-22. Position tab.

- *Menu Position:* Set the position of the menu relative to the slice that activates it. Use the position icons as well as X and Y coordinates. You can also position the menu by hand later by moving the objects on the canvas. The position icons from left to right are: Set menu position to the bottom-right of slice, Set menu position to the bottom of slice, Set menu position to the top of slice, and Set menu position to the top-right of slice.
- *Submenu Position:* Set the position of submenus relative to the respective button that activated them. Use the position icons (as described above) or use the X and Y coordinates.

o) Click on the Set menu position to the bottom of slice icon. See figure 9-23.

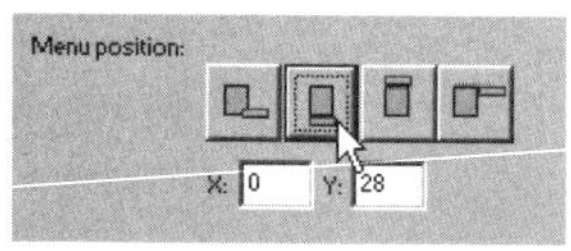

Fig. 9-23.* Set menu position to the bottom slice *icon.

p) Click on the Done button in the lower right-hand corner of the window.

q) If you need to reopen the editor to make adjustments, simply double click on the Show Pop-Up Menu action in the Behaviors panel, or right-click on the slice and select Edit Pop-Up Menu from the list.

r) Press the F12 key to preview the page within your default browser. Move the mouse over *Button 1* to display the pop-up menu you just created. See figure 9-24.

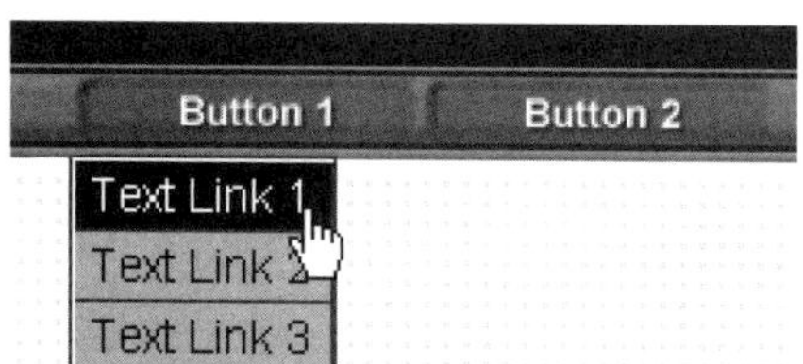

Fig. 9-24. Preview of pop-up menu as seen within a browser.

s) Close the browser window.

t) Select the Pop-Up Menu action in the Behaviors panel. Select the *Button 1* slice and click on the Remove Behavior button (Minus icon) to delete the Set Pop-Up Menu behavior.

Set Text Status

Let's conclude this guided tour of behaviors with a look at the Set Text Status behavior. Text status allows you to customize the text in a web browser's status bar, located at the lower left of the browser window. This area usually flashes URLs and server commands. However, with the Set Text Status behavior, it is possible to use JavaScript to send custom text to the status bar.

1. Let's add the Set Text Status behavior to a slice.
   a) Select the *Button 1* slice on the canvas.
   b) Click on the Add Behavior button on the Behaviors panel.
   c) Select Set Text of Status Bar from the menu.
   d) In the window that appears, type in the message *This is button 1*. Click on the OK button to close the window.
   e) Press the F12 key to preview the page within your default browser. Move the cursor over *Button 1* to display the text in the status bar in the lower left-hand corner of your browser window. See figure 9-25.

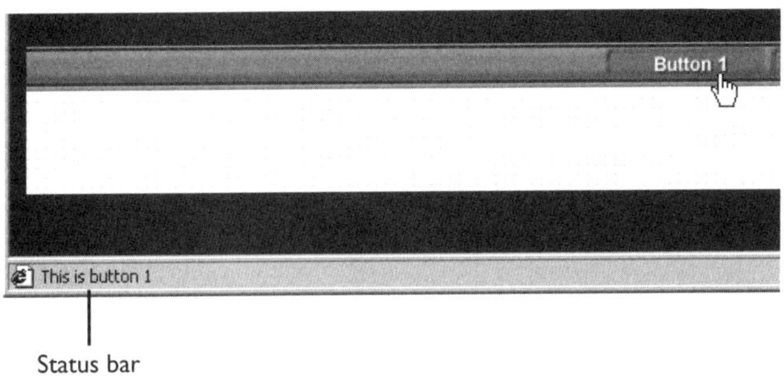

Fig. 9-25. Preview of the status bar in a web browser.

   f) Close the file without saving it.

Now that you have been introduced to the functions of each behavior in the Behaviors panel, let's get some practical experience using the Swap Image behavior to build a menu for our *San Francisco Travel Guide* web site. Practice Exercise 9-1 takes you through this process.

Practice Exercise 9-1: Building a Menu Using Swap Image Behaviors

Description

In this exercise, you will create a simple vertical menu and an image area below the menu. Swap images will appear in the image area. Once this exercise is completed, you will have learned to:

- *Create Swap Image behaviors with disjointed rollovers*

Preview of Completed Exercise

Before beginning the exercise, let's take a look at the buttons in their completed state so that you can clearly see what it is you are about to build.

1. Select File | Open and locate the *Chapter 9* folder on the companion CD-ROM. Find the file named *Exercise9_1(complete).png*. Double click on this file to open it.
2. Click on the Preview tab to preview the completed exercise. Move the mouse over each button to see a corresponding graphic for each button. (See figure 9-26.) This effect is being created with the Swap Image behavior. You may want to hide the *Web* layer in order to see the canvas images more clearly.

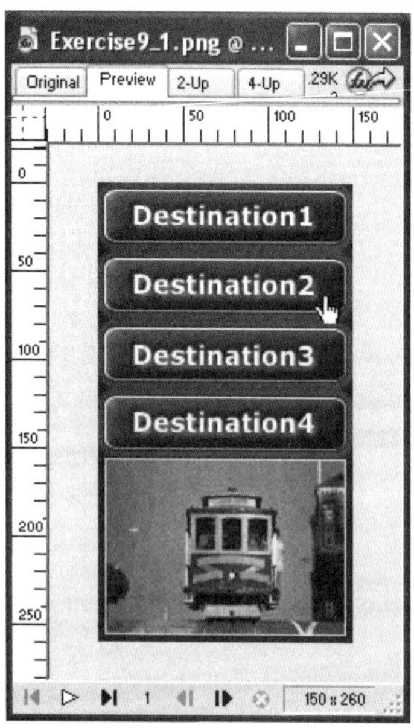

Fig. 9-26. Completed canvas showing images related to each button.

Step-by-Step Instructions

1. We'll start by creating a new file.
   a) Select File | New to open a blank canvas. Set the canvas width to 150 and the height to 260. Leave the Resolution at 72. Set the background color to #003366 (Dark Blue).
   b) Save this file into your *SaveWork* folder with the file name *Exercise9_1.png*.
2. The first thing we need to do is create the button graphics that will be used with the Swap Image behaviors.
   a) In the Layers panel, rename the *Layer 1* default layer as *Buttons*.
   b) Using the Rectangle tool, draw a rectangle on the canvas. Establish the following settings in the Properties panel.
      - *W:* 142
      - *H:* 30
      - *X:* 4
      - *Y:* 4
      - *Fill Color:* Linear; click on the Fill swatch and change the left gradient marker to #006699 and the right gradient marker to #003366. See figure 9-27.
      - *Stroke Color:* White
      - *Stroke Size:* 1, 1-Pixel Soft
      - *Rectangle Roundness:* 36

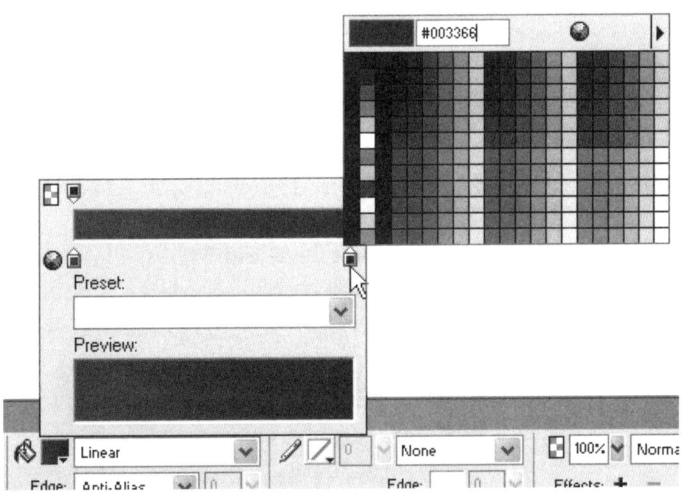

Fig. 9-27. Gradient editor from Fill Color used to set left and right color markers.

3. With the basic shape created, let's now add some effects to complete the button.
   a) In the Properties panel, select the Effects button (+ icon), and then select Bevel and Emboss | Inner Bevel and establish the following property settings.
      - *Bevel Edge Shape:* Smooth
      - *Width:* 12
      - *Contrast:* 75%
      - *Softness:* 3
   b) Now let's add a glow effect to embellish the edges of the button and set it off from the background. Click on the Effects button, select Shadow and Glow | Glow, and establish the following property settings.
      - *Width:* 2
      - *Color:* #FFFFFF (white)
      - *Opacity:* 40%
      - *Softness:* 2
      - *Offset:* 1
4. Let's add some placeholder text on the button.
   a) Select the Text tool. Establish the following settings in the Properties panel.
      - *Font:* Verdana (or other sans serif font)
      - *Font Size:* 15
      - *Font Style:* Bold
      - *Font Color:* White
   b) Click anywhere on the canvas and type *Destination 1*.
   c) Use the Pointer tool to center the text on the button rectangle.
5. Now let's add an effect to the text to blend it in with the button.
   a) With the text object selected, click on the Effects button and then select Bevel and Emboss | Inset Emboss. Leave the default settings.
   b) The text now looks like it is inset, or carved into, the button. See figure 9-28.

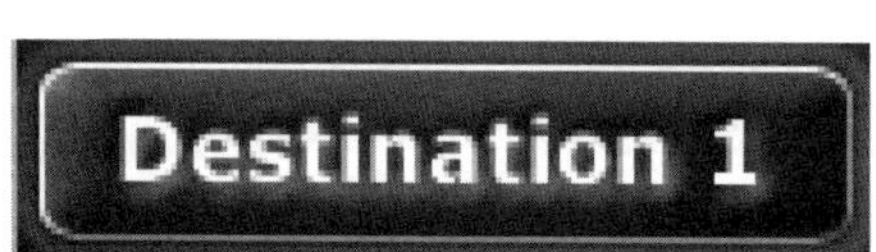

Fig. 9-28. Completed button with inset text and beveled outside edge.

·T/P·

Even though the button rectangle and text are grouped, you do not have to ungroup the object in order to change the text. Simply select the Text tool and highlight the text that needs to be edited.

6. Now let's make the next four buttons based on the first button.
   a) Select the text and the rectangle on the canvas (or in the Layers panel) by using the Pointer tool and holding down the Shift key as you select both of them.
   b) Group the text and rectangle by pressing Ctrl + G (Mac: Cmd + G).
   c) Clone the object by pressing Ctrl + Shift + D (Mac: Cmd + Shift + D). The cloned object is now on top of the first button and is currently selected.
   d) In the Properties panel, establish the following settings for the coordinates of the cloned button.
      - *X:* 4
      - *Y:* 43
   e) Select the Text tool and change the text in the button you cloned to read *Destination 2*.
   f) Select the group object for the *Destination 2* button. Clone the *Destination 2* button by pressing Ctrl + Shift + D (Mac: Cmd + Shift + D). The cloned object is now on top of the second button and is currently selected.
   g) In the Properties panel, establish the following settings for the coordinates of the cloned *Destination 2* button.
      - *X:* 4
      - *Y:* 82
   h) Select the Text tool and change the text to read *Destination 3*.
   i) Select the group object for the *Destination 3* button. Clone the *Destination 3* button by pressing Ctrl + Shift + D (Mac: Cmd + Shift + D). The cloned object is now on top of the third button and is currently selected.
   j) In the Properties panel, establish the following settings for the coordinates of the *Destination 3* button.
      - *X:* 4
      - *Y:* 121
   k) Select the Text tool and change the text to read *Destination 4*. With all four buttons created, your canvas should look similar to that shown in figure 9-29.
   l) Save the file in the *SaveWork* folder.

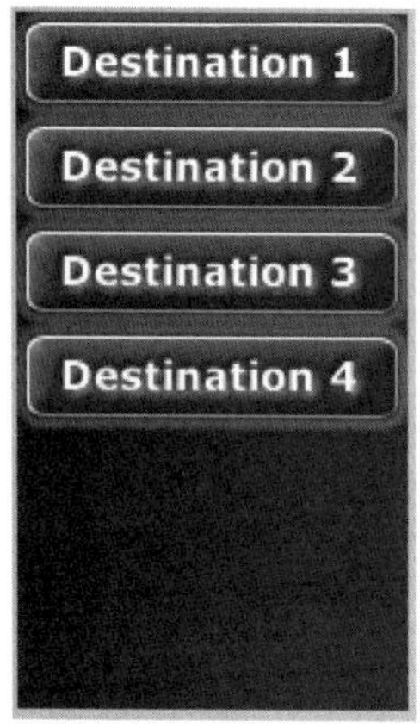

Fig. 9-29. Four finished buttons on canvas.

7. Now let's create the framework for the area where the Swap Image behavior will be viewed when we mouse over the buttons.
   a) In the Layers panel, create a new layer above the *Buttons* layer and name it *Image Frame*.
   b) Using the Rectangle tool, draw a rectangle below the buttons. Establish the following settings in the Properties panel.
      - *W:* 142
      - *H:* 100
      - *X:* 4
      - *Y:* 154
      - *Fill:* No Color
      - *Stroke Color:* White
      - *Stroke Size:* 1-Pixel Soft

Next, we need to import the images that will used for the Swap Image behavior. We will import each image to a different frame and line each up to the frame graphic we just created. Before we do that, however, we need to do a little prep work. Let's start by adding our slices and frames and then placing the images.

8. Let's add slices to define the different areas that will activate the Swap Image behaviors.
   a) Select the Slice tool from the Web toolbox and draw a horizontal slice over the *Destination 1* button. Try to cover the entire button area. See figure 9-30.

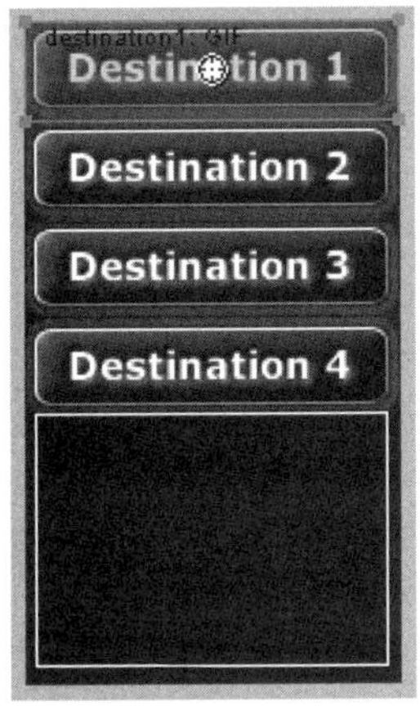

Fig. 9-30. Slice drawn over **Destination 1** *button.*

b) In the Properties panel, change the name of the slice to *destination1*, as shown in figure 9-31.

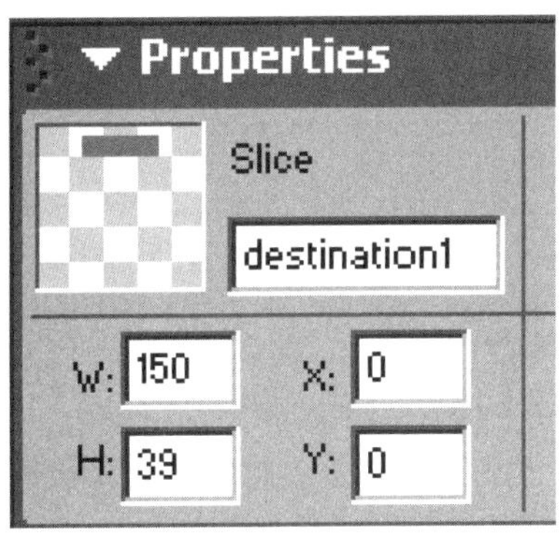

Fig. 9-31. Rename the slice in the Properties panel.

c) Draw slices over the three remaining buttons. Name these slices *destination2*, *destination3*, and *destination4*, to correspond with the button names. Be careful to not overlap any of the slices.

d) Draw a final slice over the white rectangle (image frame) under the buttons.

e) Rename this slice *frame*. You should now have five slices on your canvas and in the Frames panel.

9. Now let's set the *Buttons* layer to be shared across all frames.

   a) Double click on the *Buttons* layer. Do not change the name, but in the lower left-hand corner of the window that opens place a check mark in the Share Across Frames option. You should see an icon appear on the layer next to the *Buttons* label. See figure 9-32.

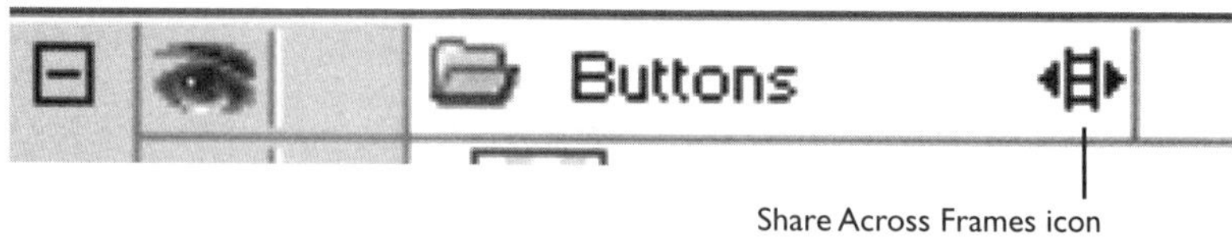

Fig. 9-32. Share Across Frames icon on the **Buttons** *layer.*

b) Repeat step 9a for the *Image Frame* layer.

10. Select the Frames panel tab so that we can add some new frames.
    a) From the Frames Options menu that opens, select Add Frames.
    b) In the Add Frames window that opens, add four frames after the current frame. Click on the OK button. You now have a total of five frames.
    c) Click on *Frame 1*.

11. Now let's import the graphics and place them in different frames.
    a) In the Layers panel, add a new layer between the *Image Frame* layer and the *Buttons* layer. Name the new layer *Images*.
    b) Collapse all layers. Lock all layers except the *Images* layer. Hide the *Web* layer.
    c) Select the *Images* layer. Press the Ctrl + R keys (Mac: Cmd + R) to import the first image. Browse for the *Image1.jpg* file in the *Chapter 9* folder. Click the Pointer tool on the white frame portion on the canvas to place the image there.
    d) Line the image up so that it sits directly under the white frame border of the rectangle.
    e) In the Layers panel, make sure the *Bitmap* sublayer is selected and in the upper left-hand corner of this panel set the opacity to 25%. See figure 9-33.

Shortcut

Use the X-Y coordinates in the Properties panel to precisely align the image with the rectangle's coordinates.

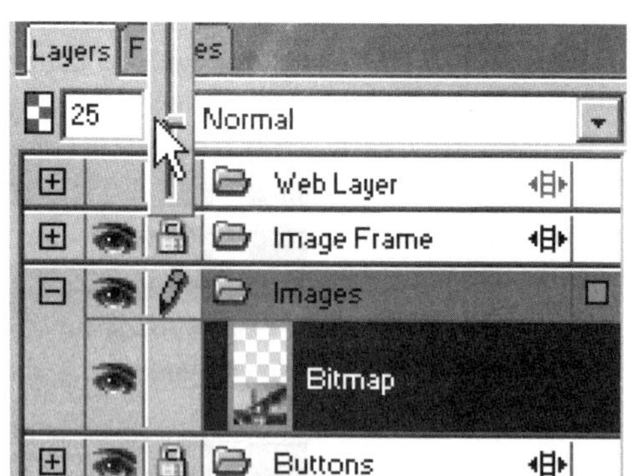

Fig. 9-33. Change the opacity of the **Bitmap** *sublayer.*

TIP

Instead of clicking on the Frames panel to select a frame, remember that the Layers panel has a Frames menu at the bottom left of the panel that can be used to toggle between frames.

f) Toggle to *Frame 2*.
g) Make sure the *Images* layer is selected. Press the Ctrl + R keys (Mac: Cmd + R) to import the *Image2.jpg* file from the *Chapter 9* folder. Click the Pointer tool on the frame portion on the canvas to place the image there.
h) Align the image with the rectangle, but leave the Opacity set at 100.
i) Toggle to *Frame 3*.
j) Make sure the *Images* layer is selected. Press the Ctrl + R keys (Mac: Cmd + R) to import the *Image3.jpg* file from the *Chapter 9* folder onto the *Images* layer.
k) Align the image with the rectangle, but leave the Opacity set at 100.
l) Toggle to *Frame 4*.
m) Make sure the *Images* layer is selected. Press the Ctrl + R keys (Mac: Cmd + R) to import the *Image4.jpg* from the *Chapter 9* folder onto the *Images* layer.
n) Align the image with the rectangle, but leave the Opacity set at 100.
o) Toggle to *Frame 5*.
p) Make sure the *Images* layer is selected. Press the Ctrl + R keys (Mac: Cmd + R) to import the *Image5.jpg* file from the *Chapter 9* folder onto the *Images* layer.
q) Align the image with the rectangle, but leave the Opacity set at 100.
r) Return to *Frame 1*.

12. Now that all graphics are in place, all we have left to do is add the Swap Image behaviors to the slices.
    a) Show the slices by selecting the Show Slices and Hotspots button in the Web toolbox or by clicking on the Eye icon in the *Web* layer.
    b) Unlock the *Web* layer.
    c) Select the *destination1* slice.
    d) In the Behaviors panel, click on the Add Behavior button.
    e) Select the Add Swap Image behavior from the list.
    f) In the Swap Image window, select the slice named *frame* from the list, or from the slice preview.
    g) Make sure the frame number is set to *Frame 2*. (See figure 9-34.) By selecting the *frame* slice and *Frame 2*, the photo imported into *Frame 2* will be displayed when a user places the cursor over the *Destination 1* button.

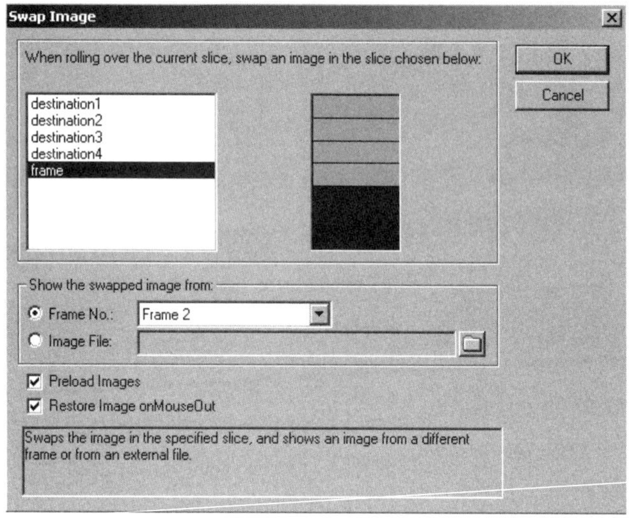

Fig. 9-34. Swap Image window for the **destination1** *slice.*

h) Click the OK button. Look at the canvas. There is now a light blue curved line connecting the *Destination 1* button to the frame sublayer where the graphic will be displayed. (See figure 9-35.) This line will not show when the *Web* layer is hidden.

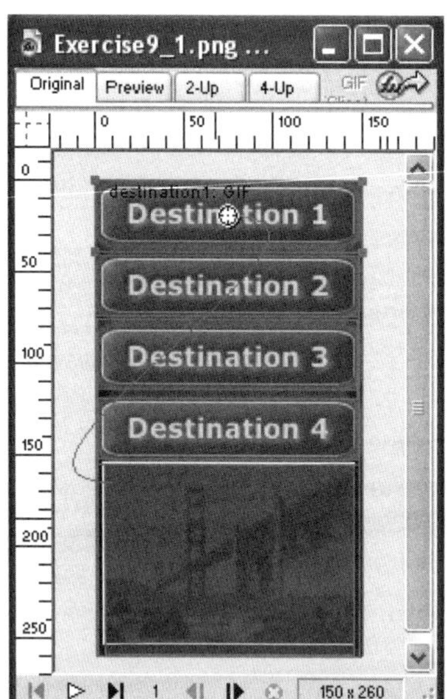

Fig. 9-35. Light blue curved line on canvas, within the **Web** *layer,* **frame** *sublayer.*

i) Select the *destination2* slice.

j) In the Behaviors panel, click on the Add Behavior button.
k) Select the Swap Image behavior from the list.
l) In the Swap Image window, select the slice named *frame* from the list, or from the slice preview.
m) Set the frame number to *Frame 3*. By selecting the *frame* slice and *Frame 3*, the photo imported into *Frame 3* will be displayed when a user places the cursor over the *Destination 2* button.
n) Click on the OK button.
o) Select the *destination3* slice.
p) In the Behaviors panel, click on the Add Behavior button.
q) Select the Swap Image behavior from the list.
r) In the Swap Image window, select the slice named *frame* from the list, or from the slice preview.
s) Set the frame number to *Frame 4*. By selecting the *frame* slice and *Frame 4*, the photo imported into *Frame 4* will be displayed when a user places the cursor over the *Destination 3* button.
t) Click on the OK button.
u) Select the *destination4* slice.
v) In the Behaviors panel, click on the Add Behavior button.
w) Select the Swap Image behavior from the list.
x) In the Swap Image window, select the slice named *frame* from the list, or from the slice preview.
y) Set the frame number to *Frame 5*. By selecting the *frame* slice and *Frame 5*, the photo imported into *Frame 5* will be displayed when a user places the cursor over the *Destination 4* button.
z) Click on the OK button.

13. Let's preview the completed file.
    a) Save the file.
    b) Select the Preview tab in the Document window. Hide the *Web* layer.
    c) Place the cursor over each button to preview the Swap Image behaviors.
    d) Select the Original tab to exit preview mode.
    e) To preview the file in a web browser, press the F12 key. Place the cursor over each button to preview the Swap Image behavior in your web browser.
    f) Close the web browser.

In Practice Exercise 9-2, we will build on this completed exercise and add another behavior to each button: the Set Status Text behavior.

Practice Exercise 9-2: Adding Status Text to a Button

Description

In this exercise, we are going to add status bar messages to the button rollovers. The purpose of status text is to give the viewer more information about the content of the site as they browse. By the end of this exercise you will learn to:

- *Add and customize the Set Text of Status Bar behavior*

Preview of Completed Exercise

Before beginning the exercise, let's take a look at the buttons in their completed state so that you can clearly see what it is you are about to build.

1. Use the menu option File | Open and locate the *Chapter 9* folder on the companion CD-ROM. Find the file named *Exercise9_2(complete).png*. Double click on this file to open it.
2. Press F12 to preview the document in a web browser. Roll the mouse over each button and note the status text in the status bar at the lower left of the web browser. See figure 9-36.

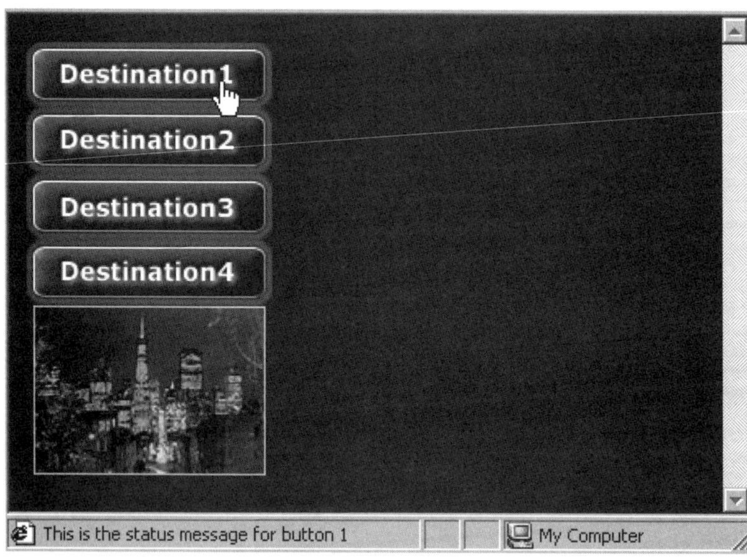

Fig. 9-36. Status bar in a web browser.

Step-by-Step Instructions

1. Continue working with the file from the previous exercise. Or if you would rather work with our version of the previous exercise, select File | Open and browse in the *Chapter 9* folder on the companion CD-ROM. Find the *Exercise9_1.png* file and double click to open it.

2. Now let's add a status message to the first slice.
   a) Make sure the *Web* layer is visible and select the *destination1* slice.
   b) Click on the circle icon in the middle of the slice to access the Behaviors pop-up window, and then select the Add Status Bar Message option.
   c) In the entry field that opens, type in *This is a status message for button 1*. Click on the OK button to close the window.
   d) To make the message disappear from the status bar when you roll off the button, click on the Add Behavior button in the Behaviors panel and select Set Text of Status Bar.
   e) In the entry field that opens, leave the message area blank and click on the OK button.
   f) In the Behaviors panel, click on the triangle next to the *onMouseOver* event, next to the blank status bar action. Select *onMouseOut*.
   g) Repeat steps *a* through *f* for the remaining three button slices.
   h) Select File | Save As and name the file *Exercise9_2.png* and save it into the *SaveWork* folder.

3. Preview and save your work.
   a) Press the F12 key to preview the status message behaviors in your web browser.
   b) Close your browser when you have tested the behaviors to your satisfaction.

CHAPTER 10

Taking Behaviors Further: Building Buttons and Navigation

Chapter Topics:

- *Introduction*
- *Building Navigation Structures in a Header Graphic*
- *Practice Exercise 10-1: Using Simple Rollovers in a Menu*
- *Practice Exercise 10-2: Adding Pop-up Menus to Rollovers*
- *Practice Exercise 10-3: Button Symbols and Navigation Bars*
- *Next in the Process*

Introduction

Via the use of behaviors, Fireworks MX has made it easier than ever to create buttons, pop-up menus, and tab-based navigation systems for your web sites. As you learned in the Chapter 9, behaviors represent an easy means of achieving a professional-looking and functioning web site.

In this chapter, we will further explore behaviors by using three methods for producing Fireworks navigation structures. By the end of the chapter you will be able to:

- *Create buttons and animated rollovers*
- *Build navigation bars with multiple buttons states*
- *Create pop-up menus with a few clicks of a button*

Building Navigation Structures in a Header Graphic

The focus of this chapter is the creation of a header graphic that will be used for navigation in an HTML frame set. We will use simple rollover behaviors, pop-up menu behaviors, and button symbols and their default behaviors to produce a working series of menus. In addition to working with behaviors, we will look closely at strategies for producing navigation features using Fireworks MX. We will use artwork from the home page of the *San Francisco Travel Guide* web site created in previous chapters. In Practice Exercise 10-1, we will work with the Simple Rollover behavior in the creation of a web site menu.

Practice Exercise 10-1: Using Simple Rollovers in a Menu

Description

Before the development of helpful programs such as Fireworks and Dreamweaver, web designers spent hours building buttons and writing JavaScript code in order to produce reliable rollover effects. Now, instead of writing code, web designers rely on the built-in behaviors in programs such as Fireworks MX. In this exercise, we will work with the Simple Rollover behavior to create a menu for the travel guide web site interface.

Preview of Completed Exercise

Before beginning the exercise, let's take a look at the buttons in their completed state so that you can clearly see what it is you are about to build.

1. Use the menu option File | Open and locate the *Chapter 10* folder on the companion CD-ROM. Find the file named *Exercise10_1(complete).png*. Double click on this file to open it.
2. Click on the Preview tab to view the completed exercise. Mouse over both header link buttons to see the Simple Rollover behavior applied to the button slices. (See figure 10-1.) You may want to hide the *Web* layer in order to see the canvas images more clearly.

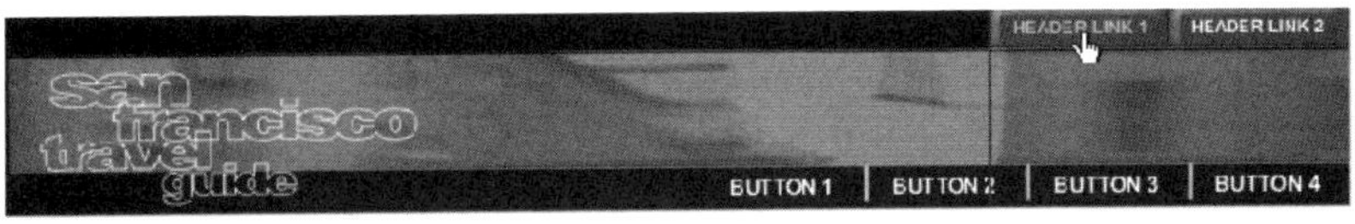

Fig. 10-1. Completed exercise on the canvas.

Step-by-Step Instructions

1. We will start with a new file.
   a) Create a new file by selecting File | New. Set the canvas dimensions at 770 x 110 and leave the Resolution at 72. Select a Custom background and set the color to black. We set the width just under 800 pixels to make sure the primary graphics will fit within an 800 x 600 browser window. Remember that when you set the width, you need to compensate for the browser interface, so setting it just under 800 should allow plenty of room.
   b) Save the file in your *SaveWork* folder, naming the file *Exercise10_1.png*.
2. Let's import some artwork to set up the interface for the header graphic.
   a) Rename the default *Layer 1* as *Interface*.
   b) Select File | Import and browse for the *Interface.png* file in the *Chapter 10* folder on the companion CD-ROM.
   c) Click to place the graphic in the upper left-hand corner of the canvas. In the Properties panel, establish the following coordinate settings.
      - *X:* 0
      - *Y:* 0
   d) Add a new layer above the *Interface* layer and name it *Logo*.
   e) Select File | Import and browse for the *Logo.png* file in the *Chapter 10* folder on the companion CD-ROM.
   f) Click to place the graphic in the upper left-hand corner of the canvas. In the Properties panel, establish the following coordinate settings.
      - *X:* 20
      - *Y:* 32

NOTE

A frame set is an HTML page that actually splits a browser window into multiple web pages that fit together. You have probably visited a page where the navigation stayed fixed in a sidebar or in the header while content in the main frame was changed. This is an example of a frame set.

g) Lock the *Logo* and *Interface* layers. The imported graphics should look familiar, because we have used them in previous exercises.

3. Now that the background is locked in place, let's start to work on the buttons. We will create the Up (default) state of the buttons first.
   a) Add a new layer above the *Logo* layer and name it *Button Text*.
   b) Select File | Import and browse for the *Button_text.png* file in the *Chapter 10* folder on the companion CD-ROM.
   c) Place the graphic in the upper right-hand corner of the canvas. With all of the imported text still selected, establish the following coordinate settings. Your canvas should then look like that shown in figure 10-2.
      - *X:* 410
      - *Y:* 2

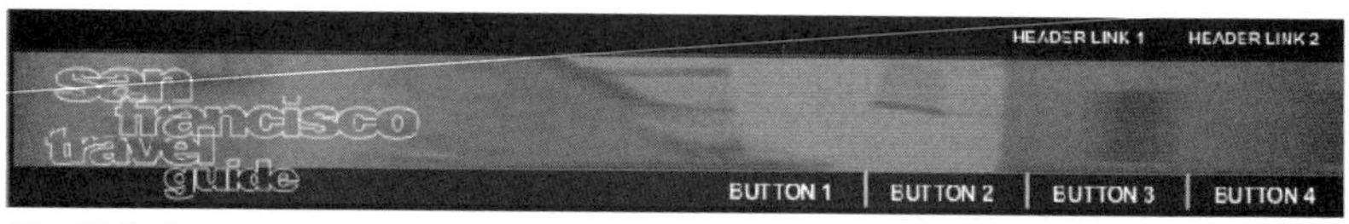

Fig. 10-2. Exercise in progress.

4. Now let's draw a background graphic for the button text. In this exercise, we are working with just the two buttons at the top right of the header. We will use a simple rectangle with some subtle effects that will make the buttons look clickable.
   a) Add a new layer below the *Button Text* layer and name it *Top Buttons*.
   b) Using the Rectangle tool, draw a rectangle on the *Top Buttons* layer. Establish the following settings in the Properties panel.
      - *W:* 90
      - *H:* 15
      - *X:* 570
      - *Y:* 4
      - *Fill Color:* #000000 (black)
      - *Stroke Color:* No Color
   c) Make sure you do not deselect the rectangle. Obviously, it is impossible to see a black shape on a black background, so let's add a beveled effect to the rectangle to make it visible. In the Properties panel, click on the Effects button (+ icon), select Bevel and Emboss | Raised Embossed, and establish the following settings. The embossed effect should render a subtle glow along the top edge of the button shape.

- *Width:* 4
- *Contrast:* 75%
- *Softness:* 3
- *Show Object:* Unchecked

d) Select the button you just created and clone it by using the keyboard command Ctrl + Shift + D (Mac: Cmd + Shift + D).

e) The cloned copy is now on top of the original image and is now selected. In the Properties panel, establish the following coordinate settings. Your canvas should then look like that shown in figure 10-3.

- *X:* 672
- *Y:* 4

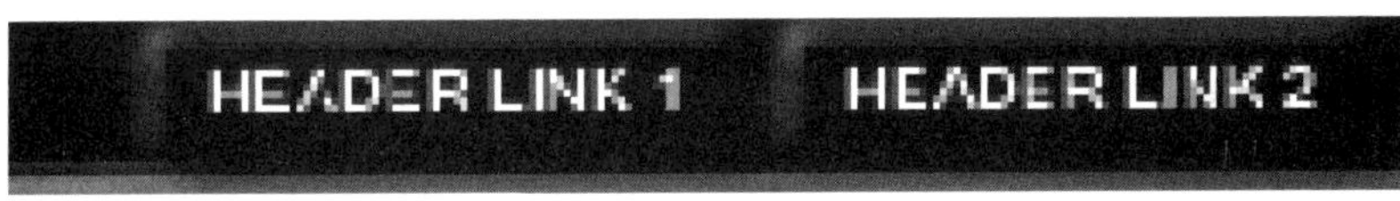

Fig. 10-3. Header buttons completed.

5. As we saw in the guided tour in Chapter 9, the rollover graphic for the Simple Rollover behavior is stored on *Frame 2*. Because our document has just one frame, we need to add a second frame to the document.

   a) First, we need to make sure the content of the *Interface* layer is shared across *Frame 1* and *Frame 2*.

   b) Unlock the *Interface* layer and double click on the layer name to access the layer properties. In the lower left-hand corner, place a check mark in the Share Across Frames check box. Press the Enter/Return key to close the window. You should now see the Share Across Frames icon to the right of the layer name.

   c) Repeat step 5b for the *Logo* layer (unlock it first) and the *Top Buttons* layer.

   d) Let's add a second frame. In the Frames panel click on the New/Duplicate Frame button.

   e) Click on *Frame 1*. Click on *Frame 2*. Note that all graphics were copied to *Frame 2* except for the button text. The reason for this is that the *Button Text* layer is not shared across frames, and therefore the content of the layer resides only in *Frame 1*.

   f) Click on *Frame 1*. Select the header link text box (it contains both header link 1 and header link 2) at the top right of the header. Press Ctrl + C (Mac: Cmd + C) to copy the text box.

   g) Click on *Frame 2* in the Frames panel and paste the text box into *Frame 2* using the keyboard shortcut Ctrl + V (Mac: Cmd + V).

h) With the text box selected in *Frame 2*, change the text color in the Properties panel to #66FF00 (light green). When you roll the mouse over the button, the text will be highlighted in green, as it is in *Frame 2*.

i) Return to *Frame 1*.

6. Now that we have our two frames created, we need to set up our slices and attach the Rollover behaviors to the image slices.
   a) Select the Slice tool from the Web toolbox and draw a slice over the Header Link 1 button. Make sure to include the entire button area, including the beveled edges.
   b) In the Properties panel, change the name of the slice to *header1*.
   c) Draw a second slice over the Header Link 2 button. Make sure to include the entire button area, including the beveled edges. Also make sure that you do not overlay the *header1* slice.
   d) In the Properties panel, change the name of the slice to *header2*.

·TIP·

Note that we did not draw slices over the enter image area. We only drew them over the areas that will need behaviors attached to them. Fireworks will by default export areas outside the slices.

7. The last step is to add the Simple Rollover behaviors to the slices.
   a) Using the Pointer tool, select the *header1* slice. Click on the white circle in the middle of the slice to access the Behaviors pop-up menu.
   b) Select Add Simple Rollover from the list. This behavior does not require any customization because it simply adds a swap image for *Frame 2* and a swap image restore.
   c) Select the *header2* slice. Click on the white circle in the middle of the slice to access the Behaviors pop-up menu.
   d) Select Add Simple Rollover Behavior from the list.
8. Let's preview and save the file.
   a) Select the Preview tab.
   b) Roll the mouse over the active buttons to see the Simple Rollover behavior. You may want to hide the *Web* layer to see the buttons more clearly.
   c) Click on the Original tab.
   d) Save the file. You will use it in the next exercise.

In Practice Exercise 10-2, you will combine behaviors by layering a Pop-Up Menu behavior over a Simple Rollover behavior. This exercise will allow you to create menus and submenus that work in conjunction with the *OnMouseOver* event.

Practice Exercise 10-2: Adding Pop-up Menus to Rollovers

Description

In this practice exercise, you will add pop-up menus to the button rollovers you just created. Because the primary buttons are already built and the slices are in place, this is an easy task. Fireworks MX has enhanced the controls for the pop-up menu in the Pop-Up Menu editor to make the process a snap. By the end of this exercise you will be able to:

- *Add and customize a Pop-Up Menu behavior*

Preview of Completed Exercise

Before beginning the exercise, let's take a look at the menus in their completed state so that you can clearly see what it is you are about to build.

1. Use the menu option File | Open and locate the *Chapter 10* folder on the companion CD-ROM. Find the file named *Exercise10_2(complete).png*. Double click on this file to open it.
2. Press the F12 key to preview the completed exercise in a web browser. Mouse over each header link button to see the Pop-Up Menu behavior applied to the button slices, as shown in figure 10-4. Note that the submenu pops up upon selection of Header Link 1 | Menu 1.

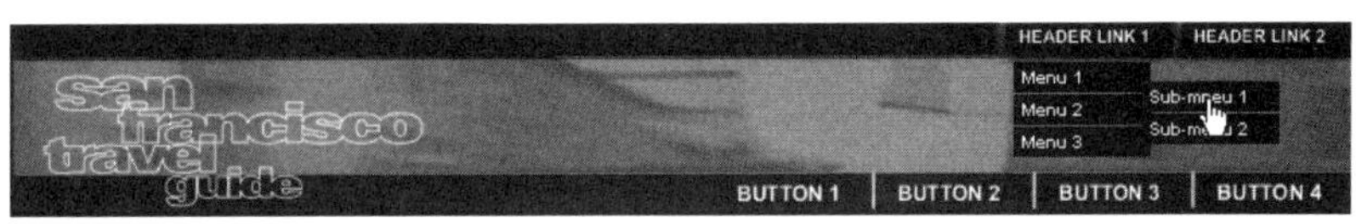

Fig. 10-4. Preview of the completed pop-up menu.

Step-by-Step Instructions

1. We will continue to use the file saved from the last practice exercise.
   a) Open your version of the file from your *SaveWork* folder, or perform step b.
   b) If you prefer, you can use our completed version of the file. Select File | Open and browse in the *Chapter 10* folder on the companion CD-ROM. Double click on *Exercise10_1.png* to open this file.
   c) Save the file in the *SaveWork* folder with the name *Exercise10_2.png*.
2. Let's now add the first pop-up menu to the *header1* slice.

a) Select the *header1* slice. When you see the white circle appear in the center, click on it to access the Behaviors menu.
b) Select the Add Pop-Up Menu option from the list.
c) The Pop-Up Menu editor appears.

3. Now let's establish the Content tab property settings in the Pop-Up Menu editor.
   a) Double click in the first row of the Text column and type *Menu 1*. Press Enter/Return.
   b) A second row was added, with the entry field open. Type *Menu 2*. Press Enter/Return.
   c) A third row was added, with the entry field open. Type *Menu 3*. Press Enter/Return.
   d) Double click the cursor in the Link column next to *Menu 1* and in the open entry field type #. Press Enter/Return.
   e) An open entry field is now open in the Link column next to *Menu 2*. In the open entry field, type #. Press Enter/Return.
   f) An open entry field is now open in the Link column next to *Menu 3*. In the open entry field, type #. Press Enter/Return. Click the cursor on the white area in the window to close the entry field.

NOTE

When used as a link, the pound sign (#) is simply a reference to the existing page. This is used as a placeholder for a link.

4. Before we move on to the next button, let's add a submenu to the first menu item.
   a) The Pop-Up Menu editor is still open.
   b) Select the *Menu 1* item in the Text list and click on the Add Menu button (+ icon) to add a row under the *Menu 1* item.
   c) Double click on this new line and establish the following settings.
      - *Text:* Sub-Menu 1
      - *Link:* #
   d) Your Pop-Up Menu editor should now look like that shown in figure 10-5.

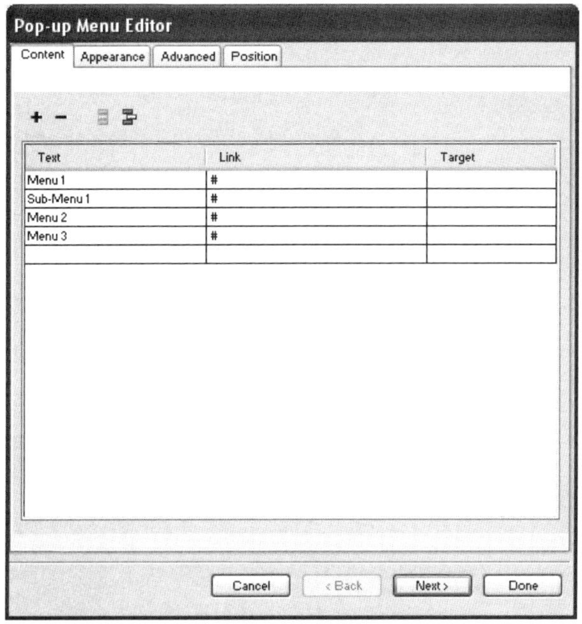

Fig. 10-5. Pop-up Menu editor in progress.

e) Click on *Sub-Menu 1* to select it and then click on the Indent button, shown in figure 10-6. Note the indented view in the list. This indicates that the item is now a submenu of the item above it.

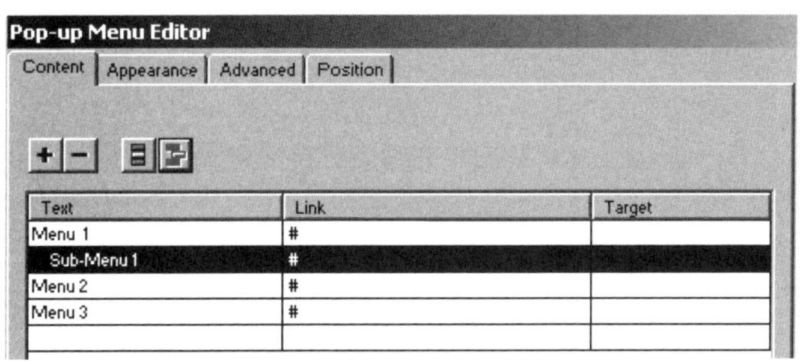

Fig. 10-6. **Sub-Menu 1** *indented.*

f) With the *Sub-Menu 1* line still selected, click on the Add Menu button. A second indented submenu item is added automatically. Establish the following settings.

- *Text:* Sub-Menu 2
- *Link:* #

g) Click on the Next button, or click on the Appearance tab.

5. Now let's adjust the Appearance tab properties in the Pop-Up Menu editor.
   a) Establish the following settings.
      - *Cells:* HTML
      - *Alignment of Pop-Up Menu:* Vertical Menu
      - *Font:* Arial, Helvetica, sans serif
      - *Size:* 10
      - *Style:* Bold
      - *Alignment of Text:* Left Justified
      - *Up State Text Color:* #FFFFFF (white)
      - *Cell Color:* #000000 (black)
      - *Over State Text Color:* #FFFFFF (white)
      - *Cell Color:* #39086B (dark blue/purple)
   b) Your Appearance tab should now look like that shown in figure 10-7.

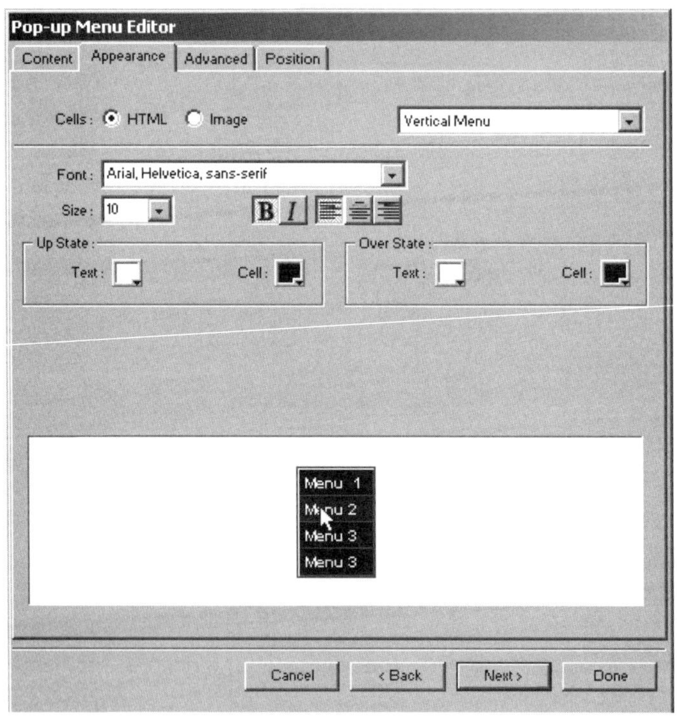

Fig. 10-7. Appearance tab properties.

   c) After making these adjustments, take a look at the preview pane below the Appearance options to see how the menu looks.
   d) Click on the Next button, or on the Advanced tab.

6. Now let's adjust the Advanced tab properties in the Pop-Up Menu editor.
   a) Establish the following settings.
      - *Cell Width:* 80 pixels (set the Automatic option to Pixels in the pull-down menu next to Cell Width)
      - *Cell Height:* 17 pixels (set the Automatic option to Pixels in the pull-down menu next to Cell Height)
      - *Cell Padding:* 3
      - *Cell Spacing:* 1
      - *Show Borders:* Unchecked
   b) Note that the border disappears from the editor preview. Your Advanced tab should now look like that shown in figure 10-8.

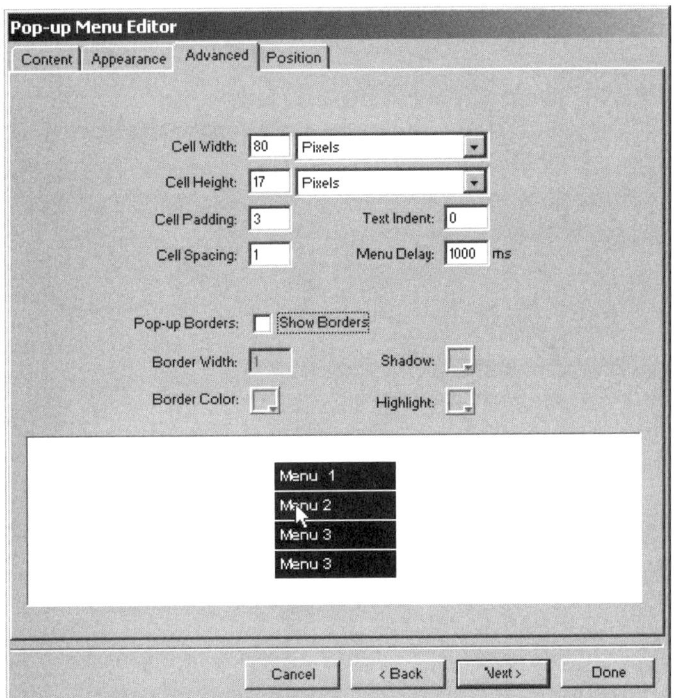

Fig. 10-8. Advanced tab properties.

   c) Click on the Next button, or on the Position tab.

7. Finally, let's adjust the Position tab properties in the Pop-Up Menu editor.
   a) Establish the following settings.

Menu Position:

- *X:* 10
- *Y:* 25

Submenu Position:

- *X:* -5
- *Y:* 11

b) Your Position tab should now look like that shown in figure 10-9.

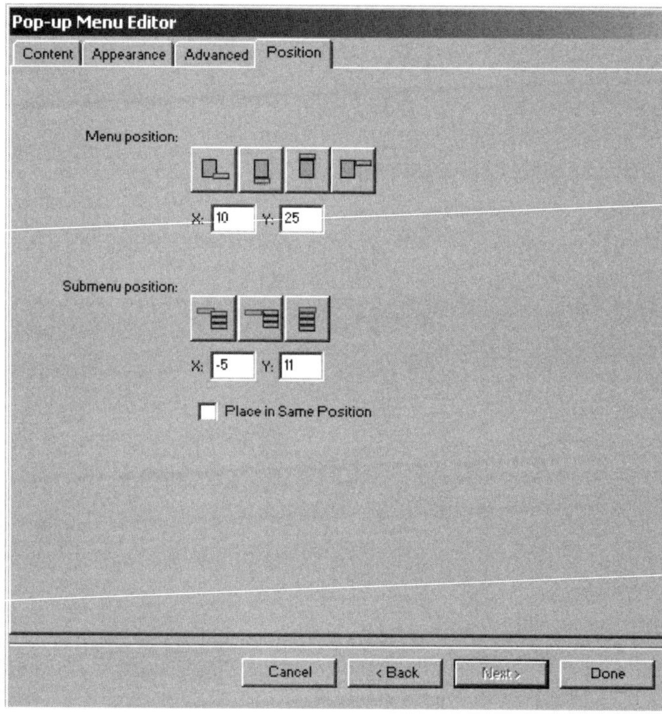

Fig. 10-9. Position tab properties.

·TIP·

You must set the submenu position from the editor. However, the menu position in relation to the slice can be set by hand using the menu preview associated with the slice. Simply click and drag the menu outline to move it to a new position.

c) Click on the Done button to exit the menu and return to the Document window. Note that the slice is still selected and that there is now a Pop-Up Menu behavior attached to this slice in the Behaviors panel.

d) The settings are complete. If you need to edit this menu again, you can simply select the slice, click on the white circle, and select Edit Pop-Up Menu from the behaviors shortcut menu.

8. One slice down; one slice to go. Let's add a Pop-Up Menu behavior to the *header2* slice as well. This time around it will be a lot easier, as Fireworks MX saves the settings from the last menu application.

a) Select the *header2* slice. Click on the white circle in the center to access the Behaviors menu.
b) Select Add Pop-Up Menu from the list.
c) The Pop-Up Menu editor appears.
d) On the Content tab, as you did before, add three menu items with the following values.
    - *Text:* Menu 1, Link: #
    - *Text:* Menu 2, Link: #
    - *Text:* Menu 3, Link: #
e) Click through the tabs (Appearance and Advanced) to confirm that the settings are the same as those you set in the previous menu.
f) On the Position tab, the settings have been reset to 0, 0. Adjust this by reentering the values from the previous menu, as follows.
    - *X:* 10
    - *Y:* 25
g) Click on the Done button to exit the editor and return to the Document window.

9. Let's preview and save the file.
    a) Press the F12 key to launch a preview of the HTML page.
    b) Roll over the active buttons with the mouse to see the pop-up menus and the submenu.
    c) Close the browser to return to Fireworks.
    d) Save your file in the *SaveWork* folder.

For the final practice exercise, we will create a navigation bar using button symbols. This will create a rollover effect with a Down state, similar to the effect created in the guided tour in Chapter 9.

Practice Exercise 10-3: Button Symbols and Navigation Bars

Description

In this exercise, we will simplify the creation of a navigation bar by building buttons within button symbols. Button symbols have the following advantages over creating buttons in the document using frames.

- *Slices are automatically associated with them*
- *Rollover and Nav Bar (navigation bar) behaviors are automatically associated with them*

- *No manipulation of the Frames panel is required*
- *Can be duplicated in the library*
- *Text is easily updated in the designated editing area in the library*

In this exercise, we will turn the button text on the bottom right of the header into simple rollovers using buttons symbols.

Preview of Completed Exercise

1. Use the menu option File | Open and locate the *Chapter 10* folder on the companion CD-ROM. Find the file named *Exercise10_3(complete).png*. Double click on this file to open it.
2. Press F12 to preview the completed exercise in a web browser. Mouse over each button to see the Pop-Up Menu behavior applied to the button slices and to see the rollovers in the lower navigation bar. Note the inclusion of a sound effect with the buttons. The completed exercise will appear as shown in figure 10-10.

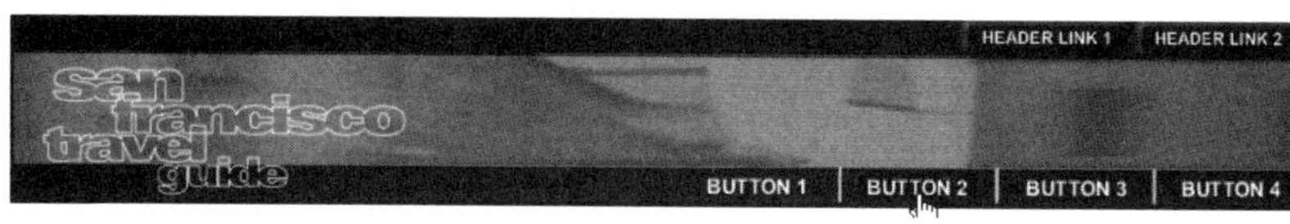

Fig. 10-10. Completed exercise shown in a web browser.

Step-by-Step Instructions

1. We will continue to use the file saved from the last practice exercise.
   a) Open your version of the file from your *SaveWork* folder, or perform step b.
   b) If you prefer, you can use our completed version of the file. Select File | Open and browse in the *Chapter 10* folder on the companion CD-ROM. Double click on *Exercise10_2.png* to open this file.
   c) Save the file in the *SaveWork* folder with the name *Exercise10_3.png*.
2. Let's clear the existing text box for the lower buttons and prepare to make our first button symbol.
   a) Select the text box that contains the text for buttons 1 through 4. Use the Text tool to delete all text and blank spaces, except for the text *Button 1*.

Shortcut

The keyboard shortcut for Convert to Symbol is F8.

b) Using the Pointer tool, select the Button 1 text box and then select Modify | Symbol | Convert to Symbol.

c) In the Symbol Properties window, name the symbol *Button 1* and check the Button behavior type. Click on the OK button to close the window.

d) Right-click (Mac: Ctrl + click) on the *Button 1* symbol and select Symbol | Edit Symbol from the menu. The editing window for the *Button 1* symbol opens. See figure 10-11.

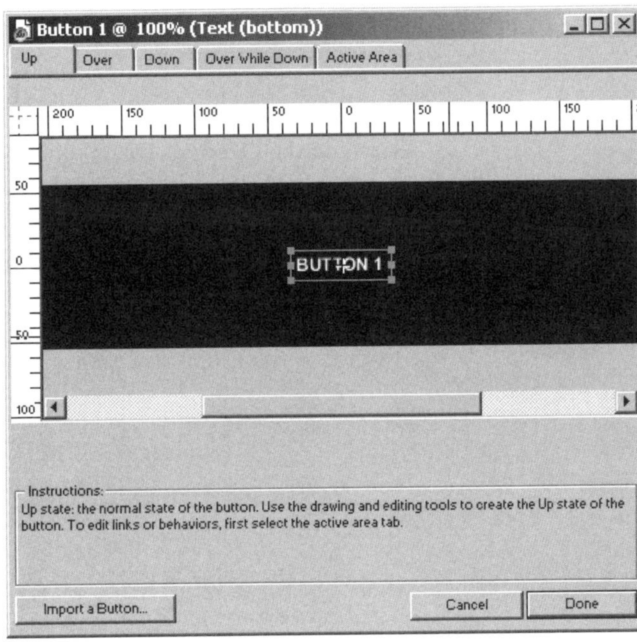

Fig. 10-11. Button symbol editing window with five tabs.

Button Symbols

Button symbols automatically have a number of button states with associated behaviors. At the top of the Button Symbol window, note that there are five tabs, as outlined in the following. (See figure 10-10.) Note the function of these tabs.

- *Up:* Default state of the button when the page first loads.
- *Over:* Rollover state of the button when the mouse cursor is moved over the button's active area.
- *Down:* This is a Nav Bar state and marks the user's current selection. It remains down until another button is clicked, whereupon it returns to the Up state.

- *Over While Down:* Nav Bar state (optional). This is a Rollover state for the button when the Down state is active.
- *Active Area:* The slice area around a button that designates the active area for button events. By default, the symbol creates an active area just large enough to surround button graphics.

We are going to create different button states for the symbol. We will leave the text as the default associated with the Up state, and then add a tab-style highlight associated with the Over state. This will create the illusion of an animated tab that follows the cursor upon rollover and connects the button to the base of the header interface.

1. Let's edit the Over tab.
   a) Click on the Over tab. This is similar to working on different frames, without having to worry about inserting the behaviors (because they are already associated with each button state).
   b) Click on the Copy Up Graphic button (lower right-hand side of the window) to copy the graphic from the *Up* frame to the *Over* frame.
   c) Using the Rectangle tool, draw a rectangle. Establish the following settings in the Properties panel.
      - *W:* 70
      - *H:* 50
      - *X:* -36
      - *Y:* -10
      - *Fill Color:* #000000 (black)
      - *Stroke Color:* No Color
      - *Rectangle Roundness:* 25
   d) We cannot see the black rectangle we just created because the canvas is black. Right-click (Mac: Ctrl + click) on the canvas in the Symbol Editing window and select Modify Canvas | Canvas Color. Select white.
   e) The button text is covered by the black rectangle. Drag the *Rectangle* sublayer and place it beneath the *Text* sublayer in the Layers panel. This will change the stacking order of the sublayers and will reveal the text.
   f) Change the canvas color back to black. Right-click on the canvas in the Symbol Editing window and select Modify Canvas | Canvas Color. Select black.
   g) Click on the Done button in the lower right-hand corner of the window to exit editing mode.

·TIP·

When working in symbol editing mode, the X and Y coordinates are relative to the center of the symbol, which is marked in the editing area with crosshairs.

·TIP·

You can use layers and frames when working in library mode, just as you would in the Document window. If you do this, the layers and frames are relative to the symbol only.

   h) Back in the Document window, note the slice marks that have automatically been added around the *Button 1* symbol.
   i) We can only see the Up state. Click on the Preview tab and roll the mouse over the *Button 1* symbol to view the Over state. Because we used a Button symbol, we do not have to add any behaviors to the slice since they are automatically built into the symbol.
   j) Click on the Original tab.

2. Next, let's create the other three buttons by duplicating the first symbol in the library.
   a) Select Window | Library to open the Library panel.
   b) In the Library panel, select the *Button 1* symbol and duplicate it by dragging it to the New Symbol button (+ icon) at the bottom of the panel, as shown in figure 10-12. Note that a second symbol, named by default *Button 2*, appears in the library. This is a great trick. Fireworks will name duplicate symbols sequentially if the name ends with a number.

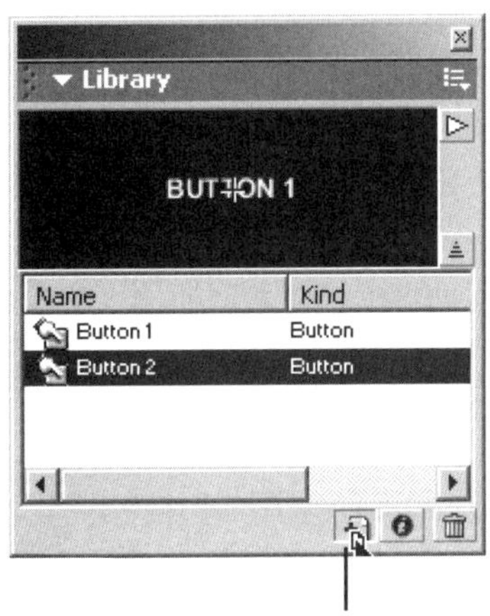

Fig. 10-12. Duplicate symbol.

   c) Repeat step 2b two more times for a total of four button symbols.
   d) Click on *Button 2* in the Library panel and double click on the preview pane to quickly enter symbol editing mode.
   e) The editing window for *Button 2* opens.
   f) Using the text tool, on the Up tab, change the text from *Button 1* to *Button 2*.
   g) Click on the Done button. A prompt window appears, asking if you want to update the text across all frames. Click on the Yes button. This changes the text in the *Over* frame automatically.

h) Repeat steps e through g on *Button 3* and *Button 4* to update the text to correspond with the button names.

3. Now that we have four buttons created in the library, let's place copies of the remaining three buttons on the canvas.
   a) Hide the *Web* layer if it is not already hidden. This will make it easier to see what we are doing while placing the buttons on the canvas.
   b) Select *Button 2* in the library and drag an instance (copy) of it to the stage.
   c) In the Properties panel, establish the following coordinate settings.
      - *X:* 504
      - *Y:* 88
   d) Select *Button 3* in the library and drag an instance of it to the stage.
   e) In the Properties panel, establish the following coordinate settings.
      - *X:* 598
      - *Y:* 88
   f) Select *Button 4* in the library and drag an instance of it to the stage.
   g) In the Properties panel, establish the following coordinate settings.
      - *X:* 690
      - *Y:* 88
   h) The navigation bar graphic has the same appearance as it did when we first started, with the exception that each button is now a separate button symbol.
4. Let's now preview what we have so far.
   a) Click on the Preview tab to view the completed rollovers.
   b) Roll over the button symbols to test them.
   c) Click on the Original tab when finished testing.
5. Let's complete the file by adding a Down state to the Nav Bar behavior. As we saw in the Chapter 9 guided tour, we can add the Nav Bar states manually via the Behaviors panel. However, button symbols simplify things yet again by building this functionality into the button editor. In fact, all you have to do is draw a graphic on the Down state and check the Include In Nav Bar option.
   a) First, we will need to add a Down state graphic into each symbol. This will be easy to do because of the tab-style menu. We will simply copy a graphic from the *Over* frame to the *Down* frame. Select *Button 1* in the library and double click on the preview to launch the editing window.
   b) Click on the Down tab to move to the *Down* frame.

c) Place a check mark in the check box Include Nav Bar Down State, located in the upper left-hand corner of the window. Click on the Copy Over Graphic button (lower right-hand side) to copy the *Over* graphic to the *Down* frame.

d) If you want to make sure the black rectangle was copied from the Over state, right-click (Mac: Ctrl + click) on the canvas in the editor and select Modify Canvas | Canvas Color. Change the color to white. After you have verified it is there, change the canvas color back to black.

e) Click on the Done button to exit the editing window and return to the Document window. The *Button 1* instance on the stage is automatically updated.

f) Repeat steps 5a through 5e to add the Over state for *Button 2*, *Button 3*, and *Button 4*. You now have a fully functional navigation bar menu.

6. Now let's preview and save the file.
   a) Press F12 to launch a preview of the HTML page and sliced graphics.
   b) Roll over the Nav Bar buttons and click on them. Note the behavior of the Down state.
   c) Close the browser when you are finished and return to Fireworks.
   d) Save your file in the *SaveWork* folder.

·TIP·

The Down state is intended to be used primarily for frame set functionality. However, if you want to export the Nav Bar behavior to multiple web pages, you can check the Multiple Nav Bars HTML Pages option in the HTML Settings option of the File menu.

Next in the Process

At this point you have completed the exercises, but you may be wondering what to do next to finish the header graphic. You already have most of the skills you will need. If you are ready to finish the project, there are several things you can now do on your own:

- *Check slice settings and compression quality across all slices*
- *Add other slices and behaviors*
- *Export all slices and HTML*
- *Import the HTML and slices into Dreamweaver or other HTML editor for fine-tuning*

CHAPTER 11

Working with Efficiency and Consistency

Chapter Topics:

- *Introduction*
- *Guided Tour 11A: Working with Styles*
- *Guided Tour 11B: Working with the Library*
- *Guided Tour 11C: Working with the History Panel*
- *Guided Tour 11D: Working with Commands*
- *Guided Tour 11E: Batch Processing*
- *Guided Tour 11F: Working with the Project Log*
- *Guided Tour 11G: Working with Find and Replace*
- *Guided Tour 11H: Working with the URL Panel*

Introduction

The central theme of setting up your Fireworks MX environment to work efficiently and with consistency will be carried through this chapter and into the next. As you have probably already observed as you have been working on practice exercises, the repetition of tasks is a very common part of the design process. For example, in the last chapter you set up behaviors for one button, and then turned around to do the same thing for the next three buttons.

We want the buttons to look the same (except for the text) and to function in a similar manner. In other words, it is very important to maintain consistency in design appearance and functionality from page to page in web design, and in many other types of design applications. One major aspect of achieving this consistency is through the accurate repetition of tasks from one object to the next (similar) type of object.

Many of the panels and commands you will work with in this chapter will help your development efforts become more streamlined by minimizing and standardizing these repetitive tasks from file to file. Undoubtedly you will find these streamlined methods extremely valuable when developing large web sites and working with a team, but even with smaller projects they will allow you to focus more on creativity and less on mechanics.

This chapter consists of a series of guided tours designed to introduce you to Fireworks panels that will help you to become more efficient. In particular, these panels are all used to streamline the work process and manage multiple Fireworks files. By the end of the chapter you will be able to:

- *Create, export, and import style settings for fill and stroke color presets*
- *Create, export, and import reusable graphics, buttons, and animations in the library*
- *Create, export, and import custom commands using the History panel*
- *Handle bulk file processing with the Batch Processing feature*
- *Manage project files using the Project Log feature*

Guided Tour 11A: Working with Styles

A style is simply a set of properties you define so that you can then consistently apply those properties to objects. In Fireworks MX, a style applied to any object includes detailed settings regarding the appearance of that object. Perhaps the most familiar use of styles would be their application to text objects. For example, in that you want text in your application to be consistent each place you use it, you might want to define a style that uses a particular font, size, color, and text attribute (such as bold or italic). Styles can be created and applied to other objects as well – perhaps establishing a particular type of fill, color, texture, and stroke width for all rectangles you create. All of these settings associated with an object may be stored in a single style and applied as a group to any other object.

The portability of styles is what makes them so useful. You could spend hours recreating common characteristics among a group of objects by hand. However, by saving the style of a prototype image, it can be applied easily to any number of images. Once applied to the other images, each image's settings can be refined individually.

In this guided tour, you will learn to use the Styles panel to store and manage saved styles and presets. Let's take a look at the features of the Styles panel.

1. Select File | New to open a blank file with the dimensions 500 x 500. Leave the resolution at 72 and set a white background.
2. Select Window | Styles to open the Styles panel. (See figure 11-1.) The Styles panel is stored in a panel group named Assets, along with the URL and Library panels. You can change the arrangement of these panel groups by dragging the Styles panel off the Assets panel.

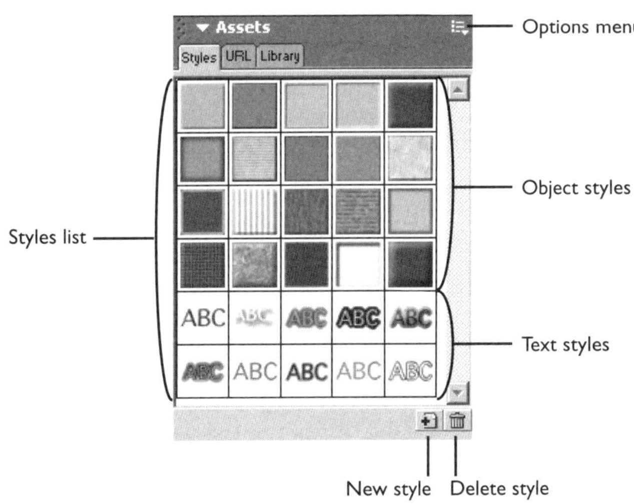

Fig. 11-1. Styles panel.

   a) The lower part of the Styles panel contains a graphic preview of each style.
   b) Styles are added and deleted from the panel using the New Style and Delete Style icons, shown in figure 11-1.

c) As with all panels, the Options menu is located in the upper right-hand corner of the panel.

3. Let's create a simple shape for experimenting with the application of styles.
   a) Using the Rectangle tool, draw a square shape on the canvas about 2 inches across. Use the Shift key as you draw to constrain the shape to a perfect square.
   b) Do not worry about the square's color at the moment.

4. Take a closer look at the Styles panel.
   a) There are two general types of styles in the panel: Object styles and Text styles. The Object styles are noted with a square icon, and the Text styles with an ABC icon. Although these two style types are basically the same, the Text style also stores font-specific information (such as font, size, and alignment).
   b) With the square selected on the canvas, apply different styles to it by clicking on some of icons in the Styles panel.
   c) Watch the Properties panel as you apply the styles. Note the change in Fill and Stroke settings, as well as the change in the Effects list in the Properties panel. Each style has unique properties that are automatically applied to the square.

5. Next, let's look at how to create a new style.
   a) Select the second style in the first row and apply it to the square. We will make some changes in the applied style's settings and save the changes as a new style.
   b) With the square still selected, establish the following settings in the Properties panel.
      - *Stroke Width:* 10
      - *Stroke Color:* #333300 (dark olive)
      - *Inner Bevel Width:* 6
   c) You should see a more box-like frame effect now, as shown in figure 11-2. Save the style by clicking on the New Style button (+ icon) at the bottom of the panel.

Fig. 11-2. New stroke settings.

TIP

Both Object styles and Text styles can be applied to any type of object. If a Text style is applied to a regular shape, such as a square, the text information is ignored. If an Object style is applied to text, it affects the text as expected, but without making any typesetting changes, such as font settings.

CAUTION

Styles in Fireworks are not linked after they are applied to an object. Usually when you hear the term style, this is a reference to a dynamic link from the style definition to the object the style is applied to (which can be automatically updated by editing the original style). However, in Fireworks, styles are not linked to the style definition after they are applied. In other words, if you make a change to a style in the Styles panel, it does not update any objects where the style was applied.

d) The New Style window, shown in figure 11-3, appears and asks you to name the style and the style properties you want to save. Note that you have options for the fill, stroke, effects, and text characteristics. If you uncheck any of these settings, when you apply the style to an object, the style will not override the unchecked object settings. In this case, the style will ignore any text settings. Establish the following settings in this window.

- *Name:* myStyle
- *Properties:* use defaults

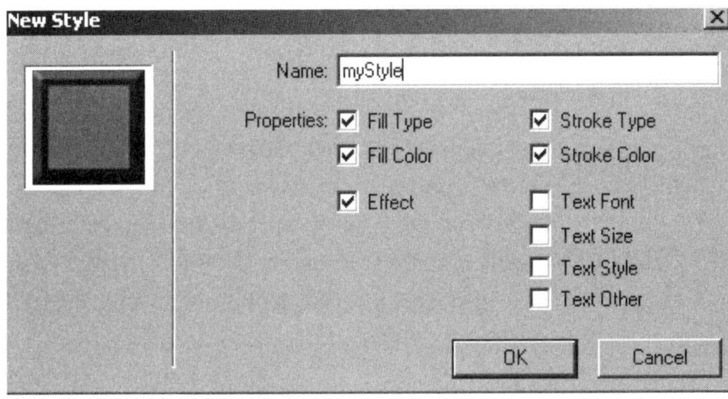

Fig. 11-3. New Style window.

e) Click on the OK button. You should see the new style appear at the bottom of the Styles list, as shown in figure 11-4. Now you can apply this style to any object just as you did with the other styles.

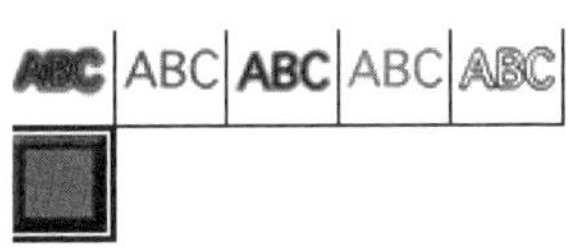

Fig. 11-4. The new style in Styles panel.

f) To delete a style, select its icon in the panel and then click on the Delete Style button (Trash Can icon) at the bottom right of the panel.

g) To manage styles, use the Style Options menu in the upper right of the panel. Click on the menu icon to view the menu options, which are as follows.

- *New Style:* Creates a new style from a selected object's properties. Performs the same function as the New Style button we just used to add a style to the panel.
- *Edit Style:* Launches the Edit Style window, which is the same window you saw when you first converted an object's

properties into a style. This window allows you to adjust the style name and turn on and off the stroke, fill, effect, and font characteristics for the style.

- *Delete Styles:* Deletes selected styles.
- *Import Styles:* Imports saved style settings from an external file.
- *Export Styles:* Exports current styles to an external file.
- *Reset Styles:* Resets the Styles panel to its default presets.
- *Large Icons:* Makes Styles icons larger.

h) Save this file, as it will be used in the next guided tour.

Guided Tour 11B: Working with the Library

While we have already worked with the Library panel in previous chapters dealing with symbols, in this tour the focus will be on strategies for using the Library panel to streamline your workflow. As we learned previously, the library is like a filing cabinet for reusable assets called symbols. A symbol is simply a master copy of an object that is stored in the library. Symbols even have their own separate editing area, distinct from the document canvas.

Working with Symbols

Symbols can be used as many times as you like, by dragging a copy of a symbol from the library to the canvas. The copy of a symbol is called an instance of the symbol. Instances always share the characteristics of the parent symbol stored in the library, but instances can also have unique properties applied to them on the canvas. If the parent symbol is updated in the library, all instances of that symbol inherit the update automatically. Let's review the Library panel.

1. Continue working with the previous file.
2. Select Window | Library to open the Library panel, if it is not already open. By default, the Library panel is stored in a panel group named Assets, along with the Styles panel and the URL panel.
3. Let's convert the square to a symbol.
   a) Select the square drawn on the canvas in the previous guided tour.
   b) Now convert the square to a symbol by pressing the F8 key.
   c) The Symbol Properties window appears. As you may remember from previous chapters, you can enter a name for the symbol, as well as choose from three behavior types for the symbol in this window. The following are the three behavior types.

TIP

If you would like to revert to the default arrangements of panel groups (or sets) on your screen, select Commands | Panel Layout Sets | Monitor Resolution to revert to the defaults.

- *Graphic:* Stores static graphics as symbols for reuse and export to other files.
- *Animation:* Creates a symbol that can be animated with the animation properties in the Properties panel. Options include Animate Move, Direction, Rotation, and Transparency.
- *Button:* Creates a button symbol with built-in Up, Over, Down, Over While Down, and Active Area states. The JavaScript behaviors and slice area (Active Area state) are automatically added to a button symbol.

d) Name the symbol *square1* and leave the behavior set to Graphic. Click on the OK button.

e) On the canvas, new selection markers appear around the square, as shown in figure 11-5.

Fig. 11-5. Selection markers around the square.

f) The *square1* symbol also now appears in the Library panel list and preview pane.

4. Let's review some of the features of the Library panel that allow you to manipulate symbols. Examine the Library panel, shown in figure 11-6, which includes the following options.

    - *New Symbol:* To create a new symbol, click on the New Symbol button on the lower right of the panel. The editing area for the symbol automatically opens in a new window.
    - *Symbol Properties:* Select the symbol in the Library list and click on the Symbol Properties button (i) in the lower right of the Library panel.
    - *Delete Symbol:* To delete a symbol from the library, select the symbol in the Library list and click on the Delete Symbol (Trash Can icon) button in the lower right of the panel.

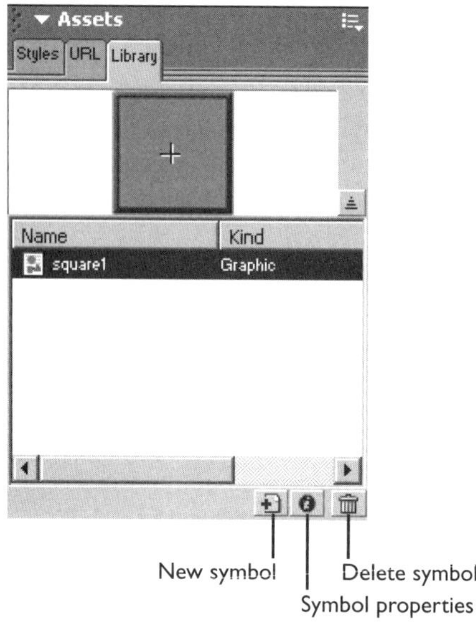

Fig. 11-6. Library panel.

·TIP·

If you cannot see the entire canvas, use the Zoom tool to zoom out (make canvas smaller) on the canvas. Select the Zoom tool in the View toolbox and hold down the Alt key (Mac: Opt). When the plus (+) sign on the magnifying glass turns to a hyphen (-), click on the canvas to zoom out.

5. Let's now add a few more instances of the *square1* symbol to the canvas so that we can learn to work with instances.
   a) Add a new instance of the *square1* symbol to the canvas by clicking on and then dragging the symbol preview from the library to the canvas. Continue to add instances until there are four copies on the canvas.
   b) Arrange the instances so that each sits separately in a corner of the document, as shown in figure 11-7.

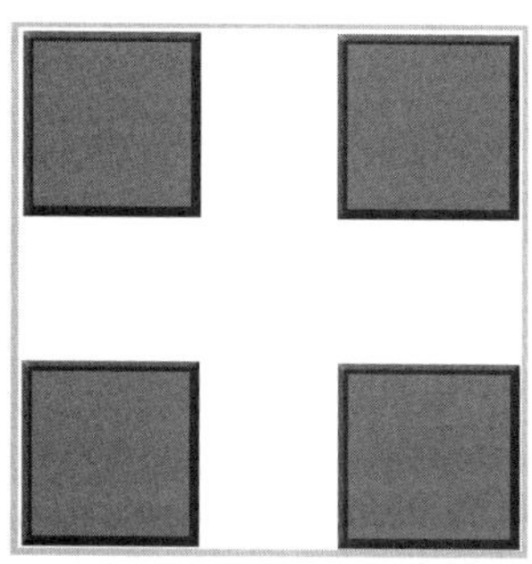

Fig. 11-7. Instances of the* square1 *symbol arranged on the canvas.

6. Note that each instance looks like the parent symbol in the library. Let's change the appearance of each by altering its physical properties one at a time.

a) Select the square in the upper left-hand corner. Select the Scale tool in the Select toolbox and use the handles to make the square smaller. Hold down the Shift key while you drag the bottom right-hand corner handle toward the center of the square, to constrain the proportions of the object as you scale it. See figure 11-8.

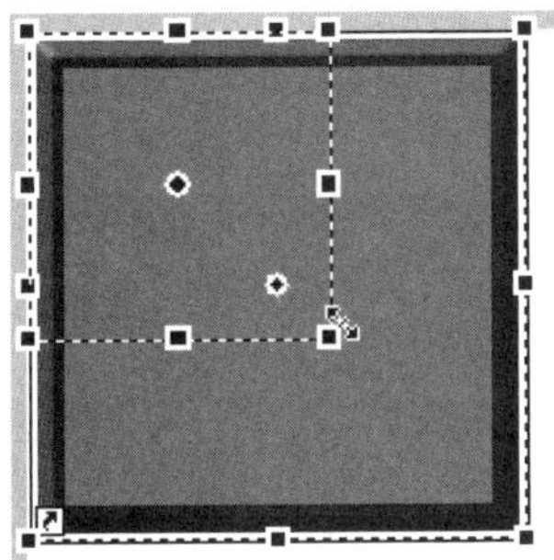

Fig. 11-8. Scaling the first square.

b) Using the Pointer tool, select the square in the upper right-hand corner and apply a Drop Shadow effect in the Properties panel by clicking on the Add Effects button and then selecting Shadow and Glow | Drop Shadow. Establish the following settings.

- *Distance:* 7
- *Opacity:* 65%
- *Softness:* 3
- *Angle:* 229

c) Using the Pointer tool, select the square in the lower left-hand corner and apply an Inset Emboss effect in the Properties panel by clicking on the Effects button and then selecting Bevel and Emboss | Outer Bevel. Establish the following setting.

- *Color:* #333300

d) Using the Pointer tool, select the square in the lower right-hand corner and change the opacity setting of the object to 50%. Use the slider above the Effects button in the Properties panel to adjust the opacity.

7. We have adjusted instances on the canvas, but what happens to these changes if we make a global change to the parent symbol in the library? Let's edit the symbol and apply the changes to see the effects on the instances on the canvas.

a) Select the *square1* symbol in the Library list and then select Edit Symbol from the Library Options menu.

TIP

Working with symbols and instances is a common process with many Macromedia products, such as Flash, FreeHand, and Dreamweaver. Familiarizing yourself with symbols here will help you with those other products as well.

Shortcut

You can also enter symbol editing mode by selecting Edit in the Symbol Properties window, by double-clicking on the symbol preview or instance in the library, by right-clicking (Mac: Ctrl + clicking) on the instance and selecting Symbol | Edit Symbol, or by selecting Modify | Symbol | Edit Symbols.

b) You should now see the symbol in the Symbol Editing window. You can work within this window just as you have been working in the main document window. You can add layers and frames and use any tools from the toolbox. Select the square on the canvas in the Symbol Editing window and use the Properties panel to change the Fill color to red # CC0000.

c) Close the window and note that all four instances on the canvas have been updated automatically. The properties unique to each instance on the main canvas remain the same. That is, the scaled image, shadow, outer bevel, and opacity properties remain the same. This demonstrates that instances are connected to the parent symbol in the library, but can be customized to a degree once they are added to the canvas.

Exporting Libraries

After this crash course in working with symbols and instances, let's move on to other library features. Libraries are saved with the document in which they are created. If you want to manage groups of libraries, perhaps to create an archive of symbols, you can export the symbols as an external file. Fireworks saves exported symbols as a standard Fireworks PNG file, which can easily be shared with other users.

1. Let's try exporting symbols in a library.
   a) Click on the Library Options menu icon in the upper right-hand corner of the panel and select Export Symbols.
   b) In the Export Symbols window that appears (see figure 11-9), select the symbols you want to export. In our current case, there is only one symbol in library. Select the *square1* symbol.

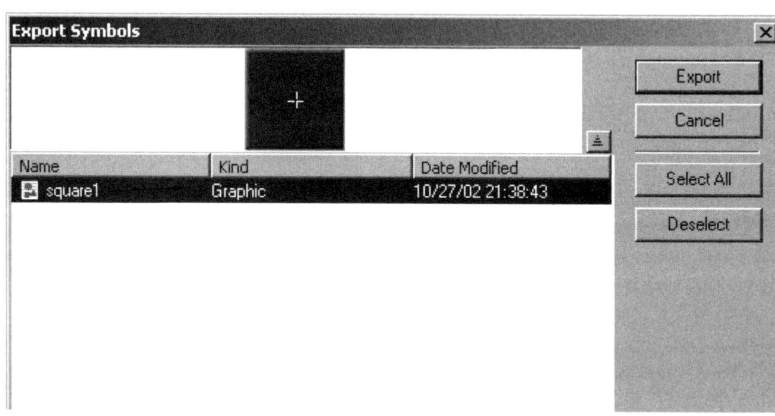

Fig. 11-9. Export Symbols window.

c) Click on the Export button. Use the Save-in window to locate the *SaveWork* folder on your computer and save it with the name *Custom Rectangle.png*.

d) Let's create a new blank file and import this symbol into it.

e) Select File | New to create a new file with any dimensions.

f) To import the exported symbol into the new file, click on the Library Options menu and then select Import Symbols. Browse in the *SaveWork* folder for the *Custom Rectangle.png* file you just saved.

g) An Import Symbols window opens and asks which symbols in the file to import. This window also shows you a preview of a selected symbol.

h) There is only one, but go ahead and click on the Select All button. Click on the Import button. The *square1* symbol is imported into the blank files's library.

i) Without saving it, close this file when you are finished.

Guided Tour 11C: Working with the History Panel

·TIP·

By default, the History panel stores the previous 20 actions applied to the Fireworks canvas. You can change this number by selecting the Edit | Preferences menu and typing in a new number of steps in the Undo Steps field. You will need to restart Fireworks to apply this change.

The History panel has a few impressive uses. First, it records all steps you make while working in a Fireworks document, and allows you to undo and replay steps. You can always use the Edit | Undo command, but the History panel stores a list of previous steps and allows you to navigate directly back to the step you are interested in. In addition to undo and redo capabilities, the History panel steps can be used to create commands without writing a script. To create a command, simply select a series of steps and save them as a command. Creating custom commands allows you to automate repetitive tasks and save time in the production process.

1. Let's take a look at the History panel. Open a new blank file with a canvas size of 500 x 500 and a white background.
2. Select Window | History to open the History panel. By default, the History panel is grouped with the Frames panel, but it can be moved to any other panel grouping. As you can see, it is currently blank because we have just opened a new file. See figure 11-10.

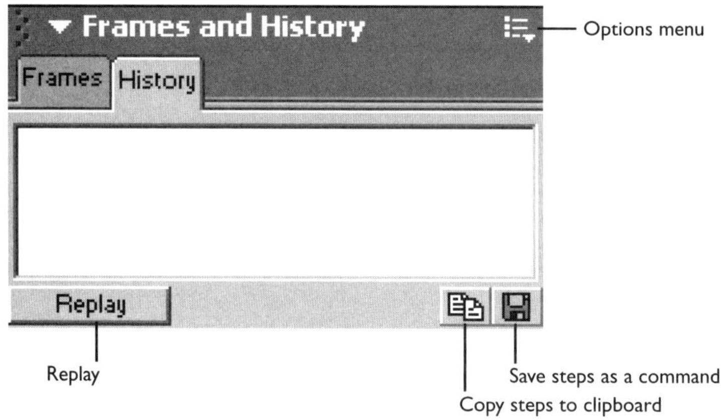

Fig. 11-10. History panel.

The History panel has the following three buttons at the bottom that control features in the panel.

- *Replay:* Replays selected steps in the History panel.
- *Copy steps:* Copies selected steps to the clipboard.
- *Save steps:* Saves selected steps as a command.

3. Let's create a shape with some formatting and watch the effects of our actions on the History panel.
   a) Select the Polygon tool from the Vector toolbox. Remember, the Polygon tool is a hidden tool selected by clicking and holding on the Rectangle tool until the pop-up menu appears.
   b) In the Properties panel, establish the following settings.
      - *Fill:* #FFCC00
      - *Stroke:* None
      - *Shape (far right in panel):* Polygon
      - *Sides (far right in panel):* 5
      - *Angle:* 30
   c) Draw a polygon in the middle of the canvas by simply clicking the tool on the canvas and dragging the cursor as you keep the mouse button down. You should now have a polygon figure that looks something like that shown in figure 11-11.

Fig. 11-11. Polygon on the canvas.

d) In the Properties panel, click on the Effects button (+ icon) and then select Shadows and Glow | Drop Shadow. Establish the following settings.

- *Distance:* 25
- *Opacity:* 15%
- *Softness:* 6

e) Now take a look at the icons listed in the History panel. (See figure 11-12.) The slider bar and tab to the left of the steps is the Undo marker. The slider tab always sits at the most recently applied step unless you move it up the list. If you move the marker up to a previous step, the file reverts to that step.

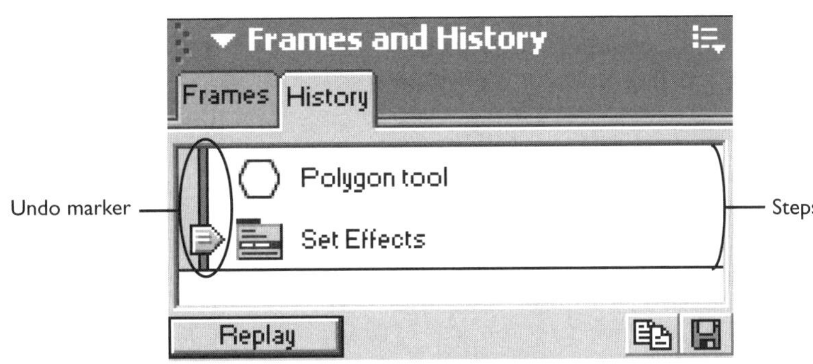

Fig. 11-12. History panel with steps and Undo marker.

f) Drag the Undo marker back one step. The Drop Shadow effect disappears because it was the last step applied.

g) Drag the marker back to its original position, next to Set Effects. The Drop Shadow effect reappears. The History panel gives you visual access to undoing and redoing steps during editing. This is a very convenient feature to work with.

Shortcut

You can replay a step or series of steps by selecting the steps and then clicking on the Replay button. Alternatively, you can use the Replay Selected Steps commands in the History Options menu. This applies the selected steps to a new object.

4. In addition, you can replay selections from steps and apply these steps to another object. Let's look at an example.
   a) Draw another polygon on the canvas.
   b) Select the *Set Effects* step in the History panel by clicking on it. You should see it highlight in blue.
   c) Click on the Replay button at the bottom left of the panel. Note that the *Set Effects* step with the Drop Shadow effect was applied to the new polygon without having to reenter the shadow properties.
5. The History panel stores a limited number of steps while the Fireworks document is open. When you close the document, the history is cleared. To save a step for use later, you will need to save the step (or steps) as a command. Let's save the *Set Effects* step as a preset shadow that we can apply to an object in any Fireworks document.
   a) Select the *Set Effects* step in the History panel. It should now be highlighted in blue.
   b) Open the History Options menu, located in the upper right-hand corner, and select select the option Save as Command. (Another way of saving the command is to click on the Save Steps as Command button – the floppy disk icon – in the lower right-hand corner of the panel.)
   c) The Save Command window now opens. Name the command *Preset Shadow 1*. (See figure 11-13.) Click on the OK button.

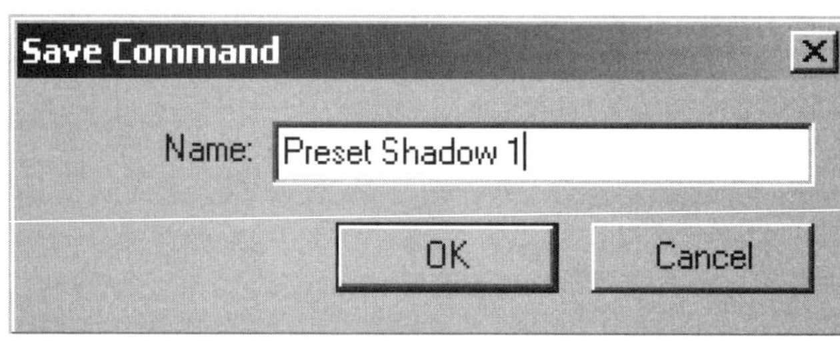

Fig. 11-13. Save Command window.

   d) Select the Commands menu and note that *Preset Shadow 1* has now been added to the bottom of the Commands list. See figure 11-14.

TIP

Fireworks MX stores the commands you create via the History panel in the *Fireworks MX* folder in the *Applications Data/Support* folder. These are user-specific commands unlike the master commands stored in the *Configuration* folder.

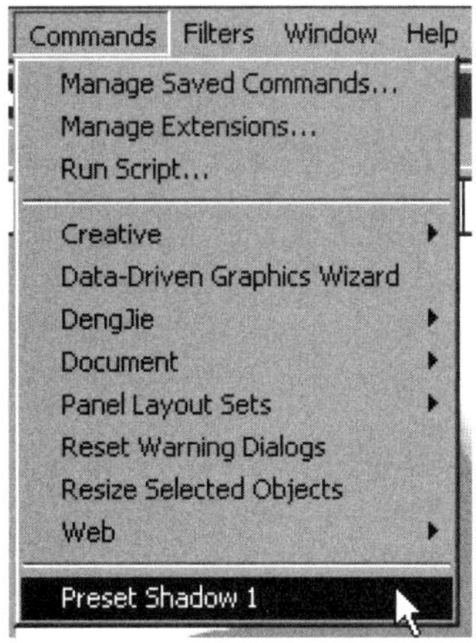

Fig. 11-14. Commands menu with* Preset Shadow 1 *command added.

CAUTION

The History panel does have some limitations when creating commands. Some steps, such as drawing shapes using the bitmap tools, cannot be recreated using the History panel. These steps appear with a red X icon next to them in the list. Other steps, such as changing selections during a process, will produce unpredictable results when used as a command. These steps are underlined in the list.

  e) Draw a new polygon on the canvas and then select Commands | Preset Shadow 1. The shadow preset is applied to the shape.

The History panel also has the ability to copy steps to the clipboard. Copying to the clipboard actually copies the Fireworks scripting commands to memory, and therefore they can be pasted into a text editor. In the text editor, the steps appear as JavaScript code that can be edited and modified.

6. Finally, let's clean up the History list.
   a) Save the file in the *SaveWork* folder, using *History* as the file name.
   b) Select Clear History from the History Options menu. The previous steps have been deleted.
   c) Close the file.

Guided Tour 11D: Working with Commands

Commands are prebuilt scripts that perform specific functions when applied. Commands can be designed to control almost anything in the Fireworks MX environment. They are launched and managed by the Commands menu, and as we saw in the previous tour, commands can be created using the History panel very easily. In addition, commands can be built by hand using JavaScript for those with scripting experience. New to Fireworks MX is the ability to add SWF files created in Flash to commands as a user interface.

1. Open a new blank file with a canvas size of 500 x 500 and a white background.
2. Let's create another simple shape with which to experiment.

a) Select the Polygon tool. In the Properties panel, establish the following settings.

- *Fill Color:* #3300CC
- *Stroke:* None
- *Shape:* Polygon
- *Sides:* 3
- *Angle:* 30

b) Draw a triangle in the center of the stage.

3. Let's look through the Commands menu and experiment with various commands.

a) Select the Commands menu and take a look at the following command categories. See figure 11-15.

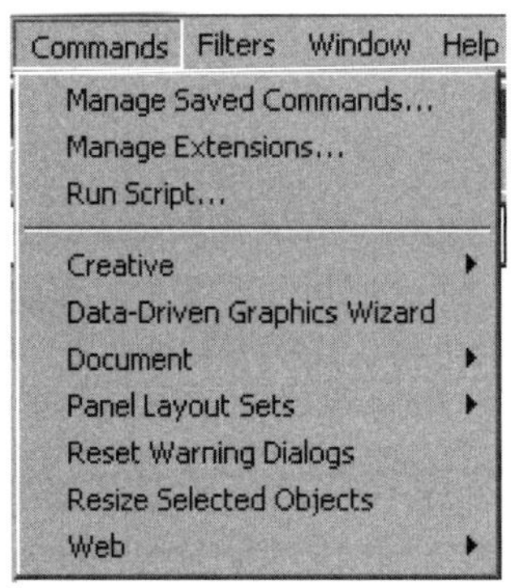

Fig. 11-15. Commands menu.

- *Creative:* Contains commands such as Add Arrowheads, Add Picture Frame, Convert to Grayscale, Convert to Sepia Tone, and Fade Image.
- *Document:* Contains commands that adjust an object's relationship to layers or frames, including Distribute to Frames, Hide Other Layers, Lock Other Layers, and Reverse Frames.
- *Panel Layout Sets:* Contains commands that affect the panel layouts in the Fireworks interface. You can save your own setting or reset to a size of 1024 x 768, 1280 x 1024, or 800 x 600.
- *Web:* Contains commands for adjusting web settings. Commands include Create Shared Palette (for defining a palette for a set of images) and Select Blank Alt Tags/Set Alt Tags, for adjusting <Alt> tag values associated with slices.

b) In addition, there are the following commands, which do not have associated submenus.

- *Data-Driven Graphics Wizard:* Template commands for creating data-driven graphic templates powered by XML content. This is a new SWF command.
- *Reset Warning Dialogs:* Resets all "Don't Show Again" warnings so that they appear when needed.
- *Resize Selected Images:* Visual interface for resizing and fine-tuning image sizes on multiple selected objects. This is one of the new SWF commands.

4. Let's test some of the creative commands.
   a) Click on the Triangle icon that you created in step 2b and select Commands | Creative | Fade Image.
   b) In the window that appears, select any of the Fade Image settings displayed. Click on the OK button.
   c) The Fade Image command has added a mask to our object. This command can be used as a substitution for building custom masks.
   d) Select Commands | Panel Layouts Sets | 1024 x 768. The panels reset to the specified size.
5. Finally, let's look at the options for managing commands.
   a) Select the Commands menu and view the first three settings at the top of the menu list. See figure 11-16.

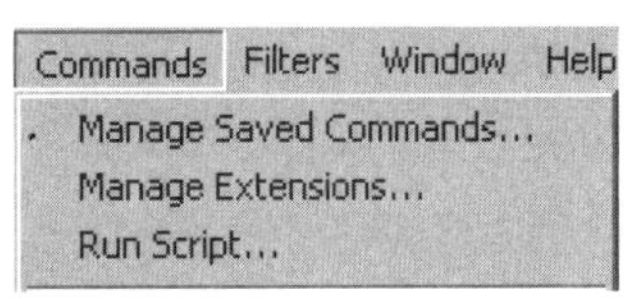

Fig. 11-16. Menu options for managing commands.

The following describe these controls.

- *Manage Saved Commands:* Opens a window box with controls for renaming or deleting any saved command. Saved commands are those saved from the History panel, or commands you manually install in the user configuration files in the *Application Data/Support* folder.
- *Manage Extensions:* Launches the Extensions Manager for control over all acquired extensions, as well as the preset Fireworks commands. All commands available from the Commands menu can be added or removed using the Extensions Manager.

- *Run Script:* Allows you to run a JavaScript (JSF) file saved externally to the Fireworks configuration files. This option allows you to store scripts remotely. Use this option to launch scripts saved from the batch processing command, covered in detail in the Guided Tour 11E.

b) Select Commands | Manage Saved Commands and view the window that appears. Note that the *Preset Shadow 1* command installed from the History panel guided tour is currently the only command saved. See figure 11-17.

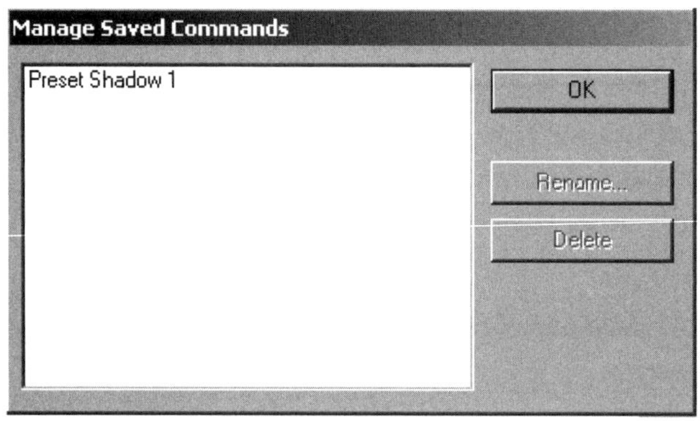

Fig. 11-17. Manage Saved Commands window.

c) Select the *Preset Shadow 1* command. Click on Delete to remove the command.

d) The *Preset Shadow 1* command has been deleted in the Commands menu.

e) Close the file.

Guided Tour 11E: Batch Processing

When discussing optimization of repetitive tasks, batch processing is one of the most powerful utilities in Fireworks. With batch processing, you can select a series of files to process with certain commands, and then create a routine to run them automatically. Basic tasks (such as scaling, exporting, and the find-and-replace function) can be automated across any number of files. For complex actions, custom scripts can also be created and executed on any number of files.

1. To get started, let's launch the Batch Processing wizard.
   a) Select File | Batch Process. The Batch Processing wizard opens. (See figure 11-18.)
   b) There are three steps in this wizard that walk you through the selection of files to batch and the routines for running them.

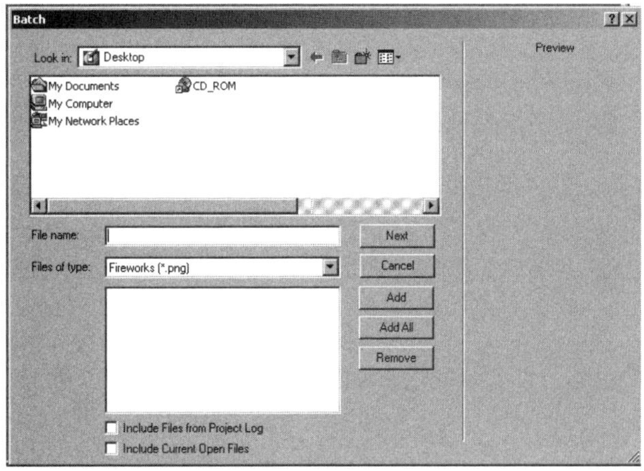

Fig. 11-18. Batch Process window.

2. The first step is to choose which files should be included in the batch.
   a) Set Files of Type to All Files. With the default PNG setting, you cannot see any other types of images, such as JPEG images.
   b) Browse in the *Chapter 11* folder on the companion CD-ROM and open the *images* subfolder. There are eight JPEG images in the *images* subfolder. Click on the Add All button to select all eight images.
   c) Before we move on, note the options located at the bottom of the window: Include Files from Project Log and Include Current Open Files. Include Files from Project Log allows you to include any files in the log whether they are currently open or not. Include Current Open Files will include all files open in Fireworks. Do not choose either of these options. The window should now look like that shown in figure 11-19.

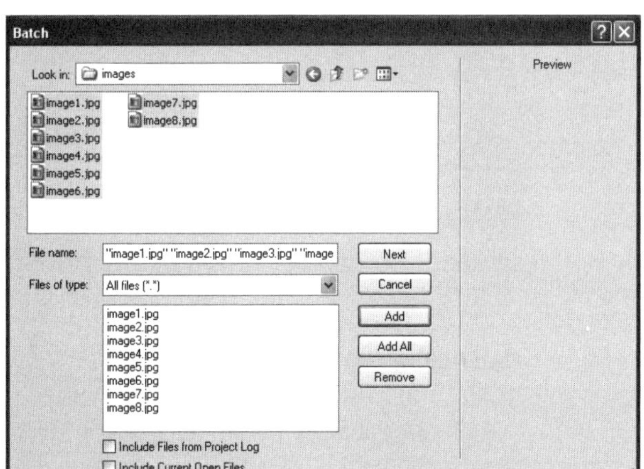

Fig. 11-19. Batch Process window with files selected.

d) Click on the Next button to move to the second step. A new window has opened.

3. The second step is to choose which batch options to run on all files.
   a) Let's examine the batch options listed in the new window, as follows.
      - *Export:* Allows you to adjust export file types and compression settings.
      - *Scale:* Allows you to scale files to a set size, a fixed area, or a percentage.
      - *Find and Replace:* Allows you to batch process any of the Find and Replace features, including text, fonts, colors, URLs, and nonweb-safe colors.
      - *Rename:* Allows you to add a new prefix or extension to any existing file name.
      - *Commands:* Allows you to apply any command in the Commands menu. This is an expandable or collapsible menu.
   b) You can select more than one option if you wish. Add an option by clicking on it to select it and then pressing the Add button. Go ahead and select Scale and click on the Add button. You should see the option added to the list on the right. See figure 11-20.

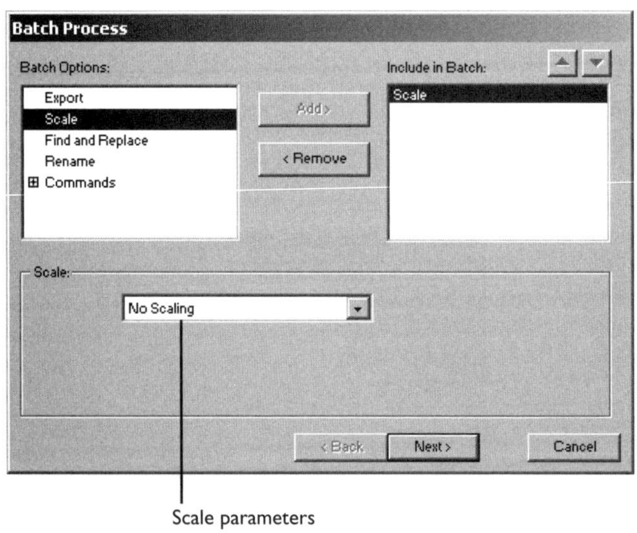

Fig. 11-20. Adding Scale to the batch.

   c) In the Scale Parameters menu, located in the bottom portion of the window, select Scale to Fit Area and then set the width to 150 and the height to 75. See figure 11-21.

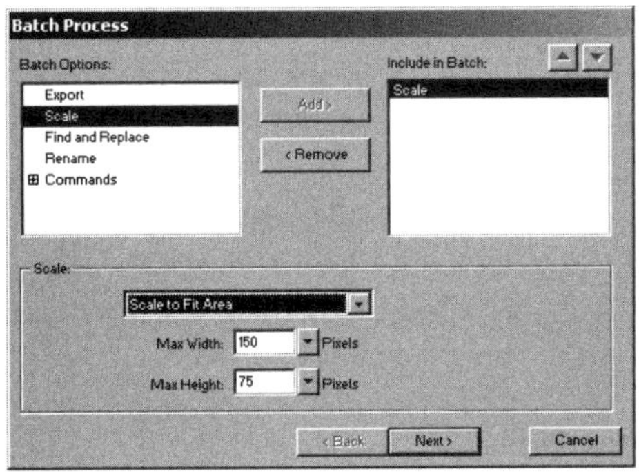

Fig. 11-21. Scale parameters in the Batch Process window.

d) Go back to the Batch Options in the upper left, and click on the Plus (+) icon next to the Commands options. Select the Convert to Grayscale option and then click on the Add button to add this command as well.

e) If you wanted to remove an option from the list, you would select it and click on the Remove button. However, do not remove any options from the list at this point.

f) Click on the Next button to move to the third step.

4. The third step is where you choose your options for saving the processed files.

   a) First, however, let's start with a quick review of the options for saving, which follow. See figure 11-22.

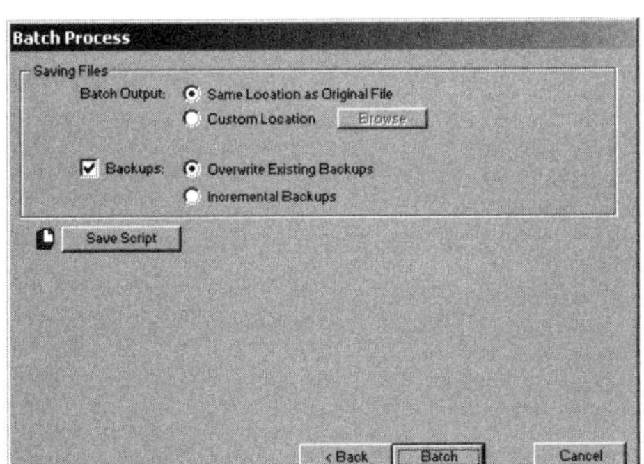

Fig. 11-22. Saving file options.

- *Same Location as Original File:* The default action is to write over the existing files.
- *Browse for a Custom Location:* Allows you to save the batched files to a different location.

- *Backups (On or Off):* If Backups is checked, Fireworks will save a backup version of the original files. If this feature is unchecked, Fireworks will write over the original file with the new file without saving a backup.
- *Overwrite Existing Backups:* If this option is checked, Fireworks will overwrite existing backup files if the batch is run multiple times.
- *Incremental Backups:* If this option is checked, all backup versions will be saved and numbered incrementally to mark the version number.
- *Save Script:* Will save the current batch process script to the Commands menu.

b) Click on the Custom Location button and browse for the *SaveWork* folder to save the images to your hard drive. Click on the Select button at the bottom of the window to select the *SaveWork* folder.

c) Click on the Batch button. The Batch Progress window opens and updates with a display of how many images are complete. When finished, the window alerts you to a successful batch-processing attempt.

d) Click on the OK button.

e) Select File | Open and open the *image1.jpg* image in the *SaveWork* folder.

f) Select File | Open and open the *image1.jpg* image in the *images* subfolder within the *Chapter 11* folder on the companion CD-ROM. As you can see by looking at both images, the original image was a much larger, color image. By applying the Scale and Grayscale conversion in the process of batch processing, the image was automatically converted to a smaller, black-and-white image.

·TIP·

If you save the batch process script, you can run the batch by simply dragging a copy of the script over the Fireworks icon on your desktop or by dropping it onto an open Fireworks document.

If you need to run a complex task through batch processing, you can do so by building a custom command using the History panel, or alternatively using JavaScript. Once the command is saved to the Commands menu, it is available in the first step of the Batch Processing wizard.

CAUTION

Commands that require selections may not work during a batch process. Try to choose commands that do not require object selection.

Guided Tour 11F: Working with the Project Log

The Project Log is a tool used to help track changes to files altered by the Find and Replace or Batch Processing command. Find and Replace coupled with Batch Processing allows you to search and modify large numbers of files automatically. This is a great time saver for large projects or graphics-intensive web sites. While you make wholesale changes and modification to files, it is sometimes possible to inadvertently modify files that should not have been changed.

The Project Log panel allows you to register certain files to watch and report on if there are any changes. If files are registered with this panel, a list of file names will be stored, along with the date and time they were modified and on what frame they were modified. This report helps track down files that were incorrectly processed, and reverts files to the correct version. The Project Log also offers a shortcut for re-exporting the files in the list with the last saved export settings. This allows you to navigate through changed files, and to update selected files and re-export them quickly.

In addition, the Project Log makes accessing stored files extremely easy. You can open files listed in the Project Log by double clicking on them, or you can run a batch process or find-and-replace function on the list without having to search for the files. Let's take a closer look at the Project Log.

> **TIP**
>
> The Rectangle, Polygon, Rounded Rectangle, and Ellipse tools are stored in the same location in the Vector toolbox. Click and hold on the tool to display the menu associated with each tool.

1. First, we need to create three files to register with the Project Log. Once we register the files, we can perform tasks on them and see how the log updates. Each file will consist of a basic shape filled with the same color.
   a) Create a new file with a canvas size of 500 x 500 and a white background.
   b) Use the Rectangle tool to draw a square in the center of the canvas about three inches in width. Fill the square with a blue color #0000FF and no stroke.
   c) Save the file in the *SaveWork* folder as *square.png*. Close this file.
   d) Create a second new file with a canvas size of 500 x 500 and a white background.
   e) With the Ellipse tool, draw a circle in the center of the canvas about three inches in diameter. Fill the circle with a blue color #0000FF and no stroke.
   f) Save the file in the *SaveWork* folder as *circle.png*. Close this file.
   g) Create a new file with the canvas size of 500 x 500 and a white background.
   h) Draw a five-pointed polygon with the Polygon tool in the center of the canvas, about three inches in width. Fill the star with a blue color #0000FF.
   i) Save the file in the *SaveWork* folder as *star.png*. Close this file.
2. Let's take a look at the Project Log.
   a) Select Window | Project Log to open the Project Log panel. (See figure 11-23.) This panel is grouped with the Find and Replace panel by default. Find and Replace is examined in the next guided tour.

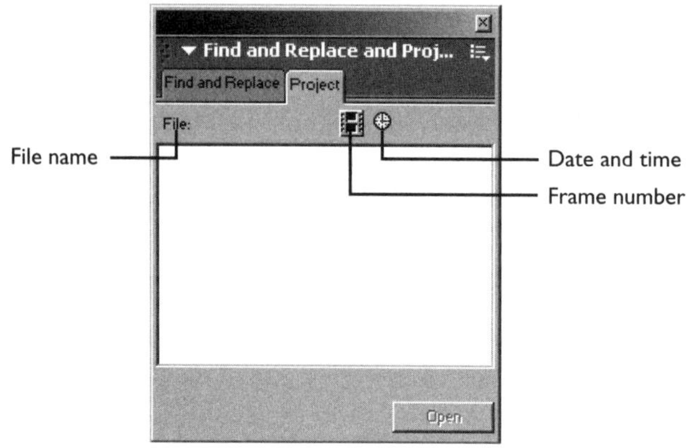

Fig. 11-23. Project Log panel.

b) At first glance, you might notice that there is not much to the Project Log. The primary space on the panel is reserved for the file list. Each line within the file list will have three elements, corresponding to the three icons at the top of the panel, as follows.

- *File Name:* Name of the source file that has been modified.
- *Frame Number:* Frame number that has been modified.
- *Date and Time:* Date and time of the modification.

c) In addition, note the Open button at the bottom of the panel. This button gives you a shortcut to opening any file in the list.

TIP

Registering files with the Project Log is a handy way of accessing all files you are working on without having to open them all at once.

3. Now let's register with the Project Log the three files we prepared for this tour.

a) From the Project Log Options menu, located in the upper right of the panel, select Add Files to Log.

b) In the window that appears, browse for the *square.png*, *star.png*, and *circle.png* files located in the *SaveWork* folder. Shift-click on each file to load them all at once. Click on the Done button.

c) The three files now appear in the Project Log list. (See figure 11-24.) Note that there is no information under the Frame or Date and Time columns stored in the Project Log. This is because no modifications have been performed to the listed version.

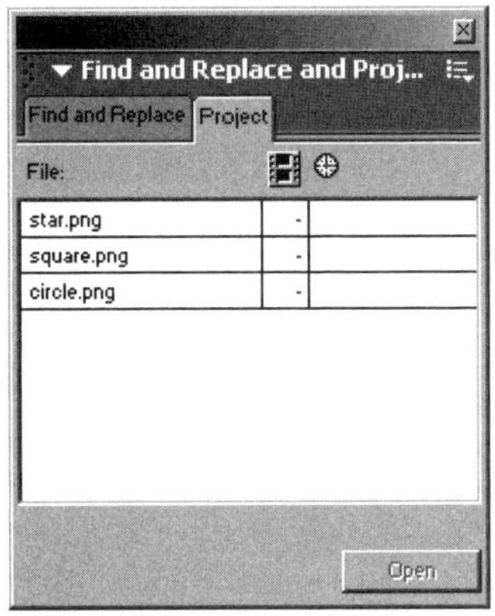

Fig. 11-24. Project Log list.

   d) Before we move on, take a look at the process for removing files from the Project Log. Do not remove any files at this point, but if you did want to remove a file, you would select the file by clicking on the name in the list and then selecting Clear Selection from the Options menu. This will remove any selected files. You can also remove all files at once by selecting Clear All from the Options menu.

4. Let's now open the three files and perform a find-and-replace procedure on them to see how it affects the list.
   a) Shift-click to select the three file names in the Project Log. They are highlighted in blue when selected.
   b) Click on the Open button at the bottom of the panel. All three files open. If you select the Window menu and look at the very bottom of the menu, you will see that the three files are listed as being opened. You can select any of the files displayed here to place that file on top.
   c) Click on the Find and Replace tab next to the Project Log tab. See figure 11-25.

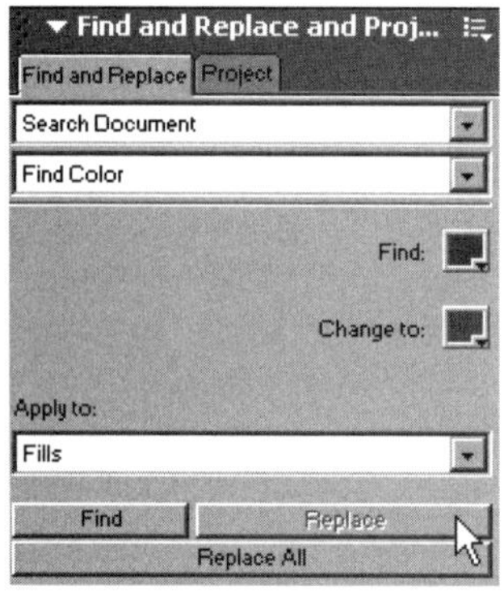

Fig. 11-25. Find and Replace panel.

d) Establish the following settings in the Find and Replace panel.

- *Search in:* Search Project Log
- *Change Attribute:* Find Color
- *Find:* #0000FF (blue)
- *Change to:* #CC0000 (red)
- *Apply to:* Fills

e) Click on the Replace All button. Fireworks now runs through the files in the Project Log and finds the blue fill color and replaces it with red. A window appears and notifies you that three changes have been made. Click on the OK button.

f) Click on the Project Log tab and note that new entries have been added to the list. (See figure 11-26.) This time, the list shows the file names, the frame on which the modification was made, and the date and time of the modification. You will see similar updates when you perform other find-and-replace tasks.

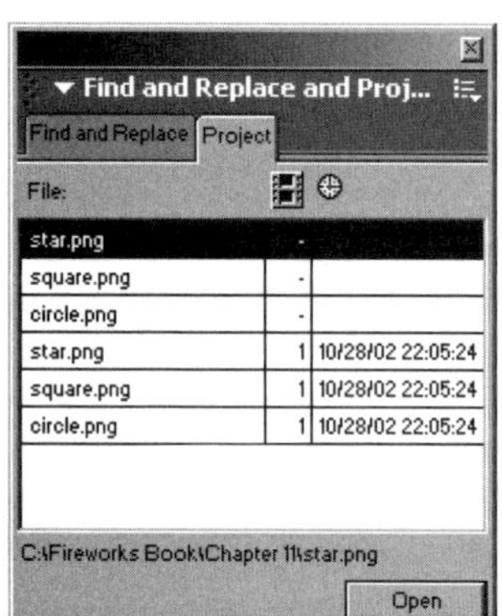

Fig. 11-26. Project Log showing new entries.

g) Close the file.

Guided Tour 11G: Working with Find and Replace

In the previous tour, you experimented with the Find and Replace feature while working with Project Logs. In Chapter 4, we used this feature to control colors. In Guided Tour 11E, you learned that this type of function can also be performed using batch options. In this tour, we will focus on the options available within the Find and Replace feature. Once you understand how to set up the search parameters, Find and Replace is a very simple feature to use.

CAUTION

Find and Replace will not work on flattened image types such as GIF, JPEG, and BMP. These and similar file types do not contain editable objects.

Find and Replace can be used on single or multiple files, depending on the search settings specified. You can search for and modify text, URLs, fonts, and colors. Find and Replace will only work on Fireworks PNG files or other editable vector files, such as a FreeHand file. Let's take a closer look at the Find and Replace panel.

1. The Find and Replace panel should already be open from the last guided tour. If it is not, select Window | Find and Replace. By default, it is grouped with the Project Log. See figure 11-27.

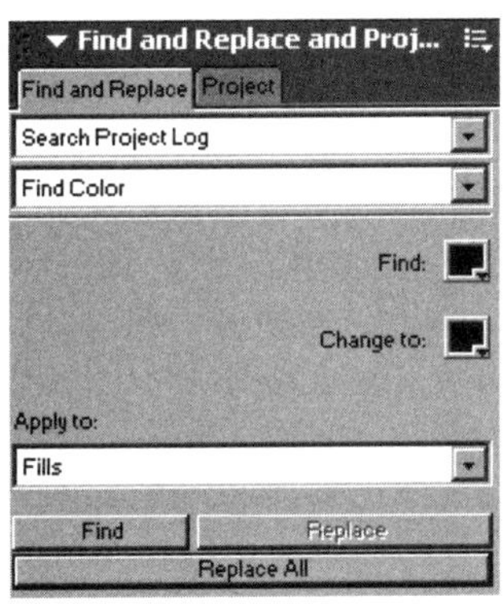

Fig. 11-27. Find and Replace panel.

2. Click on the pull-down menu in the top field in the panel. See figure 11-28.

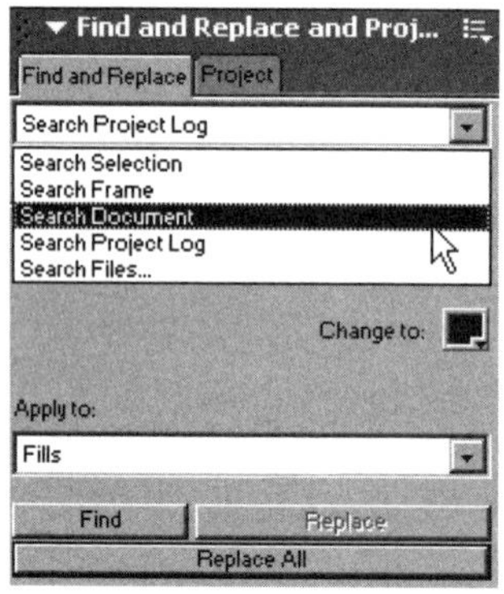

Fig. 11-28. Search In options.

a) Note the search options listed in the menu. Your selection here will determine where to search. Let's review the list, as follows.

- *Search Selection:* Searches only among currently highlighted objects in the active document.
- *Search Frame:* Searches only within the current frame.
- *Search Document:* Searches within the active document.
- *Search Project Log:* Searches files listed within the Project Log.
- *Search Files:* Allows you to browse for a selection of files to search.

b) Select the Search Document option.

3. Click on the pull-down menu in the second field to set the Find option.

   a) Note the list of search attributes in the Find option menu. Your selection here will determine what to search for. Options include Find Text, Find Font, Find Color, Find URL, and Find Non-Web216. See figure 11-29.

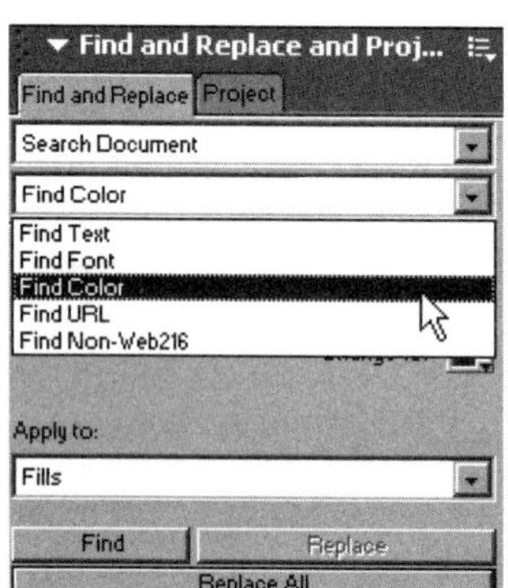

Fig. 11-29. Search attributes.

b) Select Find Text and review the properties that appear, as follows.

- *Find:* Type in the word or words to search for.
- *Change to:* Type in the replacement text.
- *Whole Word:* Finds the text only if it is not part of another word..
- *Match Case:* Creates case-sensitive searches.
- *Regular Expressions:* Allows you to search through text based on a pattern instead of specific text. For example, you could search for a range of sale prices based on the pattern of the digits.

c) Select Find Font from the Search Attribute options. Review the properties that appear, as follows.

- *Font List:* Select a font to search for.
- *Font Style:* Select a font style to search for.
- *Min/Max:* Select minimum and maximum point sizes to search for. This limits the search if you only need a specific font size setting.
- *Change to:* Set the font, style, and size to change the font to.

d) Select Find Color from the Search Attribute options. Review the properties that appear, as follows.

- *Find:* Choose a color to find from the swatches.
- *Change to:* Choose a replacement color.
- *Apply to:* Choose to apply the change to fills only, strokes only, fills and strokes, effects, or all properties.

·TIP·

While the swatches are visible, you can also sample colors from the visible area of the document using the Eyedropper tool.

e) Select Find URL from the Search Attribute options. Note that properties that appear are the same options as the Find Text options. Review the properties that appear, as follows.

- *Find:* Type in the word or words to search for.
- *Change to:* Type in the replacement text.
- *Whole Word:* Finds the text only if it is not part of another word.
- *Match Case:* Creates case-sensitive searches.
- *Regular Expressions:* Allows you to search through text based on a pattern instead of specific text. For example, you could search for a range of sale prices based on the pattern of the digits.

CAUTION

Find Non-Web216 only works on vector objects. It will not work on image objects such as imported bitmaps.

f) Select Find Non-Web216 from the Search Attribute options. Review the property that appears, as follows.

- *Apply to:* Choose to apply the change to fills only, strokes only, fills and strokes, effects, or all properties.

TIP

In general, it is considered good practice to first set up your search parameters. You then click on Find to find the first instance. Click on Replace to replace that instance's attributes. If this first pass works as expected, select Replace All to replace all instances. Otherwise, undo the replace, reset your attribute settings, and try again.

4. After you have set the Search In and the Search Attributes fields, the only thing left to do is to search. You have the following three buttons available at the bottom of the panel. These control the actual search.
    - *Find:* Searches the specified target for the next instance of the specified attribute.
    - *Replace:* Replaces the selected instance with new attributes.
    - *Replace All:* Finds and replaces all instances with the specified attributes.
5. One last thing to note about Find and Replace. If you are going to use this feature on multiple files that are not open, such as files listed in the Project Log, you have the option of saving backup files when overwriting.
    a) Open the Find and Replace Options menu and select Replace Options.
    b) Note the window that appears. You can set the following options.
        - *Save and Close Files:* This option is checked by default. If you uncheck it, Fireworks will open each file and perform the search and replace, and then leave the files open without saving them.
        - *No Backups:* This option allows Fireworks to overwrite the original file when saving.
        - *Overwrite Existing Backups:* Saves only the most recent backup copy of a file when changes are made.
        - *Incremental Backups:* If this option is selected, all backup versions will be saved in a folder called *Original Files,* and numbered incrementally to reflect the version.
    c) Click on the Cancel button.
    d) Close the files and the Find and Replace panel.

CAUTION

When you use Find and Replace to modify files that are not open, the changes are made to the unopened files and they cannot be undone using Edit | Undo. Using the Project Log allows you to track changes and revert to previous versions of the modified files.

Guided Tour 11H: Working with the URL Panel

Universal resource locators (URLs) are simply text paths that act as addresses used to locate web pages. If you use the Internet, anytime you type in *http://www* you are typing in a URL. In Fireworks, URLs can be added to hotspots, buttons, and slices. Previously, you learned how to create a slice, select it, and enter a URL for it in the Properties panel. URLs can be included with slices, hotspots, and buttons to link to other web pages.

With the URL panel, you can manage libraries of links so that they can be reused and shared with a workgroup. This is an invaluable tool for larger sites with a lot of links, or for creating a standard set of placeholder links for designing sites. URL libraries are accessible from all Fireworks documents. You may store new URLs in the default *URLs.htm* library or create your own custom-named URL libraries. Let's take a closer look at the URL panel.

1. Select File | New and browse in the *Chapter 11* folder on the companion CD-ROM. Locate the *Tour_11H.png* file. Double click on the file to open it.
2. Select Window | URL to open the URL panel. The URL panel is grouped in the Assets panel group with the Library and Styles option. See figure 11-30.

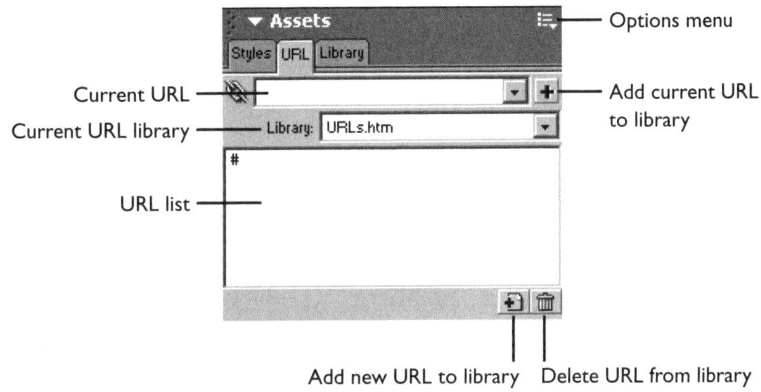

Fig. 11-30. URL panel.

3. In the *Web* layer, select the *button1* slice using the Pointer tool. Make sure you can clearly see the URL panel, the Properties panel, and the slice on your screen. Adjust the location of these panels if you need to.
4. Now let's explore the URL panel.
   a) The structure of the URL panel is fairly simple. The major portion of the panel is reserved for the URL list displayed by the current URL library.
   b) Let's review the options, as follows.
      - *Current URL Menu (chain link icon):* Enter a new URL here or edit a URL selected from the list. If an object is selected without a URL, this field will display No URL (NoHref).
      - *Add Current URL to Library button (+ icon):* This button will add the URL in the Current URL field to the library list selected in the Library field.
      - *Current URL Library Menu:* Allows you to switch the display between the default *URLS.htm* and any URL library you may have created or imported.
      - *URL List:* List of URLs in the selected URL library.

- *Add New URL to Library button (lower right):* Launches a text dialog and allows you to enter a new URL to be included with the current library.
- *Delete URL from Library (trash can):* Removes selected URLs from the current URL library.

5. Let's create a new URL library and populate it with placeholder links.
   a) In the URL panel, select New URL Library from the URL Options menu. See figure 11-31.

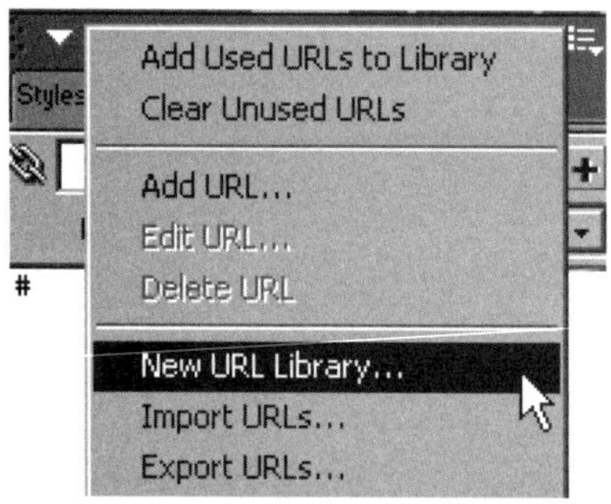

Fig. 11-31. New URL Library in the URL Options menu.

   b) In the window that appears, name the library *placeholders*. Click on the OK button.
   c) Note that the current library switches to *placeholders.htm*. Click on the Library pull-down menu and note that the default *URLs.htm* is still available in the list. You can toggle back and forth between multiple libraries in the URL panel. Leave the selection set to *placeholders.htm*.

6. Now let's add a few URLs to the menu.
   a) Click on the Add New URL to Library button, located in the bottom right of the panel. In the window that appears, type in *page1.html*. (See figure 11-32.) Click on the OK button.

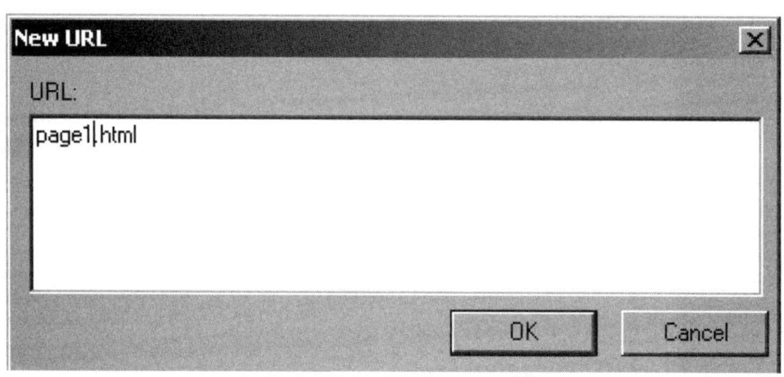

Fig. 11-32. Add* page1.html *to library.

b) Repeat the previous step to add *page2.html* and *page3.html.*

c) All three URLs should be listed in the URL panel. See figure 11-33.

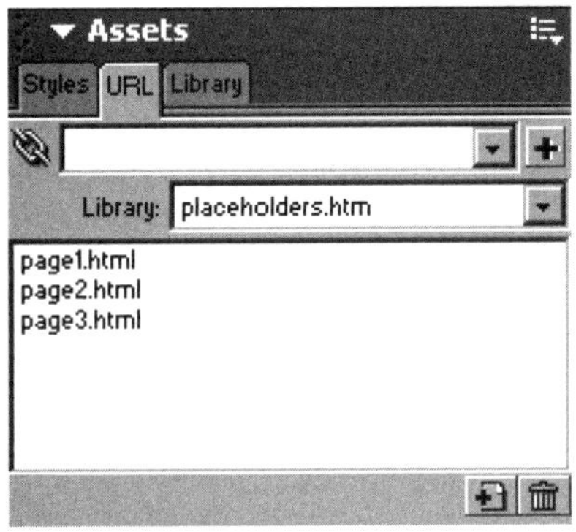

Fig. 11-33. URLs in the URL panel.

d) Select the *button1* slice if it is not already selected, and select *page1.html* in the URL list. The Current URL field in the URL changes to reflect the selection. In the Properties panel, the Link field also shows *page1.html.* See figure 11-34.

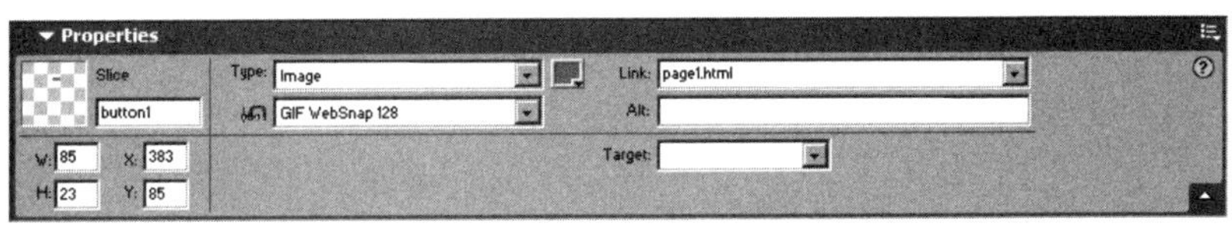

Fig. 11-34. Link in the Properties panel.

e) Click on the Link field in the Properties panel. You can select links from the current library using the Link field in the Properties panel as well. Select *page2.html.*

7. To edit a URL, select an item in the URL list in the URL panel and then select Edit URL from the URL Options menu.

8. To remove a URL, select it in the list and click on the Delete URL button (Trash Can icon) on the lower right of the panel.

9. Let's take a look at the last few options in the URL Options menu list.

   a) Click on the Options menu icon in the upper right of the URL panel. The options menu should appear.

   b) Note the following options.

      - *Add Used URLs to the Library:* Adds any URL used in the current document to the current URL library.

- *Clear Unused URL: Clears* URLs that have not been applied to slices or hotspots in the current document from the current URL library.
- *Add URL:* Adds a URL to the current URL library.
- *Edit URL:* Edits a selected URL from the current URL library.
- *Delete URL:* Deletes a selected URL from the current URL library.
- *New URL Library:* Creates a new URL library.
- *Import URLs:* Imports a URL library.
- *Export URLs:* Exports a URL library.

All URL libraries are stored in HTML files in the Fireworks user configuration files on your hard drive. Like the Project Log, you can open the HTML files in a web browser and print this file if necessary. URL libraries are stored in the *URL Libraries* folder in the *Application Data/Support* folder.

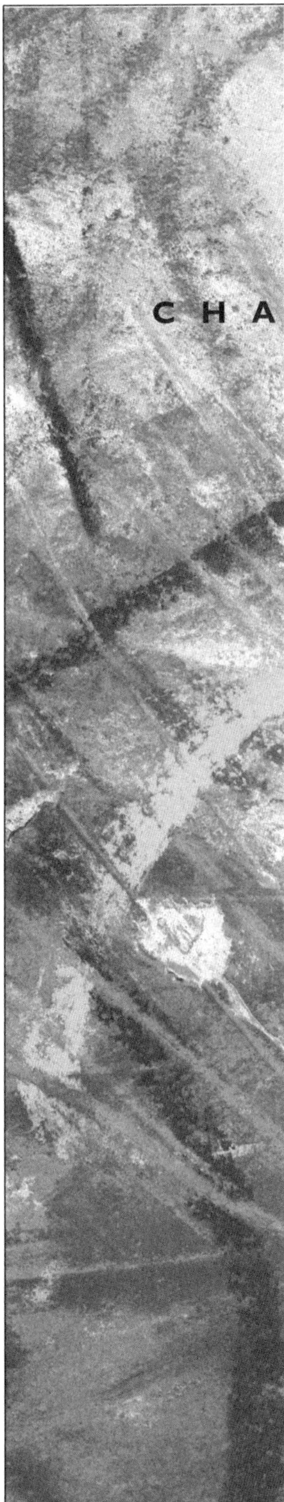

CHAPTER 12

Fireworks and Other Applications

Chapter Topics:

- Introduction
- Fireworks and Other Applications
- Tips for Working with Fireworks Images and Other Applications
- Tips for Working with Fireworks HTML with Other Applications
- Guided Tour 12A: Using Alternate Export File Types
- Guided Tour 12B: The Quick Export Menu and Other Applications

Introduction

Although Fireworks MX has many tools that can be used for both web and print design, most designers use Fireworks as just one program within a suite of software programs used to get a job done. With this in mind, Fireworks MX has been upgraded to better integrate with other standard design software and supported file formats. This enhancement means greater flexibility in a design and production environment. In this chapter, we will look at how to use images and HTML created in Fireworks MX in other programs. By the end of this chapter you will be able to:

- *Use Fireworks images in other applications*
- *Understand how to export Fireworks files so that they can be used in other applications*
- *Select appropriate export settings, depending on the final destination of the Fireworks file*

Fireworks and Other Applications

In any discussion of *how* Fireworks interacts with other development tools, we need to first consider what information is shared or exported to other applications. In Fireworks, there are two general categories: images and HTML. In that these two elements are the products of your work in Fireworks MX, it is important to explore alternative export files types, the Quick Export menu, and import file format specifics for applications such as Dreamweaver, Flash, FreeHand, and more.

Tips for Working with Fireworks Images and Other Applications

The following are some general tips for handling the preparation and export of vector and bitmap graphics. In addition, Fireworks MX features a cross-application graphic editing feature called Launch and Edit, which allows you to manipulate graphics created in Fireworks from other programs where these files have been imported.

Handling Vectors

Vector graphics are flexible and will travel from application to application, maintaining their editable paths until rasterized. The following are a few tips for working with vectors.

1. The Edit | Copy command has been enhanced so that vector shapes copied from Fireworks MX and pasted into other MX software, such as Flash MX, now maintain their exact appearance. In order to do this, the vectors are flattened to bitmaps and no longer consist of editable paths.
2. The Edit | Copy Path Outlines command allows you to copy and paste vector paths into any software capable of editing vector graphics. The editable vector is retained, although some appearance styles may be lost.
3. Exporting in Illustrator 7 format allows you to import into any vector editing software. Illustrator 7 is a commonly supported vector format incorporated into most design software. The Export command in FreeHand uses the Illustrator 7 format as well.

Handling Bitmaps and Maintaining Editable Files

Bitmap graphics are also fairly simple to pass between applications. The common export formats in Fireworks MX are supported by most development applications. As for the master Fireworks PNG file, you can open the PNG in Flash MX, or export it as a Photoshop file. Either option will maintain layers and editable objects. The following are a few tips for working with bitmaps.

1. Flattened bitmaps—such as JPEG, GIF, PNG, TIFF, BMP, and PICT (Macintosh only)—do not preserve editable layers. These file formats are almost universally supported by a variety of software programs and can be opened or imported in most graphics and presentation software.
2. Flash MX can open or import Fireworks PNG files and maintain layers, editable vectors, text, and bitmap images.
3. Exporting in Photoshop format maintains layers and editable objects as well.

NOTE

Behaviors and web objects cannot be imported into Flash MX.

Launch and Edit Settings

Flash MX, Dreamweaver MX, HomeSite, Director, and FrontPage are all enabled with the Fireworks Launch and Edit feature. This feature allows you to launch Fireworks from inside another application in order to edit or optimize the image that was imported from Fireworks. When you have completed the modification in Fireworks and close it, you are automatically returned to the application with the updated file. The Launch and Edit preferences in Fireworks control what happens to the PNG source file when launching Fireworks editing mode from another application.

Take a look at how the Launch and Edit settings in the Fireworks Preferences can be customized.

NOTE

Dreamweaver ignores the Launch and Edit preferences in all instances unless editing a single image. In instances where Dreamweaver is editing a Fireworks table, Dreamweaver will automatically launch the source PNG file.

1. Open the Fireworks preferences by selecting Edit | Preferences. The Preferences window opens.
   a) Click on the Launch and Edit tab in the Preferences window. See figure 12-1.

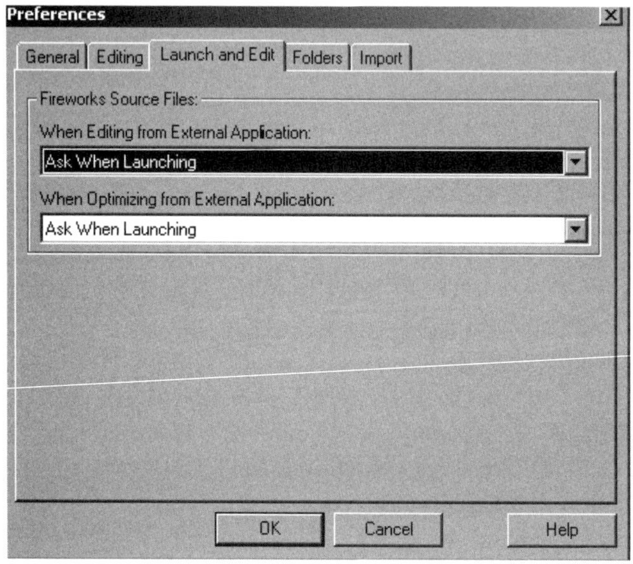

Fig. 12-1. Launch and Edit tab in the Preferences window.

   b) The following two fields appear on the Launch and Edit tab.
      - *When Editing from External Application*
      - *When Optimizing from External Application*
   c) Both fields have the following three options.
      - *Always Use Source PNG:* Always performs the modification on the source file.
      - *Never Use Source PNG:* Always applies the modification to the applied graphic.
      - *Ask When Launching:* Lets the user define which option to use each time Launch and Edit is used. This is the default for both fields.
   d) Click on the Cancel button.

Tips for Working with Fireworks HTML and Other Applications

Fireworks HTML consists of tables, URLs, <*Alt*> tags, JavaScript, and image maps. As we have seen in previous chapters, this code is generated behind the scenes during export. Once exported, the HTML code gathers all behaviors, image slices, links, and other elements from the *Web* layer and creates a text-based page that gives the web browser directions on how to display and interpret all elements in order for the page to function correctly.

Because Fireworks is not a web page editor, we need ways to transport the HTML code and images for use in other applications, or to convert the HTML to a PNG file. Let's look at some of the general features that can be used when working with other HTML or web development applications.

Reconstitute Table

Reconstitute Table allows you to convert an HTML table and graphics into a Fireworks PNG file. This allows you to load an HTML page in Fireworks and then convert it to a master PNG file. Fireworks leaves slices separate in order to mark the table borders in the *Web* layer. This is perfect for those times when you have the web site files but the master PNG files are not accessible. The following is the process for using this command.

1. To use Reconstitute Table, select File | Reconstitute Table.
   a) In the window that appears, browse on the companion CD-ROM to the *Chapter 12* folder, and find the file *splash.html*. Select the file and click on the Open button. The *splash.htm* page is linked to a number of image files that are located within an *image* folder, located within the *Chapter 12* folder on the companion CD-ROM.
   b) The file appears as a PNG file with slices marking the previous table borders. The sliced graphics appear as separate objects on a layer named *Shared Layer*, and each graphic has a corresponding slice in the *Web* layer. You can now edit the file as necessary.

TIP

When using Reconstitute Table, you can select all graphics on the *Shared Layer* layer and select Flatten Selection from the Layers Options menu to merge them into one image.

HTML Setup

Let's take a look at the HTML setup within the context of matching source code to different HTML editors.

1. Select File | HTML Setup from the menu and look at the General tab. See figure 12-2.

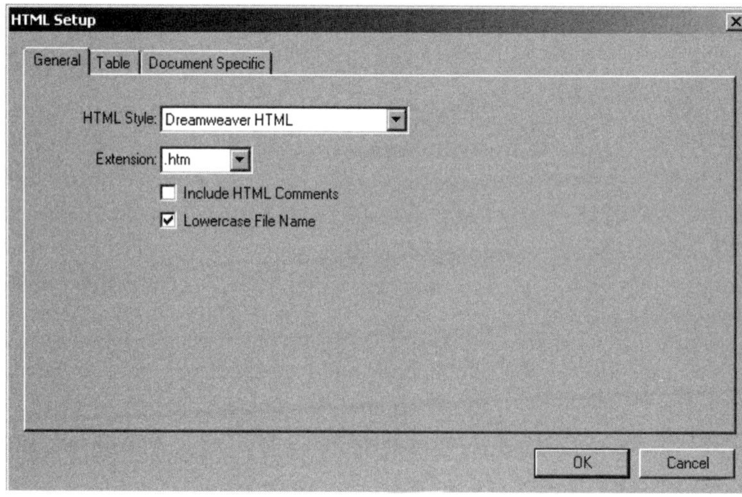

Fig. 12-2. HTML Setup window.

a) Select the HTML Style field. A menu appears, containing the following options.

- *Dreamweaver HTML*
- *FrontPage HTML*
- *Generic HTML*
- *GoLive HTML*

Use the Generic HTML setting if you are not using any interactive elements such as Rollover or Nav Bar behaviors. If you do have interactive elements, it is advisable to select your target web editor from the list. Interactive elements export differently from Fireworks based on the selected HTML style. Adjusting this setting each time you export to a different editor will be your best bet for avoiding compatibility problems.

b) XHTML is a new standard that is a combination of HTML and XML (Extensible Markup Language). Fireworks MX will import and export XHTML. If you wish to do this, choose one of the following three XHTML selections.

- *Dreamweaver XHTML*
- *Generic XHTML*
- *GoLive XHTML*

c) Click on the Cancel button to close the window.

·TIP·

Dreamweaver MX also imports and exports XHTML.

Update HTML

Update HTML allows you to update Fireworks HTML that has been placed in other files, such as Dreamweaver files. The following are general steps for updating Fireworks HTML.

1. Make the desired modifications to a Fireworks file that has already been exported and used in a Dreamweaver or GoLive site.
2. Select File | HTML Setup from the menu and then select the HTML Style option that matches the editor file type that contains the Fireworks HTML.
3. Select File | Update HTML. Browse in the window that appears for the file to be updated. Select it and click on the Open button.
4. Another prompt appears that asks for your preferences for overwriting the file you are updating. Choose from the following options.
    - *Replace Images and Their HTML:* Updates both images and HTML by overwriting the previous file.
    - *Update Images Only:* Updates the images only, by overwriting them.
5. Select a preference and click on OK. Another window appears and asks which images directory to use. Browse for the correct folder and click on the Select button. The files are saved and the HTML is now updated.

Copy HTML to the Clipboard

The Copy HTML to Clipboard command allows you to copy and paste HTML code directly into the editor of your choice. Those users who have experience hand-coding HTML can then directly manipulate the pasted code in the editor. To use Copy HTML to Clipboard, perform the following.

1. You should still have the *splash.html* file open. If not, open any Fireworks file, preferably one with slices and content on the *Web* layer. Select Edit | Copy HTML Code. Copying the code in this manner copies the generic code to the clipboard. Click on the Cancel button.
2. You can also use Quick Export to specify HTML code written for a particular program.

Quick Export

The Quick Export button is located in the upper right-hand corner of the Document window. Go ahead and click on it. A menu now opens. (See figure

12-3.) You can now make the selection you need for exporting the document in the compatible format.

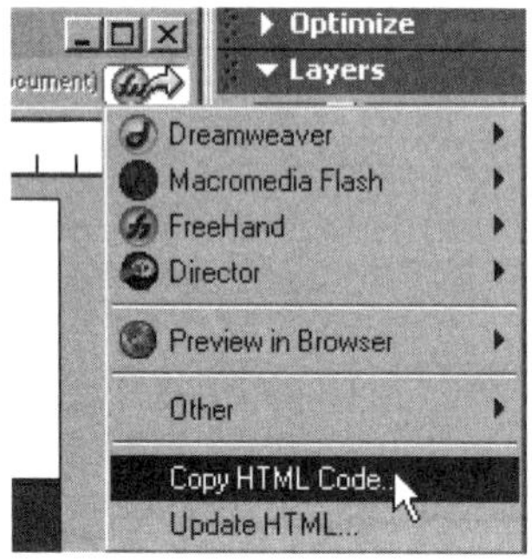

Fig. 12-3. Quick Export button in the Document window.

1. From the menu, you can select Copy HTML Code to copy the generic code, or select one of the other programs formats. Once you have copied the code in any manner, you can open any text editor and paste in the code for further editing.

Roundtrip HTML

Roundtrip HTML is a new feature that is enabled in Dreamweaver, FrontPage, and HomeSite. Changes made to Fireworks-generated HTML code in these applications are also preserved in the original Fireworks PNG document. The result is that both files reflect changes made in either location, which allows for seamless editing between these applications.

CAUTION

If major changes are made to a Fireworks table in Dreamweaver, Fireworks may not be able to read the new updates during the roundtrip conversion. It is recommended that you make table edits by launching Fireworks from Dreamweaver.

In Guided Tour 12A, we will look at export file types that we have not covered in previous chapters. Understanding these file formats can be very helpful when working between different programs.

Guided Tour 12A: Using Alternate Export File Types

Before we get into the shortcuts for exporting file formats that are compatible with different applications, let's look at the standard export file type options. These settings are often overlooked, but understanding the file choices available is valuable when working on a wide range of print, multimedia, and web design projects. This tour is a review of the Export options as an introduction to alternate settings that go beyond images and HTML export.

1. You should already have the *splash.html* file open. If you do not, open any one of the sample files you have created in previous practice exercises, or open a blank file in order to view the export options. Select File | Export

from the menu and click on the Save as Type field. Take a look at your choices displayed here. See figure 12-4.

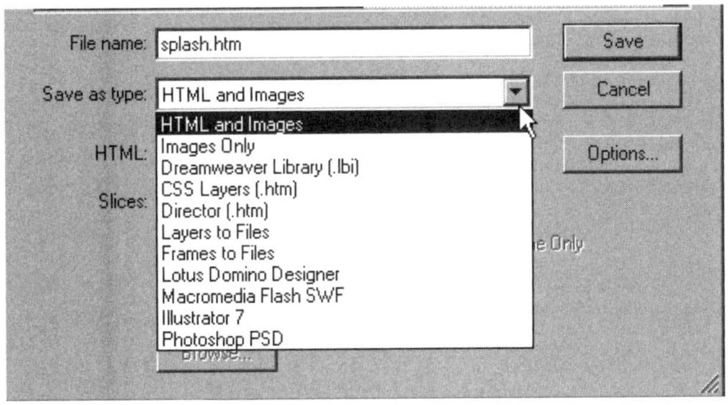

Fig. 12-4. File type choices.

We have already explored the first two choices listed. HTML and Images exports Fireworks HTML and images to a specified location. Images only does just what the name implies—saves only the images.

2. The next option is Dreamweaver Library (.lbi). Dreamweaver libraries hold graphics that can be reused and updated in a web site and are very similar in function to the Fireworks library. This option allows you to create a library of images and place it in a site in Dreamweaver. Repetitive elements such as logos and taglines can be managed and updated very easily in a Dreamweaver library. If you are not a Dreamweaver user, you can skip forward to the next file format.
   a) Select Dreamweaver Library (.lbi) from the Save as Type menu.
   b) Dreamweaver libraries are created in the root folder for any site that uses libraries with Dreamweaver. Fireworks can also save a library file to this folder as long as you specify the correct location. As soon as you select Dreamweaver Library, a window appears prompting you to browse for the target *Library* folder. Click on the OK button.
   c) In the next window, browse for the *Library* folder in the root folder of the site that will use the file. Create a folder named *Library* if one does not already exist.
   d) Highlight the folder and click on the Select button.
   e) Fireworks now creates the library of images.

CAUTION

The prompt does not appear if the current directory is labeled *Library*.

3. The next export option is CSS Layers (.htm). A layer in dynamic HTML is a container that can be exactly positioned, hidden, or shown. Layers are used to create animations in JavaScript and to build effects such as menus and tool tips. By exporting your Fireworks document with this feature,

each Fireworks element will be stored on a separate layer in the code. This code can be used in other applications as well.

a) Select CSS Layers (.htm) from the Save as Type menu. The following settings appear.

- *Source:* Select from Fireworks layers, frames, or slices for the original source the CSS layers will be created from.
- *Trim Images:* Trims the size of the layer to the image size.
- *Put Images in Subfolder:* Creates a subfolder for the images.
- *Current Frame Only:* Saves images from the current frame only. This setting is grayed out if there is only one frame in the document.

b) Choose your settings and click on OK. The images are saved in the specified folder, and the layers are saved in code in the HTML document that was exported with the images.

4. The next export option is Director (.htm).

a) Select Director (.htm) from the Save as Type menu. The Director options are almost the same as the CSS Layers options, as follows.

- *Source:* Select from Fireworks layers or slices for the original source the CSS layers will be created from. Unlike the CSS Layers file type, Fireworks does not allow you to choose frames for the Director type.
- *Trim Images:* Trims the size of the layer to the image size.
- *Put Images in Subfolder:* Create a subfolder for the images.
- *Current Frame Only:* Saves images from the current frame only. This setting is grayed out if there is only one frame in the document.

b) Choose your settings and click on Save. The HTML and images are saved to the location you specified.

5. The next export option is Layers to Files. This option saves each Fireworks layer to a separate file.

a) Select Layers to Files from the Save as Type menu. The following options are available.

- *Trim Images:* Trim the size of the file to the size of the objects on each layer.
- *Current Frame Only:* Only saves images from the current frame. This setting is grayed out if there is only one frame in the document.

b) Click on Save. Fireworks now saves the separate images from each layer with the export settings currently specified in the file.

6. The next export option is Frames to Files. This option saves each frame to a separate file, and is very handy for splitting up an animation or button states.
   a) Select Frames to Files from the Save as Type menu. There is only one option available.
      - *Trim Images:* Trim the size of the file to the size of the objects on each frame.
   b) Click on Save. Fireworks saves the separate files and names them *fileName_f01.gif*, *fileName_f02.gif*, and so forth.
7. The next option on the list is Lotus Domino Designer. Lotus Domino uses a format called Image Wells to create an effect similar to Fireworks frames within a single file. Instead of separate frames, Image Wells contains four graphics side by side, separated by a single pixel. Using this option will enable Lotus Domino Designer to use Fireworks graphics for things such as rollover effects.
   a) Select Lotus Domino Designer from the Save as Type menu. The following source options are available.
      - *Fireworks Frames:* Exports the top four frames of the Fireworks document as a file.
      - *Fireworks Layers:* Exports the top four layers of the Fireworks document as a file.
      - *Fireworks Slices:* Exports the first four frames of each slice as a file.
      - *Trim Images:* Trims the size of the file to the size of the objects on each layer.
      - *Current Frame Only:* Saves images from the current frame only.
   b) Click on Save. Fireworks now saves the single Image Well file.
8. The next option on the list is Macromedia Flash SWF. SWF files can include animations and vector graphics. They are characterized by small file sizes and are displayed with the widely distributed Flash Player. SWF files can be embedded in web pages or imported into other applications that support the SWF format.
   a) Select Macromedia Flash SWF from the Save as Type menu.
   b) There are no settings available. However, note the Options button. (See figure 12-5.) Click on the Options button to open the SWF Export Options window.

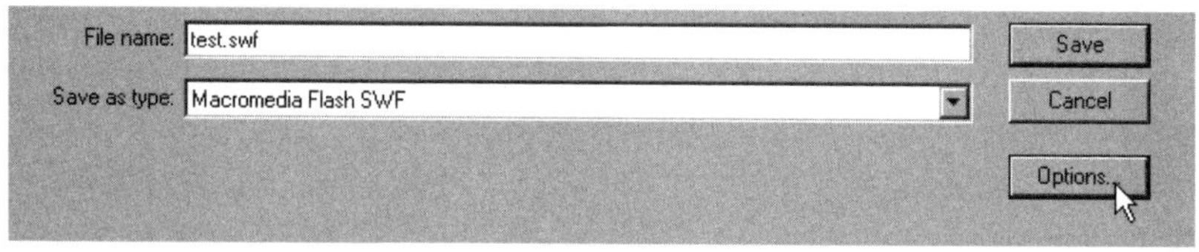

Fig. 12-5. Options button shown in Macromedia Flash SWF type choice.

c) As shown in figure 12-6, the SWF Export Options window has the following options.

- *Objects*
  - *Maintain Paths:* This option maintains editable paths, but discards appearance settings such as effects and formatting.
  - *Maintain Appearance:* This option flattens the image into a bitmap to maintain the appearance. Editable paths are lost.
- *Texts*
  - *Maintain Editability:* Maintains text editability, but discards effects and style formatting.
  - *Convert to Paths:* Maintains style formatting by converting the text to paths. Text can no longer be edited as text, but can be edited as a path.
  - *JPEG Quality:* Sets the bitmap export quality (0 to 100, where 100 is best quality).
  - *Frames:* Select All, or choose a range of frame numbers to include in the SWF file.
  - *Frame Rate:* Set the SWF frame rate here. The default in Flash is 12 frames per second. The default in Fireworks is 15.

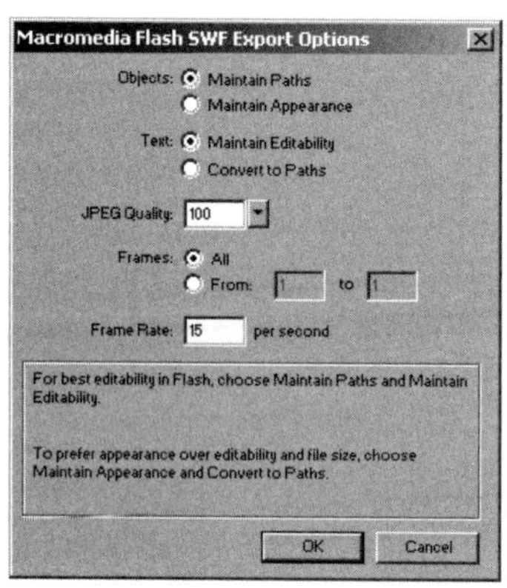

Fig. 12-6. Macromedia Flash SWF Export Options window.

d) Click on Save. Fireworks now saves the SWF file with your settings applied.

9. The next export option is Illustrator 7. This option has has no additional settings because the file is simply saved with Illustrator formatting and the file extension *.ai*. Illustrator 7 is a widely accepted format for importing and exporting vector files. This format can also be used to export vectors from FreeHand.

10. The final export option is Photoshop PSD. This option allows you to reconfigure the Fireworks file to the Photoshop format while maintaining as much editability as possible in relation to the original file. The ability to go back and forth between Fireworks and Photoshop is a useful feature for designers who use a wide range of programs.

    a) Select Photoshop from the Save as Type menu. Note the settings, as follows.

    - *Settings*
        - *Maintain Editability over Appearance:* Converts the layers to Photoshop layers and renders effects and text so that they are editable in Photoshop. This is the default and recommended setting.
        - *Maintain Fireworks Appearance:* Flattens text and effects to maintain the original appearance.
        - *Smaller Photoshop File:* Flatten layers, text, and effects for the smallest file size possible.
        - *Custom:* Allows you to mix and match your own settings from the options that follow. These options are grayed out unless Custom is selected as the setting.
    - *Objects (Grayed out unless Custom is selected as the setting)*
        - *Convert to Photoshop Layers:* Converts each Fireworks object to a Photoshop layer and converts Fireworks masks into Photoshop layer masks.
        - *Flatten Each Fireworks Layer:* Flattens all objects in a Fireworks layer to create a single Photoshop layer.
    - *Effects (Grayed out unless Custom is selected as the setting)*
        - *Maintain Editability:* Maintains any Fireworks editable effects as closely as possible in Photoshop. If there is no matching effect, the Fireworks effect is discarded.
        - *Render Effect:* Flattens effects to preserve appearance.
    - *Text (Grayed out unless Custom is selected as the setting)*

- *Maintain Editability:* Maintains the editability of Fireworks text when exported to Photoshop. Discards any styles incompatible with Photoshop.
- *Render Text:* Renders text as an image. The appearance is preserved, but text can no longer be edited.

b) Click on Save and Fireworks saves the PSD file.

Now that we have gone over all of the export types available, let's turn to the Quick Export options.

Guided Tour 12B: The Quick Export Menu and Other Applications

The next stop on our tour through Fireworks MX will be to explore the new Quick Export feature, located on the Document window. At the beginning of this chapter, there was a description of the function of this feature. However, this handy utility allows users to easily export images and/or Fireworks HTML to any application. As you will see in this tour, specific applications (such as Flash, FreeHand, and Dreamweaver) have enhanced features and exporting capabilities. We will look briefly at the highlighted applications in the menu and how they integrate with Fireworks MX.

1. Open a new blank file if there is not one already open. Set the canvas to 500 x 500 and the background to white.
2. Look in the upper right-hand corner of the Document window for the yellow icon with the arrow. (See figure 12-7.) This is the Quick Export button.

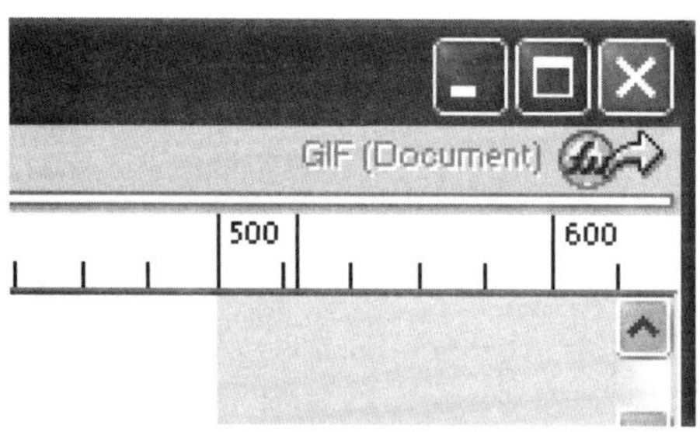

Fig. 12-7. Quick Export button.

a) Click on the Quick Export button to view the menu.
b) Note the grouping of options for Dreamweaver, Flash, FreeHand, and Director. We will tour through each selection and explain features associated with each software program.

Dreamweaver

1. Highlight Dreamweaver in the Quick Export menu to reveal the Dreamweaver submenu. See figure 12-8.

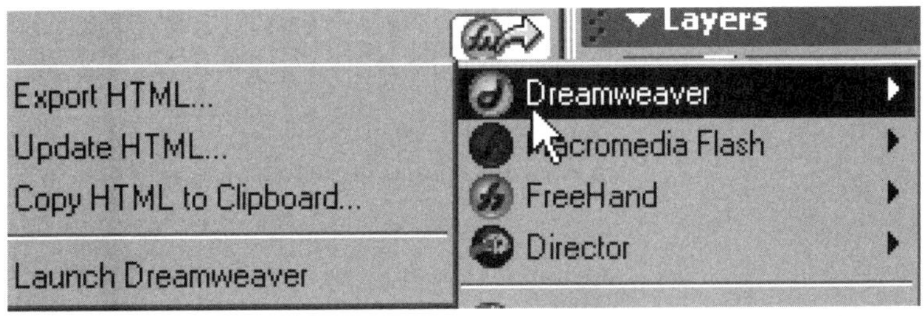

Fig. 12-8. Dreamweaver submenu opens to the left when using the default workspace settings.

   a) In the Dreamweaver submenu, review the following options.

      - *Export to HTML:* Exports the Fireworks document with the Dreamweaver HTML style automatically set.
      - *Update HTML:* Searches for and updates a previously created Dreamweaver file with the Dreamweaver HTML style automatically set.
      - *Copy HTML to Clipboard:* Copies Dreamweaver HTML to the clipboard to paste into Dreamweaver's code editor.
      - *Launch Dreamweaver:* Launches the Dreamweaver application.

2. The following are Dreamweaver integration features supported by Fireworks:

   a) Fireworks and Dreamweaver blend editing together seamlessly with Roundtrip HTML and the Launch and Edit command. Launch to Fireworks from within Dreamweaver to edit images, tables, web objects, and other elements. These modifications are automatically updated in existing Dreamweaver files when complete.

   b) A new Dreamweaver MX feature is the ability to create Fireworks image placeholders within Dreamweaver. These placeholders can then launch into Fireworks, with their predefined size, for further rendering. Upon completion, the image is then automatically updated in the Dreamweaver file.

   c) Export the Fireworks file as a Dreamweaver library to predefine assets for a site.

   d) The Update HTML command can be used to update Dreamweaver files from Fireworks without launching Dreamweaver.

e) Both Fireworks MX and Dreamweaver MX can import and export the XHTML file type.

Macromedia Flash MX

1. Highlight Macromedia Flash in the Quick Export menu to reveal the Flash submenu. See figure 12-9.

Fig. 12-9. Flash submenu opens to the left when using the default workspace settings.

   a) In the Flash submenu, review the following options.
      - *Export SWF:* Shortcut for exporting an SWF file. The SWF options window appears after choosing this selection. (See figure 12-6.)
      - *Copy:* Copy selected objects to paste into Flash.
      - *Launch Macromedia Flash:* Launches the Flash application.

2. The following are Flash integration features supported by Fireworks.
   a) The Launch and Edit command in Flash allows you to launch Fireworks to update images in Flash.
   b) Fireworks PNG files can be opened into Flash MX, and editable objects and layers are maintained. Vectors, bitmaps, animations, and multistate buttons can be imported into Flash.
   c) Fireworks is able to export PNG 32 files that support transparency in bitmap graphics that are to be imported into Flash.
   d) Fireworks exports JPEG, GIF, PNG, and SWF file formats, which can also be imported into Flash.

FreeHand

1. Highlight FreeHand in the Quick Export menu to reveal the FreeHand submenu, shown in figure 12-10.

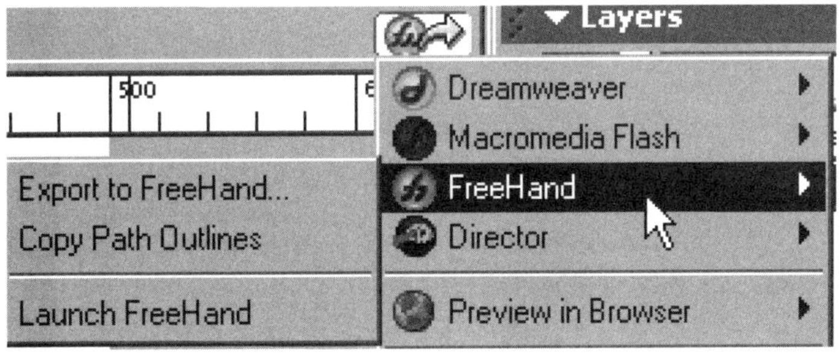

Fig. 12-10. FreeHand submenu opens to the left when using the default workspace settings.

a) In the FreeHand submenu, review the following options.

- *Export to FreeHand:* Exports the Fireworks file in Illustrator 7 format, which can then be imported into FreeHand.
- *Copy Path Outlines:* Copies vector paths for the selected object. The paths can then be pasted directly into FreeHand.
- *Launch FreeHand:* Launches the FreeHand application.

2. The following are FreeHand integration features supported by Fireworks.
   a) Share vector shapes freely back and forth between Fireworks and FreeHand. Note that some appearance formatting, such as effects, may be lost.
   b) Using the Copy Path Outlines command, copy and paste paths between applications.
   c) Using the Copy command, copy and paste vectors as bitmaps to maintain appearance.
   d) Import FreeHand file types into Fireworks with adjustable options for file handling.

Director

1. Highlight Director in the Quick Export menu to reveal the Director submenu. See figure 12-11.

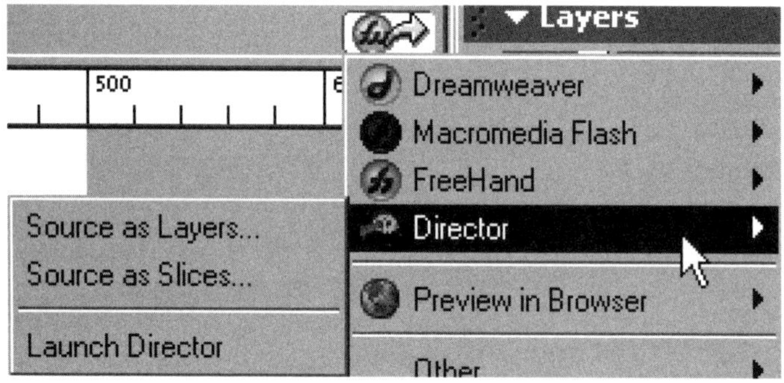

Fig. 12-11. Director submenu opens to the left when using the default workspace settings.

a) In the Director submenu, review the following options.

- *Source as Layers:* Exports each layer in the Fireworks document as a separate image, and exports an HTML file with CSS layers.
- *Source as Slices:* Exports each slice in the Fireworks document, along with the HTML table code.
- *Launch Director:* Launches the Director application.

2. The following are Director integration features supported by Fireworks.
   a) The Launch and Edit command is available in Director. Launch and Edit can also allow roundtrip optimization control on images from Director.
   b) File | Export from Fireworks preserves interactivity, such as behaviors, slices, and layered images.
   c) Freely import JPEG, GIF, and PNG 32 into Director.
   d) Fireworks PNG 32 supports transparency for use with images to be imported into Director.

Preview in Browser

1. Highlight the Preview in Browser option in the Quick Export menu to reveal the Preview in Browser submenu. (See figure 12-12.) We have already used the F12 key command for Preview in Browser, but here is another option that is also convenient to use. You can set up and launch your primary and secondary browsers from this location.

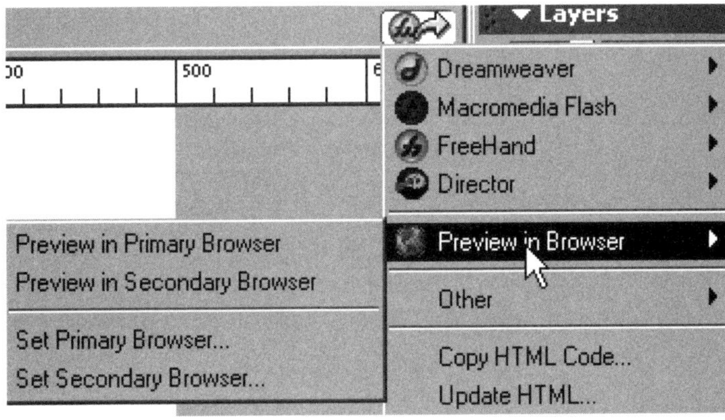

Fig. 12-12. Preview in Browser submenu opens to the left when using the default workspace settings.

a) In the Preview in Browser submenu, review the following options.

- *Preview in Primary Browser:* Preview the artwork on the canvas in your preferred, primary browser. This browser is also launched by the keyboard shortcut F12.
- *Preview in Secondary Browser:* Preview the artwork on the canvas in another browser. This browser is also launched by the keyboard shortcut Ctrl + F12 (Mac: Cmd + F12).
- *Set Primary Browser:* Specify the preferred browser. This browser is also launched by the keyboard shortcut F12.
- *Set Secondary Browser:* Specify a second browser for preview. This browser is also launched by the keyboard shortcut Ctrl + F12 (Mac: Cmd + F12).

Other Options

1. Highlight the Other option in the Quick Export menu to reveal the Other submenu. (See figure 12-13.) The Other category contains a collection of non-Macromedia applications that have export shortcuts as well.

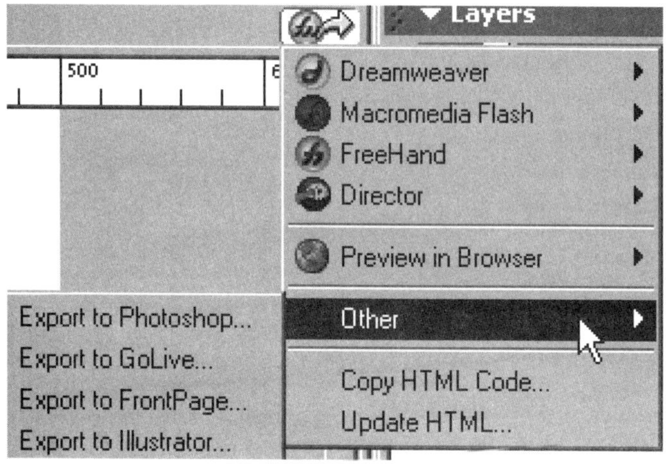

Fig. 12-13. Other export submenu opens to the left when using the default workspace settings.

2. The first option in the Other submenu is Export to Photoshop. This option will launch the export settings, with Photoshop as the file type. Set the export options as described in the previous guided tour. The following are Photoshop integration features supported by Fireworks.
   a) Maintain layers, masks, and editable text while importing Photoshop files to Fireworks or exporting Fireworks files to Photoshop.
   b) Use the Photoshop export options to specify the conversion of the Fireworks file to a Photoshop file.
   c) Import editable Photoshop 6 text into Fireworks.
   d) Import Photoshop 5.5 and lower filters and plug-ins into Fireworks.
   e) Drag and drop a Photoshop document onto a Fireworks document to open it in Fireworks.
3. The next option in the Other submenu is Export to GoLive. GoLive is an Adobe HTML editor similar to Dreamweaver. Using this setting will preserve interactivity such as behaviors once the file is opened in GoLive. The GoLive HTML style is automatically set when this option is chosen. GoLive shares the same basic HTML integration features that were discussed throughout this chapter.
4. The next option in the Other submenu is Export to FrontPage. FrontPage is the Microsoft HTML editor similar to Dreamweaver and GoLive. Those working with FrontPage and GoLive will discover that it actually has a closer integration with Fireworks than GoLive. The reason for this is that FrontPage shares Roundtrip HTML editing and Launch and Edit graphic editing with Fireworks. The FrontPage HTML Style is automatically set

when this option is chosen. The following are FrontPage integration features supported in Fireworks.

a) Fireworks and FrontPage have been designed to support a seamless workflow with Roundtrip HTML and Launch and Edit graphic editing. Launch to Fireworks from within FrontPage to edit images, tables, web objects, and other objects. Modifications made in Fireworks are automatically updated in FrontPage when completed.

b) FrontPage shares the basic HTML integration features that we have discussed throughout the chapter.

5. The last option in the Other submenu is Export to Illustrator. This exports the file in the Illustrator 7 format, which can be imported into a wide range of programs.

TIP

Macromedia HomeSite also has strong Fireworks integration features. Similar to Dreamweaver and FrontPage, it has Roundtrip HTML editing capabilities, as well as Launch and Edit graphic editing capabilities.

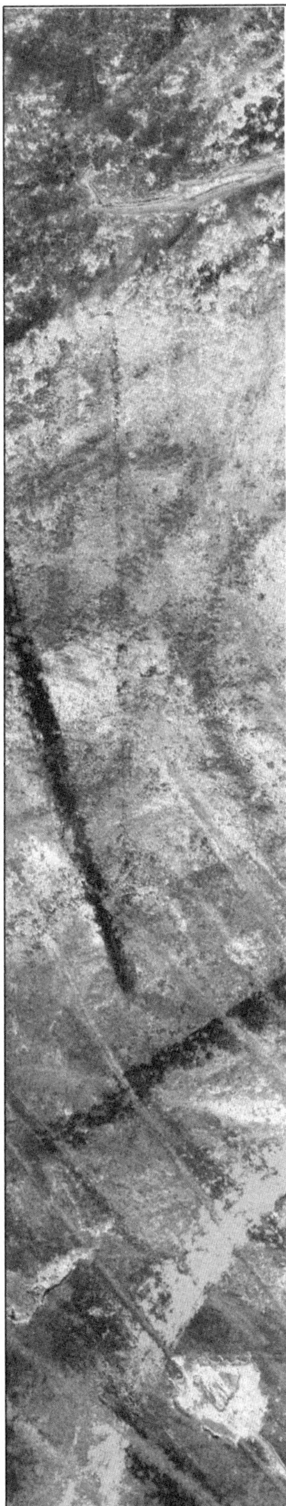

INDEX